Behaving as a Christ-Believer

Itero

Reprints in the Service of the Scholarly Community

www.ehs.se/itero

Series Editor

Thomas Kazen

No. 5

Rikard Roitto

Behaving as a Christ-Believer

A Cognitive Perspective on Identity and Behavior Norms in Ephesians

Enskilda Högskolan Stockholm

Itero – Reprints in the Service of the Scholarly Community

Books still in demand should not get out of print, and with today's techniques there is no defence. With the reprint series *Itero*, the Biblical Studies department at Stockholm School of Theology would like to make books available for free online and at a very low cost in print. Part of the background is the fact that several faculty members have published their studies in series that were cancelled. With the publishing market in constant flux, series migrate, and volumes still in demand can suddenly become unavailable. This is unsatisfactory. In collaboration with the authors, we are now republishing a number of such volumes and we will consider publishing other out-of-print titles, for which authors hold the copyright. This is entirely a non-profit project. Files may be downloaded at *www.ehs.se/itero* and books can be bought through most major internet bookshops.

University College Stockholm – Stockholm School of Theology

University College Stockholm (Enskilda Högskolan Stockholm) is a major Swedish provider of education in Human Rights and Democracy, as well as in Theology/Religious Studies. EHS offers Bachelor's Master's and Doctoral programmes. The university college was founded in 1993 through a merger of educational institutions with roots dating back to 1866. *Stockholm School of Theology* is the common designation for the two theological departments: Religious Studies and Theology, and Eastern Christian Studies. *Stockholm School of Human Rights and Democracy* is the designation for the programmes in Human Rights and Democracy.

Reprint edition. Previously published by Eisenbrauns.

ISBN: 978-91-8890-617-5

Cover design by Carl Johan Berglund. Typeset in EB Garamond.
Printed by BoD – Books on Demand, Norderstedt, Germany.

Stockholm School of Theology
University College Stockholm
Åkeshovsvägen 29, 168 39 Bromma, Sweden
www.ehs.se

Preface to the Itero Reprint Edition

I am grateful for this opportunity to make my revised thesis available for scholars again. Thanks to the series editor, Thomas Kazen, and designer, Carl Johan Berglund, for creating this series of reprints, which hopefully will take many scholarly contributions out of the valley of the shadow of amnesia!

Bromma in November 2021

Rikard Roitto

Table of Contents

Text Study: Identity and Behavior Norms in Ephesians 145

Preface

This publication is a revised version of my doctoral thesis, which I defended at Linköping University, 11th December 2009.

I am most thankful for the fortunate circumstances, the blessing and the good will of those around me that have allowed me to write this dissertation. In 1998, when I was a student at Lund University, I decided to write my graduation thesis in the summertime and Docent Håkan Ulfgard, who became my supervisor but was a stranger to me back then, kindly offered to supervise me at this odd time of the year. The following summer I was ordained to be a pastor for Svenska Missionskyrkan (Mission Covenant Church of Sweden) and moved to Linköping to minister there. Not long after that, Håkan Ulfgard accepted a position as a Senior Lecturer at Linköping University. The way things developed, this coincidence was most fortunate for me. Ulfgard asked me to fill in for him at a number of classes at the university, and quite soon he recommended me to a group of scholars who wrote an application for a major research project (see below). I was included in the project application, the project was accepted and so I had the funding necessary to begin my Ph.D. studies. Now, seven years and three paternity leaves later, I would like to thank those who have helped and inspired me.

First of all my gratitude goes to my supervisor Håkan Ulfgard. He has supported me and guided me in every way, encouraging me to develop both research skills and teaching skills. My strengths he has allowed to bloom and where I needed to improve he has fostered me. His thorough and continuous feedback on my texts has allowed a process of growth throughout my time as a doctoral student. Most importantly, however, he has been a good friend.

My dissertation is part of a larger research project, *Christian Identity: The First Hundred Years,* funded by Riksbankens Jubileumsfond and led by Professor Bengt Holmberg, Lund University. Holmberg was also my assistant supervisor. Besides including me in the research project, he has given me encouragement and competent feedback on my thesis, for which I am most thankful, particularly in the later stages of writing. The other participants in the project were Th.D. Bo Brander, Lund University, Professor Samuel Byrskog, Gothenburg University (at the time), Th. Lic. Fredrik Ivarsson, Gothenburg University (at the time), Docent Dieter Mitternacht, Lund University (at the time), Assistant Professor Anders Runesson, McMaster University, Docent Mikael Tellbe, Örebro Theological Seminary, Docent Runar Thorsteinsson, Lund University (at the time), and Docent Håkan Ulfgard, Linköping University. Being the only Ph.D. student in my discipline at my university, it was most valuable to meet the project group regularly to discuss and receive constructive critique. I am particularly thankful for the help I received from Mikael Tellbe, who read and evaluated my thesis in the final review and gave me valuable suggestions.

At Linköping University I have participated in the cross-disciplinary research environment of Identity and Pluralism at the Department of Culture and Communication, with participants from the disciplines of Applied Ethics, Cultural Anthropology, Philosophy, and Religious Studies. Particularly I would like to thank Ph.D. Senior Lecturer Jan Willner, who gave me important advice about the chapter on hermeneutics (chapter 3).

In the autumn of 2005 I spent a few months at the University of St Andrews, Scotland, under the supervision of Professor Philip Esler. Professor Esler kindly kept his promise to supervise me, even though he had just begun his work at the Arts and Humanities Research Council. He used his weekends to give me most qualified supervision, encouraged me to aim high and helped me get my method straight. Professor Esler also introduced me to Stephen Reicher, Professor of Social Psychology at St Andrews, who gave me informal supervision. Professor Reicher's broad vision and extensive competence in the field of social psychology helped me see how I could further develop the method of my study. I am most grateful to Professor Esler and Professor Reicher, whose supervision was a breakthrough for the method of my study.

I would also like to express my appreciation of Professional Translator Lars Jämterud, who proofread the manuscript meticulously and made several improvements. Moreover, I am grateful to Riksbankens Jubileumsfond, who financed our research project. Lastly, I would like to express my gratitude to STINT for financing my stay at St Andrews.

Introduction

The Pauline letter to the Ephesians and other texts of the early Christ-movement present behavior norms which vary considerably from one text to another. Many of these behavior norms were quite conventional in the first century Mediterranean world and not unique to the Christ-movement. Yet the norms are typically presented as expressions of the identity as Christ-believers. Why? How was the relation between social identity and behavior norms constructed in the early Christ-movement? How did the Christ-believers in the early Christ-movement experience their identity "in Christ" as both causing and requiring certain behaviors?[1]

The purpose of this study is twofold: First, I will *discuss how the cognitive sciences can provide a theoretical framework* to answer the questions above. The aim is to provide an analytical perspective, which is founded on cognitive research on how human minds handle identities and behavior norms. Second, I will *apply this framework to the Pauline letter to the Ephesians* in order to present a new understanding of the letter, particularly of the relation between identity and behavior norms as expressed in the text. In the analysis of Ephesians, I will also discuss the potential group dynamic effects of Ephesians, assuming hypothetically that its construction of identity and behavior norms was embraced by local communities of Christ-believers.[2]

---

[1] I will argue in chapter 3.1 that we cannot access the experience of the subjects of the past directly, but we can analyze the cognitive patterns which governed their experience by studying how texts express cognitive patterns.

[2] Note that when this study uses the term "group" and "group dynamics" it will primarily refer to groups small enough to allow direct interaction between its members, e.g., a local community of Christ-believers rather than the global Christ-movement. Some group dynamic effects are only relevant on the level of

Why, of all possible texts, have I chosen Paul's letter to the Ephesians? First, Ephesians expresses the relation between identity as a Christ-believer and behavior norms in a most elaborate way. Although scholars have always recognized the relation between "theology" and "ethics" in Ephesians, they have not been able to explain fully how the author imagines the relation between the two. I believe that the perspective developed in this study has the capacity to explain the thinking of Ephesians better than previous studies. Second, Ephesians is a text that is difficult to connect to a particular crisis or occasion. Therefore many scholars have given up any attempt to discuss the relation between the text and the social reality of those who used the text. Yet Ephesians seems to both reflect and construct real communal life, since it deals extensively with practical ethics. With the perspective developed in this study, we gain new tools to approach the relation between the text and social reality in a more systematic way than previous studies.

The progression of the investigation reflects the study's twofold purpose. First, I investigate how cognitive sciences, particularly cognitive psychology, can help us to analyze the relation between identity and behavior norms (chapters 3 to 12). My ambition is that the theoretical framework developed in this chapter will be applicable to many different texts (not only Ephesians). Subsequently, I use the insights gained in the theoretical part of the study to develop a new understanding of how Ephesians constructs the relation between identity and behavior norms, and how this potentially relates to social reality (chapters 13 to 18). Readers of this study will most likely either be interested in cognitive perspectives on the early Christ-movement or the Pauline letter to the Ephesians, but not necessarily both. The division of the study into two parts rather than a continuous presentation of theoretical insights from cognitive sciences throughout the analysis of Ephesians is intended to help the reader concentrate on the issues of greatest interest to him or her. The analysis of Ephesians is of course dependent on the theoretical chapters, but the insights from the theoretical chapters of the study are briefly recapitulated throughout the

---

smaller groups, while other group dynamic effects are relevant for large groups, too.

analysis of Ephesians. The study differs from the average historical study in the theoretical chapters being almost as long as the chapters applying the theories to Ephesians. This arrangement is necessary in order to thoroughly discuss theoretical, methodical and epistemological issues, since the use of cognitive research in historical studies is still a rather new and unexplored field.

In order to demonstrate the broader relevance of the approach in the ancient Mediterranean context and in the early Christ-movement, I have intentionally taken illustrative examples from ancient sources other than Ephesians in the theoretical part of the study.[3]

---

[3] Longer quotes from the Bible in English translation are based on the *New Revised Standard Version* (NRSV), but I have modified NRSV when necessary for the scholarly discussion. In translations of shorter phrases I have retained the vocabulary of NRSV to a large extent, but otherwise made my own translations.

1 Using Cognitive Psychology

1.1 How and Why Does This Study Utilize the Cognitive Sciences?

The cognitive sciences are, broadly speaking, the sciences of the mind.[4] How do our minds process and structure sensual inputs, memories, thoughts, emotions, attitudes, decisions, etc.?[5] What are the capacities, constraints, variations and universals of the mind? How does the mind relate to the body and to the material, social and cultural context? How is culture, society and group dynamics formed by our cognitive setups and vice versa? These are some of the questions discussed in the broad field of the cognitive sciences. The cognitive sciences are not only psychological sciences, but a multi-disciplinary network of sciences, including for instance neuroscience, philosophy, artificial intelligence, linguistics, psychology, social psychology and anthropology. However, this study will focus mainly on different branches of cognitive psychology and sciences that study the social and cultural consequences of the character of our minds, such as social identity theory and cognitive anthropology. As opposed to behavioral psychology, which assumes that the mind is an inaccessible "black box," cognitive psychology assumes that the processes of our minds can be understood and conceptualized. As opposed to psychodynamics, which has often

[4] Thagard 2007. Thagard writes "cognitive science" (singular), meaning the sum of all cognitive sciences. I will, however, write "cognitive sciences" (plural), meaning the many different branches of cognitive science.

[5] Note that in this study I do not use "cognition" in the narrow sense, meaning only "rational thought." Rather, "cognition" is all processes of the mind.

focused on qualitative methods and interpretations, cognitive psychologists typically (but not always) formulate their hypotheses in ways which can be tested by means of quantifiable experiments. These different psychological traditions do, however, overlap in both theory and method, and no sharp dividing lines can be drawn between the traditions. Cognitive anthropology does, for example, frequently use qualitative field studies rather than experiments as its research method, but aims to make its theories coherent with what cognitive psychologists have concluded from their experiments.[6]

At first glance, it might seem problematic that a historical study utilizes a science that uses experimentation as its most important practical method. A historian cannot make experiments on dead subjects. This study will, however, work in analogy with the methods of cognitive anthropology. As a historian, I will have to carry out a "field study." In other words, I will conduct a hermeneutical reading of texts, but use explanations and analytical categories that are informed by the results from the cognitive sciences in a heuristic manner.[7] As I will argue below in chapter 3.1, there is good reason to believe that we as *homo sapiens sapiens* have many cognitive capacities and constraints in common with the first Christ-believers.

There are several reasons for this study to utilize the cognitive sciences. First, this study is a study of the mental constructs governing the experience of identity and behavior norms in the early Christ-movement. Cognitive science is a research paradigm that has within its various sub-disciplines has analyzed just about the whole range of the human experience, from details of individual cognition to the dynamics of entire cultures, with theoretically continuous perspectives. These sciences can therefore help us piece together the interaction between culture, group dynamics, narratives, spirituality, morality, beliefs about what causes humans to act, etc., into a coherent account of how identity relates to behavior norms. The constructs that we find in texts from the early Christ-movement can be understood with reference to the

[6] E.g., Sperber 1996; Whitehouse 2004.

[7] I agree with Esler 2000; Horrell 2000; Theissen 2007: 15–19 that psychology and social sciences have to be used as "hermeneutical" or "heuristic" tools in relation to historical texts.

properties of the human mind—a mind which is embodied and interacts with a material, social and cultural world. This enables the historian to discuss the relation between artifacts (e.g. texts), experience and social reality in a more qualified manner.

Second, this study asks how we can understand constructs of identity among subjects from the past. Some historians innocently think that we can understand the experience of subjects from other epochs and cultures through empathetic studies of textual artifacts. Other historians suspiciously deny the possibility of cross-cultural understanding. The cognitive sciences can help us find a way forward in this debate, since there are many studies on the cognitive universals and variations of human cognition. This gives the historian an opportunity to start his/her analysis from more substantiated assumptions about the cognitive capacities of the subjects of another time and culture (see chapter 3.1).

Third, rephrasing the traditional analytical vocabulary of "theology and ethics" into "identity and behavior norms"—the latter of which are concepts inspired by socio-cognitive psychology—helps the historian avoid several assumptions that the traditional vocabulary tends to prompt (see chapter 2.1).

1.2 Cognitive Psychology and Other Psychological Disciplines in Biblical Studies

Psychological biblical criticism has often been accused of inducing untenable historical interpretations, and not without reason. I will, however, argue that cognitive psychology can reverse the situation and improve rather than distort certain kinds of historical investigations.

As one reads *Psychological Biblical Criticism*, Andrew Kille's overview and theoretical introduction to how psychology has been used to analyze the Bible, it is striking that Freudian and Jungian psychology have dominated the scene, followed to some extent by other psychoanalytical perspectives.[8] Some precursors to cognitive

---

[8] Kille 2001. See also Rollins 1999. Other prominent works in the field are e.g. Ellens and Rollins 2004; Kille and Rollins 2007; Theissen 1983; 2007; Theissen and von Gemünden 2007a.

psychology, such as developmental psychology, have been used to some extent, but modern cognitive psychology has played a very modest part.[9] This is odd, since cognitive psychology has increasingly become the dominant paradigm in psychological research. In the last decades, there has been a "cognitive turn" in psychology.[10]

Kille, who writes in order to promote psychological biblical criticism, admits that the use of psychology—that is, psychoanalytical psychology—in order to understand historical subjects, has largely been a failure and that criticism has been warranted.[11] "[P]sychology has a very limited value as a tool for studying history, especially ancient history."[12] Kille identifies several difficulties that have caused the exegetical, historical-critical, use of psychoanalytical psychology to be speculative.[13] First, the biblical texts do not contain the data necessary for psychoanalysis. Second, scholars have often ignored the redactional processes of the texts, which increase the distance to figures like Jesus and Moses. Third, scholars have often ignored the cultural, social and historical context in their psychoanalytical readings. In short, psychoanalytical psychology seems to be a paradigm that easily (but not necessarily[14]) inspires overt eisegesis and symbolic readings mounting to allegory. There are probably easier historical questions to ask than how subconscious psychodynamic processes and possible childhood traumas determine the personality of an individual who we only know through

---

[9] Not much has changed in this respect between the publication of Kille 2001 and Kille and Rollins 2007. Theissen and von Gemünden 2007a does, however, show an increased interest in cognitive psychology and other cognitive sciences.

[10] Thagard 2007 for a short historical overview.

[11] Kille 2001: 5–7.

[12] Kille 2004: 24.

[13] Kille 2001: 13–15, 22–23.

[14] For instance, Halperin 1993; Theissen 1983 are mentioned by Kille as examples of how one can overcome these problems through careful methodological considerations and thorough attention to the historical context. Theissen 1983 does even get some recognition from Berger 2003: 2–3, who is otherwise critical of the use of modern psychology in the study of experience in the New Testament.

texts.[15] According to Kille, psychological biblical criticism, formed largely by psychoanalytical perspectives, has rather had its greatest successes in for instance narratological, existential, religion-critical, and therapeutic analyses; that is, readings of the world "of the text" and "in front of the text" rather than "behind the text."[16] These topics seem to be more accessible for analysis with the help of psychodynamic psychology than historical-critical issues.

In contrast to the often skeptical reception of psychological approaches in the community of biblical scholars, social-scientific approaches have been more accepted.[17] The main reason for this, as far as I can see, is that the use of these models has inspired credible historical interpretations. Scholars who use social scientific approaches have not been more successful than scholars who use psychological approaches in establishing—on a theoretical level—that these theories and models, developed for and through analysis of present day societies, are valid for ancient societies. On the contrary, the potential danger of applying a theory based on contemporary observations on ancient texts has been one of the most important arguments of the skeptics.[18] The defenders of social scientific theories have argued that it seems reasonable to assume a certain amount of continuity in social patterns, either between cultures or within the Mediterranen culture across time.[19]

---

[15] Rebell 1986: 16–18. Rollins 1999: 136–139 argues that this is an achievable goal, but I am afraid that the danger of eisegesis is substantial. The only biblical person who might be psychoanalyzed with some success is Paul, since a number of his own compositions are available to us, see Theissen 1983.

[16] Kille 2001: 23–27.

[17] E.g. Blasi, Duhaime and Turcotte 2002; Esler 2005; Holmberg 1990; Horrell 1999a; Malina 2001; Rohrbaugh 1996 for useful overviews of social-scientific exegesis.

[18] See Horrell 1999b for an overview of the scholarly discussions. Another important argument against the employment of social-scientific methods is that the historical texts do not always contain enough social data. That is, similar arguments have been used both against the use of social-scientific approaches and against the use of psychological approaches.

[19] E.g. Malina 2001: xii briefly states that he presupposed that it is reasonable to assume continuity within the Mediterranean culture across the centuries. Esler 2005: 4 states that "users of models ... do accept the existence of certain

However, since we can never know beforehand whether a certain model is applicable in another context, the acceptance of these approaches should come from their success in shedding new credible light on the meaning of the texts.[20] This heuristic approach is sound and has yielded most interesting results, but leaves us with weak theoretical justification for the use of these models.[21]

Recently, Gerd Theissen has defended the value of using psychology in historical analysis of biblical texts in his book *Erleben und Verhalten der ersten Christen: eine Psychologie des Urchristentums*.[22] Theissen acknowledges that there are limits to what kinds of analyses the sources allow. However, psychology can be used in two ways, according to Theissen: First, it can be used to ask better and more revealing questions to the texts. Second, psychology can be used as (heuristic) *analogies* to understand the experience of past subjects. Theissen's arguments are

---

regularities in social life, even though these regularities fall short of 'social laws'" but does not discuss why these regularities exist.

[20] E.g. Holmberg 1978: 5, quoting Theissen 1974: 37, argues that the usefulness of social-scientific models must be determined "by observing it used on the available sources." Malina 2001: 23 invites the reader to see if the ancient texts seem to validate the usefulness of his models. Esler 2005: 4 argues that "one must judge a model by whether or not it is helpful."

[21] Zetterholm 2003: 13–14, referring to Berger and Luckmann 1966, however, spells out the basic theoretical argument that other scholars' use of social-scientific approaches seem to imply. He argues for the use of social-scientific models by referring to the "biological constitution" of mankind. Since it is the nature of humans to create social patterns, we should expect similarities in these social patterns across cultures, Zetterholm argues. It is therefore justified to use models based on observations in one society and use them heuristically on other societies. Zetterholm does not, however, argue in detail for the biological foundation of the models he uses. This is not surprising, since he leans on Berger and Luckmann, who wrote in 1966 and therefore did not have the same empirical support for their assertion as present scholars do. (As Luomanen 2007: 207–208 points out, Berger and Luckmann were mainly interested in the cultural factors that formed knowledge and less interested in the innate properties of the human mind.)

[22] Theissen 2007: 20–32. Already in Theissen 1983 he discussed these problems. See also Leiner 2007; Theissen and von Gemünden 2007b.

similar to those used by biblical scholars who use social-scientific methods. However, if one insists that subjects of the past are fundamentally different from us, then the analogy approach is not applicable. Rather, any attempt to use analogy would risk inducing anachronistic readings. Theissen does, however, rightly point out that there are biologically innate and therefore cross-culturally universal psychological capacities and constraints, which we share with the historical subjects. Therefore we have theoretically grounded reason to believe that there is continuity between us and them. (As Theissen does so, he refers to evolutionary cognitive research, which has scrutinized the universals of the human mind more thoroughly than psychodynamic research has.[23]) Based on this insight about innate cognitive capacities, which I will develop throughout this study, I would like to make a suggestion, which is a bit less cautious than that of Theissen: Our minds should not only be treated as analogous to the minds of the past—we should recognize that they are *the same* in certain basic respects, because of the biologically innate constraints and capacities of our minds (see chapter 3.1). Analogies and similarities, which appear at the more complex levels of cognition and social interaction, are there because both our and their minds create culture with the same basic cognitive capacities.

Cognitive psychology has something to offer in the area Kille targets as the weak spot of psychological biblical criticism—the exegetical, historical-critical, study of the Bible.[24] That is, cognitive psychology can be an aid to gain understanding of historical subjects. Cognitive

---

[23] Theissen 2007: 25 n. 33. Theissen 1983 treats psychodynamic, cognitive and learning psychology as equal and complementary. In Theissen 2007, however, he thinks of cognitive psychology as the approach that can unify the other approaches: "Dazu werden Theorien aus lerntheoretischen, psychodynamischen und kognitiven Ansätzen herangezogen. *Ihre Vorbindung wurde durch die kognitive Wende in der Psychologie seit den 70er Jahren ermöglicht*" (p. 40, emphasis added).

[24] Kille 2001: 23, 31 is very sparse in his dealings with cognitive psychology as a tool for interpretation, but suggests, for instance, that studies of memory processes may enlighten the process of oral transmission and how language influences cognition and action. This only scratches the surface of the potential of cognitive psychology.

psychology asks very basic questions about the human mind: How do we categorize? How do we construct causality? How do we understand agency, intentionality and dispositions? How do we think in narratives and how do we use the narratives in problem-solving? How do we construct analogies and metaphors? How does motivation and goals modify cognition? What is the relation between language and cognition? These kinds of questions bring us very close to the linguistic expressions of the texts and help us discuss how the texts are the expressions of cognitive processes, which in turn are the fruit of interaction with the material, social and cultural world. Cognitive psychologists frequently discuss to what extent cognition is innate and to what extent it is culturally determined, which takes us beyond just asserting that there probably is some continuity between us and the subject of the past in our cognitive makeup as a justification to use cognitive psychology as an analytical tool.[25]

Although cognitive psychology has not been the dominating approach in psychological biblical criticism, several studies have utilized cognitive psychology in order to understand the subjects of the past.[26] Gerd Theissen's book *Psychological Aspects of Pauline Theology* is often mentioned as one of the most important early contributions to psychological criticism.[27] Theissen integrates cognitive psychology with behaviorist learning theory and psychodynamics. In Theissen's study, as well as in other studies by for instance Philip Esler, Walter Rebell and Dieter Mitternacht, social aspects of cognition have been used to analyze the texts.[28] Both social cognition research and social identity theory have proved to be powerful tools for understanding how texts may have corresponded to a historical social situation. Particularly Esler's use of

---

[25] As Kille 2001: 14 points out, continuity between our and their way of thinking is an implicit assumption in *all* historical-critical exegesis, not just in psychological Biblical criticism, since we assume that we can read their texts and interpret them intelligibly.

[26] Although I mention a number of studies here, I will not attempt to cover the scholarly history of cognitive perspectives on the Bible.

[27] Theissen 1983 (translated to English in 1987) summarized and evaluated by Mitternacht 2004. Cf. n. 23.

[28] Esler 1998; 2003; Mitternacht 1999; Rebell 1986.

social identity theory, most importantly in his books *Galatians* and *Conflict and Identity in Romans: The Social Setting of Paul's Letter,* has had many followers in biblical studies.[29] Socio-cognitive approaches will be important in this study, too.

Other aspects of cognitive psychology have also been used in biblical studies, the book *Explaining Christian Origins and Early Judaism: Contributions from Cognitive and Social Science,* edited by Petri Luomanen, Ilkka Pyysiäinen and Risto Uro, being the most extensive volume so far exploring new aspects of how cognitive sciences can be used in biblical studies.[30] Hugo Lundhaug and Vernon Robbins have used cognitive blending theory in order to understand metaphor and integration of theological concepts.[31] Cognitive research on memory transmission within groups has been used by, for example, Samuel Byrskog and Philip Esler to understand how Jesus and Paul were remembered.[32] Kimmo Ketola and Risto Uro have used cognitive ritual theories in order to analyze rituals in Judaism and the Gnostic movement.[33] István Czachesz has used cognitive epidemiology theory in order to understand what factors may have contributed to the spread of the early Christ-movement.[34] This is but a small sample of how cognitive psychology can be used as an analytical tool for biblical studies.

---

[29] E.g. Byrskog 2005; Hakola 2007; Horrell 2007b; Jokiranta 2005; Jokiranta 2007; Luomanen 2007; Marohl 2008; Shkul 2009; Tellbe 2009. (I have not aimed at finding every article or monograph that uses social identity theory to analyze biblical texts. These are just examples, intended to illustrate the increasing popularity of the approach.)

[30] Luomanen, Pyysiäinen and Uro 2007a; Uro and Czachesz forthcoming, may become the starting point of a movement of biblical scholars who take interest in what we may call "cognitive biblical criticism."

[31] Lundhaug 2007a; 2007b; Robbins 2007.

[32] Byrskog 2008; Esler 2007.

[33] Ketola 2007; Uro 2007.

[34] Czachesz 2007a; 2007b. Czachesz has written a large number of articles, in which he uses cognitive sciences to analyze different aspects of the early Christ-movement.

1.3 Using Behavioral Sciences to Understand Identity and Behavior Norms in Ephesians

In Ephesians, the recipients are initially described as chosen "to be holy" (1:4), which is followed by three chapters of "theology" or "identity narrative" (1:3–3:21). The first and second half of Ephesians are then bridged by the exhortation to "lead a life worthy of the calling to which you have been called" (4:1), followed by three chapters, which contain mainly (but not only) paraenesis (4:1–6:20). It is therefore not surprising that many have argued that Ephesians makes some kind of connection between on the one hand theology, ecclesiology or identity, and on the other hand, ethics or behavior norms. The author obviously thinks that being a Christ-believer (identity) implies a certain lifestyle (behavior norms).

Although earlier scholarship on Ephesians did not use the analytical category of "identity," Ephesians has frequently been seen as a discourse on the unity of the *ekklēsia,* which is implicitly an identity theme.[35] The first scholar (at least to my knowledge) to explicitly articulate that the purpose of Ephesians is to "reinforce their sense of Christian *identity*" was, however, Andrew Lincoln in his commentary on Ephesians.[36] He argues that the author aims to inspire the recipients to adhere to ingroup beliefs and norms and act accordingly. Lincoln argues that the first epideictic[37] half of the letter is intended to increase the appreciation of their identity, while the second deliberative[38] half is intended to inspire action, which is in conformity with their identity. Lincoln's position has since then been embraced and modified in, for instance, the

[35] See e.g. Hoehner 2002: 97–98, 102–104 for an overview of scholarly suggestions that the author intends to promote the unity of the *ekklēsia,* perhaps in the face of some internal conflict or external pressure.

[36] Lincoln 1990: lxxv, emphasis added.

[37] A praising or blaming oratory genre intended to influence the audience to appreciate certain values and reject others, often in a ceremonial setting.

[38] An oratory genre intended to inspire the audience to take a certain future course of action, often in a political setting.

commentaries on Ephesians by Ernest Best and Margaret MacDonald.[39] Best slightly modifies Lincoln and argues that the purpose of the letter is "maturation." MacDonald is more willing than Lincoln to discuss possible extra-textual circumstances that might have occasioned the text and proposes that the letter is intended to strengthen the identity of the recipients, who are perhaps under pressure from the surrounding world. While Lincoln and Best do not use any social-scientific concepts in order to understand identity formation, MacDonald uses several sociological and anthropological models in her analysis.[40]

No other study on Ephesians has made use of the same range of cognitive perspectives that this study will use. However, a few scholars have recently analyzed this identity formation in Ephesians with the aid of social identity theory, one of the theories of importance to this study, too (see chapers 5 to 10).

Minna Shkul's revised publication of her dissertation *Reading Ephesians: Exploring Social Entrepreneurship in the Text* is the most extensive of these studies.[41] She uses a range of social-scientific models, including social identity theory, to understand the author of Ephesians as an "entrepreneur of identity." Shkul focuses especially on the ethnic relations in Eph 2, where she emphasizes that the text leaves the reader with gaps to fill in as regards the relation to Israel. Shkul does, however, not only analyze chapter 2 but examines how the author builds identity throughout all chapters of Ephesians. Her social-scientific perspective has led her to ask many questions similar to the questions of this study, and I approve of many of the conclusions in her study.

Daniel Darko's revised publication of his dissertation *No Longer Living as the Gentiles: Differentation and Shared Ethical Values in Ephesians 4.17–6.9* also uses social identity theory to a limited extent.[42] He refutes the apparently contradictory scholarly suggestions that Eph 4:17–5:20 represents a separatist and introversionist attitude, while 5:21–6:9 (the

---

[39] Best 2004: 22; MacDonald 2000: 18–22. Others who have suggested that the purpose of Ephesians is identity formation after Lincoln include O'Brien 1999: 57; Sampley 1993: 23; Snodgrass 1996: 23; Talbert 2007: 12–15.

[40] MacDonald 2000: 1–4. See also MacDonald 2004.

[41] Shkul 2009.

[42] Darko 2008.

household code) represents an attempt at apology and integration. Instead, Darko argues, the passages form a coherent rhetorical unit, which aims to create a distinct identity and an ethos of unity and cooperation for the group. These efforts are neither separatist nor apologetic. Darko's use of social identity theory is basic but fruitful. His problem overlaps the problem of this study to some extent and I find many of his conclusions sound.

However, although both Shkul and Darko use social identity theory (or at least parts of the theory), they do not use the same wide range of cognitive psychology as I will use in this study. The shift in analytical approach to cognitive psychology in this study will enable us to better integrate the reading of the linguistic expressions in the text with the theoretical framework, since the cognitive approach of this study provides us with analytical questions that facilitate such close readings. Linguistic expressions of causal beliefs will be particularly closely examined and discussed in relation to the cognitive framework of this study. The use of attribution research (see chapter 6) will also improve our understanding of the relation between identity and behavior norms. This will result in a more detailed understanding of how the relation between identity and behavior norms is constructed in Ephesians. Shkul's and Darko's quite recently published studies came to my attention at a late stage of this study and therefore I primarily engage with their studies at points where I have found them particularly illuminating and at certain points where we disagree.

Besides Shkul and Darko, Philip Esler and Samuel Byrskog have written articles that employ social identity theory to understand how Ephesians forms identity and behavior norms.[43] Esler utilizes social identity theory together with studies about collective remembering to explore how Paul is remembered as an exemplar of suffering and imprisonment in deutero-Pauline literature, including Ephesians. Byrskog uses social identity theory to explore how the paraenetic and the theological material in 4:1–16 are interwoven in such a way as to make the norms of unity in the passage an expression of the Christ-

---

[43] Byrskog 2005; Esler 2007. Byrskog's article is published in Wolter 2005, a volume entitled *Ethik als angewandte Ekklesiologie: Der Brief and Der Epheser*.

believers' identity. Both these studies contribute to the understanding of the identity forming rhetoric in the letter.

The novelty of the present analysis of Ephesians compared to earlier research is not that it points out the existence of a connection between identity and behavior norms. Nor does the innovation concist in the mere idea of using behavioral sciences in the analysis. Rather the novelty of the present analysis is a) that it scrutinizes in detail how the letter creates a coherent cognitive system of identity, ingroup narratives, prototypical attributes and behavior norms, and b) that the study engages more strongly with cognitive approaches than previous studies in order to do so. Therefore, this study will be able to interpret the construction of the relation between identity and behavior norms in Ephesians in a new way.[44]

[44] A contrasting example to the method of this study is Malan 2006, an article entitled "Identity, ethics and ethos in Ephesians." Malan re-narrates the ethical content of Ephesians thematically and makes some effort to understand this ethics as a part of their identity in Christ, trusting his scholarly intuition on the relation between identity and ethics. His narrative is indeed coherent with the content of Ephesians and I have no major objections to the conclusions he is able to draw with his intuitive method. Nevertheless, his study has no illuminating analytical concepts that explain how ethics is a part of identity and therefore he cannot create the analytical distance necessary to get a more thorough and systematic understanding of the early Christ-believers' experience as described by Ephesians.

2 Introductory Notes on Terminology

2.1 Why "Identity," "Narrative" and "Norms" Rather Than "Theology" and "Ethics"?

The traditional way of analyzing the meaning of behavior norms in the early Christ-movement has been to ask how the ethics or the morality of the first Christ-believers was motivated by their theology. In this study, however, I will re-conceptualize the question into a question about the interaction between social identity, norms and ingroup narratives. When this study uses the term "identity," it will primarily refer to social identity. Social identity is the individual's identity as belonging to a context (e.g., "I am a Christ-believer," see chapter 5.2 for further discussion). Social identity can be contrasted with, on the one hand, individual identity (e.g., "I am Paul"), and, on the other hand, the abstracted identity of a group or a movement as a whole (e.g., "Israel is the people of God"). Norms are the group's shared ideas about proper attitudes, beliefs, behaviors, etc. (see chapter 2.2). A narrative is basically a cognitive construct connecting events into temporal and causal chains. This means that narratives are not just a literary genre, but a way to think about and comprehend life—including theology (see chapter 11). The concepts of "social identity," "narrative," and "norms" are more readily compatible with cognitive psychology than "theology" and "ethics" are, and will therefore be more adequate for the present study. This is the main reason to use this non-traditional vocabulary. There are, however, also other reasons. Without doubt, the traditional formulation of the problem in terms of theology and ethics has produced much valuable and relevant research. The formulation does, however, have a number of problems:

First, "theology and ethics" is a phrase that often (but not always) lacks association to social context, while "social identity and behavior norms" clearly signals that the norms are integrated into the perception of "who we are." In a modern context, ethical conduct is often considered to be an individual matter. One should derive one's conduct from one's own ethical deliberation. In contrast, the texts from the early Christ-movement often understand behavior as an expression of one's social identity as a Christ-believer.[45]

Second, we easily (but not necessarily) equal theology with theory and ethics with application, as if ethics was the outcome of theology. This is often how the relation is rhetorically presented in the texts of the early Christ-movement and throughout history. Our cognitive and rhetorical structuring of the relation between the two often goes from indicative (theology/narrative) to imperative (norm).[46] For instance, the narrative "in the way you judge, you will be judged" motivates the norm "do not judge" (Matt 7:1). However, in the social life of the group where narratives and norms are formed, ingroup narratives interact dialectically with norms. In the continuous negotiation for ingroup identity in relation to new intergroup and intragroup challenges, new norms are as likely to modify the narratives as the narratives are likely to inspire new norms. The vocabulary of identity, narrative and norms, taken from social psychology, helps us interrupt the intuition that theology precedes practice.

Third, "theology" is sometimes (but not always) associated with theoretical propositions about the divine, rather than with the narrative about God and the ingroup. The various texts of the early Christ-movement typically explain the value and meaning of being a Christ-believer in narrative form. They tell the narrative about what God has done, particularly through Christ, and what relation the Christ-believers have to God. When God is described as someone with character traits, it is often to explain why God acts in a certain way or why the recipients

---

[45] See chapter 6. Cf. Esler 2003: 21 who argues similarly. Esler also points out that "theology" is an anachronistic term. Since scholars frequently use etic analytical terms, this is not a valid objection against using the concept of "theology." Nevertheless, we should not think that the authors of the early Christ-movement thought of themselves as "theologians."

[46] See chapters 6.1 and 11.1.

should act in an analogous way.[47] Research in the cognitive science of religion has shown that our intuitive thinking about supernatural agents (e.g. gods) in everyday situations is very far away from abstract philosophical descriptions of the divine.[48] Rather, God is primarily experienced as an anthropomorphous, powerful, and interested agent, often with superior moral insight, who interacts with humans and expects humans to act in certain ways. In the words of Todd Tremlin:

> *Person* is the only natural ontological category that the mind possesses for comprehending the type of entities that gods are said to be. ... It is only theologians and religious specialists who represent them as radically "Other." But people who present them as radically different from the category *Person* make them incomprehensible and irrelevant as well. Mel Gibson's portrait of the "Passion of the Christ" will always be more compelling than Paul Tillich's obtuse depiction of God as the "Ground of Being."[49]

When the divine is perceived as an interested agent, it is very effortless for the human mind to motivate behavior with reference to the divine.[50] This anthropomorphic intuitive thinking about God is formed as a narrative. The term "myth," used by Gerd Theissen in his analysis of the emergence of Christianity, is therefore better than "theology," since it emphasizes the narrative character of the representation of the divine.[51] But myth is also a partly problematic term in relation to behavior norms, since it is typically only used for narratives about the divine.[52] The narratives of the divine were certainly an important part of the ingroup narrative but the ingroup narrative also included the narratives about the history, character and value of the group itself, the narratives of the group members' past before they became group members and the narratives about outgroups. All these narratives were intertwined and together formed the narrative rationale of their identity. Hence, rather

[47] See e.g. chapters 6.4 and 11.2.

[48] Barrett and Keil 1996; Boyer 2001: 322–327; Tremlin 2006: 74–182.

[49] Tremlin 2006: 96.

[50] Boyer 2001: 193–231.

[51] Theissen 1999: 2.

[52] Myth: Encyclopedia Britannica Online.

than "theology" or "myth," I will use the term "ingroup narrative(s)" to refer to all the narratives that provide the narrative rationale of the group.

Fourth, "ethics" tends to be narrower than "norms" and "practical ethics" narrower than "behavior norms." Theissen differentiates between "ethics" and "rites," which both include prescribed behavior.[53] The distinction between ethics and rites certainly has analytical value, but what this study needs is a term that includes all kinds of normative behavior. There are a number of behavior norms which do not fall easily into either ethics or rites, such as purity regulations, social gestures and aesthetics. For example, when a woman in one of the recipient communities of 1 Peter avoided glamorous jewelry, she imagined herself to be as pious as the biblical Sarah, replacing the outer beauty with inner beauty before God (1 Pet 3:3–6). Is her clothing behavior ethical, ritual, aesthetical, a bit of everything or something else entirely? Likewise, is it a rite or a social gesture to greet each other with a holy kiss (e.g. Rom 16:16)? The terms "norm" and "behavior norms" are terms that include all kinds of norms that are important for the identity in Christ.

2.2 Definition of "Norms" and "Behavior Norms"

In this study, "norms" will be defined in congruence with the vocabulary in social psychology, particularly social identity theory. (On social identity theory, see chapter 5.2 below.) In his broad introduction to social psychology, Rupert Brown defines norms as "a scale of values which defines a range of acceptable (and unacceptable) attitudes and behaviors for members of a social unit."[54] Scholars in the social identity theory tradition define norms similarly: John Turner et al. define it as "any shared standard or rule that specifies appropriate, 'correct', desirable, expected, etc., attitudes and conduct."[55] Jose Marques et al. define it as "propositions that prescribe beliefs, perceptions, and

---

[53] Theissen 1999: 2–4.

[54] Brown 2000: 56.

[55] Turner et al. 1987: 13.

behaviours of group members."[56] In the definitions by Turner and Marques et. al above, there are two shared components. There is a behavioral component, how one should behave. This component is the only visible and audible (etc.) component, from which the presence of the other components in other group members has to be inferred. There is an attitude component, how you should evaluate and feel about matters. Finally, in Marques et. al., there is also a belief component, what one should hold to be true and how one should interpret the world. Accepting certain truths is certainly a part of what one should do as a Christ-believer. Much social identity research has more or less ignored the belief component. A notable exception is Daniel Bar-Tal, who has emphasized the importance of what he calls "group beliefs."[57] Group beliefs are beliefs about the goals of the group and "beliefs which provide a rationale for the group's existence."[58] For example, the narrative belief that Christ had risen from the dead was a very central group belief providing a rationale for the existence of the Christ-believing group. Based on the discussion above, I propose the following definition of norms and behavior norms:

Norms are cognitions about proper behavior, attitudes, goals and beliefs, which are shared and sanctioned by a group.

Behavior norms are norms about observable *behavior (as opposed to attitudes, goals and beliefs, which are not directly observable, but can only be attributed to others on the basis of their behavior).*As we will see in chapter 6, we have reason so single out behavior norms from other norms, since a central aspect of this study is attribution theory, research about how we humans infer what attitudes, goals, and so on, other people have based on how we see them act and appear.

Philip Esler, who has analyzed Paul's letters to the Romans using social identity theory, argues that one should call norms "identity descriptors."[59] As we will see below, this is true to a large extent, since most of the norms expressed in the texts of the early Christ-movement

---

[56] Marques et al. 2001: 402.

[57] Bar-Tal 1990; 1998.

[58] Bar-Tal 1998: 112.

[59] Esler 2003: 20–21, 323–330.

are presented as typical for the ideal Christ-believer. But even though most norms in the New Testament are presented as aspects of the ideal Christ-believer, it is not always necessary to equate norms and identity descriptors. There can be intragroup norms which are not included in the ingroup prototype (i.e., the cognition of the ideal Christ-believer, see chapter 5).[60] "Norms ... do not necessarily have to be group beliefs. Norms may regulate group members' behaviour without being considered as characteristic of the specific group."[61] Therefore, I will use the term "norm" rather than "identity descriptor," in order to be open for the possibility that some expressed norms are described as primarily just practical. Having said that, we can expcect norms that are not seen as identity descriptors to be far less common in our texts, since there would have been no reason to bring them up as long as they were adhered to. Moreover, if people did not adhere to these norms, the urge to convince them to act according to group norms would often have inspired the authors to transform these norms into identity descriptors, in order to give the argument greater impact.

Finally, there is one more reason not to replace the term "norms" with "identity descriptors." Doing so would to a certain extent make the answer to the question in this thesis inherent in the definition. I cannot ask the question about the relation between practical behavior norms and identity and use a definition of norms that partly assumes the answer right from the outset.

---

[60] Marques et al. 2001 make a distinction between denotative and prescriptive group norms. Denotative norms are norms that are a part of the identity prototype. These norms are included in the group's shared image of the prototypical group member. Prescriptive norms are norms which regulate group dynamics without being included in the identity prototype.

[61] Bar-Tal 1998: 96. Bar-Tal uses the term "group belief" to denote norms and other beliefs that are considered "as defining their 'groupness'" (p. 94).

2.3 Why "Christ-believer," "Identity in Christ" and "Christ-Movement" Rather Than "Christian" and "Christianity"?

This study will use the term "Christ-believer" rather than "Christan," "identity in Christ" rather than "Christian identity" and "Christ-movement" rather than "Christanity."[62] (Occasionally, in relation to authors who use the term "Christianity," I will use that vocabulary while discussing their research.)

"Christ-believer" is inspired by the expression ὁ πιστεύων επὶ/εἰς τῷ Χρίστῷ/τὸν Χριστόν and similar expressions, which are frequently used in texts from the early Christ-movement (e.g., Matt 18:6, Mark 16:16; John 3:16; Acts 2:44; Rom 10:11; Eph 1:19; 1 John 5:1). Χριστιανός, "Christian" occurs only rarely in the first century (Acts 11:26; 26:28; 1 Pet 4:16) and probably originated from outside the movement.[63] In contrast, variations of expressions such as ὁ πιστεύων επὶ τῷ Χρίστῷ, which can be paraphrased "Christ-believer," were quite common self-designations. Having said that, however, I do not think that scholarly salvation lies in the invention of a flawless terminology. In the words of Bengt Holmberg:

> It is true that anachronisms can creep in through careless use of terms. However, words are not receptacles that automatically contain every meaning that anybody ever put into them ... The label *Christianoi* or "Christians" need not by itself signify a group outside Judaism any more than a term like *Pharisaioi* does.[64]

---

[62] E.g. Esler 2003: 12 argue for this vocabulary. Tellbe 2009 entitles his study *Christ-Believers in Ephesus*. Also Runesson 2008 argues against the term "Christianity" and "Christian" for the first century movement, but suggests "Apostolic Judaism" and "Christ-fearer." I will not reiterate the entire scholarly discussion about proper terminology here.

[63] Horrell 2007a for a recent discussion.

[64] Holmberg 2008: 4. Lieu 2004: 1–7 is a good example of how a scholar can discuss the problems of the term "Christian" and then use the term fruitfully anyway.

It does, however, fit my scholarly aesthetic to use this designation which is inspired by emic terms. It is a reminder that large portions of the Christ-movement during the first century considered themselves to be a continuation of the covenant rather than a "third race" in opposition to Judaism, and that many dogmatic formulations and organizational patterns were very different from post-Nicaean Christianity.[65]

Consequently, this study will use the term "Christ-movement," meaning the movement consisting of Christ-believers. Χριστιανισμός, "Christianity" is a term which is even later than Χριστιανός, appearing first in the beginning of the second century in the texts of Ignatius of Antioch (Ign. *Magn.* 10:1, 3; Ign. *Rom.* 3:3; Ign. *Phld.* 6:1). I prefer "Christ-movement" before "Jesus movement," since Gerd Theissen, who first used the term "Jesus movement," used it to designate the movement in Palestine consisting of household communities and "wandering charismatics" who traveled throughout Palestine and preached the Kingdom.[66] "Christ-movement" is intended to be a term for the entire movement, not only the Palestinian movement. The choice to call it a "movement" is, however, inspired by Theissen's terminology. "Movement" signals that the different Christ-believing groups had something in common, although they were not hierarchically organized. The title "Christ" is almost omnipresent in the texts from the movement emerging from Jesus.[67] It is the most common title indicating that the members of the movement typically[68] thought that Jesus was something more than an ordinary human. Moreover, to use "Christ-movement" rather than "Jesus movement" signals that although the movement had not yet fully become what would later be called "Christianity," it is, nevertheless, the historical precursor to Christianity.

---

[65] Runesson 2008.

[66] Theissen 1978.

[67] Χριστός is used in every New Testament writing except 3 John. All Apostolic Fathers use the title. (Search performed with BibleWorks 7.) Besides 3 John, "Christ" is not used by e.g. *Gos. Thom.* Cf. the "antichrists" who deny that Jesus is Christ, according to 1 John 2:18, 22.

[68] Cf. the discussion below in chapter 4 on culture as frequently distributed beliefs.

"Identity in Christ" is inspired by the frequent Pauline metaphor of being ἐν Χριστῷ, "in Christ" (e.g., Rom 6:11),[69] and by the similar metaphor of the vine in the Gospel of John (John 15:1–9). The term is perhaps unduly Pauline, but less clumsy than "identity as a Christ-believer." The term does, however, have merits. It indicates that the identity was typically believed to be more than membership in an association, that it brought the Christ-believer into a privileged relation to God "in Christ." For the sake of variation, the term "Identity as a Christ-believer" will occasionally be used, too.

---

[69] Neugebauer 1961: 65–71, 131–133 for complete references to ἐν Χριστῷ in Pauline literature.

Theory: A Cognitive Perspective on Social Identity and Behavior Norms in the Early Christ-Movement

The purpose of chapters 3 to 12 is to explore how cognitive research can provide a theoretically continuous perspective on the construction of the relation between social identity and behavior norms in the early Christ-movement. The goal is to create a discourse, based on cognitive psychology, which will be able to shed new light on the many classical problems in biblical studies that the question of this study raises.

First, we need to discuss how cognitive psychology may contribute to the problem of the extent as to which we can understand the subjects of the past (chapter 3).

Second, since the early Christ-movement can be understood as a (sub-)culture, we need to have a concept of culture, which is coherent with cognitive psychology (chapter 4).

Third—and most importantly—we need to explore the relation between identity and behavior norms from a cognitive perspective (chapters 5 to 10). What is a social identity and on what cognitive capacities are our social categories based (chapter 5)? How do we explain and moralize about behavior, particularly the causes of behavior (chapter 6)? What are the particular cultural patterns of explaining behavior in the ancient Mediterranean world (sections 6.2–6.4)? What intergroup and intragroup dynamics shape and are shaped by identity and behavior norms (chapters 7 and 8)? What factors are important for the individual's identification with a group (chapter 9)?

Fourth, we need to understand the importance of narratives in the formation of identity and behavior norms from a cognitive perspective (chapter 11). How can narratives imbue social identities and behavior norms with meaning?

3 Cognitive Research and Historical Investigation

The primary question of this historical investigation is not what happened in the early Christ-movement, but *how historical subjects constructed* their identity in Christ. The question entails a study going from subject to subject across time and culture, since it asks how *we* can understand *their* cognition. As a secondary endeavor, this study will also ask hypothetical questions about how their cognitive patterns both were formed by and influenced their social reality, since the construction of social matters is always "in the flesh" and cannot be justly understood without reference to the world outside the text.[70] Therefore, two principal questions arise: First, in what sense is it possible to understand cognitive constructs which govern experience across time and culture (chapter 3.1)? Second, how can we hypothesize about the relation between texts, the cognition of historical subjects and their social reality (chapter 3.2)? Cognitive research provides help for the historian to answer these questions.

Although historians disagree on to what degree and in what way the narratives produced by historians correspond to the past,[71] they

---

[70] The expression "in the flesh" is taken from Lakoff and Johnson 1999, who emphasize that all human cognition is founded in our biological constitution and our sensual experience of the world.

[71] Carr 1961 is typical for the modern historian's ethos as he insists that although the historian makes a subjective interpretation, the interpretation nevertheless relates to the past. Other historians, such as Jenkins 1991; 2003, do, however, argue that history is a discourse that reflects the present and says very little about the past. Provoked by "postmodern" historians such as Jenkins, yet others, such as Evans 1997, have defended the referential nature of history

generally agree that the duty of the historian is to present an interpretation of the historical artifacts that is as *coherent* as possible.[72] We expect a historical investigation to present an interpretation, which is coherent with the examined artifacts. However, that is not all we expect—we also expect the historian's account to be coherent with our broader knowledge about other artifacts from the context of the artifacts examined. Therefore, we bring related texts and archeological findings, as well as philology and scholarly historical narratives about related historical events, social, cultural and political circumstances, etc., into the coherence puzzle. However, not even this is the whole truth about what we expect of a coherent historical account—we also expect a historical investigation to be *coherent with our general expectations about humans*. For instance, the resurrection of Jesus would not be problematic as a historical event coherent with the textual artifacts, unless it was incoherent with our expectation about human beings. Most of our expectations about human beings are, however, not related to their physiological capacities but to their capacities as agents and subjects of experience. We expect a historical narrative to be coherent with reasonable assumptions about humans as mental and social entities.

Many historians simply use their intuitions about human agents when they assemble the pieces of their historical puzzle. They trust that their own intuitive competence, in virtue of being human, provides them with correct assumptions about how the historical subjects must have functioned. Birger A. Pearson even belittles scholars who do not use their intuition and claims that obsession with method will only divert the attention from the real work of historical investigation.[73] Such

---

writing. In the following, I will argue that a historical account is constructed rather than objective, but still refers to the past.

[72] Megill 2004. Clarification: a coherent account must not claim that the artifacts are coherent in relation to each other. Rather, the historical account is sometimes coherent in virtue of pointing out incoherencies in and between artifacts. By "coherent" I mean both "consistent," i.e., "without self-contradictions" and "congruent," i.e., "linked together into a (subjectively experienced) whole."

[73] Pearson 1997: 214–225. Pearson argues that a certain amount of mental automation (i.e., learned intuition) is necessary in order to perform historical

intuitions will often do just fine, but the potential danger of bringing unwarranted presentism, anachronism and personal preferences into the analysis is apparent. Historians have therefore increasingly brought systematic knowledge about the human mind and human social behavior into the coherence puzzle.[74] Sociology, anthropology, psychology, literary theory, etc., provide hermeneutic tools, which suggest that some ways of making a coherent interpretation of historical artifacts are more reasonable than others. Biblical exegesis has certainly been enriched in the 20th century by these cross-disciplinary influences.[75] We need only to think of the tremendous impact of Bruce Malina's book *The New Testament World: Insights from Cultural Anthropology,* which established an anthropological perspective on such important notions as collectivity, honor, shame, and purity among New Testament scholars.[76] Malina's emphasis is more on the difference than on the similarity between us and the subjects living in the ancient Mediterranean environment, since his object is to overcome anachronistic interpretations of the texts. (Malina does not, however, claim that we lack similarity with subjects from the ancient Mediterranean world.[77]) In contrast to his approach, this study will begin with what is similar between us and them and then pinpoint the differences. We are biological beings, who are culturally configured. An appreciation of what is similar between us and first century Christ-believers is just as important as is an appreciation of the differences for a proper understanding of how they constructed their social world. Although I do not believe that our cognitive capacities and constraints determine culture and history, I do think that our biologically inherited cognitive capacities have certain constraints and tendencies which influence the

---

analysis. Although I agree with him that a certain amount of automation is practically necessary, due to the limited capacity of even a scholar's mind, we must not jump to the conclusion that we should not form our automations by systematic knowledge about human behavior and thinking, rather than by the intuition we have acquired through our personal experience.

[74] Megill 2004.

[75] See the discussion in chapter 1.2 for references.

[76] Malina 2001 (originally 1981).

[77] Malina 2001: 7–11.

way we create culture. Therefore, it is a good start for cross-cultural understanding.

I do not argue that the universal aspects of human life are the most intriguing aspects of the past. On the contrary, it is the particular which interests the historian. My claim is simply this: If we structure our understanding of the experience of the subjects of the past around cognitive universals, we are in many cases in a better position to understand their particulars. Indeed, if we are to talk about "understanding" in the sense that we to some extent can understand how they constructed their reality and what their texts mean, we have to assume that they are like us in certain respects.

3.1 Understanding across Time and Culture

Can we understand the cognitive constructs of people who took part in the early Christ-movement through interpretation of texts that were produced and used by them? What kind of understanding of the subjects in the early Christ-movement is it reasonable for us to claim?

It may seem evident that communication with public representations such as words and gestures leads to our understanding each other.[78] If I ask you to please send me the potatoes, you seem to understand what I mean well enough to send me the potatoes. Humans are able to cooperate and create enormously complex civilizations. This collective effort would not have been possible if understanding had been largely illusory.

From an evolutionary perspective, effective communication and understanding provide an enormous advantage in the task of survival.[79] Nevertheless, the argument that it would be advantageous does not prove that it therefore must be so. Evolution does not aim teleologically at the perfect constitution, but selects among random deviations, which

---

[78] Sperber 1996: 56–76 points out that the private representations in our minds (e.g. beliefs) must be expressed in public representations (e.g. speech, texts), before they can be transformed into private representations in other people's minds. This process may be more or less successful and result in more or less similar representations in the minds of communicators.

[79] Deacon 1997: 28; Dunbar 1996; Pinker 1994; Tremlin 2006: 73–86.

means that our actual cognitive constitution is not necessarily the most beneficial one.[80] We need to recognize that psychologists have an epistemological problem when they wish to prove that intersubjectivity is often real and not illusory, since they try to investigate mental states, which only the subjects themselves can access directly.[81] There is, however, an increasing amount of research from social psychology, developmental studies and neuroscience, which indicates that people who interact regularly tend to share similar (but not identical) cognitive patterns, that is, similar beliefs, emotions and values.[82] More specifically, we have reason to believe that linguistic and bodily interaction can function to reach intersubjective understanding.[83] But does this mean we can understand subjects from the past by reading their attempts at communication?

In the 1930s-1940s, the philosopher of history Robin George Collingwood argued that history was not primarily a science that should reconstruct the events of the past, but a science that should aim at understanding the minds of the past.[84] Collingwood believed that such historical imagination was quite possible, arguing that one does not have to enter the minds of historical subjects in order to reach empathetic understanding of the values and beliefs of the subjects of the past. According to Collingwood, the historian should (and can) reenact the experience of past subjects in his or her own mind.

Although much cognitive research affirms the possibility of empathetic intersubjective understanding and shared cognitive patterns, as discussed above, this research also shows that shared cognition arises most easily in circumstances where there is close social intercourse.[85] The

---

[80] Deacon 1997: 28–39.

[81] Praetorius 2004. Praetorius does, however, argue that we have sufficient reason to believe that linguistic reports about mental states may be trusted.

[82] See Decety and Sommerwille 2003 for an overview. See also Baars 2003 on neuroscience. The most concrete evidence comes from cognitive neuroscience, where brain scans reveal that brain activity correlates with subjective experience.

[83] E.g. Malle and Hodges 2005; Verhagen 2005; Zlatev et al. 2008.

[84] Collingwood 1946; 1999 (posthumous publications), summarized by D'Oro 2006.

[85] Decety and Sommerwille 2003.

historian cannot take part of such intense intercourse with the subjects of the past; communication is crippled. We cannot ask the authors of historical texts for clarification. Moreover, we and the historical subjects do not entirely share cognitive configuration, since we belong to different cultures. Consequently, we can hardly internalize the cognitive patterns of historical subjects to the extent that we can reenact their thoughts, values and emotions in the way Collingwood argued. Particularly the intuitive cognitive patterns, which are not the result of deliberate reasoning, are difficult to reenact, since we are basically incapable of overriding our own intuitions.[86] The transfer of mental representations through historical artifacts will always result in a less than perfect understanding, which cannot be called "empathetic reenactment."

Many historians, who are aware of these problems, still retain Collingwoodian optimism. James Dunn, for instance, is aware of the problems in his study of the experience of the Spirit among the first Christians. He acknowledges that experience is subjective, that the sources are scant and that he has to overcome inter-cultural differences.[87] Nevertheless, he is convinced that simply "a sympathetic study" of the texts will help him overcome the difficulties.[88] In short, Dunn does not take the epistemological and methodological consequences of his own insights seriously.

After Collingwood, many philosophers have been less optimistic about the possibility of historical imagination in the Collingwoodian sense. Hans-George Gadamer, one of the most important philosophers of hermeneutics in the 20th century, criticized Collingwood for

[86] Chaiken and Trope 1999. According to the dual-process theory, our minds have two kinds of mental processes. One is deliberate and conscious, the other is intuitive and unconscious and therefore not possible to control through deliberation. Since the latter kind is unconscious, a historian cannot fully appreciate to what extent his intuitions differ from those of a historical subject.

[87] Dunn 1975: 2–5.

[88] Dunn 1975: 3. A few pages later, he does, however, note that "perhaps it [i.e., the study of historical experience] requires an interdisciplinary competence (in theology, psychology, sociology and anthropology for a start) that too few possess" (p. 5). Dunn is certainly right, but he does not follow his own insight.

underestimating the importance of the historian's preunderstanding in his/her interpretation of historical artifacts.[89] Gadamer did, however, not conclude that the historian produces thoughts which are only a product of his/her own preunderstanding. Rather, the preunderstanding of the historian interacts with the historical material in a hermeneutical dialectic, so that the historian gradually reaches a "fusion of the horizons (*Horizontverschmeltzung)* of the author and the interpreter."[90]

Gadamer's hermeneutics, in the respect described here, is nowadays standard hermeneutics and many historians, such as Edward Hallet Carr in his famous George Macaulay Trevelyan lectures in 1961, see the historian as someone in dialogue with the historical artifacts.[91] Few modern historians would claim that historians produce objective descriptions of the past. Rather, historical understanding is always reached from a certain perspective.[92]

In contrast, historian Keith Jenkins has gone to the opposite extreme of Collingwood and argues for a minimum of referential qualities in the historian's narrative.[93] According to Jenkins, the historian does not

---

[89] The critique of Collingwood in Gadamer 1975 has been summarized by Vardoulakis 2004. Vardoulakis does, however, conclude that Gadamer partly misrepresents Collingwood and that Collingwood's historical imagination actually is not that far away from Gadamer's *Horizontverschmeltzung.*

[90] Vardoulakis 2004: 9. Gadamer, although methodologically often similar to Jaques Derrida, did not share Derrida's declaration that authorial intention was beyond reach, see Michelfelder and Palmer 1989.

[91] Carr 1961: 1–24.

[92] Gaddis 2002.

[93] Jenkins 1995, who considers himself a "postmodern" historian, criticizes Carr, suggesting that Carr is inconsistent when he insists that history reconstructs the past. See also Jenkins 1991; 2003. "The past and history float free of each other, they are ages and miles apart," Jenkins 1991: 5. "[T]he historian's narrative is not representing the once actuality at all in the sense of presenting it *again* ... because *all* proposals can only be deemed relatively plausible *not* in relation to 'the past' as such but with regard to other historian's proposals or texts—that is intertextually—then when it comes to 'judging' historian's presentations/proposals *the past literally does not enter into it*; only the texts matter historically. Consequently, we are free to make of the past what we will, without

primarily understand subjects and events of the past, but rather constructs something new, when he or she interacts with historical artifacts. History in Jenkins' sense is not a discipline that says anything about the past, but a discipline that constructs interpretations of historical artifacts.

I agree with Gadamer that the historical interpretation is typically a fusion of horizons rather than an objective description of the past, and that the goal of reenactment of the minds of the past is untenable. Yet I would like to contest Jenkins' idea that historical understanding has insignificant referential qualities in relation to the past, just because historical understanding is constructed and biased rather than objective. Constructed does not equal non-referential. Historical understanding, just like other kinds of knowledge, can be constructed, biased *and yet* referential. Gadamer was quite optimistic that the hermeneutical process could lead to an understanding of authorial intent.[94] After all, the historical subjects had the same innate linguistic capacity as we have and their texts were typically designed to communicate.[95] But if we discard the goal of reenactment and emotional empathy as well as the illusion of objectivity, as I did above, in what sense are we justified to talk about an understanding of the subjects of the past? In the following, I will use the insights of cognitive psychology in order to approach an answer.

Gadamer debated his hermeneutic approach extensively with Jürgen Habermas.[96] Although they agreed that interpretation is dependent upon preunderstanding, Habermas argued that Gadamer did not appreciate enough how careful deliberation could help the scholar scrutinize and criticize his/her own culturally learned preunderstanding. Habermas was generally critical of the postmodern paradigm and developed a "theory of communicative action," which among other things aimed at

---

any kind of 'original past' that can count decisively to stop us," Jenkins 2003: 41–42, emphasis original.

[94] According to Gadamer 1989: 117–118, hermeneutics is "the art of grasping what someone has really wanted to say."

[95] Cf. the excursus on linguistic universals and cross-cultural understanding at the end of this section.

[96] The so called "Habermas-Gadamer Debate" has been summarized by Mendelson 1979.

enabling intersubjective understanding through deliberation. A central component in this theory was to develop a "reconstructive science," which analyzes the universal[97] structures of human thinking that are the prerequisites of any human understanding.[98] If such universal structures of human understanding exist and we are able to recognize these structures, then it is possible to find common ground in our understanding between us and the subjects of the past. We could then use our knowledge about universal cognitive structures of the human mind to interpret the artifacts. Thus, by starting from the universal structures that the cultural specifics of the past are built on, we would have the possibility of reaching some degree of understanding the subjects of the past.

This understanding is not a reenactment of their minds, nor emotional empathy, but an intellectual analysis of textual expressions of the cognitive structures which produce their subjective experience. Only at a secondary stage might this analysis induce a certain amount of "empathy," once we understand their experience as the fruits of cognitive structures, which we share with them. This "empathy" is, however, not the primary aim of the study. Rather, the goal is an analysis of how they structured their cognition. Having said that, the analysis does not have explanatory value in virtue of being objective. Just because we analyze texts in terms of something universal, it does not mean that our knowledge about these universals is not constructed. Knowledge about universal characteristics of the human mind, as constructed as this knowledge is, has explanatory value for historical investigations, not in virtue of being objective, but in virtue of starting from structures we share with the subjects of the past. In short, our historical investigation produces an account that in a constructed way

---

[97] "Universal" should not be interpreted as "every human subject without exception," since we must recognize that individuals can have varying cognitive capacities. We need only to think of autism or psychosis. Rather, "universal" should be interpreted as "typical in all cultures."

[98] E.g. Habermas 1984; 1990. Alford 1985 summarizes and evaluates Habermas' reconstructive science. Alford aptly shows that Habermas' theory is problematic in many respects. In this context, however, I will only emphasize the interpretative value of knowledge about universal human cognitive structures.

refers to cognitive constructs, which produced experiences for subjects of the past, since we structure our historical interpretation of the artifacts around shared patterns of cognition.

But do we have reason to believe that there are universal features of the human mind?[99] Features that would enable understanding of subjects across time and culture? Cognitive psychology is the most obvious choice of scholarly discipline, if we are looking for universal cognitive structures.[100] Cognitive scientists generally recognize the brain, the place where the mind happens, as a biological entity. As the cognitive linguistic scholars George Lakoff and Mark Johnson phrase it, we have "embodied minds."[101] Our minds are the products of a genetic code, which we humans largely share and the configuration of our minds is to a large extent dependent on our bodily experience. Our minds are of course also culturally configured, but the configuration can only take place within the possibilities of the innate structures of our brains.[102] These genetically innate preconditions, which make us human, have not changed significantly over the last few thousand years. Therefore, we can find basic processes of emotions, knowledge formation and interpretation that are essentially the same across time and culture.

---

[99] Not very surprisingly, postmodern author Lyotard 1984 denies the possibility and desirability of universals and consensus in a postmodern world and criticizes Habermas accordingly (pp. 65–66). The debate between Habermas and Lyotard is wider than the problem posed here—universals of the human mind—but, as will be argued below, a general rejection of universals does not take the biological nature of the human mind seriously.

[100] Habermas discusses Noam Chomsky's theory of language, Lawrence Kohlberg's theories of moral development, Jean Piaget's theory of genetic epistemology and psychodynamics as a universal structure of the human mind, see Alford 1985. Habermas' choice of theories to lean on is, however, inadequate for the needs of this study. As will hopefully become clear in this study, there are many branches of cognitive psychology that are better starting points for a cross-cultural analysis of experience.

[101] Lakoff and Johnson 1999.

[102] Tomasello 1999: 13–55.

The term "innate" needs some clarification, since it has been understood in many ways.[103] As I will use the term, "innate" does not mean that babies are born with certain capacities fully developed, nor that it is impossible to create an environment for babies that would prevent these capacities from developing or that no individuals may be born with cognitive handicaps. "Innate" does, however, mean that most humans are genetically predisposed to develop certain cognitive capacities under many different cultural circumstances.[104] Certain cognitive patterns are typical for the human race, as they appear in most humans in all or almost all cultures and develop reliably in almost all children. For instance, humans learn language far more easily than any other species.[105]

The debate among cognitive psychologists is not mainly about whether such species-typical cognitive patterns exist, but what the cause of these regularities is. Tom Simpson et al. describe the debate:[106] One position, the "nativist" position, is that the brain is modular, that is, we are born with specialized cognitive "modules," which develop under almost any circumstances. These modules are the fruit of evolutional adaptations and explain why human cognition is surprisingly regular in spite of cultural variations. The opposite position, the "empiricist" position, is that the human brain is best characterized as a general learning device, that cross-cultural regularities are not as great as the nativists suggest, and that regularities are better explained by other factors than specialized modules. In between these two positions, there are all kinds of suggestions that combine nativism and empiricism. The flexibility of the human mind seems to warn against at least the strongest forms of nativism. However, there seems to be enough support for the thought that innate cognitive patterns are due to domain specific capacities in our brains, at least to some extent.[107] Cognitive research

---

[103] Griffiths 2002.

[104] Carruthers, Laurence and Stich 2005–2008 for a thorough overview of research on innateness in recent decades.

[105] See the excursus at the end of this section, particularly n. 115.

[106] Simpson et al. 2005.

[107] See Carruthers, Laurence and Stich 2005–2008. See also e.g. Hirschfeld and Gelman 1994; Pyysiäinen 2003: 197–233; Tremlin 2006: 53–72.

indicates that the brain is not only characterized by a general intelligence, which handles all cognitive processes. Rather, the brain has biologically innate domain-specific cognitive capacities, which are apt to handle specific tasks that make us fit for the environment we live in. It is not crucial for this study to subscribe to a specific interpretation of how modular and hard-wired the human mind is. The important point is just that we humans as biological beings are born with certain cognitive capacities and constraints.

In light of the regularities in human cognition, it becomes unsustainable to assume that the mind is an infinitely formable general purpose device—a popular implicit assumption in much hermeneutically oriented science, such as history, anthropology and literary criticism.[108] The anthropologist Maurice Bloch, who is informed by cognitive psychology, rightly argues that "anthropologists have grossly exaggerated cultural variation. ... [T]he traditional questions of cultural anthropologists concerning very broad areas of knowledge should be rephrased from 'How are these things learned?' to 'How is culturally specific knowledge produced out of universal predispositions?'"[109] Analogically, an important aspect of this study is to ask: "How is the culturally specific construct of identity and behavior norms in the early Christ-movement produced out of universal predispositions?"

Petri Luomanen, Ilkka Pyysiäinen and Risto Uro, in the introduction to the edited book *Explaining Christian Origins and Early Judaism: Contributions from Cognitive and Social Science,* have rightly pointed out that cognitive psychology may enrich our understanding of the early Christ-movement and other branches of early Judaism by pointing out universal cognitive processes.[110] In contrast, Klaus Berger has argued that all modern psychology is useless for the study of the early Christ-

---

[108] Pinker 1994: 404–430 criticizes this imagination of the mind as flexible without limit.

[109] Bloch 1998: 5.

[110] Luomanen, Pyysiäinen and Uro 2007b. See also Martin 2005; 2007. Martin has been involved in several projects that seek to explore the merits of using the cognitive sciences in history writing, e.g. Martin and Sørensen 2009; Whitehouse and Martin 2004.

movement and that the historian must construct a "historical psychology," which is not dependent on modern psychology.[111] Berger's position is untenable. If we, as Berger does, "call into question any atemporal approach" to the human mind,[112] we would have to conclude that we cannot hope to understand anything of the textual artifacts of the early Christ-movement, since they have no thought patterns in common with us. Nevertheless, Berger assumes that he can read their texts and understand them. Is linguistic competence not an innate psychological skill, which we share with the first Christ-believers? Berger reacts mainly against psychoanalytical interpretations of the biblical texts and it might be true that some forms of psychology, such as Freudian and Jungian psychology, are not suitable for historical investigation.[113] However, in contrast to Berger, I suggest that if we are to argue for any kind of understanding of subjects and textual artifacts of the past, we have to assume that we share basic mental capacities with them. If we start our analysis from insights about cognitive patterns, which we share with the first Christ-believers, we can then also appreciate more fully in what sense we are different from them.

In this study I will argue that a number of cognitive skills are innate and therefore shared by us and the first Christ-believers. These are categorization (see chapter 5.1), causal thinking (see chapter 6), attribution of intentions and characteristics to agents (see chapter 6.1), narrativization of experience (see chapter 11) and analogical (metaphorical) thinking (see chapter 11.2). I will discuss these capacities in the chapters below. I will also argue that some cognitive tendencies are not universal and that there is good reason to think that the first Christ-believers differed from us in many respects. In yet other cases, I will argue that they construct knowledge in a way similar to us, although it is not necessarily a cross-culturally universal pattern. In short, I will be careful to avoid anachronism and only claim innateness if there is good reason to do so.

---

[111] Berger 2003.

[112] Berger 2003: 3.

[113] Cf. chapter 1.2 above.

> *Excursus: Linguistic universals and cross-cultural understanding.* Most historians basically just assume that we can understand the sentences in texts from other times and cultures, provided that we have access to the grammar of the language and the semantic field of the words. Is that the case? To my knowledge, no one would argue that the capacity to communicate through language is not cross-culturally universal. It might, however, be possible that different languages shape the cognition to such an extent that we cannot really grasp the thinking of speakers of other languages.[114] There are, however, great structural similarities in language across cultures and children all over the world learn language in a similar pace and order.[115] This evidence indicates that our brains have language processing skills, which all languages are dependent on. Therefore, as George Lakoff argues, although speakers of different languages have different systems of conceptualization, they still have the same conceptualizing capacity.[116] Thus, Lakoff concludes, it is possible to learn other languages and understand what speakers of other languages mean, even in cases where the two languages conceptualize a certain sphere of knowledge differently. I will therefore assume, like most historians do without even discussing the problem, that whatever differences there are in thought structure due to language, it can be approximately bridged by careful deliberation on the relation between cognition and linguistic expressions.

In sum, many basic properties of human cognition are biologically innate and cultural variations in cognition are formed by minds with these biological preconditions. We share many cognitive features with

---

[114] Whorf 1956 is paradigmatic for this relativist position, while Chomsky 1957; 1965 is paradigmatic for the universalist position. For an evaluation of Whorf, see Lakoff 1987: 304–337.

[115] E.g. Deacon 1997; Gleason 2000: 18–19, 421–422; McCabe 1997; Pinker 1994; Stein and Albro 1997; Turner 1996. Note that although many theorists agree that the human brain is strongly predisposed to learn language, they disagree on the nature of this predisposition. The original suggestion by Noam Chomsky that there is a "universal grammar" as the result of a specialized language centre in the brain is frequently questioned. It is, however, not necessary for this study to delve into these intricate matters.

[116] Lakoff 1987: 311–317.

the first Christ-believers, since they, just like we, are humans. If we use knowledge about these cognitive capacities in order to make better assumptions about how they probably organized their experience cognitively, we can to some extent bridge the divide of time and culture and better understand their culturally unique construction of identity and behavior norms.

The discussion in this section has obvious contact with the debate among biblical scholars whether it is a good idea to use social-scientific (sociological, anthropological, etc.) theories to analyze biblical texts, and how these social-scientific models should be used. The defenders of social-scientific methods have claimed that although there are no "social laws," there are nevertheless regularities in the social life of humans.[117] While I agree that this is the case, there has been some confusion as to *why* we should assume such regularity. My analysis above suggests that at least one of the reasons is that humans across cultures create culture and social patterns with the same basic innate cognitive capacities. Research about cognitive universals might therefore advance this discussion. For instance, social identity theory, which has been used by Philip Esler and many others,[118] is based on the innate human capacity to categorize, as I will argue below (see chapter 5). Therefore, we have good reason to use at least parts of this theory in our analysis of biblical texts. Other social patterns, such as the social dynamics of honor and shame in the Mediterranean world, described initially to biblical scholars by Bruce Malina,[119] seem to be more dependent on the distribution of these patterns among the minds of the subjects through learning, since they only appear in some cultures. These kinds of patterns, which are more dependent on distribution through learning, will still be typical within that culture, but they will probably exhibit more intra-cultural variation than social patterns governed by innate cognitive capacities (cf. chapter 4).[120]

---

[117] Esler 2005 for an overview of the debate. See also the discussion in chapter 1.2.

[118] See nn. 28 and 29.

[119] Malina 2001: 27–57.

[120] Lawrence 2003 has recently scrutinized the claims in Malina's work, from the suspicion that Malina has suggested an overtly uniform set of models of the

3.2 Imagining the Social Reality of the Past

The experience of the first Christ-believers took place in real life and their behavior norms were norms about real social situations. They were, just like we are, biological, social and cultural beings and their cognition was formed in relation to the world they lived in. The texts produced by the subjects of the past were formed by factors outside the texts themselves, as they were experienced by the authors. However, although we can assume that the experience of the early Christ-believers was formed by their social reality, can we, as historians, gain some insights into this social reality "behind" the texts by reading them?

Our mental representations of our social reality as well as our linguistic statements about this social reality are pragmatic and interested constructs.[121] The texts from the early Christ-movement seldom give us straightforward, disinterested reports about social realities. On the other hand, if a text aiming at handling some social issue had not related to social reality at all, that text would have been irrelevant to the recipients. Although some historians argue for a

---

first century Mediterranean culture. Some of her objections are valuable correctives. On the whole, however, she does affirm the value of Malina's use of anthropology in the interpretation of the New Testament.

Philip Esler and David Horrell have debated the correct use of social sciences in the interpretation of New Testament texts in e.g. Esler 2000; Horrell 2000. They both agree that there are no "social laws" and that social sciences should be used heuristically. However, they disagree on whether the social scientific models should mainly be considered as a way to overcome anachronistic readings (Esler) or a way to open the historian's eyes to new perspectives (Horrell). Their discussion is very useful to anyone who is interested in the use of any social and psychological science in the interpretation of the Bible. However, the discussion lacks differentiation between a) basic social patterns, which can be explained mainly by innate cognitive dispositions, and b) culturally specific patterns, which must be explained mainly by the distribution of the patterns through learning and therefore may vary within and between cultures, since these cultural patterns can be more or less distributed and dominant among the minds of the population.

[121] See chapter 6.1.

virtually arbitrary relation between text and reality,[122] this is not a plausible description of how humans typically configure their cognition (and thereby linguistic statements) in relation to their social reality. Our cognitive and linguistic capacities are such that they enable us to both interpret and manipulate our surroundings. This is also true of the texts of the early Christ-movement, which are interested and strategic linguistic expressions of cognition—they often aim at both interpreting and manipulating their surroundings. Thus, if we want to understand the texts, we must often speculate about what the texts relate to.

Nevertheless, in spite of the principal reasons to assume a pragmatically constructed correlation between text and reality, we are certainly often skating on thin ice when we speculate about the social realities of the early Christ-movement. Do the texts reveal enough to disclose the social reality which they relate to? Scholars who investigate the social reality of the early Christ-movement have reason to be cautious, due to the sparse and frequently polemic, idealizing and prescriptive rather than descriptive sources. For instance, Paul's letter to the Galatians is certainly pragmatically related to a social situation, but nevertheless extremely difficult to mirror-read, since the rhetoric obviously aims at influencing by means of a tendentious description of the situation.[123]

Judith Lieu, in her multi-faceted analysis of "Christian identity" in the first and second centuries, expresses serious doubt about whether we can really know anything about how the communities of Christ-believers understood their identity, by reading texts from the movement.[124] She does not question the ability of a modern historian to understand the texts; that is, her problem is not related to the hermeneutical discussion about "fusion of horizons." On the contrary, she distances herself from the accusation that her interpretation is only "conditioned by a twenty-first century agenda" and treats the texts as situated in their historical and cultural context.[125] Neither does Lieu question that the texts were

[122] Clark 2004: 138–145. Cf. n. 93.

[123] E.g. Mitternacht 1999; Nanos 2002.

[124] Lieu 2004. Cf. Lieu 1996.

[125] Lieu 2004: 302.

typically both formed by and formed real communities and social experiences. On the contrary, she affirms that this was most probably often the case.[126] Rather, the problem for Lieu is the nature of the historical evidence.

> [By reading texts] we can catch partial, but only partial, glimpses of the wider range of social experience than that directly represented by the texts. Indeed, when we attend to the voice of the text, often that of a particular author, we may not always be confident of how far it is articulating an existing consensus, or how far it is engaged in construction …[127]

From this insight, she draws the methodological conclusion that she will not engage in speculation about how the communities of Christ-believers constructed their identity, but only how the texts themselves construct identity.[128]

I acknowledge that Lieu has pinpointed an important problem. But does her methodological conclusion improve her understanding of the texts? I agree with Lieu that the constructions of identity in the texts are more accessible to the historian than is the social reality of the early Christ-believing communities. I could, in principle, adapt Lieu's cautious method and only ask how the texts themselves express the relation between identity and behavior norms. Indeed, this will be a central task in this study. Many of the texts of the early Christ-movement are, however, so blatantly in dialogue with realities outside the text that we are bound to misunderstand the texts unless we ask what they are in dialogue with. Lieu recognizes this problem with her method.

> Even a modicum of realism … is bound to ask what, if anything, is the referent of these texts. Focusing on the texts, we have been (rightly) unable to silence the voices of those who provoked and received them … and so we are bound to ask what, if anything, is the referent of their experience and how may it be articulated.[129]

---

[126] Lieu 2004: 27.

[127] Lieu 2004: 9.

[128] Lieu 2004: 60–61.

[129] Lieu 2004: 310.

We are caught in a dilemma. On the one hand, speculation about the social realities which the texts refer to is bound to be very fragile, at best a simplification of that reality, at worst a fantasy. On the other hand, attempts to isolate the text from that social reality is bound to misinterpret the dialogical character of the text. What is most hurtful to a historical understanding of the texts: to speculate about their social context or to avoid speculation? The answer to this question is dependent on what question we as historians ask the texts.

In the case of this study, the posed question involves behavior norms, which can only be meaningful in relation to a social reality. Behavior cannot be treated as a textual phenomenon. (And, frankly, neither can social identity.) I will therefore not take the same methodological route as Lieu, although I agree with her description of the problem, since it is impossible to discuss how behavior norms are constructed as a part of the identity in Christ without reference to the practical social dynamics of these norms. Therefore, I will engage in what might be called *hypothetical history*.[130] I will ask: In what social context(s) could the author possibly have suggested these norms? How would these norms have functioned if they were embraced by a community? The result of this hypothetical reconstruction is not history *wie es eigentlich gewesen*, but history as it typically could have been. The hypothetical history should be *coherent* with a) social-scientific and psychological research, which provides us with knowledge about what social dynamics and subjective needs usually form the social reality of a group, b) knowledge of culturally typical social and cognitive patterns in the ancient Mediterranean world, and, most importantly, c) the text and other related artifacts. Moreover, the hypothetical history should be no more detailed than what is necessary to imagine as a reasonable social situation that the texts are in dialogue with.

We need to conceptualize how we should assess the probability that the cognition expressed in a text from the early Christ-movement expresses something that to some extent was or became the shared cognition of one or many Christ-believing communities. To assess to

---

[130] Cf. Zetterholm 2008 who suggests that all historical reconstructions are hypothetical and can only be tested as to whether they are coherent with the evidence.

what extent the recipient community actually accepted and lived according to the message in a text is indeed very difficult, unless we have documents telling us how the text was received. Unfortunately, the typical situation is that we have a text, say Paul's letter to the Romans, but no record whatsoever of how the letter was received by the intended recipients. In principle, the letter may have fallen on deaf ears. Only rarely do we have other texts, which give us hints about the reaction of the intended recipients. One such case is Paul's second letter to the Corinthians, which gives the impression that Paul himself thinks he had some success in convincing them with his first letter to them (and other to us unknown communication) (e.g., 2 Cor 1:23–2:11; 7:2–16), but not total success (2 Cor 10–13).[131] Hints about the reception of a text from sources that close in time are not very common. More frequent is affirmation from later generations that secondary readers of the texts appreciated the message, such as in 2 Peter 3:15–16, where Paul's letters are considered authoritative. What later generations thought is, however, at best a very indirect hint of what the intended recipients thought.

However, social identity theory and social cognition research can help us find questions that will help us estimate whether it seems reasonable or not that the recipients shared or came to be influenced by the author's views. From that point of view, the problem comes down to three sets of questions, outlined below. The difficulty in answering these questions will vary in relation to different texts. There will still be no certain answers, but the questions help to sort out what seems to be a more a reasonable answer than the alternatives:

1) Does the author seem to be ingroup for the recipients? One of the most basic features of intergroup dynamics according to social identity theory is that the ingroup tends to consider the outgroup to be different and lower in status than the ingroup.[132] An author who is considered outgroup will therefore probably not have much success, no matter what

---

[131] Many, e.g. Furnish 1984: 5–12, suggests that 2 Cor is a redactional product, which would explain the change in tone in chapters 10–13.

[132] E.g. Tajfel and Turner 1979. See also discussion in chapters 7.1 and 7.2 below.

his arguments are. Usually, both the author and the recipients of the texts we have from the early Christ-movement would consider themselves Christ-believers and they are therefore potentially experienced as part of each other's ingroup. However, for various reasons, the recipients might have reasons to categorize themselves at a subcategory level in relation to the author or declare the author deviant:[133] "You are not the same kind of Christ-believer as we are." Hence, the author would be perceived as deviant or outgroup. Therefore one has to ask questions such as:

- Does the text indicate that there is a conflict situation between the author and the recipients, which would make the recipients inclined to declare the author outgroup or deviant?
- Is the author socially close to the recipients or does he write from a position where he is easy to dismiss as outgroup or deviant?

2) Does the author seem to be prototypical in the eyes of the recipients? According to social identity theory, the ability to present oneself as prototypical, that is, as embodying group ideals, is the basis for influence in the group.[134] If the author is able to present himself as prototypical of the identity in Christ, he is in a position where he can prescribe norms and beliefs, since he embodies the truth. Even if the author is considered ingroup, he is not automatically considered prototypical. Therefore one has to ask, for instance:

- Are there signs in the texts that the author might not be considered prototypical by the recipients, such as defensive or self-promoting passages?

3) Does the message in the text seem to take its starting point in the recipients' current cognition? One of the findings from cognitive psychology is that well developed cognitive structures resist change.[135] If a message

[133] On social subcategories, see chapter 5.1–5.2. On deviants, see chapter 8.2.

[134] E.g. Turner 2005. See also chapter 8.3.

[135] E.g. Augoustinos, Donaghue and Walker 2006: 81–83; Fiske and Taylor 1984: 171–178. See also chapter 7.3.

deviates too much from what the recipients already think they know, the usual response will be to ignore it as something false, but if the message starts with what they think they know, they will usually be more open to adding new knowledge to the existing knowledge structure and even modify it. Cognitive structures usually change slowly.[136] It is possible to cause abrupt changes in a cognitive system if the recipient is presented with massive proof that the current cognitive system is flawed. However, it would be bold to imagine that distant communication through texts could have such massive impact very often. Therefore one has to ask such questions as:

- Is it reasonable to think that the author knows the recipient group's cognitive system—for instance language conventions, ingroup narratives and ingroup ideals—well enough to take a relevant starting point in his argument? Is there reason to doubt that the message has bearing on the recipient's current situation?[137]
- When the author criticizes behavior, does he seem to refer to an ingroup prototype that the recipients would agree on, that is, something they "know," in order to prove his point?
- Does the author affirm at least parts of the group's self-image before he criticizes other parts? (Usually a positive self-image is part of the group's shared cognition, so anyone who criticizes that image is in conflict with precious aspects of what the group members think they know.)

I will use these questions, together with a discussion about the known usage of the Pauline letter to the Ephesians, in order to assess how likely it is that the vision of the ideal Christ-believer expressed in

[136] Fiske and Taylor 1984: 171–178.

[137] Reasons for a message to be irrelevant for the current situation and the current cognitive structure could be e.g. a) that the author does not have enough knowledge about the recipients and their situation (e.g. because he writes from a distance), or b) that the author feels obliged to include traditional material which is difficult to apply to the current situation (e.g. Jesus-sayings in the synoptic Gospels).

Ephesians—or at least a similar vision—was embraced by some communities of Christ-believers.

In sum, the topic of this study, identity and behavior norms, necessitates speculation about the social situations that the texts relate to, if we are to understand why identity and behavior norms are expressed in the way they are in the texts. I will call such speculation *hypothetical history*. This hypothetical history should be coherent with relevant factors and no more elaborate than necessary. Moreover, although we seldom know anything about the reception of a text, we can use social identity theory and social cognition research to assess whether it is likely that the text reflects and successfully constructs identities and norms of the recipients.

4 The Culture of the Early Christ-Movement as Shared Cognition

The shared understanding of the relation between identity in Christ and behavior norms was part of what we may call a "culture" or a "subculture," molded within the rich and varied ancient Mediterranean culture. However, "culture" is an elusive concept. Is it possible to talk about a unified culture of the entire early Christ-movement or even of a single community of Christ-believers? Conversely, is it possible to deny cultural patterns within the early Christ-movement?

One of the classic problems of cultural anthropology is that it seems unrealistic to talk about uniform cultures with distinct borders, but equally unrealistic to deny that there are cultural phenomena. Cognitive anthropologists, beginning with Dan Sperber and followed by for instance Bradd Shore, Maurice Bloch, Claudia Strauss and Naomi Quinn have argued for a very attractive (and perhaps apparent) solution to this problem: a cultural phenomenon exists to the extent that interacting individuals share similar cognitions, which guide their interaction.[138] Culture is something in our minds. Cultural meaning is "the typical (frequently occurring and widely shared aspects of the) interpretation."[139] It is of course also extended into in our external representations (texts and other kinds of artifacts), but the external representations mean nothing until they are interpreted by minds. The cognitions of the minds in a culture could be said to have a Wittgensteinian family likeness. For example, in the ancient Mediterranean world a majority of people accepted for instance the household, the *ethnos*, honor and shame, virtue and vice, natural sex

[138] Bloch 1998; Shore 1996; Sperber 1975; 1996; Strauss and Quinn 1997.

[139] Strauss and Quinn 1997: 6.

differences, a spiritual reality, etc. Even though none of these matters were uncontested, these were concepts governing the social interaction and most people had to relate to them, whether affirmatively or not—they were cognitive schemata (i.e., mental representations[140]) widely recognized and thus cultural. In the early Christ-movement, members of communities shared beliefs and norms and their relations were determined by these shared cognitions. In other words, they too had a culture.

The advantage of this understanding of culture becomes clearer if we compare it to the "objective" and "textual" understanding of the culture of the early Christ-movement, which Gerd Theissen uses in his book *A Theory of Primitive Christian Religion* (original title: *Die Religion der ersten Christen: Eine Theorie des Urchristentums*), also published under the title *The Religon of the Earliest Churches*.[141] Theissen defines religion as "*a cultural sign system* which promises a gain in life by corresponding to an ultimate reality."[142] Moreover, religion "is an *objective* sign-system."[143] In defining religion as "a cultural sign system" that is "objective," he analyses the religion of the Christ-movement as a kind of linguistic system. Theissen subscribes to the same textual, objective and methodologically anti-subjective view of cultural symbolic systems as his source of inspiration for this definition, Clifford Geertz, does.[144]

---

[140] A "schema" is "a cognitive structure that represents organised knowledge about a given concept or type of stimulus.", Fiske and Taylor 1984: 140.

[141] Theissen 1999 (published by both SCM Press and Fortress press).

[142] Theissen 1999: 2, emphasis added.

[143] Theissen 1999: 2, ephasis added.

[144] Theissen writes that the inspiration for his definition of religion comes from Clifford Geertz's view of religion, see Theissen 1999: 2, n. 2. Geertz 1973: 90 defines religion as "(1) a system of symbols which acts to (2) establish powerful, pervasive, and long-lasting moods and motivations in men by (3) formulating conceptions of a general order of existence and (4) clothing these conceptions with such an aura of factuality that (5) the moods and motivations seem uniquely realistic." When reading Geertz, it is notoriously difficult to pinpoint his position, both because he is vague, and because he tends to change his opinion from one text to another. When I discuss Geertz in this chapter, however, it will be an interpretation of Geertz in line with Theissen's own usage of him. One might argue that Geertz can be understood differently, but for the

Many, for instance cognitive anthropologists Claudia Strauss and Naomi Quinn and cognitive psychologist Ilkka Pyysiäinen, have argued that Geertz's textual concept of culture is ontologically unintelligible.[145] Meaning can only exist in the mind. Meaning cannot just abstractly float around in some textual reality or be stored in cultural objects independently of people's interpretations: "Cultural objects, texts included, do not have any intrinsic meaning. They merely provide cues that direct people's attention, thus underdetermining their own interpretation."[146] Before I advance on this issue I must, however, empathically underscore that it does not seem to be Theissen's intention to place culture "above" our minds when he uses this terminology. He often refers to psychological mechanisms in order to explain how the culture of the early Christ-movement developed and changed. Nevertheless, there are problems inherent in the theory of culture that he leans on.

It may sometimes be fruitful to conceptualize complex phenomena, like culture, in an abstract way, and this is probably Theissen's intention when he uses the textual approach to religion. Theissen uses a textual understanding of culture in order to introduce the idea that the religion of the early Christ-movement is a "semiotic cathedral," a cultural

---

purpose of discussing Theissen I will assume the "objective" interpretation of Geertz' definition of culture which has inspired Theissen. Ever since the days of Ferdinand de Saussure, the "father" of linguistics, the word "sign" is used to denote a semiotic conception of language and culture which is a "social fact," denying (at least methodologically) that since language must be in people's minds, the meaning of the sign can vary between individuals and change as the result of interaction. "[W]hat can be chosen is already determined in advance. No individual is able … to modify in any way a choice already established in the language." "[A] language exists as a social fact", Saussure 1960: 71, 77. Also Meeks 1986 uses Geertz's understanding of culture in order to understand the morality of the first Christians, but compared to Theissen his use of Geertz is superficial.

[145] Pyysiäinen 2003: 25–53; Strauss and Quinn 1997: 12–23. In this paragraph, I base my critique of the objective and public approach to cultural meaning on these accounts, but the references in their studies indicate that their critique is quite common.

[146] Pyysiäinen 2003: 33.

language with grammatical "rules." According to Theissen, the semiotic cathedral has a grammar that holds "basic axioms" and "basic motifs" which set up positive and negative rules for what kinds of signs may or may not be assigned to the cathedral.[147] The signs of the cathedral—myth, rite and ethics—revolve around these basic axioms and basic motifs. For example, the basic motif of renunciation of status, or change of position, is actualized both in myth: Jesus renounced his high position to save humanity; in rite: for example, feet-washing; and in ethics: for example, that leaders should serve and that followers of Christ should accept loss of status. The different basic motifs of the semiotic cathedral "recur in different themes, genres and spheres of tradition."[148]

The basic motifs are regulative, that is, they serve as criteria for what is and what is not an expression of the semiotic cathedral.[149] The users of this cultural language are able to "test successfully whether a statement is an element of its own system or represents an alien element," just like users of ordinary language can know whether a sentence is correct or not.[150] His thesis is that Gnostics and others were excluded because they did not speak the language properly and introduced incompatible elements into the semiotic cathedral.[151]

But the associative patterns of recurring "basic motifs" which Theissen outlines can scarcely be treated as grammar in the sense that they can make clear distinctions between what is an element of the cathedral and what is not. Theissen has been inspired by George Lindbeck, when he argues that religion is a grammar.[152] Lindbeck leans indirectly on Noam Chomsky when he proposes a rule-theory of religion, where religions have an underlying "deep grammar" of rules which regulate the religion in question.[153] Noam Chomsky proposed a model of the brain as biologically equipped with the mechanisms for

---

[147] Theissen 1999: 5, 274–282.

[148] Theissen 1999: 271–272.

[149] Theissen 1999: 4–5.

[150] Theissen 1999: 5.

[151] Theissen 1999: 274.

[152] Lindbeck 1984, see Theissen 1999: 4, n. 7.

[153] Lindbeck 1984: 79–88.

grammar, which explains the deep-structure of syntax and which is behind every language.[154] However, whether Chomsky is right or not about language acquisition, it is a problematic move to transpose a theory about grammatical deep-structures designed for actual language to a theory of culture and religion.[155] Chomsky was able to demonstrate and define consistent deep-structure rules for how the different components of language could and could not be connected, but Theissen is not able to establish such distinct rules, only a number of highly flexible basic motifs. As Pascal Boyer remarks, "cultural anthropology has not so far produced any cultural phenomenon which would even approach the standards of certainty and stability which are familiar to linguists."[156] Early Christ-believers could certainly recognize many ideas as alien to their culture, and I am convinced that Theissen has discovered something important when he pinpoints a number of basic motifs. It is, nevertheless, misleading to propose that the users of religious and other cultural sign system always are able to make sharp distinctions between what does and does not belong to the semiotic system, as if it was as defined as a language. For instance Tertullian, *Val.* 4, claims that the gnostic Valentinus was a candidate to become a bishop, which might be an indication that the otherness of his teachings was not evident to everyone.

The idea of "basic axioms" and "basic motifs" is the reason that Theissen employs the conceptualization of culture as a language with grammar. His findings of recurring motifs are indeed important, but do we really need a textual and objective concept of culture, if we want to hang on to the fruitful idea of basic motifs?

If we treat Theissen's basic motifs as shared cognitive schemata, we can hold on to his idea about basic motifs, but drop the problematic conceptualization of culture as a grammar with rules.

---

[154] Chomsky 1957; 1965.

[155] From an interview with Chomsky about the metaphorical use of his concept of deep structure: "… I simply stopped using the term because it was being so widely misunderstood. 'Deep structure' was a technical term. … I've been appalled by what I've read on how 'deep structure' is used.", Olson and Faigley 1991.

[156] Boyer 1993: 11.

First, an objective concept of culture cannot account for intra-cultural variation, since culture is somehow "above" the subjects. Again, this is not Theissen's intention, but nevertheless it is what comes out of such a model of culture.[157] If we instead use the understanding of culture as distributed beliefs, we can overcome the pseudo-dichotomy between uniformity and diversity in the construction of identity and behavior norms within the early Christ-movement. We do not need to assume that there is one uniform set of cognitive representations, which everyone shared univocally. A more plausible imagination is that certain cognitive patterns were widely shared within an interacting population of the movement, both within and in between communities of Christ-believers. Some cultural phenomena were more established and uncontested than others. There were several versions of cognitive schemata, shared by different intermingling subgroups. With this understanding of culture, we can imagine shared perceptions of identity and behavior norms and yet conceptualize how people could challenge and reinterpret dominant patterns.

Second, a concept of culture as public text implicitly assumes that cultures are distinct entities with firm and clear borders. Assuming clear cultural borders does not always fit the intermingling of several subgroups within the Christ-movement. Assuming that culture is distributed cognition, however, there is no need to always assume a definite border. There may very well be, for instance, Christ-believers with Johannine influences, partaking in worships in communities with a Pauline tradition. This did not, however, stop the social dynamics of the Pauline tradition to mainly be governed by that tradition's understanding of their identity.

Third, Theissen's grammatical and textual approach overestimates the regulative and stabilizing capacity of cultures. With a textual approach to culture, it is difficult to discuss why cultures change, since culture is understood as objective, "above" the individuals. Theissen's book is a book about change and development and his textual model of culture is perhaps not the most adequate, when one aims to explain change. But if we understand culture as shared cognition, we can lean on

[157] Cf. Räisänen 2000: 146 whose judgment is that Theissen's "choice of a semiotic approach may have led to an overemphasis on 'system.'"

cognitive research, which has explored the conditions for stability and change in a way which is coherent with our understanding of culture. Cognitive research has, for instance, shown that cognitive schemata tend to be most open to change when they are new and based on limited experience.[158] New schemata are based on concrete experience, but as the number of experiences which are handled by the schema grows, that schema tends to become more stable, abstract and general. We can therefore expect the stability of the schemata of the Christ-movement to increase as time passes. Well developed schemata resist change (unless they are proven insufficient by overwhelming experience).[159] We can also expect the most central thematic schemata to go from concrete to abstract. The basic motifs, which I think Theissen is right to identify, are best seen as highly abstracted schemata which are the accumulated result of a large number of experiences in the movement. Once a schema has become well developed and stable, it can be used for regulatory activity, such as judging whether an instance is true or false; typical or atypical. The basic motifs of the primitive Christ-movement could therefore often have the regulatory effect, which Theissen argues that they had, but only in an approximate way, since abstract schemata are often imprecise and therefore open to interpretation.[160]

Fourth, a cognitive understanding of culture gives us a good starting point to explain why and how basic motifs spread and were reused creatively in ever new contexts within the movement. A textual and objective understanding of culture has no intrinsic mechanism to explain creativity, which is something that modifies the culture, since the "text" of the culture precedes the thoughts and actions of individuals. Theissen is absolutely no stranger to creativity in his study, but again, his model of culture does not answer how creativity, which changes culture, may

---

[158] Fiske and Taylor 1984: 173–175.

[159] Fiske and Taylor 1984: 171–173. Much could be said about the conditions which promote change also in established schemata, but the space here does not allow for that.

[160] Fiske and Taylor 1984: 146, 151; Sperber 1996: 70–74. Sperber observes that religion and other beliefs that do not refer directly to empirically observable matters, are more flexible and malleable than beliefs, which are directly based on sense perception.

come about. How did the first Christ-believers use their culture in order to create new cultural patterns, which could interpret and handle new situations? Creativity and interpretation are obviously cognitive processes. Creativity is still one of the most enigmatic capacities of the human mind, but analogical thinking and conceptual blending are central in this process.[161] We humans transfer knowledge from one domain in order to solve problems in another, or we blend knowledge from multiple domains in even more complex processes of creativity. We will discuss these processes further in chapter 11.2 when we try to discern how ingroup narratives may have been a creative resource in handling new situations.

In sum, if we imagine culture as shared cognition, we have a good starting point to discuss the relation between social identity and behavior norms. In the practical work of analyzing texts, we need to imagine the text as a text in dialogue with a culture, both drawing from it and constructing it. Identity and behavior norms are shared and constantly negotiated perceptions within the group. With this view, we can use a wide range of cognitive research on intragroup challenges, creativity in adaptation to new circumstances and so on, in a way which is coherent with our concept of culture.

---

161 Fauconnier and Turner 2002; Gentner, Kokinov and Holyoak 2001. See chapter 11.2.

5 Social Identities and the Self in a Collectivistic Culture

What do the cognitive sciences have to say about how we think about social identities and the behavior norms we associate with these identities? This is the most important aspect of the theoretical framework of this study, and it will be discussed in chapters 5 to 10. Throughout this discussion, these theories will be integrated with the ancient Mediterranean context through examples and reflection about innate universals and cultural variation. We begin by reflecting upon how we form social identities, particularty how we should understand the social self in the collectivistic culture of the first century Mediterranean.

5.1 How We Categorize

> Every living being categorizes. Even the amoeba categorizes the things it encounters into food or nonfood, what it moves toward or moves away from. The amoeba cannot choose whether to categorize; it just does. The same is true at every level of the animal world. Animals categorize food, predators, possible mates, members of their own species, and so on.[162]

Categorization is one of our most basic skills. It is difficult to even imagine how a culture could do without categorization. Different cultures do of course produce different categories, but the cognitive mechanisms behind the processes of categorization are innate.[163] Social

---

[162] Lakoff and Johnson 1999: 17.

[163] Medin, Unsworth and Hirschfeld 2007 review the growing field of cross-cultural research on categorization and shows that although there are indeed cross-cultural differences, categorization exists in all cultures. In some areas,

identity theory and self-categorization theory takes this human skill as the starting point for a discussion about group dynamics. Hence, we need to discuss briefly how humans categorize.

In the classical theory of categorization, all objects of a certain category share certain properties, which are both necessary and sufficient for making an object belong to a category.[164] For example, all birds have wings and lay eggs, etc. However, cognitive research on categorization has discovered that this view does not entirely capture how we actually categorize.[165] For instance, some categories have no definite borders. When does red stop being red? Having said that, many categories do have some quite distinct properties. For instance, birds must lay eggs to qualify as birds. Nevertheless, all categories, including those with distinct properties, have members that are better examples than others of that category. For example, robins and sparrows are better (i.e., more typical) examples of birds than penguins.

Prototypicality. Eleanor Rosch, the great pioneer on cognitive research on human categorization, introduced the insight that all categories in our minds center on a *prototype*, that is, a representation of the ideal or typical member of the category.[166] For instance, the cognition of "red" has a prototypical centre, although no definite border. The centre of a category (its prototype) is as important as its borders (necessary criteria) for our understanding of a category.

Context sensitivity. We should, however, be careful not to reify the prototype, since it is not a static construct in our minds. Rather, the prototype is the emerging effect of our cognitive structures in a certain

---

such as the categorization of animals, plants and social categories, there are important cross-cultural similarities, which indicate that categorization is partly a domain-specific cognitive skill.

[164] Taylor 2003: 19–40.

[165] Lakoff 1987: 5–11; Taylor 2003.

[166] E.g. Rosch 1978 summarized in Lakoff 1987: 39–55. Experiments on infants give strong support for the theory that the prototype effect is innate, see Goswami 1998: 25–33 for an overview. The universality of the prototype effect is recognized also by many scholars who devote their energy to finding cross-cultural differences, e.g. Norenzayan, Choi and Peng 2007: 571, 588.

context and therefore changes with the context.[167] For instance, the prototypical dog is quite different when one talks about pets and when one talks about security. Therefore, it might be better to talk about "prototypicality" or "prototypical effects" than to talk about a "prototype," in order to avoid reification.[168] I will, however, use "prototype" occasionally, since it is convenient, well aware that the prototype changes with the context.

Hierarchical organization. One thing that cognitive research on categorization has in common with the classical view is that we often arrange categories into hierarchies. There, the category on a level "above" is more inclusive than the category on a level "below": For example, entity, thing, furniture, chair, kitchen chair.[169] The more specific levels are often modeled on the characteristics of the more general level, from which modifications are made and more specific characteristics are added. For instance, a chair is made to sit on, while a kitchen chair is made to sit on in the kitchen.

Both the prototype and the ordering of categories into hierarchies are relevant for our understanding of social categories, too. Social identities, just like all categories, center on prototypes and can be ordered hierarchically.

5.2 Social Identity as Categorization

Just like humans inevitably categorize non-human entities, we categorize ourselves and each other. For example, some research suggests that automatic race and gender classifications seem to be a universal and almost unavoidable phenomenon, due to the automatic processes of categorization in our minds.[170] Other social categories, such as the identity in Christ, are culture-specific, but equally important once

---

[167] Lakoff 1987: 68–76; Ungerer and Schmid 1996: 43–55.

[168] Lakoff 1987: 68–76 uses the phrase "prototypical effects" while self-categorization theory frequently uses "prototypicality", e.g. Turner et al. 1987. Cf. Luomanen 2007: 213–214, 219–220.

[169] Taylor 2003: 48–53. Hierchical organization of categories exists in all cultures, see e.g. Atran 1989.

[170] Cosmides, Tooby and Kurzban 2003.

learned.[171] As regrettable as some may find our tendency for categorization, especially in the case of race and gender, it is a part of our makeup, and it is a means to handle our social context.

Social identity theory, introduced by Henry Tajfel, is based on the universal human capacity to categorize.[172] Tajfel proposes that a group or a social category exists because people categorize themselves as members of the group. The group exists because people believe in it and identify themselves with it. The group has certain characteristics because people share a certain way of thinking about, feeling about and evaluating their group. Tajfel demonstrated our affinity for group belonging by a series of experiments called minimal-group experiments. He showed that when people were categorized into groups they immediately started to discriminate in favor of their group, even though they had not even met the other group members and even though the group membership had no positive connotations whatsoever.[173]

Tajfel proposed that in intergroup situations, people act in terms of the group rather than in terms of their personal self.[174] Once people have categorized themselves and identified with the group, they compare themselves with relevant outgroups and seek positive distinctiveness.[175] The drive for positive self-evaluation (on the group level), according to Tajfel, is what inspires groups to act and to interpret reality in certain

---

171 Cf. Hirschfeld 1995.

172 Tajfel 1972; 1974; 1978; 1982; Tajfel and Turner 1979. Nguyen 2008: 1–2, in the introduction to his study of identity in Paul's letters to the Corinthians, quickly dismisses social identity theory as a "*modern* model" and sets out to "construct an *ancient* model or grid" for identity. Although he does not explicitly criticize biblical scholarship that uses "modern" theories, he seems to be unaware that social identity theory is an application of the universal cognitive capacity for categorization. There are aspects of social identity theory whose cross-cultural validity need to be discussed in the following sections, but Nguyen's swift dismissal of the theory as "modern" is unwarranted.

173 Tajfel et al. 1971.

174 Tajfel 1974.

175 Tajfel 1981; Tajfel and Turner 1979.

ways.[176] As a result, groups tend to exaggerate the similarity within the group (intragroup similarity), to overstate the difference between themselves and other groups (intergroup difference) and to give negative and uniform evaluations of competing groups (stereotyping). Tajfel developed his model, partly in reaction to earlier research on social cognition, which had focused mainly on how an individual experiences the social situation, rather than the group dynamic effects of our cognition. His goal was to create a model that could be used in concrete contexts to understand how and why groups, not just individuals, acted and interpreted reality.

In the footsteps of Tajfel, John Turner (et al.) developed the *self-categorization theory*.[177] The key idea of the theory is that "cognitive representations of the self take the form, amongst others, of self-categorizations, i.e., cognitive groupings of oneself and some class of stimuli as the same (identical, similar, equivalent, interchangeable and so on) in contrast to some other class of stimuli."[178] What is new about self-categorization theory, compared to social identity theory, is that it elaborates the cognitive processes which cause group processes. Most importantly, self-categorization theory develops the idea that the group (just like any category) has a prototype. That is, the group members share perceptions about the ideal group member. Moreover, self-categorization theory suggests that social categories, just like other categories, can be ordered in hierarchies.[179] For instance, the social category "New Testament scholar" could be categorized as a subcategory to the category "scholar".

Since self-categorization makes more elaborate assumptions about the cognitive processes that lie behind group formation, it makes way for the study of intragroup dynamics. On the whole, however, social identity theory and self-categorization theory are very similar. The two theories are often referred to as the "social identity perspective". In this

---

[176] The universality of the self-esteem hypothesis has been questioned, see discussion in chapter 7.1.

[177] Turner et al. 1987. Many of the ideas were presented already in Turner 1982; 1985.

[178] Turner et al. 1987: 44.

[179] Turner et al. 1987: 117-141.

study, when I make reference to "social identity theory," I will use it inclusively, since it is generally not useful to see the two theories as separate. When I refer to "self-categorization theory" it will be because there is a reason to emphasize the shift in focus between the theories.

Today social identity theory research comprises a wide spectrum of analyses of group processes, based on the social identity theory approach. As mentioned in chapter 1.2, Philip Esler has pioneered the use of these theories in the field of biblical criticism, for example with his books on Galatians and Romans.[180]

5.3 Social Identity as Dyadic Relations

Bruce Malina argues that the typical Mediterranean person has a "dyadic personality," that is, an understanding of himself or herself as interconnected with others.[181] As a biblical scholar, it might be easy to assume that the Bruce Malina's concept of the "dyadic personality" is more or less the same as Philip Esler's use of social identity theory, since they both deal with social self-construals in relation to the early Christ-movement. However, Malina's suggestion is based on the research by Harry Triandis et al. in the field of cross-cultural psychology.[182] They discovered that people in Eastern, more "collectivistic" cultures, to a larger degree than Westerners, understood themselves as interconnected to others in a network of "dyadic" face-to-face relations. Social identity theory, on the other hand, has explored how people understand themselves as members of a category. In other words, people can conceptualize their belonging either as belonging to a network of relations or as belonging to a category. These are two different kinds of cognitive constructs. Masaki Yuki shows that Eastern cultures tend to conceptualize their belonging in the "dyadic" fashion, while Westerners tend to conceptualize their belonging in the categorial fashion.[183] This

---

[180] Esler 1998; 2003.

[181] E.g. Malina 2001: 58–80.

[182] E.g. Triandis 1989; Triandis et al. 1988. See also Markus and Kitayama 1991.

[183] Yuki 2003.

could possibly mean that there could exist cultures where only one of these modes of relatedness exists. Possibly, either Malina or Esler has used a model of Mediterranean culture, which does not fit. Yuki does not wish to make absolute distinctions between East and West, however. In a recent article, he and Kosuke Tekemura highlight how intragroup relatedness and intergroup distinctiveness exist in both Western and Eastern cultures.[184] In other words, it is possible for both Easterners and Westerners to relate socially in both the dyadic and the categorial manner. Therefore, it is best to assume that individuals can identify on the individual, relational as well as on the categorial level, depending on the situation.[185] There is, as far as I can see, good reason to assume that both the relational and the categorial mode of identification existed in the ancient Mediterranean culture. For example, the household identity of a wife must be understood in both ways. Within the household, the wife held a unique role and had dyadic relations to other household members. In society at large, "wife" was a category many women belonged to. These two levels interacted so that the prototypical expectations on the category "wife" influenced the role as a wife within the household.

How, then, should we analyze the social identity of the early Christ-movement? As a network of relations or as a category? The answer depends on the texts we analyze and the questions we ask, but frequently both are relevant. For example, the narratives in the Gospels seem to assume both categorial and dyadic relationships. The Pharisees, for example, are typically portrayed as a collective category, which are in opposition to Jesus and his disciples. However, intragroup—within the category of Jesus and his disciples—the narrative portrays dyadic relations, most prominently the relation between Jesus and Peter. I would suggest that both models of social belonging are relevant for the study of the early Christ-movement. However, I have found that the categorial level of identification, explored by social identity theory, is more fruitful for the question that this study poses, since I do not primarily ask about how interpersonal dyadic relations within the early

---

[184] Takemura and Yuki 2007.

[185] Brewer and Gardner 1996; Deaux and Martin 2003.

Christ-movement relates to behavior norms, but how belonging to the Christ-movement relates to behavior norms. Moreover, although both the relational mode and the categorial mode of identification without doubt were relevant for the social life of the early Christ-movement, I would estimate that the sources from the early Christ-movement have more to say about behavior norms in relation to the categorial than the interpersonal level of belonging. Ephesians, which I will analyze in this study, definitely has more to say about identity on the categorial than on the dyadic level.

5.4 The Self in Christ as Stereotyped and Interdependent but Not Lost

According to social identity theory, when a person sees herself as a group member, she tends to "depersonalize" or "self-stereotype" herself.[186] That is, she experiences herself to be similar to the ingroup prototype, since she categorizes herself as a member of the ingroup. The group is the currently salient perception of what the individual experiences herself to be. Hence, the interests of the group are her own. As we will discuss in chapter 9, the degree of identification and self-stereotyping can vary depending on commitment to the identity and how well the identity fits into a certain situation, but we begin by discussing the effect of a rather strong identification with a social category.

Some early research in the field of social psychology about depersonalization tended to see this process as a kind of loss of the self: the individual ceases to monitor herself and subdues herself anonymously into mindless crowd behavior.[187] Stephen Reicher et al. contrast this research with the analysis of depersonalization in social identity theory.[188]

---

[186] "Depersonalized" and "self-stereotyping" are terms used in Turner et al. 1987. "Deindividuation" is used in much earlier research, e.g. Le Bon 1896; Zimbardo 1969.

[187] Reicher, Spears and Postmes 1995. See also n. 186.

[188] Reicher, Spears and Postmes 1995. Reicher builds on earlier research, see e.g. Turner et al. 1987; Abrams and Hogg 1990, but I refer to Reicher's article

The self—that is, my perception of who I am—is not a unitary cognitive construct according to social identity theory.[189] Rather, the self has several subsystems, a) personal identity and b) social identities. "Thus, in becoming part of a group, individuals do not lose all sense of self, rather they shift from the personal to the social level of identification ... The criterion for action shifts from the personal to the social categorical level."[190] When a social category component of the self is salient in a person's mind, that social identity is "who I am." The individual still experiences herself as an individual, but the experience of "who I am" is formed by her current conceptualization of herself as a group member. The interest of the group *is* the interest of the individual, and the norms of the group *are* the norms of the individual. This understanding of what happens to the self when one identifies with a group has implications for how we understand the rather collectivistic culture of the ancient Mediterranean world.

Ancient Mediterranean culture was largely a collectivistic culture.[191] The term "collectivistic" in "collectivistic culture" is used here according to its use in both cross-cultural psychology and social identity theory. In terms of cross-cultural psychology, a collectivistic culture is a culture where the self is understood not as distinct, but interdependent and integrated with others.[192] In terms of social identity theory, it is a culture where people tend to categorize themselves as members of various social categories, rather than in terms of their personal identity. As I argued above in chapter 5.3, these two levels of social identification are not the same, but both are relevant for the understanding of the collectivistic nature of the ancient Mediterranean world. In collectivistic cultures, people are socialized into the value that it is not my unique features that are valuable and stable, but the features of the social context to which I

---

because it pinpoints the difference of social identity theory in relation to other strands of research.

[189] Reicher, Spears and Postmes 1995: 176.

[190] Reicher, Spears and Postmes 1995: 177. On the concept of the self, see also Abrams 1999; Hogg and Abrams 1988; Turner et al. 1994.

[191] Malina 2001: 58–76. On the concept of culture, see chapter 4.

[192] Markus and Kitayama 1991.

belong. Therefore, who I am, what I feel, think, do, etc., is and should be a function of my salient social identity and my role within the group. (This definition of a collectivistic culture is a theoretical position at one end of a spectrum and we would be wrong in denying all individualistic tendencies in antiquity, cf. the discussion about Cicero below.) In the ancient Mediterranean world, honor and shame were typically given to each individual to the extent that they excelled in the expectations of their social category.[193] An honor-shame culture, especially in its more agonistic form, could easily collapse into ever escalating spirals of violence, which occasionally actually happened.[194] Typically, however, egoistic aggression would not merit honor. Halvor Moxnes argues that "[a]s society became more complex in the Hellenistic period there was a need for less competitive and aggressive values and attitudes in order to keep the city-state (πόλις, *polis*) united."[195] The overarching vision was a society or a group in *homonoia* (ὁμονοία, lat. *concordia*), "same-mindedness."[196] The agonistic competition for honor was governed by *homonoia* norms that promoted harmony and ascribed honor to those who contributed to the group rather than those who competed in a destructive way with others in the group. The picture of the community as a body, where different parts interacted in harmony and needed each other was a widely used picture of society.[197] In terms of social identity theory, the city-state, the *ethnos*, the household, the identity in Christ, etc., were considered to be superordinate social identity categories, within which different subordinate identities should be defined in relation to the superordinate category.[198] In terms of dyadic relations, every person and every group was to accept their role in relation to other

---

[193] For Biblical studies of honor and shame, see e.g. DeSilva 1995; Lawrence 2003; Malina 2001; Moxnes 1996; Neyrey 1998. Lawrence 2003 has a fairly recent overview of the field. On Roman honor, see Barton 2001. On Greek honor, see Cairns 1993.

[194] Barton 2001: 88–111.

[195] Moxnes 1996: 34.

[196] On *homonoia*, see Thraede 1994.

[197] E.g. Plato, *Leg.* 628c ff.; Aristotle, *Pol.*, 1253a, Cicero, *Off.* 3.22; Seneca, *Ira* 2.31.

[198] See chapters 5.1 and 9.1.

parts of the community. In this collectivistic mindset, virtues and behavior norms were defined in relation to one's specific role or subordinate category. A few examples: Plato's *Republic* depicts the ideal state in perfect harmony. Every individual is conceptualized as belonging to society on the superordinate level and on the subordinate level as belonging to the group of either guardians, auxiliaries or producers. Only the guardians excel in the virtue of wisdom and only the auxiliaries excel in the virtue of courage (*Rep.* 427d-445b).[199] A small elite of the best should govern all the others in order to obtain a harmonious society. Also Cicero attributes different duties to different social roles. In his four-personae theory in *On Duties,* he says that man has four *personae,* one generally human *persona,* one individual *persona,* one social *persona* that chance has provided, and finally one social *persona* which is the social role we are striving for (*Off.* 1.107, 115).[200] The fact that he takes individually unique traits into consideration warns against a too uniform picture of the Mediterranean culture as only interested in duties derived from social roles. His focus is, however, more on social duties and general duties as a human. Different social roles oblige a person to do different things—young people and old people; magistrates and common people; citizens and foreigners; they all have different duties (Cicero, *Off.* 1.122–125). Likewise, Hierocles details the duties of different social categories in his *On Duties*.[201] Further, the Jewish wisdom literature praises those who fulfill their household duties and reproaches those who do not (e.g. Prov 30:21–32; 31:10–31; Sir 3:1–16; 4:1–10). (More examples of collectivistic thinking will be given below and in chapter 6.)

But does this collectivistic stance mean that the individuals in antiquity had a weaker sense of self? The unfortunate idea in early social psychology that a collective context equals loss of the self as a responsible agent,[202] made its way into biblical studies in the idea of

---

[199] See Mulgan 1968.

[200] See Gill 1988.

[201] An English translation of Hierocles, *On Duties* can be found in Malherbe 1986: 85–104.

[202] Cf. nn. 186 and 187.

"corporate personality." Henry Wheeler Robinson claimed in the beginning of the 20th century that Jewish (and Christian) texts could only be understood through the concepts of "corporate personality."[203] By this he meant that the Hebrew concept of the self was often a kind of pre-logical primitive collective self, where the action of one person could be seen as the action of the entire group. The paradigmatic example is Josh 7:1, where the whole of Israel is guilty of the transgression of Achan. He argues that people did not only see themselves as interdependent, but that they had a blurred sense of agency. His idea became very popular and was extensively used in biblical studies, but has now been refuted with compelling arguments by Joshua Porter, John Rogerson and Stanley Porter.[204] J. Porter argues that the juridical laws of the Torah consistently judges personal responsibility. More importantly, Rogerson shows that Robinson's ideas are based on sweeping generalizations and wild anthropological speculation about the primitive psyche popular in his time, which later generations of anthropologists would abhor. S. Porter basically affirms the argument of the former two and shows indignation over how several scholars have failed to leave the theories of Robinson behind. However, although Robinson's characterization of the collective mind was less successful, we cannot escape the massive impression that the Jewish people had a sense of belonging, common fate and often also collective responsibility. The critics of the "corporate personality" theory confirm the collectivistic stance in the *Tanak*, even though they want to abandon the theoretical framework of Robinson.

Richard Freund has shown how ideas of individual and collective responsibility go side by side in Jewish literature from exilic times to late antiquity.[205] He does not impose a corporate personality onto Jewish thinking when he explains his findings, but rather gives a functionalistic explanation. He argues that people were often so strongly dependent on each other in agrarian societies that it probably seemed reasonable that the group should accept collective responsibility for the actions of

---

[203] E.g. Robinson 1911; 1964, summarized by Porter 1965.

[204] Porter 1965; Porter 1990; Rogerson 1970. These articles also give an overview of the impact of the theory in the field. See also Malina and Neyrey 1996: 12–13.

[205] Freund 1997.

individual group members, under certain circumstances. "A concept of collective retributive justice and punishment may have developed to ensure the fulfilment of obligations of individuals to the group necessary to maintain an integrated economy."[206]

Dale Patrick analyses the collective responsibility in Deut 12–26 to enforce the law as rhetoric.[207] According to Patrick, the order to "purge the evil from your midst" (13:5; 17:7; 19:19; 22:21; 22:24; 24:7) is a call for national solidarity and the punishment of deviants in a historical situation when Josiah attempted to strengthen the nation. In Deut 12–26, the laws punish the individual, but the people is a) collectively responsible to punish transgressors and b) collectively accountable for the success and failure to do so, which God collectively will reward or punish, respectively. Such a rhetorical construct is intended to inspire the enforcement of the law. In the same way, the narration of the Achan-incident (Josh 7:1) is better seen as a rhetorical device to mobilize a sense of collective responsibility, rather than an expression of a vague sense of agency.

The individual in a collectivistic setting was self-stereotyped, interdependent and experienced himself/herself as integrated with others, while still being an agent. However, when an individual was seen as an agent, the value of his/her actions was measured by the standards of the group.[208] A few examples: According to Jesus Ben Sirach (second century B.C.E), every Jewish individual is especially scrutinized by God, because he belongs to the collective, which God has chosen for himself as his property (Sir 17:17–32). Another vivid example of the relationship between collective and individual is the relation between the chorus and the individual characters in the Greek tragedies. According to John Gould, the function of the chorus is often to be the voice of the shared collective experience.[209] The actors of the drama are

[206] Freund 1997: 280.

[207] Patrick 1995.

[208] "[L]iving interdependently does not mean the loss of self, the fusion of self with others, or the absence of self-interest. What it does mean is that attention, cognition, affect, and motivation are organized with respect to relationships and norms", Fiske et al. 1998: 925.

[209] Gould 1996.

individuals, but the meaning and value of their actions is disclosed by the voice of the chorus. Andrew Riggsby, in his analysis of the relation between the self and the community in Pliny the Younger (c. 62–113 C.E.), concludes: "Traditional aristocratic thinking may well have included some sort of *moi*-idea, but it was the *personne* around which their values were organised."[210]

Bruce Malina introduced a more reasonable description of the collective culture of the ancient Mediterranean world, with the concept of the "dyadic personality" (cf. chapter 5.3 above).[211] Although I find his account valuable at large, there is, however, one aspect of the collective personality as described by Malina that is untenable: he claims that the collectively oriented persons of the Mediterranean world did not find introspection meaningful and interesting, since their identity was confirmed in interaction with others.[212] Malina occasionally specifies the introspection as "individualistic" introspection,[213] but most of the time he just claims that they did not engage in introspection at all.[214] Later, he modifies his position and concedes that Greek and Roman philosophers did discuss matters like will, virtues and emotions, but maintains that such issues were absent among Jews and in the New Testament.[215] Such a sharp distinction between Greco-Roman and Jewish culture is odd in the light of the fact that Jews had been in contact with and influenced by Greek ideas for centuries. In the Second Temple era, Greek thinking influenced Jewish writers such as Philo, Josephus, Jesus ben Sirach and

---

[210] Riggsby 1998. Riggsby's terminology is taken from the classical article by Marcel Mauss from 1938 (English translation: Mauss 1985). Although Mauss's overly neat evolutional account of the development of the sense of the self is generally abandoned, many still use his distinction between *moi* (individual self) and *personne* (social self). See Carrithers, Collins and Lukes 1985 for a series of articles using Mauss as the point of departure.

[211] Malina 2001: 58–80. (Originally Malina 1981.)

[212] Malina 2001: 66–67.

[213] E.g. Malina 2001: 65. If Malina had consistently only claimed that they did not think of their dispositions as individually unique, I would have been able to agree with his description.

[214] E.g. Malina 2001: 66–68.

[215] Malina 2001: 68.

the anonymous author of the Wisdom of Solomon. I would agree that the *Tanak* texts have less elaborate introspective concepts than for instance Aristotle and the Stoics have (see chapter 6.3). Nevertheless, the thought of dispositions as the cause of action is not strange to the *Tanak*. "Because the LORD your God is a *merciful* God, he will neither abandon you nor destroy you." (Deut. 4:31, emphasis added).[216] God's disposition to being merciful is the cause of action. There was an elaborate debate in the Hellenistic era how people should handle their desires and emotions by means of virtue.[217] The Jewish wisdom tradition was perhaps less sophisticated, but nevertheless moralized about emotions and virtues.[218] "One who is slow to anger is better than the mighty, and one whose temper is controlled than one who captures a city" (Prov 16:32). A culture, which both acknowledges and moralizes about virtues and emotions as the cause of action, can hardly be characterized as not caring about "psychological motivations"[219] even if the explanations are less elaborate and more stereotypical than those of our day.

According to social identity theory, to identify with a social category is not to stop self-monitoring or engaging in introspection.[220] The individual who identifies with a social identity reflects upon him- or herself as a group member, including inner thoughts and desires, in order to be able to fulfill what he or she experiences him- or herself to be in this social identity.[221] Rather than no introspection, there is self-stereotyped introspection, where the individual evaluates feelings, thoughts and actions in relation to the prototype of the currently salient

---

216 Frequently in the Old Testament, dispositions like חמלה , "sparing" (e.g. Gen 19:16), רחום , "compassionate" (e.g. Deut 4:31), חסד , "merciful" (e.g. Prov. 11:17), קנוא , "jealous" (e.g. Exod 20:5) explain both the actions of God and humans.

217 Sihvola and Engberg-Pedersen 1998. See discussion in chapter 6.3.

218 Brown 1996.

219 Malina 2001: 66. It seems to me that Malina even contradicts himself when he later correctly claims that Matt. 5:27–30 emphasizes "the relation between the head and the hands and the feet, between one's interior, innermost self and one's outward activity" (p. 71).

220 Reicher, Spears and Postmes 1995.

221 See the discussion in chapter 6.1 about self-regulation.

identity.[222] It is quite difficult to imagine how a collectively oriented person would be able to adhere to the ingroup norms without this kind of self-regulatory mental activity. Louise Lawrence, in a thorough appraisal of Malina's theories, comes to a similar conclusion.[223] Having surveyed recent developments in anthropological studies of honor and shame she concludes:

> Whilst the management of one's appearance before others is particularly well attested in Mediterranean ethnography, this does not preclude an interest in introspection. On the contrary, the importance of one's public self being aligned to one's private intentions was a focus of moralizing.[224]

It is preferable to view the early Christ-believers as capable of introspection with a stereotypical perception of the self rather than view them as lacking in introspection.

In sum, identification of oneself as belonging to a group means that the self is experienced as similar to the ingroup prototype and interdependent on other group members, but it does not mean a loss of the self as a distinctive agent, nor that the individual stops engaging in basic introspection, not even in collectivistic cultures. Both Jews, Greeks and Romans had concepts about for instance virtues and emotions that they used to explain and moralize about behavior. These concepts helped them regulate themselves and thus fulfill the ideals of their social identities, as we will explore further in chapter 6. In many contexts of the ancient Mediterranean world, the individual felt responsible for the actions of other group members as the result of his or her identification with the group. However, the sense of collective responsibility did not diminish individual responsibility.

---

[222] The same can to a certain extent be said of our Western culture. Even if we are taught to believe that our feelings and motivations are unique, they are often quite stereotypical. We too have cultural ideas about proper feelings and motivation for different situations.

[223] Lawrence 2003: 113–141. See also Barton 2001: 202–242, discussing how the Romans moralized about sincerity.

[224] Lawrence 2003: 135.

6 Explaining the Cause of Behavior

David Hume's famous analysis of the logical non-necessity of causality is of little practical concern to us humans in our everyday lives—causality is nevertheless part of how humans *a priori* understand the world, as Immanuel Kant rightly argued.[225] Causal cognition is a cross-culturally universal and innate capacity, although it can take a variety of cultural forms.[226] Our causal cognition enables us to interpret, predict and manipulate our material and social environment, which is obviously a great advantage.

Generally, two forms of causal cognition can be distinguished in all humans: a) mechanical causality, where we think that an inanimate object changes due to external force from another object, and b) intentional causality, where we think that a living agent acts, driven by internal force, since the agent intends to do so.[227] Billiard balls and humans may both be the cause of events, but humans, as opposed to billiard balls, act purposefully. For our purpose, the intentional kind of causal cognition is of greatest interest. This kind of causal belief is often

---

[225] Hume 1739; Kant 1787, summarized by De Pierris and Friedman 2008.

[226] Sperber, Premack and James Premack 1995 for an overview of different perspectives on causal cognition. The authors of this volume generally agree that all humans have the capacity for causal cognition, although they debate how much intercultural variation there is in these causal beliefs.

[227] Premack and James Premack 1995; Sperber 1995. There is a debate whether these two are one or two different domains of knowledge. E.g. Lakoff 1987: 54–56 suggests that all causal cognition belongs to one domain of cognition, while e.g. Boyer 1995 argues that folk mechanics and folk psychology are different cognitive domains.

referred to as the "theory of mind."[228] Based on studies of how infants react to different kinds of movement, James Premack concludes that "the perception of intention, like that of causality, is a hard-wired perception."[229] We humans have an innate capacity both to intuitively perceive and to consciously theorize about what is going on in the mind of an intentional agent. Why does X act? What goals, knowledge, circumstances, dispositions, etc., causes X to act intentionally? Although we do not always manage to understand each other correctly, this capacity is immensely important in our social interaction.

Beyond this basic universality there is, however, considerable cross-cultural diversity in how we explain human behavior. Therefore, we will have to survey the variations that research on human cognition has encountered and ask which of these variations are present in the ancient Mediterranean world.[230] Before we do that, however, we need to discuss the processes of explaining and moralizing about behavior in a group context.

6.1 The Interplay between Attributions, Moral Judgment and the Ingroup Prototype

The orator, philosopher and senator Cicero (106–43 B.C.E) writes in one of his many letters to his friend Atticus: "I always attach more importance to the causes of events (*causae eventorum)* than the events themselves" (*Att.* 9.5/171). Cicero's attitude is not unique, but rather typical. Explanations of why people act and why things happen are central to our understanding of social events. The mental process of explaining behavior as the result of dispositions is called "attribution" in social cognition research.[231] We explain the cause of our own and other

---

[228] E.g. Leslie 1995; Premack and James Premack 1995. Some recent research does, however, question the idea that we humans generally have conscious "theories" about other people's intentions. Rather, our perception of the intention of others is often intuitive and unconscious, see e.g. Zlatev et al. 2008.

[229] Premack 1990: 2.

[230] See chapters 6.2–6.4.

[231] E.g. Augoustinos, Donaghue and Walker 2006: 149–185; Fiske and Taylor 1984: 20–98.

people's behavior with dispositions such as knowledge, goals, character traits and emotions. These kinds of explanations were quite frequent in antiquity, too.[232] Explaining behavior with "nature" (e.g., male/female, slave/free), social role and spiritual standing was probably more frequent in antiquity than in our days, but is in no way totally absent in modern Western culture.[233]

Historically, social cognition research has sometimes had a tendency to imagine the explaining individual as a passive and neutral interpreter of others, who just wants to understand other people's behavior.[234] It has, however, become increasingly well documented that we are frequently biased, moralizing, strategic and goal-oriented in our attributions.[235] We are more willing to attribute (malevolent) intentionality to people when we are harmed by an action than when we are not. We often prefer to attribute positive characteristics to ourselves, in order to increase self-esteem. Attributions of character traits, emotions, etc., which are thought to cause behavior, are often value-laden. To be wise is good, to be greedy is bad, etc. We are not only motivated to understand each other; we are also motivated to praise and blame ourselves and each other. Often we even make a moral judgment of an action first, without even considering factors such as intentionality and dispositions, and then attribute fitting morally loaded attributed explanations as to why people acted the way they did.[236] In short, the

---

[232] See discussion in chapter 6.3.

[233] See discussion in chapters 6.2 and 6.4.

[234] Augoustinos, Donaghue and Walker 2006: 20–21. Historically, there has been a scientific schism between social identity theory research and social cognition research (the scientific field that has explored attribution), where social identity theory has accused social cognition research of incapacity to explain how cognition is active in forming group dynamics. Hogg and Abrams 1999; Operario and Fiske 1999 give good overviews over the historical differences between the two strands of social psychology research.

[235] Augoustinos, Donaghue and Walker 2006: 164–166; Cushman, Knobe and Sinnott-Armstrong 2008; Shaver 1985: 129–133; Williams 2003.

[236] Leslie, Knobe and Cohen 2006.

process goes both from attribution to moral judgment and from moral judgment to attribution.[237]

The intertwining of attribution and moral judgment was certainly apparent in the Greek virtue ethics. *Virtues and Vices,* attributed to Aristotle (384–322 B.C.E.) but probably written in the first century B.C.E.,[238] opens with this statement:

> Fine things (τὸ κάλον) are the object of praise, base things (τὸ αἰσχρόν) of blame; and at the head of the fine stand the virtues (ἀρετή), at the head of the base the vices (κακία); consequently the virtues are objects of praise, and also the *causes* (αἴτιον) of virtues are objects of praise, and the *things that accompany* (τὸ παρεπόμενον) the virtues and *that result* (τὸ γινόμενον) from them, and their *works* (ἔργον) [i.e., behavior], while the opposites are the objects of blame.
>
> (Aristotle, *Virt. vit.* 1.1–2, emphasis added.[239])

The Greeks, who also influenced both Jews and Romans, did not just combine attributions and value judgments—they based their moral discourse on the convictionnotion that it was right to do so.[240] Virtue and vice was at the centre of their moral discussions. It is an interesting detail that the Greek word for "cause," αἴτιον, was frequently used in legal discourse with the meaning "responsibility."[241] Anyone who behaved well should be recognized as having virtue and consequently be praised.[242]

The cognitive processes between attributions and moral judgment go both ways: attributions guide moral judgments and moral judgments inspire biased attributions. Therefore, the attribution process motivates us to regulate our behavior in a way which is consistent with our self-

---

[237] Knobe 2005.

[238] Rackham 1952 thinks that the text is a simplification of Aristotelian ethics.

[239] Cf. *Nic. Eth.* 4.3.9–11, 14: "The reward of virtue is honor" (4.3.14).

[240] On Greek virtue ethics, see MacIntyre 1981: 121–164.

[241] Lloyd 1995.

[242] This attitude is quite opposed to much modern ethics, which often only asks if the behavior or the consequences of behavior are ethically right, see MacIntyre 1981: 160–161.

image and our image before others, in order to avoid *cognitive dissonance*, both before ourselves and others.[243] Cognitive dissonance occurs when we cannot create coherence between different cognitions. We want our actions to harmonize with what we consider ourselves to be. If I believe that my identity in Christ causes me to do good, I will have motivation to do good (or at least behave in a way, which allows me to think of myself as someone who does good) in order to be able to maintain my belief that I am in Christ. Conversely, if I fail to act according to the behavior norms of my group, I may have to blame myself. (Alternatively, I might a) become creative and adjust my interpretation of the ingroup norms, so that I can maintain a positive self-evaluation or b) distance myself from the group.[244]) Moreover, since I know that others in the group may make attributions about my commitment and character, I will have social motifs to act in a way that will make them think of me as a prototypical group member. In short, the indicative belief that attribute A causes behavior B, is simultaneously an imperative to do B in order to be A (or to avoid B in order not to be A).

When we communicate our attributions (rather than just think them) our motivation to praise and blame gains yet another dimension. Derek

---

[243] Bem 1967; 1972; Festinger 1957, summarized by Augoustinos, Donaghue and Walker 2006: 128–130. There are two theories which attempt to explain this self-regulation, cognitive dissonance theory, introduced by Leon Festinger, and self-perception theory, introduced by Daryl Bem. According to cognitive dissonance theory we dislike having experiences and beliefs that contradict each other. Therefore we either have to change our behavior or change our perception of ourselves in order to make our beliefs coherent. According to self-perception theory we always attribute what we believe are reasonable causes of our behavior to ourselves ad hoc, in order to explain to ourselves why we did what we did. The difference is thus that according to dissonance theory the impact between attribution and behavior is bidirectional and dialectic, but in self-perception theory, the impact always goes from behavior to attribution. While Bem's theory suggests less demanding cognitive efforts, Festinger's theory can account better for how our beliefs about ourselves can motivate behavior. Cf. Theissen 1983: 41–49. Theissen uses attribution theory and cognitive dissonance theory, but does not integrate it with social identity theory in the way this study does. On "status before others" see also chapter 8.3.

[244] Cf. chapter 9.3.

Edwards and Jonathan Potter have pointed out the highly strategic and rhetorical aspect of discourse about attribution.[245] If I tell you that "I did X out of love," I probably want to guide your process of attribution, since otherwise you might have come to the wrong conclusion about what caused me to do X. In his *Rhetoric,* Aristotle divides the possible persuasive strategies into *logos, ethos* and *pathos*.[246] When he discusses *ethos,* he is aware that there is much to win by presenting oneself as someone with good character:

> [P]roofs (πίστις) are established not only by demonstrative (ἀποδείκτικος, "apodictic"), but also by ethical (ἠθικός, "character based") arguments—since we have confidence in an orator who *exhibits* certain qualities [...] We shall incidentally bring to light the means to *appear* of such and such a character, ... for it is by the same means that we shall be able to inspire confidence in ourselves or others. (Aristotle, *Rhet.* 1.8.6, 9, emphasis added)

If you can induce the belief that a person has a good character, it will be difficult to think that he has done evil. An attribution rhetoric of this kind can also be seen in Cicero's famous defense speeches, where he repeatedly refers to the virtue, honor and past actions of the different parties in a court, including himself, in order to prove that the accused could not possibly have done what he is accused of, or at least must have had a very noble reason to do so.[247]

The rhetorical aspect of communicating attribution is particularly relevant in a group context. For example, the claim in 2 Peter against the "false teachers" (2:1) that "in their greed these teachers will exploit you with stories they have made up" (2 Pet 2:3), is hardly a neutral evaluation of the motivation of "these teachers," but rather intended to portray them as deviants who should be rejected. Not only are their actions deviant—their deviant actions are caused by deviant dispositions.[248]

---

[245] Edwards and Potter 1992: 77–126.

[246] *Logos* is rational argumentation, *pathos* is touching the feelings of the audience and *ethos* is argument of character. On rhetorical analysis, see e.g. Black 1965; Kennedy 1984.

[247] E.g. Cicero, *Cael., Mil., Arch.* and, *Roch.*

[248] On deviants, see chapter 8.2.

In a group context, we need to imagine that the processes of moral judgment and attribution are related to the ingroup prototype. The ingroup prototype is structured as a set of prototypical attributes and behaviors:[249]

> A social identity category
> is characterized by an *ingroup prototype,*
> which has an *attributed side,*
> consisting of normative beliefs, goals, character traits, spiritual states etc.
> and a *perceptible side,*
> consisting of norms of behavior and appearance

For instance, the ingroup prototype Paul describes could be summarized like this:

> Example: *Prototypical Christ-believer,* according to Paul (simplified)
>
> Attributed side:
> Beliefs: Thinks that Christ is the savior
> Spiritual states: Is in Christ; has the Spirit
> Character traits: Believing; has the fruits and the gifts of the Spirit
> Goals: Wants to do the will of God; wants community with God through Christ
> Perceptible side:
> A multitude of practical behaviors

[249] The model is also valid for the prototype (or stereotype) of various outgroups. Our cognitive schemata of both individuals and groups typically hold both attributes and behaviors, see Augoustinos, Donaghue and Walker 2006: 69–71. (The concepts of "role schema" in social cognition research is for our purposes equivalent to a social identity category, as described in social identity theory.) The attribution process is relevant both on the individual, group and societal level; see Hewstone 1989 for an overview.

Since moral judgments and attributions affect each other mutually, there is a rhetorically useful ambiguity in the causal attributions of the ingroup prototype. The prototype can both be interpreted as "is" and "should be"; indicative and imperative. For instance, the phrase קדשים והייתם in Lev 11:44, 45; 20:7, 26, holds this ambiguity. The phrase could be translated either "You are holy" (indicative) or "Be holy" (imperative).[250] "Holy" is the hallmark of the ingroup prototype of the Jewish people, so an ambiguous grammatical expression is certainly fitting. The prototypical characteristic "holy" as a description of the group (indicative) can be source of self-esteem for the group, but also for the individual, since the individual tends to see herself as similar to the prototype.[251] But "holiness" can also be a rhetorical weapon for exhortation, praise and blame, (imperative) since it can be used to measure ingroup members by. For example, a Pharisee who does not practice the Torah according to group standards can be judged as less holy (or pure, righteous, etc.), that is, deviating from the ingroup prototype. (On the group dynamic effects of the prototype, see chapters 7 and 8 below.)

After this discussion, we can note briefly that Paul did not invent the tension between imperative and indicative. Rather, it is typical for identity rhetorics. In Rom 6–7 the indicative is that the believer *is* dead to sin, since he/she is in Christ and the imperative is that the believer *should be* dead to sin, since he/she is in Christ (cf. Gal 5:24–25). This tension is only to be expected, since Paul in these chapters discusses his interpretation of their identity.[252] Every ingroup prototype is experienced

---

[250] E.g. NRSV, NIV, ESV and NASB translate קדשים והייתשם (consecutive perfect) as an imperative. One of the many possible functions of the consecutive perfect in Hebrew is to "introduce a command or wish", see Gesenius 1910: §112.4.(b). The basic function of consecutive perfect is, however, indicative. LXX manages to preserve the tension between indicative and imperative by translating the phrase in the future tense, ἅγιοι ἔσεσθε, which can have both imperative and future indicative meaning.

[251] On self-stereotyping, see chapter 5.4.

[252] Parsons 1995 surveys the research on indicative and imperative in Paul and comes to the quite common conclusion that indicative precedes imperative

as both descriptive and prescriptive by ingroup members. If there is anything particular about Paul's account, it is not the tension itself, but that he highlights the tension and gives it a particular narrative framework.

In sum, attribution is closely related to moral judgments. In a group context, discourse about attribution is a way to judge or praise the prototypicality and status of both ingroup members and outgroups. The ingroup prototype holds both character traits and behaviors. The beliefs about what causes a certain action—beliefs that are integrated in the prototype—will therefore be very important in the analysis of how the texts present the relation between identity in Christ and behavior norms.

6.2 Explaining the Cause of Behavior in the Ancient Mediterranean World

In the beginning of chapter 6 I argued that causal beliefs and attribution of intention to human agents are universal features of the human mind. However, although these aspects of causal cognition are universal, we must, nevertheless, be careful not to press our own individualistic and secularized interpretations of the causes of human behavior onto the early Christ-movement. For not only do we have beliefs about intentionality, we also have beliefs about what causes an agent to have intentions.[253] The narratives about what causes intention vary from culture to culture. I write "*narratives* about what causes intention" for

---

in Paul's thinking. This is indeed how Paul describes the initial chronological order between the two. Such an analysis does not, however, consider how the tension between indicative and imperative probably functioned in a group context. Cf. Horrell 2005: 91–95 who just like this study concludes that the tension between indicative and imperative is not very specifically Pauline, but rather typical for many social groups. Horrell's analysis is based on Clifford Geertz's discussion of "world-view" and "ethos." On identity formation in Rom 5–7, see Esler 2003: 195–242.

[253] Leslie 1995: 122 argues that we humans represent human agents as having a) mechanical properties (a body), b) actional properties (intention) and c) cognitive properties (dispositions, knowledge, emotions, etc.). It is the cultural variation in c) that I wish to explore in this section.

two reasons. First, the causal connection between events is one of the hallmarks of a narrative, as we will discuss in chapter 11.1. Beliefs about what causes intention and action could therefore be seen as mini-narratives. Second, the cultural variation in explaining behavior suggests that these explanations are typically integrated in the larger network of narratives, which are formed in different cultures.

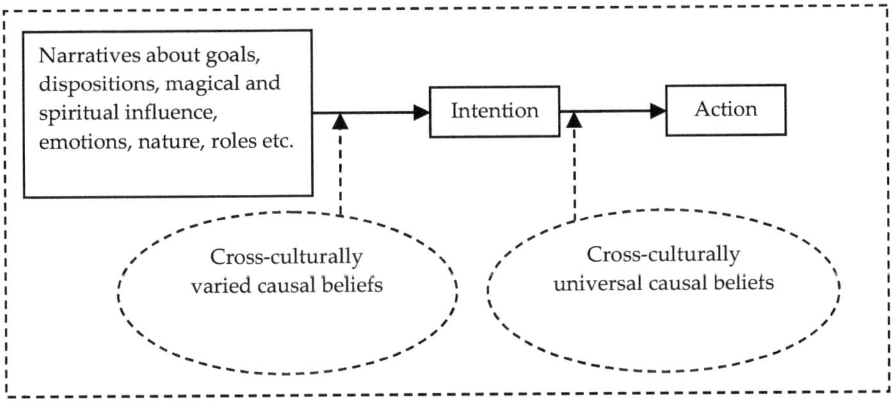

It is well attested that we Westerners like to explain events as the result of individual, long-lasting and stable character traits and goals of the people who are involved in the events.[254] It is a part of our narrative about the free individual with integrity and independent agency. Since we Westerners are probably too fond of this kind of explanation, it is often referred to as "the fundamental attribution error."[255] But even though this belief is so native to us that we barely reflect upon it, it is not the only and universal way to explain what causes a person to do something.[256] In more collective Asian cultures, people are more inclined to attribute behavior to the role they have (i.e., their social identity) and the circumstances they are in.[257] They also see dispositions as less stable

[254] Cf. n. 231.

[255] The term was coined by Ross 1977.

[256] Markus and Kitayama 1994 suggest that the preference for individuality in Western culture has dominated Western social psychology to the degree that research has neglected the interconnectedness of the self to the context.

[257] Kunda 1999: 517–556; Markus and Kitayama 1991; 1994.

and more constructed from the situation than individualists tend to do.[258]

Does this mean that people from collectivistic cultures are incapable of perceiving dispositions as the cause of action? There are indeed cultures where "trans-situationally stable" individual dispositions are not used to explain behavior.[259] (Dispositions are, however, used in the ancient Mediterranean culture to explain action, see chapters 5.4 and 6.3.) But people from more collectivistic cultures are, nevertheless, fully capable of attributing dispositions to each other.[260] In chapter 5.4 above, I argued that the self does not stop introspecting even in a collectivistic setting. In some cross-cultural research about the difference between collective and individualistic cultures as to how people explain behavior, the explanations of behavior have been categorized into merely two categories: a) attribution to goals and traits of the individual, or b) attribution to the social situation, the role, the context, the circumstances, etc.[261] This dichotomy fails to see that b) can be divided into b1) attribution to circumstances, which are external to the agent and b2) attribution to collective goals and dispositions (etc.) of groups. Tanya Menon et al. have pointed out this important distinction.[262] Her experiments show that in collective cultures, even though people do not attribute action to individual traits to the same extent, they are quite keen on attributing behavior to the disposition of groups and social categories. For example, this argument in 1 John was perfectly intelligible in the collectivistic context of the first Christ-believers:

---

[258] Choi, Nisbett and Norenzayan 1999; Miller 1984; Triandis et al. 1988.

[259] Hirschfeld 1995: 315.

[260] "A survey of ethnographic and psychological literature suggests, however, that dispositionist thinking is in no way absent in non-Western cultures, including East Asian cultures. Indeed, there is substantial evidence that East Asians do have and use dispositions in much the same way that Americans do", Choi, Nisbett and Norenzayan 1999: 54.

[261] E.g. Miller 1984. See Menon, Morris and Chiu 1999 for further examples.

[262] Menon, Morris and Chiu 1999. Cf. Choi, Nisbett and Norenzayan 1999: 56.

> [W]hoever *obeys his word* [behavior], truly in this person *the love of God has reached perfection* [disposition]. By this we may be sure that *we are in him* [social identity/spiritual status]: whoever says, "*I abide in him* [social identity/spiritual status]," ought to *walk just as he walked* [behavior]. (1 John 2:5–6)

The ingroup member is (or should be) characterized by prototypical dispositions and spiritual states, which cause his/her actions.

People do, however, sometimes explain behavior directly from social identity categories, without taking the intermediate step of assuming mental states. We sometimes explain behavior as the direct result of belonging to a certain category of people. This kind of explanation seems to be more common in collectivistic cultures.[263] When the Gospel of Mark tells us that Simon and Andrew were "casting a net into the sea [behavior]—for they were fishermen [social identity]" (Mark 1:16), the text does not bother to explain that as fishermen, they had the *goal* (i.e., a disposition) to make a living out of fishing, but presents fishing as something that those who belong to the category of fishermen just do. We should not, however, assume that this was the most common discourse in the early Christ-movement. In the case of the fishermen in this passage, we should not be too hasty to equal discourse about attributions with the full content of the author's beliefs.[264] The author may just assume that everyone knows that fishermen have goals, which causes them to fish.

Our discussion so far has overlooked what we may call "counterintuitive" causal cognition, where magic or spiritual agents cause behavior in ways which to some extent contradict our intuitions about causes.[265] In the ancient Mediterranean world, these beliefs were abundant, varied and central to how many people explained action. As

---

[263] Hirschfeld 1995.

[264] Boyer 1995 points out that it is a common mistake among anthropologists to equal public discourse with the sum of mental beliefs.

[265] Boyer 1995 suggests the term "counterintuitive causation" for those causal beliefs that have components that contradict our direct experience of the world, for instance, that magic and rituals can cause an effect on an object or a person without even being close to it.

Pascal Boyer points out, some anthropologists have called attention to the immense cross-cultural variation in religious and magical beliefs as an argument against any universality in human causal cognition.[266] Boyer does, however, show that, as diverse as these beliefs are, they are still constrained by the two kinds of causal beliefs, which cognitive psychologists have argued to be universal. Magical beliefs are basically beliefs about how inanimate things cause effects by force. The only difference is that some aspects of how this force is affected are speculative and counterintuitive. Beliefs about spiritual agents are basically constructed in the same way as beliefs about human agents. They are intentional agents with dispositions, goals, etc., just like humans. The only difference is that some aspects of how they can affect humans are speculative and counterintuitive.

I propose that all the variations of causal beliefs that have been discussed here were present in the ancient Mediterranean world. We must therefore suspect that all these variations can be part of the rhetoric about the relation between identity in Christ and behavior norms. The variations can be summarized into three themes:

a. Attribution to dispositions, that is, virtue, vice, knowledge and emotions
b. Attribution to spiritual influence and magic
c. Attribution to category, that is, role, social identity or "nature"

These causal beliefs often interact in the texts. For instance, being in Christ (c) causes one to have the Spirit (b), which causes one to have virtue (a) according to Paul. The relation between these factors can be described both as causes (indicative) and duties (imperative).[267]

---

[266] Boyer 1995. Boyer's thesis is a part of larger research program in the cognitive science of religion, which has showed that religious beliefs tend to be analogous to intuitive beliefs, but with a counterintuitive "twist." The intuitive parts of the religious beliefs make them understandable and rich in associations, while the counterintuitive twist makes them attention-grabbing and easy to remember. On the cognitive science of religion, see e.g. Atran 2002; Boyer 2001; Pyysiäinen 2003; Tremlin 2006.

[267] Cf. chapter 6.1.

Moreover, ancient texts do not only discuss how (a), (b) and (c) cause behavior, but also how behavior causes (a), (b) and (c). For instance, regular good conduct can make one more virtuous or more strongly influenced by positive spiritual forces. In short, we will discover that the causal beliefs go in just about every direction:

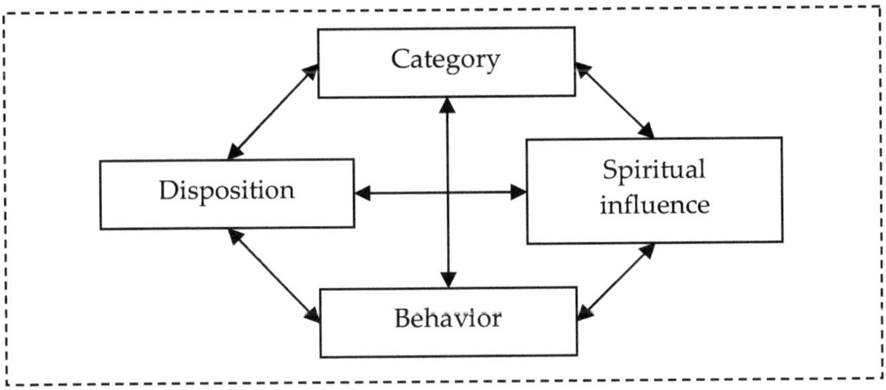

In the remainder of this chapter we will investigate how beliefs about dispositions (a) and spiritual influence (b) could function in group contexts (c). The goal of the brief survey below is not to cover all aspects of causal beliefs in the extremely diverse culture of the ancient Mediterranean world. Rather, the purpose is to outline some of the most frequently occurring patterns and discuss their social and psychological function.

In the analysis of Ephesians, I will often summarize the discussion about causal beliefs with arrows, for instance:

> *Causality:* Spirit → Power
>
> *Attribution*: Knowledge → Speaks the truth
>
> *Causality:* Idolatrizes → Is disliked by God → *Duty:* Should be reproached, marginalized or even excluded

"Causality" stands for the causal beliefs of the soft flexible kind discussed above. The first example above should be read as "the Spirit causes power" or "having the Spirit causes one to have power."

"Attribution" is really a subcategory to "causality," but I have chosen to use this word when we discover a belief where attributed traits are considered to cause visible behavior. The second example above should be spelled out as "having knowledge causes one to speak the truth." "Duty" is used to summarize the normative conclusions that can be seen in the text or that we can imagine an ingroup reasonably would have drawn from the beliefs expressed in the text. The third example should be interpreted: "Idolatry causes the idolater to be disliked by God. Therefore it is our duty (as God's clients) to reproach, marginalize and, if nothing else helps, exclude an idolater."

6.3 Attribution to Dispositions in the Ancient Mediterranean World

In his *Nicomachean Ethics,* Aristotle discusses how dispositions together with perception are the causes of intentional action:

> Now there are three elements in the soul which control action (πρᾶξις) and the attainment of truth: namely Sensation (αἴσθησις), Intellect (νοῦς) and Desire (ὄρεξις). Of these, Sensation never originates action, as is shown by the fact that animals have sensation but are not capable of [deliberate] action. Pursuit and avoidance in the sphere of Desire correspond to affirmation and denial in the sphere of the Intellect. Hence inasmuch as moral virtue is a disposition of the mind in regard to choice, and choice is deliberate desire, it follows that, if the choice is to be good, both the principle be true and the desire right, and the desire must pursue the same things as principle affirms. … Now the cause of action … is choice, and the cause of choice is desire and reasoning directed to some end. (Aristotle, *Nic. Eth.* 6.2.1–2, 4)

According to Aristotle, when a virtuous man perceives a sensation (e.g. sees or hears something), his reason and desire are harmonious in handling the perception. Both reason and desire want the same good thing, which in turn causes the virtuous man to make a good choice and act well.

The opposite is the brutish man, who reasons and desires viciously. Aristotle also discusses how desire and reason do not always harmonize, that people can desire to do the wrong thing, even though they know what is right (*Nic. Eth.* 7).

Aristotle's account is surprisingly close to some of the results of modern brain research, as described by Daniel Goleman.[268] When we decide something, both intellectual and emotional brain centers are involved and coordinated. Indeed, people with brain conditions blocking the emotional component of a decision process have a hard time deciding anything at all.[269]

Not everyone was, however, as positive as Aristotle to the role of emotions.[270] Aristotle, Plato and just about every philosopher of the Greco-Roman world, considered dispositions, virtue and vice, to be the most important ground for judging the moral value of an action,[271] but they disagreed on the value of emotions. Aristotle thinks that emotions can be trained to be virtuous and that they are part of a virtuous man's disposition. The Stoic writers[272] generally had a more negative view of emotions, usually called *pathē* (sing. *pathos, πάθος*), which they use as an umbrella term for destructive non-rational desires, aversions and emotions.[273] ("Emotions" is a somewhat misleading translation of the Stoic use of *pathē,* since the term *pathos* mainly covers destructive emotions in Stoic thinking.) In *On Anger*, Seneca (5 B.C.E.-64 C.E.) sees only destructiveness in anger, the perhaps most typical *pathos* in Stoic thinking. In explicit polemic with Aristotle, he argues that anger is not beneficial even in battle:

---

[268] Goleman 1995: 3–12.

[269] Goleman 1995: 52–54.

[270] Sihvola and Engberg-Pedersen 1998 discuss the various attitudes to emotions in Hellenistic philosophy.

[271] On Plato's and Aristotle's view on the moral value of actions, see e.g. MacIntyre 1981: 131–164. On the Stoic view, see e.g. Stephens 2006. Epicurus, however, contrary to common wisdom, argued that in order to reach happiness, virtues are purely instrumental, see O'Keefe 2006.

[272] In this brief exposé, I will primarily look at the Stoics in their later, more developed phase, which hold a kernel of common ideas "which could be called orthodox Stoicism", Sandbach 1989: 19. The Stoics are of course not all the same. They are all individual thinkers, but in the regards I intend to present here, I would concur with Sandbach's judgment that they agree reasonably well.

[273] Cooper 1998: 71.

> Again, anger (*ira*) embodies nothing useful, nor does it kindle the mind to warlike deeds; for virtue (*virtus*), being self-sufficient, never needs help of vice (*vitium*). Whenever there is need of violent effort, the mind does not become angry (*irascor*), but it gathers itself together and is aroused or relaxed according to its estimate of the need; just as when engines of war hurl forth their arrows, it is the operator who controls the tension with which they are hurled. "Anger," says Aristotle, "is necessary, and no battle can be won without it—unless it fills the mind and fires the soul; it must serve however not as a leader, but as the common soldier." But this is not true. For if it listens to reason and follows where reason leads, it is no longer anger, of which the chief characteristic is willfulness.
>
> (Seneca, *Ira*, 1.9.1–2)

This negative opinion on emotions stems from the idea among the Stoics that the psyche of man is unified, not divided into reason and emotions.[274] Man's true nature is really only reason, and emotions can be seen as basically threats to reason, dangerous disturbances which cause reason to go wrong. Instead, a man should strive for *eupatheia* (εὐπάθεια), which is not all that different from *pathos*, but is only the good aspects of emotions, which inspire virtue. *Eupatheia* is different to *pathos* in that it is a benevolent, stable, lasting attitude towards other people, which does not distort truth and reason, while *pathos* is destructive, unstable and temporary and causes false reasoning.[275] It is difficult to maintain a sharp distinction between *eupatheia* and *pathē*, but nevertheless the broad tendency among the Stoics is to give emotions a primarily negative role as the driving force behind vicious action.[276]

In the *Tanak*, we do not find subtle discussions about exactly what it is that does and should cause man to act. But we do find several references to dispositions as the cause of action as well as moralizing

[274] Brennan 1998.

[275] Irwin 1998: 225; Brennan 1998: 34.

[276] The original position of the early Stoics was that one should strive for *apatheia* rather than *eupatheia*. The doctrine of *eupatheia* can be seen as a modification of the doctrine as a response to the critique that it is impossible for man to have a total absence of emotions, see Knuuttila and Sihvola 1998: 17. This compromise somewhat obscures the relation between emotions and virtues, but the basic theme that emotions are dangerous remains.

about dispositions, as we have already discussed in chapter 5.4. The attitude towards anger and other emotions in the *Tanak* is less negative than the Stoic attitude. For example, anger is considered to be the cause of both morally right and wrong actions (e.g., Gen 30:2, 49:6; Num 11:10, 33; Deut 6:5). But, as David Aune demonstrates, in the Jewish literature of the Hellenistic era, including the texts from the early Christ-movement, we can see how the Greek conceptions of emotions are often embraced.[277] A telling example is how Matthew and Luke exclude the reference in Mark to Jesus' anger (Mark 3:4–5 // Matt 12:10–13; Luk 6:9–10; 14:3–4), as if they considered anger to be an improper emotion for the Messiah. Paul thinks that "desire" (ἐπιθυμία) causes sin and that the Torah cannot efficiently be the antidote of this flaw in the human nature (Rom 7:7–25). As opposed to for instance Philo, who was inspired by Greek philosophy and thought that rationality learned from the Torah could help man to master passion, Paul thought that only the influence of the Spirit in Christ could achieve this (Rom 8:1–11).[278] In short, the tendency to view emotions as chiefly harmful dispositions, which cause morally wrong behavior, was embraced by many Christ-believers, too.

In the initial discussion in chapter 6.2 we noted that many collectivistic cultures considered dispositions to be more malleable and open to change than individualistic Westerners do. The belief in a malleable character in need of reinforcement through education and training is easily found in many ancient texts. Both the Jewish wisdom tradition and the Greek philosophical tradition consider virtue to be something which must be learned and then constantly nurtured. For example, although some noblemen probably claimed superior virtue by birth, as dissimilar authors as Quintilian and Jesus ben Sirach are convinced that all young boys need proper training to become virtuous men (Quintilian, *Inst.* 1; Sir 30).[279]

In his *Nicomachean Ethics,* Aristotle argues that in order to reach virtue one must practice the corresponding behavior during childhood:

---

[277] Aune 1994.

[278] Aune 1994 compares Paul and Philo.

[279] On the education of children, see e.g. Osiek and Balch 1997: 156–173.

> [T]he faculties given us by nature are bestowed upon us first in a potential form (δύναμις); we exhibit their actual exercise (ἐνεργεία) afterwards. ... The virtues ... we acquire by first having actually practiced (ἐνεργέω) them, just as we do the arts. ... [W]e become just by doing just acts, temperate by doing temperate acts, brave by doing brave acts. [...] In a word, our moral dispositions are formed as a result of the corresponding activities. Hence it is incumbent on us to control the character of our activities, since on the quality of these depends the quality of our dispositions. It is therefore not of small moment whether we are trained from childhood in one set of habits or another; on the contrary it is of very great, or rather of supreme, importance.
> (Aristotle, *Eth. nic.*, 2.1.4, 7–8)

In Proverbs, the implied father exhorts his son, who has learned wisdom, to hold on to it, implying that wisdom can easily be lost:[280]

> Hear, my child, and accept my words ... I have taught you the way of wisdom; I have led you in the paths of uprightness ... Keep hold of instruction; do not let go; guard her, for she is your life. Do not enter the path of the wicked, and do not walk in the way of evildoers. (Prov 4:10–11, 13–14)

The Stoics think in the same way. Epictetus emphasizes the need for "exercise" in his *Discourses* (e.g. *Diatr.* 1.4). Marcus Aurelius promotes mental exercises to prepare oneself to act right and avoid destructive emotions (e.g. *Meditations* 2). Common to both the Jewish wisdom tradition and these philosophers is a belief that one can change one's dispositions by practice, studies and mental exercises. Over time, they see what we could call a dialectic causality between behavior and disposition. Disposition causes behavior, but yet one can behave in a way that changes one's disposition:

---

[280] Cf. Sir 6:18–37.

Dialectic causality between behavior and disposition:

Virtuous man → right action and thinking → virtue reinforced
Virtuous man → careless action and thinking → virtue undermined
Vicious man → wrong action and thinking → vice reinforced
Vicious man → trying to do and think right → slow improvement of virtue

With this dialectic, the causal beliefs simultaneously become imperatives. One must act according to one's virtues if one wishes to continue considering oneself virtuous. Given the social, moral and self-regulating function of attribution, discussed above in chapter 6.1, it is not surprising that all the authors discussed above construe disposition as something malleable, which needs to be constantly reinforced. As such, the beliefs about what causes behavior and virtue form a narrative, which has the power to express both the indicative and the imperative and thus function to imbue behavior with moral value.

Finally, although we have primarily focused on how dispositions are thought to interact with behavior in this section, we should not forget that all these writers implicitly discuss the prototype of social categories.[281] In other words, they discuss the collective ideal of a group, rather than individualistic ideals. Proverbs advises young men as a preparation for their life as heads of household. Aristotle guides the free male citizen of a Greek city-state, the nobleman.[282] The Stoics promote the ideal of the "philosopher," which is also a collective ideal. The same is true for the discussions of virtue and vice in the texts of the early Christ-movement: they typically discuss the dispositions of the prototypical Christ-believer.[283] Their advice should therefore not be understood as individualistic, just because they discuss dispositions. As we discussed in chapter 5.4, social identities were often organized into superordinate and subordinate social categories. For example, Seneca

[281] Cf. Walcot 1988 who concludes that the type of person was more important than the individual in antiquity, both in the Greek and the Roman era.

[282] MacIntyre 1981: 133, 158–159, 186–187.

[283] Cf. Malina 2001: 66, but also my critique of certain aspects of Malina's reasoning in chapter 5.4.

complains about those who do not understand that societal duties should be understood as applications of universal virtue, but nevertheless thinks that different social roles carry with them different behavioral duties (*Ep.* 94). Interestingly, Seneca does not conclude that everyone should be socially equal because we can strive for the same virtues. This is also the case in Plato's *Meno,* where Plato argues for universal virtues, but nevertheless accepts differentiated household roles (*Meno* 71–72).[284] As we can see, the attributed virtues were often considered to be components of the prototype of the superordinate category, but the behavioral consequences of these virtues were differentiated for different subordinate categories. The same tendency is apparent also in the household codes of the New Testament, where different household behaviors, depending on one's household role, are motivated with virtues taken from the superordinate category of being in Christ.[285]

In sum, explaining and moralizing about behavior by reference to dispositions is a frequent *topos* in ancient Mediterranean culture, both in Jewish and Greek texts. The concepts of virtue and vice were widely distributed thought patterns, but the role of emotions as the cause of virtuous or vicious behavior was much debated. The causal relation between disposition and behavior was frequently considered to be dialectic. There was a tension between duty (imperative) and cause (indicative) in the relation between virtue and behavior. Finally, the dispositions were typically part of group prototypes rather than individual ideals.

6.4 Attribution to Spiritual Influence in the Ancient Mediterranean World

According to much research in the cognitive science of religion, the cross-culturally most common characteristic of gods and other spiritual

---

[284] Socrates corrects Meno and explains that virtues are universal, but does not question the practical duties of different social groups, which Meno has just described.

[285] Roitto 2008. See chapter 9.1.

entities, which makes them relevant to most of us humans, is that they are *interested agents,* who interact with humans.[286] As agents they act intentionally, and as interested they interfere with our lives and have opinions about how we humans should act. The gods are anthropomorphous in the sense that they are social and moral agents, and this characteristic makes it very easy for the human mind to make rich and meaningful associations between our lives and the gods. Epicurus was certainly right in saying that if the gods did not interfere with human affairs, humans should not worry about the gods either.[287] But as opposed to Epicurus, most people in the ancient Mediterranean world did think of spiritual entities as precisely that—interested agents who interact with humans.

Given that gods and spirits do things which affect humans, what is the relation between human action and divine action?[288] The answer to

---

[286] Boyer 2001: 192–231. Cf. n. 48. The cognitive science of religion is a promising field of research, which aims to explain how religion is formed by innate human dispositions. For instance Czachesz 2007; Ketola 2007; Uro 2007 has explored how the cognitive science of religion can be used for the study of the early Christ-movement. The field is new and the epistemological status of the evolutional aspects of their theories are under debate, since both biological and cultural evolution are extremely multivariate, see Day 2007. Although I think the field is promising, I will confine my use of the cognitive science of religion to the basic proposal that the gods are considered to be interested agents in most cultures, since this is the most relevant aspect for this study.

[287] Epicurus, *Epistola ad Menoeceus, Ratae sententiae* 1. Epicurus argues that since the gods are eternal and perfectly happy, they have no interest in interfering with human affairs.

[288] Barclay and Gathercole 2006 is a very informative collection of essays about the problem of divine and human agency in relation to Paul. This section of the present study is indebted to many of the excellent analyses in their book. In the introduction, Barclay 2006 describes how the historical analysis has been distorted by Lutheran theological agendas, since it was important to read Paul as not giving human agency any part in salvation. Barclay suggests that with the new perspective on Paul, initiated by Sanders 1977, the problem is again open to debate. According to Sanders, first century Judaism was characterized by "covenantal nomism" where salvation is due to grace (divine agency), but where humans are yet supposed to act in certain ways within the covenant (human agency).

this question is as diverse as we might expect it to be, given that we are dealing with narratives about the divine, which are far from always formed by direct experience, but by tradition and interpretation. Among cultural representations, the representations about the divine tend to be the most flexible and varied.[289]

The aim of this section is to survey patterns of beliefs about how supernatural agents influence human behavior and how this in turn may become part of the identity of a group. Space allows only a few illustrative examples. For heuristic purposes, the beliefs about how supernatural agents interact with humans could be divided into two kinds: a) beliefs that supernatural agents bring messages, blessings and disasters upon humans from outside the minds and bodies of humans, and b) beliefs that the supernatural agents inspire or force human action from the inside of their minds and bodies. In b) the spiritual agents are partly analogous to dispositions, since they are imagined to be invisible causes of action, which stem from the inside of the human agent. Category a) can be divided into a1) beliefs that the supernatural agents affect people's lives in order to influence their moral choice, and a2) beliefs that the supernatural agents affect people's lives for other ends. Category b) can be divided into b1) beliefs that the supernatural agents inspire human moral behavior, and b2) beliefs that the supernatural agents use human bodies and minds according to the will of the supernatural agent. The four kinds of divine interaction with humans can be represented in a table:

[289] Cf. Sperber 1996: 70–74 who suggests that cultural meta-representations, representations based on other representation rather than on direct experience, are far more flexible and varied than representations that are constrained by direct sensory input. Religion is for most people a cultural (and learned) system of meta-representations, and to the extent that the beliefs about the divine is formed by direct religious experience, this experience itself is typically interpreted by cultural beliefs, which predate the experience. Cf. also the discussion in chapter 6.2 about how religious and magical beliefs tend to be more varied within and across cultures than other kinds of causal beliefs.

	1. Supernatural agents act out of interest in the moral choice of the affected human	2. Supernatural agents act out of other interests than the moral choice of the affected human
a. Supernatural agents interact with humans from outside their minds and bodies	a1. Supernatural agents bring moral commands, rewards and punishments (external moral intervention)	a2. Supernatural agents bring disaster and fortune according to their will (external non-moral intervention)
b. Supernatural agents inspire human behavior from inside their bodies and minds	b1. Supernatural agents influence human minds to do good or evil (internal moral influence)	b2. Supernatural agents use the human body and mind as an instrument, according to their will (internal non-moral influence)

a1. Supernatural agents bring moral commands, rewards and punishments (external moral intervention). In the Jewish tradition, God is frequently portrayed as one who decides and communicates the behavioral standards of the Jewish people who are his covenant partners (e.g., Exod 19–24).[290] Moreover, he enforces these standards with blessings and punishments, either in this life (e.g., Deut 11:13–28) or in the eschatological future (e.g., Dan 12:1–3). The Jews have a duty to act according to God's will, the Torah, since they belong to the covenant (e.g., Ps 78). However, as Friedrich Avemarie points out, knowledge of the Torah is also often considered to inspire behavior, not only to prescribe it (e.g., Ps 119).[291] In other words, the Torah (and other kinds of communication and interaction from God) comes from the outside, but

[290] Avemarie 2006.

[291] Avemarie 2006: 54–58. Cf. Westerholm 2006, who shows that many Jews were quite optimistic about the possibility of observing the Torah.

hearing the Torah causes dispositions on the inside, which in turn causes behavior. Therefore, the Torah both commands (imperative) and causes (indicative) behavior.

The gods as the standard of behavior norms and the enforcers of morality were also part of the Greek and Roman traditions. Some philosophers, such as Plato and Seneca, see God (or the *logos*) as the model of human virtue.[292] Some, but not all, believed that people would be punished or rewarded for their conduct in the afterlife.[293] In conventional Roman thinking, however, it was just one of the duties of a virtuous citizen to revere the gods. One should pay homage to the gods, in analogy with the relation of a client to his patron, but not every moral decision was supposed to revolve around the gods.[294]

The Jewish worldview and rhetoric, on the other hand, was theocentric. Every behavior had its moral value in relation to God's will and to God's commandments.[295] Josephus, in his very engaged apology *Against Apion*, puts the Jewish thinking right on the spot:

> [Moses] did not make religion (εὐσέβεια, "piety") a department of virtue, but the various virtues—I mean, justice, temperance, fortitude, and mutual harmony in all things between the members of the community— departments of religion. Religion governs all our actions and occupations and speech; none of these things did our lawgiver leave unexamined or indeterminate.
>
> (Josephus, *C. Ap.*, 2.157)

---

[292] Russell 2004. It is, however, doubtful whether it is correct to say that they imagined the moral knowledge to come from the outside. Although Stoics frequently considered God to be an agent, they nevertheless considered knowledge about "the natural law" to be the fruit of rational deliberation rather than of divine revelation in the Jewish sense.

[293] E.g. Klauck 2000: 73–75. The belief in afterlife was, however, not accepted by all, see e.g. Veyne 1987: 219–223.

[294] Veyne 1987: 207–219.

[295] Most Jewish texts in Hellenistic times use εὐσέβεια arguments, e.g. the will of God, the Torah, the covenant etc, when they argue for various norms. In this way εὐσέβεια was a dominant thought pattern. See Sanders 1992: 49–51 for examples.

In short, God (or the gods) can be seen as the cause of human action via external influence, through his commandments, through the knowledge he provides or by being an ideal himself. Moreover, God is often imagined to reward and punish human action, in order to enforce behavior according to the norms.

This imagination of divine intervention in relation to human behavior can be the narrative rationale of the identity and behavior norms of various groups. The most prominent example is the Jewish people, which in Jewish writings is often considered to have superior knowledge about God's will through God's intervention in their history. They are the inheritors of a unique moral character, which has been formed through centuries of fostering. The texts of the early Christ-movement frequently use the same kind of knowledge rhetoric in order to form identity and argue for behavior norms. For instance, Col 1:3–2:15 claims superior revealed knowledge about God's will, in order to argue for what behavior norms are proper for Christ-believers in 2:16–4:5.

a2. Supernatural agents bring disaster and fortune according to their will (external non-moral intervention). Divine intervention (and magic) is used in many cultures to explain the unexplainable, especially disasters, such as bad crops and diseases.[296] For example, in the *Epic of Gilgamesh,* the gods drown humanity, simply because they feel like doing it (*Epic of Gilgamesh* 11). In the *Tanak,* the authors often (but not always) make an effort to present God's actions as morally defendable.[297] Yet God's actions are not always intended to be a response to the morality of

---

[296] Boyer 2001: 222–226. In the Greco-Roman world, "[e]veryone … believed in daemons, in the sense of intermediate beings between God and humans, beneficent or maleficent, to whom a great many phenomena affecting one's daily life could be attributed. It has been well remarked that daemons in the ancient world filled many of the roles of germs today", Dillon 1986: 220.

[297] For instance, while the gods in *Epic of Gilgamesh* 11 have no moral grounds for their actions, God reacts to the evil of humanity in Gen 6—God's acts are perceived as morally defendable, since they punish the evil of humankind. In Gen 22, however, the author does not moralize about whether it is morally defensible of God to ask Abraham to sacrifice Isaac.

human action.[298] In the Book of Job, we learn that Job is afflicted by misfortune, not because of his moral conduct, but because of heavenly conflicts, which he cannot grasp (Job 1). When God answers Job, he states that his priority is the well-being of creation (rather than the just reward of each individual's moral conduct, Job 38–41).

Narratives about impulsive gods and Job's theology are not primarily formed in order to motivate behavior norms and group identity, but in order to handle the unexplainable injustices and misfortunes of life. These narratives may, however, initiate traditions about what ritual behavior might appease the gods. For example, when Utnapishtim makes a sacrifice in the *Epic of Gilgamesh,* the gods flock like flies, repent their impulse to drown humanity and promise never to do so again—a narrative clearly meant to promote sacrifice as prevention against misfortune.

In other traditions, however, God's intervention in human affairs is positive, regardless of human morality. A very prominent example in the Jewish tradition is how God favors Abraham, Isaac and Jacob even in situations where their moral conduct is questionable (e.g., Gen 12:10–19, 25:29–34, 26:1–22), simply because it is in God's interest to bless the ones who will be the fathers of his chosen people. This positive version of God's intervention in human affairs out of self-interest can be a narrative explaining the value of the ingroup. However, it guides behavior norms only indirectly. If the group believes that "we are those who God favors," it might actualize the question: "What is the proper conduct of those who God favors?"[299]

b1. Supernatural agents influence human minds to do good or evil (internal moral influence). According to Josephus, the different Jewish "philosophies" differed as regards how they imagined the relation between divine and human agency:

[298] Boccaccini 2006: 13–15 argues that "Sapiential Judaism" (the wisdom tradition) stressed the freedom of God to do whatever he wanted.

[299] According to Sanders 1977: 419–422, this is the motivation to act, according to Jewish "covenantal nomism." Cf. n. 288.

> The Pharisees … attribute everything to Fate (εἱμαρμένη[300]) and to God; they hold that to act rightly or otherwise rests, indeed, for the most part with men, but that in each action Fate co-operates (βοηθέω, "aid"). … The Sadducees … do away with Fate altogether, and remove God beyond, not merely the commission, but the very sight of evil. They maintain that man has the free choice (ἐκλογή) of good and evil, and that it rests with each man's will whether he follows the one or the other.
>
> (Josephus, *B.J.* 2.8.14/2.162–165)

> Now at this time there were three different schools of thought among the Jews, which held different opinions concerning human affairs; the first being that of the Pharisees, the second that of the Sadducees and the third that of the Essenes. As for the Pharisees they said that certain events are the work of Fate, but not all; as to other events, it depends upon ourselves whether they shall take place or not. The sect of the Essenes, however, declares, that Fate is mistress of all things, and that nothing befalls men unless it be in accordance with her decree. But the Sadducees do away with Fate, holding that there is no such thing and that human actions are not achieved in accordance with her decree, but that all things lie within our own power, so that we ourselves are responsible for our well-being, while we suffer misfortune through our own thoughtlessness. (Josephus, *A.J.* 13.5.9/13.171–173)

In the description by Josephus, the Sadducees emphasize the upper left corner in the table above (a1), since they emphasize the duty to do God's will, rather than divine influence on human actions.[301] The Essenes emphasize the lower right corner (b2, see below), since they think that God has preordained the fate of both good and bad.[302] The Pharisees, on the other hand, would emphasize the lower left corner (b1, i.e., this

---

300 Martin 1981 suggests that Josephus thinks that εἱμαρμένη is what rules people who are without God and the Torah. Only under God is free will possible.

301 Cf. Boccaccini 2006. The description is coherent with the opinion of Jesus Sirach (Sir. 15:1–20) who is often considered to be aligned with the Sadducees.

302 This description is coherent with the attitude in the Qumran Literature, see discussion below in subsection b2.

section), where the initiative of the divine, God and fate, is considered to inspire but not entirely determine human behavior.[303]

In many texts from the ancient Mediterranean world, we find that the distinction between divine influence and human virtue is difficult to maintain. According to Emma Stafford, personification of virtues was a common phenomenon in ancient Greece.[304] Some deified virtues had their own cults.[305] In *On the Nature of Gods,* Cicero's learned treatise about the existence and character of the divine, he reports this:

> Many other divinities have however with good reason been recognized and named ... For it was thought that whatever confers great utility on the human race must be due to the operation of divine benevolence towards men. Thus sometimes a thing sprung from a god was called by the god himself; ... In other cases some exceptionally potent force is itself designated by a title of divinity, for example Faith or Mind; ... You see the temple of Virtue, restored as the temple of Honour by Marcus Marcellus, but founded many years before Quintus Maximus in the time of the Ligurian war. Again, there are temples of Wealth, Safety, Concord, Liberty and Victory, all of which things, *being so powerful as necessarily to imply divine governance,* were themselves designated as Gods.
>
> (Cicero, *Nat. d.* 2.23/2.60–61, emphasis added)[306]

When Troels Engberg-Pedersen compares Paul and the Greek philosopher Epictetus (c:a 55–135 C.E.), he finds that they construct the

---

[303] Nothing more specific can be said about the relation between human and divine agency from Josephus' accounts. There is a tension in Josephus' two accounts of the position of the Pharisees. In *B.J.* 2.8.14/2.162–165 *God and man cooperate* in the same action, while in *A.J.* 13.5.9/13.171–173 *God is the cause* of some human actions and *man is the cause* of some. It is, however, quite possible that Josephus thought that the three different possibilities could be the case at different occasions.

[304] Stafford 2000.

[305] Stafford 2000: 17–19. There was a virtue-cult in Rome, too, see Plutarch, *Mor.* 318E.

[306] The quote does not represent Cicero´s own opinion. He just refers to the opinion of those who thinks so. He himself deified virtues as "abstraction, not personal deities", see *Nat. d.* 3.24/3.61. Cicero does, however, confirm the existence and agency of the gods throughout *Nat. d.* Cf. Stafford 2000: 19–27.

relation between divine and human agency in a similar fashion.[307] Both Paul and Epictetus consider the prototypical man to be free in relation to the world but directed towards God in a way that makes human and divine agency overlap and align. For instance, Paul writes:

> [God's agency:] But by the grace of God I am what I am, and his grace toward me has not been in vain. [Paul's agency:] On the contrary, I worked harder than any of them—though it was not I, [God's and Paul's agency together:] but the grace of God together with me. (1 Cor 15:10, NRSV modified[308])

This is of course only the case if one is a prototypical philosopher or Christ-believer, since both Paul and Epictetus acknowledge the possibility of viciousness. To be virtuous is to let the divine cause one's behavior, but the divine does not cancel the will or the choice of the human agent.

John Barclay makes a similar comparison between Paul and Philo of Alexandria (20 B.C.E.-50 C.E.).[309] Barclay emphasizes how they both see God's grace as the primary cause of any human virtue. Virtue is a gift that cannot be earned; it is only given by grace. However, both Philo and Paul think that man is capable of acting viciously, that is, act in a way which is not caused by God's grace.[310] There is an asymmetry between virtue and vice, where virtue is caused by God (mediated by the Spirit or the *logos*) but vice is not. It is implicit that the human agent has to make

---

307 Engberg-Pedersen 2006. Cf. also von Gemünden 2007 who recognizes pattern of both "autodynamische Affektekontrolle," "heterodynamishe Affektekontrolle" (divine or other external influence) and "transformationsdynamische Affektekontrolle" (changing between human and divine control over the emotions) in the first century.

308 I have slightly modified NRSV, which translates ἡ χάρις τοῦ θεοῦ [ἡ] σὺν ἐμοί with "the grace of God that is with me." NRSV chooses to accept the second ἡ, which leads to the understanding that it is only God's grace which is the agent. If we, however, choose not to accept the second ἡ, a reading which also has strong textual support according to NA27, then God's grace and Paul are the agents together. Cf. Acts 15:28.

309 Barclay 2006.

310 Rom 6–7; Gal 5:13–26; Philo, *Opif.* 72–75. Cf. Frick 1999: 139–175.

some kind of effort to remain under the influence of God. The tension between indicative and imperative is never settled.

This kind of imagination, where divine agency is the cause of human agency (indicative) but where the human is yet exhorted to let the divine influence him/her (imperative) is particularly useful in a group context. The divine becomes analogous to other dispositions, in the sense that it can function in the cognitive attribution processes and the attribution rhetoric of the group. The identity of the group is that "we are those who are under God's dominion" and the prototypical group member is one who is perfectly influenced by God. Every visible behavior can either be interpreted as the outcome of divine influence or as the outcome of some undesirable disposition (desire, disobedience, etc.) or evil spiritual influence, which translates into either prototypicality or deviance; praise or blame. A lack of positive divine influence can be attributed to outgroups, while the ingroup can gain self-esteem by thinking of themselves as those under divine influence. Within the group, the association between behaviors and divine influence (e.g. Gal 5:13–26) can function to regulate behavior norms and social dynamics in many different ways (see chapters 7 and 8 below). Again, the tension between divine influence and human moral responsibility (indicative and imperative) may seem inconsistent, but is, nevertheless, highly functional in a group context.

b2. Supernatural agents use the human body and mind as an instrument, according to their will (internal non-moral influence). Possession, where a spiritual agent takes over the body and mind of an individual is quite frequent in many cultures,[311] and ancient Mediterranean culture was no exception.[312] In possession narratives of the Synoptic Gospels, the possessed person is portrayed as a victim and no moral responsibility falls upon the possessed (e.g., Mark 5:1–20, cf. Tob).[313] If the Synoptic Gospels are at one end of the spectrum of moral judgment, the

---

[311] Klass 2003.

[312] For an overview of possession in the context of the early Christ-movement, see Sorensen 2001.

[313] Berger 2003: 51 argues that the mind of the possessed is of no importance in the Gospels.

Qumranite *Community Rule* is in the other. It is possible to place the *Community Rule* in section b1 above (internal moral influence) since the text moralizes strongly about the behavior of all non-Qumranites. I have, nevertheless, placed the text in this section, since the individual is in the end left with no moral choice. In the world view of the *Community Rule,* everyone's dispositions and behaviors are entirely determined by either the Angel of Truth or the Angel of Falsehood according to God's plan.[314] The influence is not presented as possession, but rather as the most complete divine hegemony over the entire history, where human agents are deprived of any significant choice. God is the orchestrator of world history rather than someone who works for the moral improvement of the vicious. Yet, even if those who are under the Angel of Falsehood never had any choice, they will be judged by God.[315] The narrative about God's judgment, as inconsistent as it may seem, obviously functions to provide contrasting group prototypes between the Qumranites and everyone else.[316]

In the Acts of the Apostles, some of the expressions of the Spirit, notably speaking in tongues, prophecy, exorcism and healing, are portrayed as supernatural events, in which the human agent is the mere instrument of the divine agency (e.g., Acts 2:1–9, 4:23–31, 9:31–42, 19:1–17). The intervention of the Spirit is not intended to inspire human morality but to execute God's will. Although the work is done by the Spirit in these passages, the human agent is nevertheless credited with status (i.e., prototypicality), since the deeds indicate that the Spirit can work effectively through that person, which shows that the person has prototypical characteristics.[317]

---

[314] 1QS III.13–IV.24, analyzed by Alexander 2006. Those who are under the Angel of Falsehood are sometimes called "the lot of Belial", e.g. 1QS II.5; 1QM I.5.

[315] Westerholm 2006: 94–96, 98.

[316] Cf. Jokiranta 2005; Jokiranta 2007, who has studied the Qumran Literature from a social identity perspective.

[317] In some other texts, e.g. Mark 16:17–18, John 14:12, Rom 12:6, the measure of πίστις—a prototypical ingroup character trait—is mentioned as the factor which determines how well the Spirit can work in the Christ-believer.

In these examples, the amount of praise and blame is not really determined by philosophical discussions about free will, choice and moral agency, but by the extent to which the spiritual force is considered to be a group trait. The belief in spiritual forces determining one's actions entirely can therefore function in a group context in the same way as the imagination outlined above, where divine and human agency cooperated (b1).

In sum, we have seen that there is great variety in how supernatural agents are believed to cause and demand human behavior. We have also seen that all these narratives can function in different ways in a group context to create identity, motivate behavior according to group norms and structure group dynamics. The tension between indicative and imperative, which we explored in b1, might be a problem from a philosophical or theological perspective, but it is necessary in order to give the ingroup prototype the flexibility to function in many different ways in a group context.

Now that we have surveyed cultural patterns of attribution, we may return to a more detailed discussion about social identities, behavior norms and group dynamics, from a cognitive perspective.

7 Formation of the Identity in Christ in Relation to Outgroups

In chapter 4 I argued that culture is shared cognition. The ingroup prototype is a very central part of a group's culture, that is, the group members' shared cognition. Consensus about the ingroup prototype was probably almost constantly under negotiation, both within and in between the different communities of Christ-believers, just like the ingroup prototype of any group is.[318] A measure of consensus, that is, shared cognition, is reached through processes of exchange and negotiations within the group, driven by the needs and goals of its group members in relation to various circumstances within and outside the group. There are no absolute laws that determine the formation of a group's identity. Historical developments are too complex to be entirely predicted. Nevertheless, there are recurring tendencies in identity formation, which can be explained by the cognitive setup of our minds. In this chapter we will discuss these tendencies in order to form a heuristic framework, which helps us to interpret how texts reflect and construct identity and behavior norms in relation to the challenges which faced the first Christ-believers.

---

318 Early social identity theory tended to just assume that the ingroup prototype was shared cognition within the group. Such hegemonic thinking was perhaps a defensible simplification as long as the scholarly focus was on intergroup relations, but with a growing interest on intragroup dynamics, it became increasingly important to acknowledge that shared ingroup prototypes emerge as the result of intragroup processes, see Haslam et al. 1998. Cf. Brower and Nye 1996; Cialdini and Goldstein 2004, Decety and Sommerwille 2003. Reicher and Hopkins 2001 analyze Scottish political debate and show how politicians draw on shared ideas about Scottishness in order to promote their own vision of a prototypical Scotsman.

We begin by exploring the group dynamic effects of intergroup relations. How can we use cognitive psychology to understand how the identity in Christ was formed in relation to outgroups; that is, other groups that they had to relate to? Moreover, how do texts from the early Christ-movement reflect and exploit intergroup dynamic tendencies rhetorically in order to form the identity in Christ?

7.1 The Need for Self-Esteem

Tajfel and Turner, the originators of social identity theory, argue that the formation of group ideals and beliefs is driven by the group's need for self-esteem and that groups employ all kinds of creative techniques in order to maintain self-esteem.[319] Groups tend to describe themselves in a positive light and outgroups in a less positive (but not necessarily hostile and negative) light, in order to maintain a positive self-image. For instance, the Gospels' descriptions of the Pharisees are tailored to devalue them in relation to the followers of Jesus. Increased self-esteem of the Christ-believers is most probably one of the reasons (although not the only reason) to portray the Pharisees like that.

Moreover, Tajfel and Turner claim that groups often redefine what values and characteristics are really important and create a counter-culture as a mental defense against dominant cultural values. For instance, Epictetus skillfully "deconstructs" the appreciation of wealth and oratory skills as signs of superiority in *Encheiridion,* a practical handbook of ethical advice compiled by his pupil Arrian:

> The following statements constitute a *non sequitur* (ἀσύνακτος, "illogical"): "I am richer than you are, therefore I am superior to you"; or, "I am more eloquent than you are, therefore I am superior to you." But the following conclusions are better (μᾶλλον συνακικός, "more conclusive"): "I am richer than you are, therefore my property is superior to yours"; or, "I am more eloquent than you are; therefore my elocution is superior to yours." But *you* are neither property nor elocution.
>
> (Epictetus, *Ench.* 44, emphasis original)

---

[319] Tajfel and Turner 1979.

The Jews "knew" that although the Romans were considered superior in power and the Greeks were considered superior in culture, they were both morally inferior in that they were not God's chosen people and did not have the Torah. The works of Josephus and Philo, together with propaganda literature such as *The Sibylline Oracles, The Testament of Abraham, Joseph and Aseneth* and *The letter of Aristeas,* give witness to a strong sense of being morally superior. These Jewish texts exemplify a strategy to redefine superiority in way that allowed the Jews to maintain high self-esteem.

We do not know much about what the slaves, the poor, the women and all the others whose voices have gone to posterity unheard thought. We can only imagine that they must have come up with their own strategies to find other niches of honor, nurturing counter-cultures in which they could preserve their sense of self-esteem. Carlin Barton concludes that "emotionally the slave was every bit as sensitive to insult as his master. The plebeian was as preoccupied with honor as the patrician, the client as the patron, the woman as the man, the child as the adult."[320] Allen Callahan and Richard Horsley show that from what we know about slave resistance elsewhere in history, together with numerous accounts of runaway slaves, measures to prevent escapes and occasional slave rebellions in the Roman era, it is very unlikely that the slaves of the Roman era accepted the social role imposed on them without resistance.[321] Seneca's observation that "You have as many enemies as you have slaves" shows that even the elite must have been aware that the slaves did not always accept their position in society (*Ep.* 47).[322]

Being despised by the world can even be transformed into a source of self-esteem and a sign of prototypicality within the group. For instance, the letter to the Hebrews sees shame in the eyes of the world as a sign of

---

[320] Barton 2001: 11. Barton also refers to anthropological evidence to criticize the idea that the lower strata should be less interested in honor than the higher strata, see Barton 2001: 40, n. 11.

[321] Callahan and Horsley 1998.

[322] Seneca himself naively thinks that the solution is that slaves should be treated better and that it is the harsh treatment that makes them enemies.

Christ-likeness, that is, prototypicality (Heb 11:26; 12:2; 13:13, cf. 1 Cor 1:18–31; 1 Pet 4:14–16).[323]

The drive for self-esteem can, however, not be consistently shown to govern the formation of groups, although it is certainly one of the factors.[324] Moreover, self-esteem does not seem to be an equally important factor in all cultures. For instance, one study shows that Japanese students show much less self-serving bias than Canadian students do.[325] This observation does not preclude that social identities can take the form of categories in these cultures,[326] but it shows that we cannot automatically just assume that every group seeks to improve its self-esteem in relation to other groups. However, if we take into consideration the importance of honor and shame in the first century Mediterranean world, we realize that self-esteem and self-serving bias cannot have been entirely irrelevant for the group dynamics of the early Christ-movement.[327]

7.2 The Need for Cognitive Distinctiveness

In order to for a group to experience that their group is meaningful, there must be something distinctive about it, something which is not like every other group. If this was not the case, the group would be superfluous. Therefore, consensus about prototypes and stereotypes emerges from the need for an identity which brings maximized distinctiveness to the group in the current context.[328] As a consequence,

---

[323] DeSilva 1995.

[324] Brewer and Brown 1998. For a recent overview of the increasingly complex research on the exact role of self-esteem in identity formation, see Hunter et al. 2005. Self-esteem can for the individual be maintained in other ways than by group identification and it is difficult to operationalize self-esteem, see Farnham, Greenwald and Banaji 1999; Hogg and Abrams 1990.

[325] Heine and Lehman 1997.

[326] Cf. Chapter 5.3.

[327] On honor and shame, see n. 193.

[328] Haslam et al. 1998.

the shared cognition—stereotypes and prototype—changes with the context and is not static.[329]

According to the *meta-contrast principle* in self-categorization theory, groups prefer to perceive reality in a way that makes the group identity maximally distinct.[330] This is achieved by cognitively a) maximizing the intragroup similarity of the ingroup and b) maximizing the intragroup similarity of the outgroup, in a way that c) maximizes the contrast between the ingroup and the outgroup. In this way the world is experienced as orderly and the reasons to identify with the group appear as clear: "We have something in common, they have something contrasting in common and we are different from them. Therefore our group makes sense."

This means that the question of what the prototypical Christ-believer is like needs to be asked in relation to outgroups coming into contact with the group. For instance, when the author of Hebrews paints the picture of the ideal Christ-believer, he does it in deliberate contrast to the "old covenant," probably to make the contrast clear to those who want to revert to practicing the Torah again (e.g., Heb 9; 10:1; 13:9–13). A prime example of contrastive rhetoric is the *Didache*. The first six chapters contrast the way of life (ingroup) with the way of death (outgroup). Chapter 8 contrasts the fasting and prayer of the ingroup with that of "the hypocrites": "And do not keep your fast with the hypocrites. For they fast on Monday and Thursday; but you should fast on Wednesday and Friday" (*Did.* 8.1). This seemingly arbitrary norm has an unmistakable function to create a contrast to "the hypocrites."

---

[329] For example, experiments show that in a situation of conflict with outgroups, more extreme members are seen as more prototypical, while more moderate members are considered more prototypical in a less antagonistic environment, see Haslam et al. 1995. Cf. chapter 5.1.

[330] Haslam et al. 1998; Oakes 1990; Turner 1985; Turner et al. 1987. The meta-contrast principle is based on a general tendency to maximize distinctiveness between categories in our patterns of categorization. We also tend to form categories of non-human objects after the principles of intragroup similarity and intergroup distinction, see Taylor 2003: 55–58.

7.3 Group Beliefs and Other Factors as Constraints on the Flexibility of the Prototype

The self-esteem hypothesis and the meta-contrast principle can easily give the impression that groups have an infinitely flexible self-perception, which will change swiftly with every new challenge. This would lead to absurd consequences. For instance, in a quarrel between two competing groups of Christ-believers, one group could hypothetically define themselves as non-believers in order to maximize the contrast. But this does not happen. Rather, it is always the other group, which is defined as non-believers or a deviant kind of believers. Therefore, we have to briefly discuss factors that put constraints on the flexibility of the ingroup prototype, as a corrective to a too simplified understanding of social identity theory. (This is not to say that there has ever been a fixed and entirely stable identity within the Christ-movement, just that there are stabilizing factors which are as important as destabilizing impulses for the dynamics of a group.)

First, already shared group beliefs constrain how easily the prototype can be modified in a certain direction. As we discussed in chapter 4, shared cognitive schemata, such as the identity of the group, will become more stable as they become based on a larger number of experiences. The history, narratives, memories and culture of the group are important constraining and stabilizing factors in the negotiation for identity.

Second, social and material circumstances within the group cannot be ignored when the group forms its identity. For instance, when the Gospels portray many of the followers of Jesus as poor, uneducated and marginalized, it is probably not just in order to maximize the contrast with the elite, but also because these strata of people were a factual part of the group's history and current social reality.

Third, the Christ-movement was capable of creating institutions which reinforced existing consensus. The culture of the Christ-movement developed beliefs about how the beliefs should be reinforced.[331] Leadership structures, collections of texts, education,

[331] "Some sets of representations include representations of the way in which the set should be redistributed. An institution is the distribution of a set of

regular meetings, etc., often reinforced existing formulations of their identity.

The consequence of the restraints discussed here is that anyone who wished to influence a group must take existing cognitive consensus and social reality into consideration in his or her rhetoric. If one does not start from existing consensus and social life in one's rhetoric, one is very likely to be marginalized or even defined as an outsider.[332] Successful rhetoric therefore uses existing shared cognitive resources, such as ingroup narratives and norms in order give the message and the messenger credibility.

---

representations which is governed by representations belonging to the set itself", Sperber 1996: 76.

[332] Cf. chapters 3.2 on estimating whether a text successfully influenced the Christ-movement, chapter 8.1 on the emotional stress when consensus is questioned, chapter 8.2 on marginalizing deviants, and chapter 8.3 on leadership.

8 Intragroup Dynamics in Christ

The identity in Christ, both its narratives and its norms, was formed in groups with interacting members. This chapter explores the cognitive foundation of the social dynamics within the groups of Christ-believers, which formed their identity. How does the need for cognitive certainty and affirmation of truths from others form the identity in Christ? What behavior norms are meant to increase the sense of cognitive certainty? How are deviants experienced as a threat to the group and how is this threat handled? How do group members, for instance leaders, gain the credibility they need in order to influence the group?

8.1 The Need for Cognitive Certainty and the Importance of Teaching and other Speech Norms

People like cognitive certainty. We can and must tolerate some degree of uncertainty, but we generally prefer to feel certain. We do not automatically agree within a group, but when we disagree on issues that are important for the group, we try to negotiate for "the truth" until we agree (or until we part), especially under cognitively uncertain conditions, since we are often emotionally dependent on the opinion of our ingroup for our evaluation of the world.[333] If there is any difference between cultures in how much uncertainty we can tolerate, I would

[333] This was initially discovered in experiments by Festinger, Schachter and Back 1950. Later on, Moscovici 1976 suggested that the need for a subjective experience of informational certainty was the main force behind group conformity. Hogg and Mullin 1999 suggest that uncertainty reduction should be seen as the most important factor for group identification in social identity theory as well.

argue that the collective and agonistic tendencies in the ancient Mediterranean world often made people more sensitive to ambiguous social situations, where they could not interpret the situation properly. Halvor Moxnes, leaning on anthropological studies, argues that the honor-shame paradigm caused people to be constantly uncertain about their position.[334] For someone who constantly guards his or her honor, cognitive uncertain situations are experienced as potentially undermining honor. This potential threat nurtures cultural agents in fear of cognitively uncertain situations.

Having said that, what I will discuss here is not mainly cognitive uncertainty about one's honor in social situations. Rather, I will focus on cognitive uncertainty about the rationale of the group—the beliefs that make commitment to the group worthwhile.

If cognitive uncertainty and the need to get one's cognition affirmed by others is one of the major forces behind group cohesion, one has to ask if there is something cognitively uncertain about the central claims of the early Christ-movement which potentially increased the need for consensus. The answer must be "yes." Religion answers the important questions of life by reference to a reality which is not easily verified or refuted. Moreover, the rationale of the Christ-movement—the Christ-

---

334 Moxnes 1996. Hofstede 2001: 145–208, in his very large cross-cultural survey of the attitudes among employees of IBM all over the world shows that Italy, Greece, Turkey and the Arab Countries all score high on the uncertainty avoidance index. (Hofstede discusses five dimensions of culture: tolerance for power distance (i.e., inequality), uncertainty avoidance, collectivity, gender differences and orientation towards long-term or short-term goals.) People in the Eastern Mediterranean and Arab countries, the main areas of cultural contact for the early Christ-movement, on average dislike cognitive uncertainty more than the average informant in Hofstede's study. One of the consequences of this cultural feature, according to Hofstede, is higher intolerance for deviation, especially in the field of religion. It is not unproblematic to assume that a culture keeps these kinds of attitudes over such a long time as 2000 years, but since this attitude is most easily explained by the collectivistic and agonistic character of the Mediterranean culture—a prominent feature of their culture both now and in antiquity (cf. Malina 2001)—there is reason to believe that uncertainty avoidance was as important in antiquity as it is in modern times.

narrative—was often questioned by other groups, which probably undermined the cognitive certainty of some group members.

Cognitive anthropologist Harvey Whitehouse distinguishes between an "imagistic mode" and an "doctrinal mode" of religion.[335] Imagistic religions do not emphasize narrative truth, but rather rituals and episodic experiences of the divine. Doctrinal religions, on the other hand, value semantic truths about the divine. The early Christ-movement certainly had strong elements of doctrinal religion.[336] From what we know about the early Christ-movement, the attitude towards truth about the divine seems to have been all but relative. Paul claims that all humans have "exchanged the truth of God for lies" (Rom 1:25) and therefore cannot be saved. In Galatians, he accuses Peter of departing from "the truth of the gospel" (Gal 2:14) when he budges to the Judaizers. Paul claims that he has received the gospel directly from Jesus Christ (1:12) and that anyone who teaches differently is "accursed" (ἀνάθεμα) (1:9). In Ephesians and Colossians, the author emphasizes that the Christ-believers need knowledge about God (e.g., Eph 1:17–18; Col 1:9–10; Eph 4:13; Col 2:1–4). Also in 1–2 Timothy, truth and correct teaching are highly important (e.g., 1 Tim 2:4, 7; 6:3 ; 2 Tim 2:14–26). The Gospel of John uses "truth" (ἀλήθεια) in a way which indicates that only through knowing the truth, embodied by Jesus Christ, can one be saved (e.g., 1:14, 17; 3:21; 4:23–24; 8:26, 32; 14:6; 17:17). For all we know, then, many texts indicate that the early Christ-movement did not take truth about spiritual matters lightly. This increased the need for cohesion and mutual support to confirm these truths.

Jean-Pierre Deconchy defines orthodoxy as "a social-cognitive field which is 'ideological'; that is, a field in which the main items of information are held to be 'true' although they are not capable of being validated through the use of hypothetico-deductive or experimental methods."[337] In such orthodox systems, he argues, the individual who identifies with the group actively seeks for the cognitive system to guide

[335] Whitehouse 2004; Whitehouse and Martin 2004. See also Ketola 2007 for an evaluation of the merits and problems of Whitehouse's theory.

[336] The early Christ-movement also had strong elements of imagistic religion. However, in this section I will discuss the importance of semantic "truth."

[337] Deconchy 1984: 429.

his behavior and beliefs and the institutions of the group usually provide a social control system which facilitates such affirmation. Deconchy's analysis supports the idea that people are more dependent upon social affirmation when dealing with religious truth, at least in cases where objective truth is considered important.[338]

In the texts of the early Christ-movement, we frequently find norms about speech, that is, what to say and not to say. Speech norms are behavior norms, which govern what people hear each other say within the group. Speech norms are therefore very important for the sense of cognitive certainty. A few examples: In the Gospel of Matthew, teaching the commandments of Jesus is central to the identity of Jesus' followers (28:20) and whoever teaches differently and leads other group members astray should be marginalized (5:19; 18:6). In First Timothy, the implied Paul emphasizes the importance of letting no one teach falsely (1:3–7) and that that the leaders are capable teachers (3:2; 4:6–13). First Peter exhorts them to speak "the word of God" rather than deceit (3:10; 4:11). The enormously rich theme of correct speech and teaching in the early Christ-movement can of course not be covered here. These examples do, however, show that speech norms were frequently an important part of the ingroup norms, which helped maintain cognitive certainty within the group.[339]

In sum, people are emotionally dependent on affirmation from others in order to maintain beliefs. In groups the members typically need to affirm each other's beliefs about the rationale of the group in order to remain convinced about the meaning of their social identity. The early Christ-movement emphasized the importance of truth about the divine and therefore needed to support one another to feel convinced about these truths. Hence, speech norms are very important in many texts from the early Christ-movement, since it is through speech behavior that one either affirms or undermines the cognitive certainty of other group members.

---

[338] See also Burris and Jackson 2000: 145–208.

[339] These norms can be considered to be "institutions" in the sense that they are representations governing how other representations should be reproduced, see n. 331.

8.2 Deviants

The deviant is a member of the group, not an outsider. From inside the group he or she behaves in a way which deviates from the prototype and makes claims which deviate from consensus. According to Jose Marques et al., when a group member exercises deviant behavior, the sense of ingroup similarity and contrast to the outgroup cracks; reality becomes cognitively uncertain and the meaning of the group becomes less valid.[340] We intuitively dislike cognitive dissonance and cognitive uncertainty, and our need to reproach deviants increases when we perceive the ingroup as heterogeneous with vague group boundaries.[341] Often the deviance also undermines the self-esteem of the group, since the existence of the deviant member makes it difficult to claim dignity and superiority towards outgroups. In these cases, the deviant is seen as even more provocative.[342] Moreover, deviants may undermine our chances to reach our goals, for instance people who are lazy, lie, take advantage of others, break promises and rules, give the group a bad reputation, induce schisms, etc.[343] These people are seldom appreciated. The deviant can sometimes be treated with tolerance, as long as the deviance does not concern norms that are important for the meaningfulness, the self-esteem and the goals in the current situation. However, if the deviant does things that threaten any of the above, the subjective needs of the group call for action against the deviant.

When a group member insists on a deviant course, the other group members will increase their attempts to convince the deviant by all means, and if the deviant does not budge, he or she will be relegated to

---

[340] Abrams et al. 2005; Hogg 2001; Marques et al. 2001. Cf. chapters 7.2 and 8.1. The social-scientific literature dealing with deviants is extensive, see e.g. Tellbe 2009: 137–182, who uses a wide spectrum of approaches in order to understand deviance in the early Christ-movement in Ephesos. I have, however, chosen a social identity-pespective since it is coherent with the cognitive approach of this study.

[341] Marques, Abrams and Seredio 2001. See also Abrams et al. 2005; Bown and Abrams 2003.

[342] Hogg, Fielding and Darley 2005.

[343] Cf. Kurzban and Leary 2001.

low status within the group.[344] Depending on group norms, the treatment of deviants can sometimes be even harsher, for instance with punishments, exclusion or execution. Matt 18:15–30 is a good example of institutionalization of legitimate ways to handle deviant group members: increasing reproach (vv. 15–16), exclusion (v. 17), judgment (v. 18), but forgiveness if they repent (vv. 22–30). The secondary effect of such reproach of the deviant is actually strengthened group identity.[345] To label the deviant "deviant" creates a feeling that order has been restored and the meaning and value of the group appears even clearer than before. The cognitive dislike for deviance also applies to oneself. A committed group member for whom a group identity is salient will monitor himself/herself and regulate his/her own behavior in order to be able to feel like a prototypical group member. For instance, according to Matt 18:8–9, a group member who is tempted to do something wrong should "cut off" his hand, foot and eye in order to not exercise deviant behavior.[346]

Our aversion toward deviants can also be used rhetorically. If I want the group to follow my course of action or accept my interpretation of the group's social identity rather than some competing suggestion, it is crucial to argue that my course of action or interpretation is a sign of prototypicality, while the opponents' actions and teachings are the fruits of deviance. It is therefore not easy to determine to what extent the accusations in texts from the early Christ-movement reflect real deviance from some norm and to what extent the author is constructing a deviance in order to promote a contrasting norm. For instance, the descriptions of the deviants in the Pastoral letters are almost certainly not innocent reflections of marginal teachers, but rather tendentious descriptions which resemble their position just to the extent necessary

---

[344] Brown 1988: 103–106; Schachter 1951.

[345] Marques 1990; Marques et al. 1998; Bown and Abrams 2003.

[346] Those members of the group who experience themselves to be on the fringes of prototypicality and therefore know that they might be excluded, but yet are committed to the group, are sometimes most eager to exclude those who are even less prototypical in order to establish their own position, while at the same time trying harder than others to act prototypically, see Pickett and Brewer 2005.

for the description to stick (e.g., 1 Tim 1:3–7, 4:1–3; 6:3–10; 2 Tim 2:14–19; 3:1–9; 4:3–4; Tit 1:10–16).[347] However, just because the descriptions are tendentious, we should not jump to the conclusion that the authors are only driven by will to power. On the contrary, their tendentious descriptions are probably often rooted in a genuine sense of threat against the group. The description of the deviant is therefore an indirect description of the author's vision of the identity of the group.

Finally, although the intuitive response to deviance is often that it threatens the sense of order and the goals of the group, deviance is certainly a necessary condition for change. Jesus and Paul were deviants who successfully undermined perceptions of reality. People like Paul, who insist on claiming "truth," which is in conflict with consensus, are sometimes capable of causing change within their group. The mechanism behind this is that if a group member insists on something that causes cognitive uncertainty about the group consensus, then people are motivated by the disturbing feeling of uncertainty to renegotiate the consensus in order to reach a new state of subjective certainty.[348] It is of course also possible that the one who claims dissonant opinions becomes marginalized, as we discussed above, but sometimes such a person can become an agent of change within the group.

8.3 Leadership and Influence over the Identity in Christ

Not everyone is equal within a group. In some texts from the early Christ-movement, there is an outspoken institutionalized hierarchical leadership structure (e.g., Eph 4:11–14; Tim 2:2–13; 3:2–7; Tit 1:5–9; *Did.* 15:1–2).[349] However, even in groups with an egalitarian structure, some

---

[347] Tellbe 2008; 2009: 137–182 uses labeling theory and social identity theory to analyze the rhetoric of deviance in the Pastorals and other early texts from Ephesus.

[348] Brown 1988: 106–121; Moscovici 1976. Cf. n. 333.

[349] This section has no ambition to discuss all the variations of leadership structures in the early Christ-movement. Rather, the purpose is to discuss leadership and influence more generally from a socio-cognitive perspective. On

people have more influence over the group than others. For example, although the author of 1 John does not promote strong hierarchical leadership structures (e.g. 2:20–21, 27), he writes as one with superior experience (1:1–4) to his "little children" (2:1), that is, with authority.[350] Where does this informal "charismatic" power to influence others come from?

Turner analyses influence and leadership from a social identity perspective.[351] As we discussed above in chapter 8.1, there is a tendency within groups to seek consensus, especially in cognitively uncertain conditions. In this process of negotiation for consensus, some will be more influential than others. According to Turner, the most influential group members are those who manage to present themselves as prototypical group members and thus give the impression that they embody the group consensus. Someone who embodies the consensus of the group is someone who is right and knows what is best for the group. This is the basis of a leader's influence in the group.

From the standpoint that influence comes from the ability to embody group consensus, Turner criticizes traditional views of power and influence which say that influence over people's behavior derives from control over desirable goods, which makes people dependent on whoever is in control. (These goods do not only have to be material goods, but can also be cognitive, emotional, social, etc.) This kind of power is only a part of how one can influence others. Often it is the other way around—power over goods comes from influence. This is certainly true for the early Christ-movement. The influence of the very central figures Jesus and Paul did not come from their ability to control goods, but from their ability to present themselves as embodying an ideal. Of course, we must acknowledge that household masters, who provided material goods for the Christ-believing communities, probably were rewarded with status and honor, that is, recognition of prototypicality, especially in the deutero-Pauline generation when household identities

leadership structures in Pauline and deutero-Pauline communities from a sociological perspective, see e.g. Holmberg 1980; MacDonald 1988.

350 Tellbe 2009: 197–206.

351 Turner 2005. See also e.g. Haslam and Platow 2001; Haslam 2001: 40–59; Turner 1991.

were transformed into sub-categories to the identity in Christ.[352] Once the recognition of them as being prototypical increased, they influenced the ingroup identity. Nevertheless, equally influential, if not more influential, "entrepreneurs of identity" were people who had no material goods to provide, such as Paul, Ignatius of Antioch and the Shepherd of Hermas.[353]

In short, leadership is to be able to prescribe what is right from the position of prototypicality. In order to influence consensus, one must first embody the identity of the group; in order to change consensus one must "be" consensus. The practical way to do this is to behave in a way which induces an image of prototypical qualities.[354] If a person is seen as prototypical, then people will more readily accept that this person has the right to prescribe attitudes, beliefs and actions. As we discussed in chapter 6.1, the ancient rhetoricians knew this and did their best to present themselves as virtuous in order to be persuasive. Paul is the New Testament author who promotes his prototypicality most extensively in order to influence his recipients (e.g., 1 Cor 2:1–5, 4:1–15; 2 Cor 1–6, 10–13; Gal 1:10–2:14; 6:11–17; Phil 1:12–26; 3:7–17).

According to Dominic Abrams et al. "people may use the mere occupancy of the leader role as a heuristic for assuming the leader is likely to represent the prescriptive norm."[355] Abrams et al. do not

---

[352] I have argued in Roitto 2008 that household virtues converge with virtues as Christ-believer in Ephesians, Colossians, 1 Timothy and Titus, since household identities are seen as sub-categories to the identity in Christ in these letters. In this situation, it is likely that being a household master would make it easier to gain influence within the community. Cf. the discussion in chapter 9.1.

[353] Esler 2003, who employs a social identity theory approach to leadership in his analysis of Paul's leadership in the letter to the Romans, uses the term "entrepreneur of identity" (e.g., p. 38).

[354] Cf. chapter 6.1.

[355] Abrams et al. 2008: 664. See also Turner et al. 1987: 74, where "role" is mentioned in passing as one of the factors which might influence prototypicality: "[T]he direction of effective influence within the group (who successfully influences whom) is a function of the relative persuasiveness of the members, which is based on the degree to which their response (their arguments, position, attributes, experience, *role*, etc.) is perceived as prototypical of the initial

specifically discuss how institutionalized legitimate power facilitates influence, but I would like propose that institutionalized offices should be conceptualized as subgroups or roles within the group. These subgroups or roles are associated with prototypical qualities in the shared culture of the group. Different offices can be associated with partly different prototypical qualities. For example, the office of the elder (πρεσβύτερος) is a subcategory to the category of the Christ-believer in First Timothy. Being a subcategory, it inherits the prototypical traits of the ingroup, with the addition that the elder is (or should be) closer to the ingroup prototype than the average group member.[356] In other words, when an individual becomes an elder, people will (until proven wrong) infer that he is a prototypical Christ-believer and therefore someone who has the right to prescribe attitudes, beliefs and behavior. "Let the elders who rule well be considered worthy of double honor … Never accept any accusation against an elder except on the evidence of two or three witnesses" (1 Tim 5:17–19). Such a view of the elder clearly predisposes people to see the elder as prototypical. To be seen as worthy of honor is essentially to be seen as virtuous, that is, prototypical. Nevertheless, even though the definition of leaders as a prototypical subcategory encourages people to close their eyes to a certain extent to unprototypical behavior, it still opens for the possibility to criticize and dethrone the leader if the dissonance between the ideal picture of the leader and his actual behavior is too great (cf. 1 Tim 3:1–13, Herm. *Sim.* 9.26).[357]

---

distribution of responses of the group as a whole, i.e., the degree of relative consensual support for a member." (Emphasis added.)

[356] On subcategories, see chapters 5.1 and 9.1.

[357] See Abrams et al. 2008 for a study of negative reactions to leaders who deviate too much from established group norms.

9 Being in Christ from the Perspective of the Individual Group Member

So far, we have examined socio-cognitive processes from the perspective of group dynamics. This chapter will, however, discuss the experience of being in Christ from the perspective of the individual. How does my commitment to the group of Christ-believers influence the way I act within the group? How do I decide whether the identity in Christ or some other social identity should be salient in a certain situation? Just like in previous chapters, we will also reflect upon how the answers to these questions translate into rhetoric intended to influence the cognitive processes of the individual.

9.1 Conflicting Possibilities of Identity

Most individuals can potentially think of themselves as belonging to several social categories; for instance, a first century Christ-believer might see herself as a woman, a household-member, a slave, and a Christ-believer.

We can therefore not assume that a first-century individual was entirely "stuck" with, for instance, her household identity. Collectivistic as this culture was, it was not a culture where all different identities fitted neatly together into concentric circles of belonging. In terms of self-categorization theory, social identities did not form one big hierarchy of identities, where one identity was a superordinate category to the other (see chapters 5.1 and 5.2). Kinship identities could be said to form a hierarchy of superordinate and subordinate categories: household, clan, tribe and *ethnos*. Other social identities were also available: religious groups (Christ-believers, mystic cults, Pharisees, etc.), burial societies, schools, philosophical sects (Epicureans, Cynics, etc.), associations based on occupation, patron-client-networks, etc.; all of these provided a complex web of possibilities for social identification in any given situation.[358] In the cities where the Pauline version of belief in Christ had its greatest success,[359] there was already an established pattern of joining various groups that did not coincide with the kinship structure. The individuals in such a society would have to make decisions, consciously or unconsciously, about which social identity to identify with in different situations.

I have argued elsewhere that the first generation of Pauline Christ-believers saw a conflict between household identities and the identity in Christ (1 Cor 7; Philem 16), since the category of the identity in Christ did not coincide with the category of the household, neither in prototypical ideals, nor in members.[360] In the deutero-Pauline generation, where the most influential group members lived in wholly Christ-believing households, the cognition changes and household identities become subcategories to the identity in Christ (Eph 5:21–6:9; Col 3:18–4:1; 1 Tim 2:8–3:13; Tit 2). The conflict perspective is therefore gone in the deutero-Pauline literature and instead household identities are argued for with analogies from the identity in Christ. The aim is to eliminate the conflict between household identities and the identity in Christ by subordinating household identities to the identity in Christ.[361]

---

[358] See Malina and Neyrey 1996: 158–64 for an overview over different social groupings. Malina and Neyrey do not, however, reflect upon what it meant for the individual that s/he had to make decisions about which social identity was the most appropriate in a given situation.

[359] Meeks 1983: 9–50.

[360] Roitto 2008. See also the discussion in chapter 17.3.

[361] The deutero-Pauline attitude is similar to the Jewish attitude to their covenantal "religion/piety" (εὐσέβεια) as encompassing all aspects of life, including the household, as described by Josephus, *C. Ap.* 157, quoted in chapter 6.4.

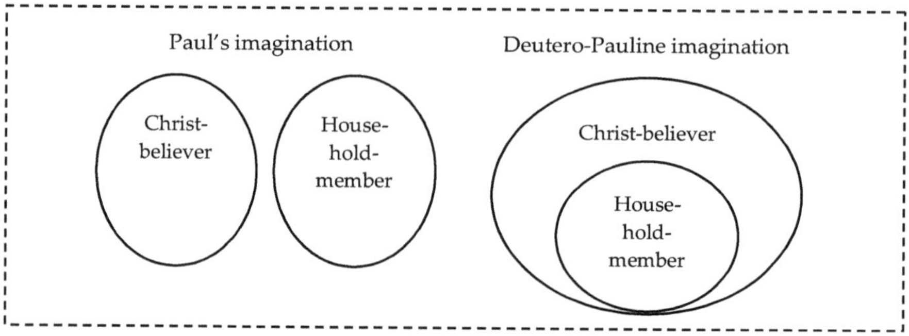

Philip Esler has analyzed how Paul organizes the relation between ethnic identities and the identity in Christ in his letter to the Romans.[362] The background to Romans seems to be that people of different ethnic origin did not always agree on the relation between *ethnos* and being in Christ. Paul redefines the covenant of Abraham and makes it a covenant of faith (Rom 4). Yet the recipients, whether Jew or gentile, do not have to cancel their ethnic identity in order to identify themselves as Christ-believers. Rather, Christ-believing Jews and gentiles are sub-categories within the category of the covenant. Paul does not create a new category of Christ-believers, which is opposed to being part of an old covenant (as Hebr 8:1–10:21 does), but redefines the covenant. The only new category, which Paul invents in great agony, is the category of the temporarily excluded non-believing Jews who will be saved in the end (Rom 9–11).

[362] Esler 2003: e.g. 29–33, 141–154, 184–194, 306–307. The short analysis here is selectively based on Esler's analysis.

Paul's imagination of the relation between ethnicity, the covenant and being in Christ

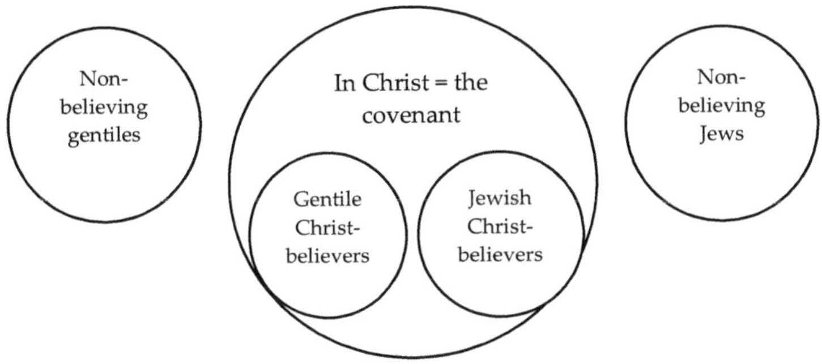

Negotiating the relation between social identities can result in many different kinds of contructs. The relation between two different social identities can be constructed in three different ways: a) as different categories, b) as the same category or c) as subcategory and superordinate category (cf. chapter 5.1). If the categories are defined as different categories, defining the relation between them is very important for an individual who belongs to both categories. Are they opposing incompatible identities or just different identities? In what practical situations should I identify with my household and my *ethnos* and in what situations should I identify with my identity in Christ? Careful attention to the relation between social categories is therefore an important part of the analysis of texts and the understanding of the potential social dilemmas these texts try to resolve.

9.2 Situation and Identity Salience

Different circumstances make different social identities *salient*. A female, Christ-believing slave would primarily have thought of herself as a slave in the face of her *mater familias*. However, when she met other Christ-believers in worship, her identity in Christ would have been the most salient one. "In Christ … there is no slave" (Gal 3:28) does not mean that she is no longer a slave, just that this identity is not (or should not be) the most relevant in the current social situation (cf. 1 Cor 7:17–24).

Penelope Oakes (et al.) argues that a social identity becomes more salient a) if there is a relevant contrasting outgroup to compare with ("comparative fit") and b) if the content of the situation matches the content of the identity ("normative fit").[363] As we encounter a new situation, our brains scan through our social identities to decide which social identity best fits the situation according to these two criteria.[364]

Oakes complements the notion of fit with the notion of accessibility; in other words, how easily accessible the identity is in the individual's cognitive structure at the moment. An identity may be more easily accessible if it has just been used or if it is very important for the individual. If an identity is very important for an individual and therefore has a constantly high accessibility, this may compensate for poor fit in different situations, since the perceiver is then highly motivated to interpret the situation as a situation that should be handled through that identity.[365] We can reasonably assume that Christ-believers were sometimes motivated to interpret every aspect of life as Christ-believers, and therefore did their best to handle also situations with poor fit with their constantly salient identity in Christ. This motivation might have inspired the often creative use of ingroup narratives in order to form and/or argue for norms for situations which had hitherto not been handled as aspects of the identity in Christ. This creative use of group narratives will be discussed in chapter 11.2.

---

[363] Oakes, Turner and Haslam 1991; Oakes, Haslam and Reynolds 1999.

[364] E.g. if one is a Christ-believer in a synagogue with Christ-believers and Pharisees and all Christ-believers claim one thing and the Pharisees claim something contrasting, then the identity in Christ has high comparative fit. If all Christ-believers claim something which fits one's normative beliefs about what Christ-believers should think, e.g. that Jesus is the Christ, and all the Pharisees claim another opinion in line with what one thinks a Pharisee would think—e.g. that Jesus is not the Christ—then the categories have high normative fit. But in situations where there are no relevant interpretative patterns connected to the identity as a Christ-believer, the identity will have no function and will probably not become salient.

[365] "[P]eople may perceive a sufficient fit of social categorizations with high chronic accessibility … even if the configuration of the stimulus persons [i.e. the persons who the individual faces] provides neither comparative nor normative fit. Under these conditions, the actual fit of such a categorization will be `overestimated'", Blanz 1999: 47.

9.3 Commitment and Behavior

Commitment can be defined as "the extent to which a group member feels strong ties with the group."[366] If an identity is salient and the group member is committed, then the group member will more probably identify with the group and thereby act according to group norms.[367] Naomi Ellemers et al. show that depending on the factors a) commitment and b) type of threat, group members tend to react in different ways:[368]

- In case of no threat:
  - *Low commitment:* Avoid involvement unless it is beneficial.
  - *High commitment:* Find meaning through group expressions.
- In case of threat to the individual from the group:
  - *Low commitment:* Affirm yourself by distancing yourself from the group.
  - *High commitment:* Get accepted by adapting typical group behavior.
- In case of threat to the group from an outgroup:
  - *Low commitment:* Save yourself by leaving the group.
  - *High commitment:* Affirm the group by stereotyping the outgroup and exalting the ingroup.

People who are committed are more often prepared to act according to group norms even when it is costly compared to people who are not that committed. Therefore it is important to understand what factors increase and reduce commitment. If we identify these factors, we can find strategies in the texts which are intended to make the recipients more committed.

---

366 Doojse, Ellemers and Spears 1999: 85.

367 Costarelli 2005 on the importance of group identity salience. Ellemers, Spears and Doosje 2002 on how high commitment motivates the individual to stay during difficult circumstances. Ellemers et al. 2005 on how commitment can make group members tolerate even the use of force by ingroup superiors.

368 Ellemers, Spears and Doosje 2002. (Clarification: The summary above this note is not a quote, but a summary.)

There is no one way to predict commitment, but I have briefly enumerated factors which usually increase commitment:[369]

a. One considers the purpose and meaning of one's group to be comprehendible and agreeable.[370]
b. One feels that one can evaluate one's group positively in relation to outgroups, that is, one's identification with the group gives self-esteem on the group level.[371]
c. One feels that one can have a positive evaluation of oneself in relation to one's ingroup, that is, one feels one gets honor, respect and appreciation.[372]
d. When the group is threatened in relation to the outgroup or the individual is threatened in relation to the ingroup, the threat increases commitment if it is already high but decreases commitment if it is low.[373] Hardship can actually make people even more motivated, because it heightens the sense that the group membership must be something very valuable.[374]
e. One is identifiable to your ingroup, that is, not anonymous.[375]
f. The group is considered to have a common fate.[376]
g. The group is considered to have a common task, for which they are dependent upon each other to solve.[377]

---

[369] This is not a complete list, just a list of factors I have found scattered throughout the social identity literature.

[370] See chapter 7.2.

[371] See chapter 7.1.

[372] Fuller et al. 2003.

[373] Spears, Doojse and Ellemers 1999.

[374] Brown 1988: 24–27 suggests that this is the result of our need to decrease cognitive dissonance. We sometimes exaggerate the value of group memberships that have caused us suffering so that we do not have to face that we have suffered for nothing.

[375] Reicher, Spears and Postmes 1995: 192.

[376] Brown 1988: 28–29.

[377] Brown 1988: 30–33.

The Shepherd of Hermas is a good example of an author who relentlessly preaches against "doublemindedness" (διψυχία[378]) and aims at increasing commitment in every possible way. He promises eternal life for those who stay committed and endure, and threatens with damnation for those who do not (e.g., Herm. *Vis.* 2.2.7–8). In other words, high costs demand high commitment but leads to high reward (cf. factor d above). He prescribes emotions and dispositions such as faith, joy and trust as an antidote to doublemindedness and grief (e.g., Herm. *Mand.* 9–10). That is, he proclaims that attitudes that might decrease commitment are deviant and sees attitudes that will increase the sense of certainty and meaning (cf. factor a above) as prototypical. He demands that people should restrict their business, so that they do not get too involved in the surrounding society (e.g., Herm. *Sim.* 1–2, 5). That is, he aims at making the identity in Christ constantly salient and asks the recipients to distance themselves from other possible social identifications. In short, Hermas is an entrepreneur of commitment. His preaching, as secteristic as it may be, aims at influencing his listeners to become more committed and detach themselves from competing loyalties.

---

[378] A search on the διψυχ-stem (διψυχία, διψυχέω, δίψυχος, etc.) in the Shepherd of Hermas gives a total of 58 hits. (Search performed with BibleWorks 7.)

10 Summary of the Functions of the Ingroup Prototype

In chapters 5 to 9 we have surveyed how socio-cognitive theories can help us understand the relation between identity and behavior norms. In these discussions the ingroup prototype has frequently recurred as an important factor in our understanding. Let us therefore summarize the multiple functions of the ingroup prototype for the social dynamics of the group and the psychology of the individual who identifies with the group:

- *Description of the group:* The prototype describes what the group is like: its character, its value, its goals, its beliefs and its norms.
- *Distinctiveness of the group:* The prototype contrasts the group with the outgroup stereotype(s) and ideally makes the group feel distinct. Therefore the prototype changes with the context.
- *Value of the group:* The prototype is used to compare the group with the outgroup stereotype(s) and explains why the group is better, which can increase self-esteem.
- *Evaluation of the group:* The prototype is the standard by which the group evaluates itself.
- *Guidance of group dynamics:* The normative ideals (behaviors, attitudes and beliefs), which are described by the prototype, guide how group members interact.
- *Self-stereotyping of the individual:* The individual group members who identify with the group strive to perceive themselves and to be perceived by others as similar to the prototype.
- *Normative guidance for the individual in the group:* The prototype prescribes norms, such as behaviors, attitudes and beliefs, for the individual.

- *Evaluation of individuals, status differentiation:* The prototype gives a standard for group members by which they can evaluate both themselves and other group members. Those who do not adhere to the norms of the prototype can be judged as deviants. Those who fulfill the norms are praiseworthy exemplars. Those members who manage to present themselves as prototypical will have more influence and status.

In short, the ingroup prototype works for both collective and individual evaluation, both for intergroup and intragroup regulation, differentiation and comparison, and has both descriptive and prescriptive functions. As we discussed in chapter 6.1, the ingroup prototype has both an attributed and a visible behavioral side. The relation between attributes and behavior (norms) is causal in both directions and explains why certain behaviors are expressions of the group's identity. All these aspects of the ingroup prototype can be used rhetorically.

11 Narrative, Identity and Behavior Norms

Together with a great number of biblical scholars I assume that narratives were an important part of the identity in Christ.[379] Narratives tell the group who they are and inspire and motivate behavior.

The narrative form of thinking is cross-culturally universal and humans most probably have an innate tendency to order and interpret experience through narratives.[380] Different cultures do of course have different narratives and different frequently recurring patterns in their narratives. I do not argue that all myths and other narratives can be nicely fitted into for example universal narrative structures or Jungian archetypes.[381] In the most basic sense, however, a narrative is an arrangement of events into coherent and meaningful temporal and

---

[379] E.g. Lieu 2004: 310–316 suggests that the narrative is the medium through which the first Christians formed their identity. See e.g. Bruner 1990; Linde 1993; Polkinghorne 1988 on how narratives form identity, help to interpret the meaning of events and create a sense of coherence in life. See Bar-Tal 1990; 1998 (also discussed in chapter 2.2) on how "group beliefs" are an important part of the identity of a group.

[380] Bruner 1990; Hogan 2003; Turner 1996.

[381] I do, however, recognize that due to our cognitive makeup some narrative structures are easier to remember than others and are therefore more likely to be retold and survive, see Sperber 1996: 98–118. For instance, narratives with straightforward causal connections are easier to remember, see Meyers and Duffy 1990. Regarding Jungian archetypes, Palmer 1997: 172–183 argues that Jungian archetypes have not been proven to be cross-culturally universal and that there even is evidence to the contrary. One of the basic problems with Jungian archetypes is that the archetypes are so vaguely defined that an empirical test of their universal existence cannot be operationalized.

causal sequences.[382] In that basic sense, much research suggests that the capacity to narrate and narrativize is cross-culturally universal. Narratives appear in all cultures and the capacity to narrate develops spontaneously in young children in a fairly predictable order if they are just given a speaking environment.[383]

In a review of understandings of narratives among literary critics, Brian Richardson acknowledges the great variety and sophistication in current scholarly analyses of literature.[384] The aim of this chapter is not to make full use of this vast field of subtle literary approaches. (I doubt that the analytical sophistication of a trained literary critic is what we should expect of an average text recipient in the early Christ-movement.) Rather, I will limit myself to some very basic notions about narratives, which are helpful in the analysis of the experienced relation between ingroup narratives and behavior norms.

11.1 Narratives Hold Causal Beliefs

Richardson recognizes two aspects of narratives which are usually acknowledged by literary theorists as typical of narratives: temporality and causality.[385] His own definition of narrative, which I agree with, is "a representation of causally related series of events."[386] When people who are not professional literary critics are asked about what they consider to be a narrative, they frequently mention temporality, causality, goal-

---

[382] See chapter 11.1.

[383] Gleason 2000: 18–19, 421–422; McCabe 1997; Stein and Albro 1997. McCabe discusses interesting cross-cultural differences in the form and emphasis of a narrative among children, but nevertheless recognizes the narrative as a universal phenomenon.

[384] Richardson 2000.

[385] Richardson 2000.

[386] Richardson 2000: 169–170. Richardson discusses how strictly the criterion of causality should be interpreted, but recognizes that in the "common sense" understanding of narrative, causality is indeed assumed. However, he does not want to limit causality to direct causality, but prefers the looser phrase "causally related."

based action by an agent, obstacles and an ending.[387] The most important of these characteristics of the narrative for this study is causality, particularly agent-driven intentional causality.[388]

Cognitive psychologists Arthur Graesser, Brent Olde and Bianca Klettke argue that the cognitive structure of a narrative has several layers in our minds: surface code (exact wording), textbase (the meaning of the words in the form of propositions), plot-level (an understanding of the chronological series of events linked together with causal explanations of why they follow each other) and the thematic level (the points or themes of the narrative).[389] The two first levels decay quickly from memory, while the other two are remembered much longer. The last two levels are of the greatest interest to us. The thematic aspect will be dealt with in chapter 11.2, but let us begin with the plot-level.

The causal links between events hold a very central position on the plot level for our understanding of a story.[390] The explanations of why one event follows another are very important if we are to experience that the narrative is coherent. Other elements such as when, where and how things happened, are also important for how we remember narratives, but not as central as the causal connections.

The ingroup narratives in the texts of the early Christ-movement hold causal beliefs about both the causes and effects of behavior. These causal beliefs are central to the normative value of different behaviors. We have already in detail discussed the beliefs about the causes of behavior (attributions) in chapter 6, and concluded that the moral value of behavior is frequently measured by the believed causes of behaviors. These causal beliefs are interwoven with other causal beliefs in the narratives of the ingroup and could even be called mini-narratives in their own right, since they are causal beliefs.

The narratives also hold motivating beliefs about the consequences of behavior, not only its causes. Certain behavior may be described as

---

[387] Stein and Albro 1997.

[388] Cf. chapter 6.

[389] Graesser, Olde and Klettke 2002.

[390] See also Meyers and Duffy 1990. On the innate capacity to construct causality, see chapter 6.

causing harm to or benefiting people or the group, that is, behavior may be considered instrumental to some good or evil end. "Those who speak in a tongue build up themselves, but those who prophesy build up the church ... if all prophesy, and an unbeliever or outsider enters ... that person will bow down before God and worship him" (1 Cor 14:4, 24–25). Paul's narrative provides causal beliefs, which affect the evaluation of charismatic behaviors. Other narratives may inform that behavior causes reward or punishment, either in this life or in eternity. For example, Hermas believes that only those who have suffered for Christ will sit on Christ's right-hand side in heaven, while the others will only be allowed to sit on the left-hand side (Herm. *Vis.* 3.1.9) and therefore Hermas hopes to suffer in order to become just like those on Christ's right-hand side (Herm. *Vis.* 3.2.1–2).

11.2 Narratives Motivate Action and Behavior Norms Through Analogy

When we hear a narrative, we frequently extract one or several themes and/or points from the narrative.[391] It is yet shrouded in mystery exactly how and why we make a certain thematic interpretation of a narrative, but experience, context as well as motivation seem to be important factors.[392] Consequently, a thematic interpretation of a narrative is highly creative and a skillful rhetorician can reinterpret familiar narratives to fit his agenda. The New Testament is full of creative interpretations of the narratives in the *Tanak,* such as Paul's surprising interpretation of Sarah and Hagar (Gal 4:21–5:1) and Matthew's frequent creative quotations from the prophets (e.g., Matt 2:17–18).

According to Roger Shank, when we put thematic "labels" on narratives in our minds, these themes then function as "indexes" to the narratives in our memories, so that we can associate to these narratives and retrieve them from memory in other situations when they might be relevant.[393]

---

[391] Graesser, Olde and Klettke 2002; Schank 1995: 84–114.

[392] Graesser, Olde and Klettke 2002.

[393] Schank 1995: 84–114; Schank and Berman 2002.

We narrativize real life events in order to understand, evaluate and remember them.[394] These real life narratives are often thematically ordered in our memory and indexed accordingly, just like narratives that we have heard. The brain does not wholly separate between real experiences and heard narratives (even if they are explicitly fictional); rather they often become conflated in our memories when they are integrated into the same memory structures, since they are thematically similar.[395] Consequently, it is quite easy for us to associate between narratives that we have heard and our own experiences. Since the brain typically organizes new experiences into existing memory structures, it is likely that new experiences will become narratively structured by narratives already existing in our minds.[396] In other words, if the narratives of my ingroup are dear to me and therefore easily accessible in my mind, they are potent interpretative patterns through which I will understand new experiences. We can only speculate about how individual Christ-believers handled everyday situations, but it is likely that the ingroup narratives became a source of guidance in their everyday decisions, if they felt that their identity in Christ was relevant for that situation.

This flexible and powerful ability to associate between narratives and narrativized experiences is best understood in terms of "analogical thinking" or "conceptual blending."[397] We frequently make assumptions about new situations through more or less conscious comparison with old situations and we frequently blend knowledge from several different domains of knowledge in order to solve problems creatively. Exactly

---

[394] Schank 1995: 114–125.

[395] Strange 2002.

[396] Schank and Berman 2002; Strange 2002.

[397] See Fauconnier and Turner 2002 on "conceptual blending." See Gentner, Kokinov and Holyoak 2001 on "analogical thinking." Blending theory develops the research in analogical thinking. While "analogical thinking" mainly denotes the transfer of knowledge from one cognitive domain to another, "blending" denotes how knowledge from several domains are combined in order to solve problems and create new knowledge. For studies using theories about conceptual blending on Nag Hammadi and New Testament texts, see Lundhaug 2007a; 2007b; Robbins 2007.

how the mind combines domains of knowledge is still not fully understood and it is probably beyond reach to reconstruct the details of this process from historical texts. Nevertheless, analogy or conceptual blending is one of our most important skills for problem solving and it seems to be typical for all humans.[398] Our ability to associate between narratives and use them creatively is probably best understood as the result of this kind of thinking.

In a group, the shared ingroup narratives are a treasure of possible associations, which can be evoked in the ingroup discourse to communicate a message. Cognitive anthropologists Claudia Strauss and Naomi Quinn recognize that central themes in a culture tend to spread from one context to another through our ability to seek an approximate fit for new situations in established schemata.[399] Paul Thagart and Cameron Shelley show that analogies can transfer not only thought patterns but also emotions from one domain to another.[400] Gerd Theissen's suggestion that there are "basic motifs" which recur in all kinds of contexts in the early Christ-movement—rites, myths and ethics—fits quite well into this picture of how narrative themes are reused in ever new situations.[401] In short, groups tend to reuse familiar themes analogically in new situations. In the following, I will focus on how thematic analogies imbue behavior norms with value and meaning in texts from the early Christ-movement.

The heroes of the ingroup narratives often function as exemplars of good dispositions and behavior through selective analogy in the early Christ-movement. The Christ-believers are repeatedly exhorted to mimic Jesus in several ways, for instance, to follow him (Matt 4:19 par.), carry the cross (Matt 10:38 par.), do the same deeds as he did (John 14:12), love like he did (John 15:12), be meek and obedient like him (Phil 2:5–11; cf. John 13:15) and suffer like him (1 Pet 2:21). They are also asked to

---

[398] Lakoff and Johnson 1980 suggest that "metaphor" (another term for analogical thinking or blending) is fundamental to all human thinking (i.e., innate). "[M]ost of our ordinary conceptual system is metaphorical in nature" (p. 4).

[399] Strauss and Quinn 1997: 118–119. Cf. Shelley and Thagard 1996.

[400] Thagard and Shelley 2001.

[401] Theissen 1999. Cf. the discussion in chapter 4.

imitate, for instance, Paul (1 Cor 4:16) and his co-workers (Phil 3:18) and the local leaders (Heb 13:7). They are asked to take historical biblical figures as role models, for example, Abraham (Rom 4; Gal 3), Sarah (Gal 4:21–32; 1 Pet 3:6) and many others (Heb 11, 1 Clement[402]). Even the archangel Michael (Jud 9) and God himself (Matt 5:48; Luk 6:36) are occasionally used as exemplars. (Many of these characters are, strictly speaking, not ingroup members, and therefore, strictly speaking, not exemplars. They are, nevertheless, important characters in the ingroup narratives and certain attitudes and behaviors become filled with value and meaning through creative analogies to the narratives.)

Readiness to suffer for one's commitment to Christ, for example, is often motivated through the use of selective thematic analogy to the suffering of Christ. Several passages in the New Testament motivate the norm of enduring suffering as Christ-believers (e.g., Matt 16:24 par.; 2 Cor 1:5–6; 4:8–11; Phil 3:10–11; Col 1:24; 1 Pet 2:18–25; 4:1, 13; Jam 1:3–4, 12). Sometimes the texts motivate through causal beliefs: a) The willingness to suffer is caused by prototypical attributed dispositions; suffering is a sign of prototypicality. b) The willingness to suffer will cause God to save that individual, but his/her avoidance of suffering will cause God to reject him/her; the willingness to suffer makes the individual ingroup or outgroup. But that is not all. In addition, the texts often present suffering for Christ as partly analogous to Christ's own suffering. The one who suffers does something, which is similar to what Christ did. Through such associations, Christ-like character traits, and emotions of doing something important and noble are transferred into the behavior of suffering for Christ's sake from the narrative about Christ's suffering. Therefore, at least some individuals were more than happy to suffer for their identity in Christ.

---

402 Esler forthcoming.

12 Recapitulation

In chapter 3 to 11 we outlined a cognitive approach to the experienced relation between identity in Christ and behavior norms in the early Christ-movement. Before we continue, let us briefly recapitulate the approach.

Cognitive sciences and historical investigation. In chapter 3 we discussed how cognitive psychology can be a good starting point for historical investigation. In section 3.1 we concluded that cognitive psychology has identified several innate cognitive characteristics of the human mind, which we most probably share with people from other eras and cultures. Since our culturally specific forms of thinking are molded and restrained by our innate cognitive setup, we can start from these common ways of thinking in order to understand the culturally specific thought patterns of the subjects of the past.

In section 3.2 we discussed the problem of the relation between the norms that are expressed in texts and social realities within the local communities of the early Christ-movement. Although all reconstructions of their social reality are speculative and hypothetic, reconstructions are, nevertheless, necessary if we are to understand behavior norms, since behavior norms are always formed in relation to real social circumstances. I proposed a way to evaluate whether it was likely that the norms of a text were ever approximately embraced by local communities.

A cognitive perspective on culture. In chapter 4 we elaborated the concept of culture. Culture was understood as shared cognition. Such an approach is ontologically clear and can explain continuity and change as well as shared and varied cognition. Moreover, if culture is considered to be shared cognition, we can use cognitive research to understand why certain themes are reused creatively over and over again, in order to inspire behavior norms.

Social identities and the self. In chapter 5 we discussed social identities. In section 5.1 it was argued that social identities are dependent on our innate capacity to categorize both humans and other kinds of objects. Categories center on a prototype, a representation of the typical or ideal category member. Moreover, categories can be ordered either as different contrasting categories or as subordinate and superordinate categories.

In section 5.2 we discussed how social identity theory and self-categorization theory understand social identities as categorization of oneself and of others. In section 5.3 we related the categorial construction of social identity to the relational construction of social identity and concluded that they were complementary levels of social identity constructs.

In section 5.4 we explored how the individual who identifies with a group self-stereotypes and experiences himself/herself as similar to the ingroup prototype. However, the ideas that a) that the collectivistic person has a murky perception of agency and b) that a collectivistic person does not engage in basic introspection, were rejected.

Attribution and morality. In chapter 6 we investigated the two main ways in which we humans construe causal relations: a) mechanical causality and b) intentional causality (i.e., agents as the cause of an event). These two basic ways to construe causality are innate and universal. The beliefs about the cause of intentions do, however, vary from culture to culture.

In section 6.1 we explored the tension between explanation and moralizing (indicative and imperative) in the process of attribution. Attributions are seldom just an interpretation, but also typically morally loaded. Communicated attributions are also rhetorically strategic. We then related the process of attribution to the ingroup prototype and argued that the ingroup prototype has an attributed side and a visible behavioral side. The relation between the attributed and the behavioral side was both descriptive and prescriptive and the prototype could therefore potentially function in several ways in a group context.

In section 6.2 and 6.3 we surveyed the two most important cultural patterns of attribution in the ancient Mediterranean culture: a) virtue and vice and b) spiritual influence. In these surveys we found intra-cultural variation. Some tendencies were, however, present in both kinds of attribution: a) the tension between imperative and indicative, b) a belief in a dialectic relation between action and attributes, and c) a connection of attributed ideals to social categories.

Group dynamics. In chapter 7 we explored how identities are formed and how this process affects ingroup norms, starting in section 7.1 with the need for self-esteem. The group's need for self-esteem in relation to other groups was often, but not always, an important factor in the formation of the ingroup prototype. The values and the self-perception of the group are formed in a way that increases self-esteem. Then, in section 7.2, we saw that the need for cognitive distinctiveness was an important factor in the formation of the ingroup prototype. According to the meta-contrast principle, the ingroup prototype and the outgroup stereotypes are formed in a way that makes the purpose and value of the group as clear as possible in relation to other groups. The rhetorical aspect of the group's need for self-esteem and distinctiveness is that we should expect authors to formulate the identity of the group in a way that aims at maximizing self-esteem and distinctiveness. Finally, in section 7.3 we discussed constraining factors, which moderated the tendency to form one's identity in relation to the current context. I argued that existing shared cognition (shared beliefs, memories, etc.), institutions and social and material circumstances to a certain extent can function conservatively.

In chapter 8 we surveyed how intragroup dynamics formed and was formed by norms. First, in section 8.1, we discussed the need for cognitive certainty and how we tend to be dependent on confirmation from other group members in cognitively uncertain situations. Religious truth is one of the areas where subjective cognitive certainty is dependent on support from the group. The early Christ-movement frequently formed norms intended to increase group cohesion and decrease cognitive uncertainty through for example teaching and speech norms.

Then, in section 8.2, we discussed how deviant ingroup members sometimes threatened the distinctiveness, self-esteem and goals of the group, which often occasioned marginalization and exclusion. Moreover, I argued that it is a common rhetorical device to portray opponents as deviant. Finally, we noted that sometimes deviants can become agents of change within the group.

In the final section dealing with intragroup dynamics, 8.3, we investigated influence and leadership. Influence and leadership comes from recognition of prototypicality. By presenting oneself and one's goals as prototypical, that is, as embodying the group ideals, other group members are more willing to listen to one's suggestions.

Being a group member. In chapter 9 we focused on what the identity in Christ would have meant for the individual and how the challenges for the individual translated into group norms. First, in section 9.1, we considered what it would have meant for the individual to navigate between different social identities and how people in the early Christ-movement constructed their identity in Christ in relation to other, sometimes conflicting, social identities, such as household identities and ethnic identities.

Next, in section 9.2, we discussed that the identity in Christ had to fit the current social situation in order to be salient for the individual. However, sometimes people are highly motivated to handle all situations, even those with poor fit, with their favorite identities.

After that, in section 9.3, we problematized the fact that people can be more or less committed to a group and therefore act more or less according to the group norms. One important task of ingroup rhetoric is to increase commitment.

Having examined various aspects of the ingroup prototype, in chapter 10 we summarized the functions of the shared cognition of the prototype for a) ingroup dynamics and b) the psychology of the individual who identifies with the group.

Narratives. Finally, in chapter 11, we examined the importance of narratives for identity and behavior norms. First, in section 11.1 we saw that the narratives provide causal beliefs, which make behavior norms a meaningful part of the identity in Christ. Then, in section 11.2, we discussed how the themes of narratives can be used analogically in order to motivate behavior and argue for new behavior norms.

We are now ready to analyze the relation between identity in Christ and behavior norms in the Pauline letter to the Ephesians with the theoretical framework that has been developed in previous chapters.

Text Study: Identity and Behavior Norms in Ephesians

The Pauline letter to the Ephesians expresses the relation between identity as a Christ-believer and behavior norms in a most elaborate way. Although scholars have always recognized the relation between "theology" and "ethics" in Ephesians, they have not been able to explain fully how the author imagines the relation between the two. I believe that the perspective developed in chapters 3 to 12 has the capacity to explain the thinking of Ephesians better that previous studies.

Ephesians is a text that is difficult to connect to a particular crisis or occasion (see chapter 14.1). Therefore many scholars have given up any attempt to discuss the relation between the text and the social reality of those who used the text. Yet Ephesians seems to both reflect and construct real communal life, since it deals extensively with practical ethics, that is, behavior norms. With the perspective developed in this study, we gain new tools to approach the relation between the text and social reality in a more systematic way than previous studies.

Besides being interesting in its own right, the text also functions as a test-case for the theoretical framework that was formed in the theoretical chapters of this study.

13 The Aim and Progression of the Analysis of Ephesians

What was it like to participate in the communal life of the congregation that Ephesians portrays? How did they narrate their identity? What were their ideals? How did they interact?

This analysis of Ephesians aims to achieve two goals (cf. the introduction of this study): The first aim is to reconstruct the relation between identity and behavior norms in Ephesians. The second aim is to discuss how the imagination of Ephesians might have functioned in a group if it came to be the shared ideal of a first century community of Christ-believers in Asia Minor. The analysis will progress thematically, with themes based on the analytical categories developed in the theoretical chapters of this study.

The most central aspect of the analysis will be the relation between attributed character traits and behavior norms in the ingroup prototype (chapter 18). However, in order to analyze the text thoroughly, we will have to begin with a few traditional historical-critical issues and a number of issues relating to identity, which will have a direct impact on how we interpret the prototype. It is rhetorically unfortunate that we cannot utilize the theoretical framework of this study fully without delay. I ask the reader to be patient. The use of the theoretical framework of this study will increase gradually through the analysis and peak in the reconstruction of the ingroup prototype.

First, we ought to ask to what extent it is probable that the norms in Ephesians, or at least a similar set of norms, were ever embraced within one or more contemporary communities of Christ-believers (chapter 14). Since the aim of the study is not only to study the identity and the norms in the text, but also to ask how this identity and these norms may have functioned in a group of Christ-believers, it is of interest to discuss why we have at least some reason to believe that the text reflects and constructs the conviction of more Christ-believers than just the author.

Second, we should have an idea about the structure, occasion, purpose and rhetorical strategy of the text (chapter 15). The author does not portray prototypical ideals without having an agenda. Rather, as is always the case, processes of attribution and formulations of prototypicality are aimed at achieving goals. We must understand this pragmatic aspect of the text in order to understand the portrait of the ingroup prototype in the text.

Third, we need to discuss the narrative rationale of the group according to Ephesians (chapter 16). How does the author tell the story about the origin and the value of the group's existence? Integrated into this narrative is the narrative about how many attributed ingroup traits are gifts from God through the Spirit. The narrative also suggests that God demands certain virtues and behaviors. Therefore, we need to understand how the author relates the character traits of the ingroup prototype to the narrative about God's initiative.

Fourth, we must examine how the text relates the identity in Christ to other social identities (chapter 17). The most important discussion is the discussion about the relation to non-believing gentiles and to "Israel" (sections 17.1and 17.2). Another problem is what the analogies between the Christ-narrative and the behavior norms in the household code have to say about the relation between household identities and the identity in Christ (section 17.3). Finally, we need to understand the relation between the subgroup of the leaders and ordinary Christ-believers (section 17.4). Some norms in the letter can only be fairly interpreted if we first determine the relation to other groups.

After these analyses we are ready to systematically scrutinize the various aspects of the ingroup prototype (chapter 18). First, we will look at the various attributed character traits and relate these traits to behavior norms and social dynamics. Then we will change the perspective and look at behavior norms and relate these norms to attributed traits.

14 The Text of Ephesians in Relation to a Hypothetical Social Context

In chapter 3.2, I argued that we are caught in a dilemma when we aspire to understand the behavior norms of the early Christ-movement. On the one hand, the relation between text and reality is difficult to reconstruct due to the character of the texts. On the other hand, behavior norms cannot be understood unless they are assumed to have a function in a social context. As opposed to Judith Lieu, who advocates an analysis of early Christian identity as it appears in the texts and the avoidance of speculation about extra-textual social realities, I concluded that minimal hypothetic speculation about the extra-textual social context of a text improved rather than distorted our understanding of identity and behavior norms in the text. Minna Shkul explicitly endorses Lieu's approach in her analysis of Ephesians and criticizes scholars such as Philip Esler and Margaret MacDonald, since they (partly) explain Ephesians by reference to reconstructions of external circumstances.[403] Shkul, just like Lieu, recognizes that the texts reasonably relate to extra-textual circumstances, but claims to analyze the author of Ephesians as an "entrepreneur of identity" who constructs identity more than he reflects circumstances outside the text. Although I agree with Shkul that texts are not purely reflective of external circumstances but also aim to form and construct,[404] I still think that some aspects of the texts, such as behavior norms, cannot be adequately understood without considering how the text both reflects and constructs its extra-textual context. In line with the principle of minimal hypothetical history, we may of course discuss how "rich" such a reconstruction of external factors needs to be

---

[403] Shkul 2009: 9-7, 13-15 criticizing Esler 2007; MacDonald 2004.

[404] See e.g. chapters 3.2 and 6.1.

in order to understand the text.[405] Nevertheless, the text does not make sense without imagining an extra-textual context. Shkul, too, assumes extra-textual circumstances (such as the notion that there actually were Christ-believing gentiles, living among non-believing gentiles) in order to explain the strategy of the text.

14.1 A Letter to Gentile Christ-Believers in Asia Minor

What external circumstances can we infer from the text by reading it? We have to acknowledge the lack of details in the letter that might reveal a particular occasion of the letter. Andrew Lincoln formulates the problem well:

> In the case of most of the letters in the Pauline corpus, scholars have usually set about reconstructing the setting of the recipients by taking the explicit statements about and references to the situation being addressed, associating these with implications that can be drawn from the particular concerns and problems of the letter, and correlating this material with other available relevant historical, geographical and social data about the place of the letter's destination. In a somewhat circular fashion this reconstruction is then employed to give sharper definition to an analysis of the letter's message and the purposes it was meant to achieve in the setting to which it was addressed. ... For such scholars, Ephesians, however, proves a source of frustration. It simply does not contain references to a specific setting or problems, and therefore other external data cannot be brought to bear in the same way as with other letters to build up a more detailed picture of the particular situation being addressed.[406]

Ephesians is a letter with no certain author, no certain date and no certain recipients. Yet it clearly gives instructions for communal life in a way that awakens our curiosity. Scholars still debate whether Paul has written the text or not, but this study will side with those who think that

---

[405] I will for instance, argue in chapter 17.2 that although MacDonald 2004 is very helpful, she nevertheless makes a too rich reconstruction of the circumstances behind Eph 2.

[406] Lincoln 1990: lxxiv.

it was written by an unknown deutero-Pauline author in Asia Minor with good knowledge of Paul's letters.[407] Since repetition of the arguments of the debate would improve neither the debate nor this study, I will not add anything to that debate but without further ado join those who favor a deutero-Pauline authorship.[408] However, it is quite a sensible working hypothesis to assume that the intended recipients did not perceive the letter as a fraud, since we have no records from the early Christ-movement suggesting that anyone suspected the letter to be forged. Rather, the evidence that we have points unanimously to a positive reception of the letter in the second century (see further discussion in chapter 14.2).[409]

Ephesians may or may not be written to Christ-believers in Ephesus, since "in Ephesus" (ἐν Ἐφέσῳ) in 1:1 is missing in a few important manuscripts.[410] We do not even know whether the author had one or

---

[407] E.g. Lincoln 1990:lix-lxxiii and Best 2004: 27–36 argue for a deutero-Pauline authorship based on the cumulative weight of important linguistic and theological differences. Hoehner 2002: 2–61 gives an exhaustive defense of Paul being the author of the letter. He disputes the idea that a majority of scholars are against a Pauline authorship of the letters by counting how many commentators side with which opinion. The result is that during the last two decades there has been a stalemate. While this head count approach is certainly interesting, it does not add proper arguments to the discussion; it mainly proves that the debate is difficult. Hoehner's proper argument for a Pauline authorship is mainly that the differences are not great enough. But he fails to give solid positive arguments for his own position (which is probably impossible) and instead surrenders to the idea that an author may change his language and theology. His strongest argument is that the text seems to have been alluded to by a number of authors around the turn of the century (Clement of Rome, Ignatius of Antioch). However, that may only prove that the fraud was very successful.

[408] I will, however, add one argument to the debate in chapter 17.3, where I will argue that Ephesians and Paul have profoundly different imaginations of the relation between household identities and the identity in Christ. This would have been inconceivable if we assume that Paul wrote Ephesians.

[409] See nn. 421 and 422.

[410] E.g. Hoehner 2002: 144–148; Schwindt 2002: 55–63 suggest Ephesus. E.g. van Kooten 2003: 197–203; Lincoln 1990: 1–4 suggest Laodicea.

several communities in mind.[411] It does, however, seem likely that it is written somewhere in Asia Minor, since it is very similar to the Pauline letter to the Colossians and since the earliest known usage of Ephesians is by Ignatius of Antioch.[412]

The recipients are addressed as gentile Christ-believers, which makes it reasonable to assume that at least the majority of them were gentile (2:11). However, since the author discusses division between Jews and gentiles (2:14–18) and since the author is probably Jewish (see discussion in chapter 17.2), it is also quite reasonable to assume that the gentile Christ-believer had some contact with Jewish Christ-believers. Perhaps they even participated in the same communities. Moreover, the recipients are assumed to be baptized (4:5; 5:26) and to live in households (5:21–6:20).[413] However, we do not need to assume that every single member of the *ekklēsia* (ἐκκλησία, "assembly, congregation, church," Eph 1:22; 3:10, 21; 5:22–33) lived in households to make sense of the text, just that it was the normal case.

In sum, the text seems to make sense if we assume that original recipients of the text were mainly gentile Christ-believers of whom a majority lived in households, probably somewhere in Asia Minor.

14.2 Were the Norms of Ephesians Embraced by Deutero-Pauline Communities?

If we wish to speculate about the social reality that Ephesians relates to and aims to transform, we should ask whether we have some reason to believe that the text actually interacts with the social reality of some community of Christ-believers. We need to assess the probability of whether the letter either reflects or successfully constructs values and beliefs that were embraced by first century Christ-believing communities in Asia Minor. This section of the analysis aims at affirming that we have

---

[411] E.g. Dahl 2000: 315–354; Percy 1946: 461–464 suggest that Ephesians is a circular letter meant for several congregations in Asia Minor.

[412] See n. 422.

[413] Cf. Best 2004: 2–3.

sufficient reason to believe that some first century communities in Asia Minor shared ideals that were at least similar to the ideals in Ephesians.

We can never know for sure how the text was received, since we have no immediate historical records of where and with what success the letter was spread. The questions that I outlined in chapter 3.2 will, however, help us assess whether it seems plausible that the letter was accepted as normative in some late first century *ekklēsiai* in Asia Minor.

Does the author seem to be ingroup to the recipients? Does the author seem to be prototypical in the eyes of the recipients? An author who wishes to impress a message on a group must be appreciated as a prototypical ingroup member in order to be credible, as we discussed in chapter 8.3. A prototypical group member embodies the identity of the group and is therefore seen as someone who is likely to express what is right and true for the group. Answering these questions will therefore help us approximate whether it is likely that the late first century recipients found the implied author—and therefore also his message—credible and authoritative.

I argued above that although the real author was probably not Paul, it is likely that the first recipients considered the letter to be written by Paul. While disputed in his own lifetime,[414] Paul seems to have enjoyed high status in the memory of Christ-believers in Asia Minor in the generations after his death.[415] Paul was often remembered as an exemplar of the identity in Christ.[416] As such he was valued as a highly

---

[414] Acts, Gal and 1–2 Cor give us evidence that Paul's authority was certainly not undisputed.

[415] On the scholarly debate whether Paul was held in high esteem or forgotten in the post-70 generations in Asia Minor, I will follow Tellbe 2009: 22–30; Trebilco 2006 who argue that Paul was held in high esteem by some groups, against the theory of Bauer 1934 that Paul was forgotten in Asia Minor after 70 C.E. (As discussed above, we do not know if the letter was addressed specifically to Ephesus, but Paul's standing in Ephesus exemplifies his status in Asia Minor in the post-70 C.E. generation.)

[416] The authors of Acts and 2 Peter (3:14–16), Clement of Rome (1 Clem 5.5-7, 47.1-3), and Ignatius (Ign. *Eph.* 12.2) admire Paul, and the almost certainly pseudonymous Pastoral epistles use Paul's post-mortal authority to give weight to their message. See e.g. de Boer 1980; Esler 2007; Shkul 2009: 142-172.

prototypical group member, a figure who embodied everything the group stood for. In the post-Pauline memory of Paul, he was probably considered more prototypical than Paul himself had ever been considered in his lifetime. In Ephesians, the author presents the implied Paul as "an apostle of Christ Jesus by the will of God" in the greeting of the letter (1:1); that is, as a prototypical ingroup member with authority. As I will develop in the analysis below, the author makes quite an effort to legitimize his message by appealing to the prototypical qualities of Paul in 3:2–13. In short, the hypothesis of a deutero-Pauline authorship of Ephesians increases rather than decreases the probability that the receiving communities would have accepted the text as authoritative, written by a prototypical ingroup member.

Does the message in the text seem to take its starting point in the recipients' current cognition? An author who wants to introduce some kind of change must start from what the recipients believe to be true, as we discussed in chapter 7.3. New input tends to be more acceptable and easier to remember if it fits our previous knowledge structures. If the message does not resonate to a certain extent with the current experience and knowledge of the recipient, the sender of the message risks being ignored as a deviant (cf. chapter 8.2). Estimating an answer to this question will therefore help us make a judgment about whether it is likely that the recipients perceived the content of the message to be relevant and true.

The author refers frequently to the narratives which were probably shared and endorsed by the group. He uses large portions of the first half of the letter to reiterate familiar and positive aspects of the ingroup identity (cf. chapter 15). He deliberately uses known Pauline thought,[417] which we have reason to believe was appreciated among many Christ-believers in Asia Minor in the post-70 generations.[418] The practical

[417] On the extensive usage of Paul in Ephesians, see e.g. Fischer 1973: 109–172; Lincoln 1990: xlvii-lviii. A few examples: The greeting in 1:2 (e.g. Rom 1:7; 1 Cor 1:3; 2 Cor 1:2; Gal 1:3), υἱοθεσία in 1:5 (Rom 8:23; Gal 4:5), ἀπολύτρωσις in 1:7, 14; 4:30 (Rom 3:24; 8:23; 1 Cor 1:30), salvation by grace and faith in 2:8 (e.g. Rom 3:21-28; Gal 2:15-3:18).

[418] Cf. n. 415.

exhortations in Ephesians have many parallels in other deutero-Pauline texts (Col, 1–2 Tim, Tit),[419] which gives us reason to believe that the author to a large extent spells out accepted practical norms. Doing so would probably make many recipients perceive the message as fairly prototypical and therefore more acceptable. We can thus assume with some confidence that the author appeals to the shared cognition of the group in large portions of the text, which would have increased the chance of the message being accepted in the group.

However, the author must reasonably have felt a need to influence the recipients, either to change or to strengthen certain behaviors and/or convictions. Otherwise he would probably not have bothered to write. On the issue of whether being in Christ is being in Israel—something that will be discussed in chapter 17.2—we have reason to suspect that the author does not represent the cognition of his intended recipients (2:11–22). Moreover, the author is probably also convinced that the recipients should strive to perfect their attitude and behavior (4:1–6:20). The author thus starts from shared cognition in order to modify it on certain points and to strengthen it on others.

Having asked these questions, one more complementary question has to be asked: *What do we know about the distribution of the text?* We have no historical sources that can give us hard evidence that the letter was received positively by anyone in the author's own generation, assuming that the text was written in the 80s of the first century.[420] Around the turn of the century we do, however, have some indications that it was used, possibly by the authors of 1 Clement, Barnabas and Hermas and most probably by Ignatius of Antioch and later also by Polycarp of

---

[419] The extensive similarities between Eph and Col are dealt with in Lincoln 1990 throughout his commentary. See van Kooten 2003: 239–289 for a recent synopsis of Ephesians and Colossians. For an overview of the paraenetical "Gemeindegut" which is used in Ephesians, see Fischer 1973: 147–172. For a cognitive perspective on the structural similarity between the household codes in Eph, Col, 1 Tim and Tit, see Roitto 2008.

[420] Lincoln 1990: lxxiii suggests that a composition around the 80s of the first century can explain both the deutero-Pauline perspective and the usage of Ephesians in Ign. *Eph.*

Smyrna.[421] The attestation of the letter around the turn of the century gives us some indication that the letter had spread with some success.

Ignatius' use of Ephesians is illuminative and provides us with two basic insights.[422] First, we can see that the letter probably did gain some influence and appreciation, since Ignatius is inspired by it. Second, we have to concede that Ignatius' theology is in no way a carbon copy of the theology found in Ephesians, although we can find many similarities. As I will argue in chapter 17.2, Ephesians thinks of the Christ-movement as a subcategory to "Israel." Ignatius, on the other hand, sees "Christianity" as something new which is opposed to "Judaism" (Ign. *Magn.* 8.1; 10.3; Ign. *Smyr.* 1.2).[423] In short, the text seems to have been used and recognized, but not necessarily by authors who agreed with the letter on every issue.

In sum, the limited evidence we have gives us reason to believe that Ephesians came to be accepted as an authoritative text written by the prototypical ingroup member Paul in some communities of Christ-believers in Asia Minor. The arguments for this are a) that Paul was remembered as a prototype of the identity in Christ in many contemporary texts, b) that the narratives and norms of the letter can be firmly placed within a Pauline tradition, that is, he articulates what in all likelihood would have been considered "true" and prototypical, and finally c) that we have some evidence that attests a positive use of Ephesians just one generation later. This does not, however, guarantee that communities that embraced the text shared the cognition expressed there in every detail. Nevertheless, it is reasonable to infer a) that the text *reflects cognition* which was shared in some communities of Christ-

---

421 Best 2004: 13–17; Hoehner 2002: 2–6. E.g. 1 Clem. 46.6 // Eph 4:4–6; 1 Clem. 59.3 // Eph 1:17–18; *Barn.* 6.11 // Eph 2:10; 4:22–24; Herm. *Mand.* 10.2 // Eph 4:30; *Barn.* 6.15; 16.8–10 // Eph. 2:21–22; Pol. *Phil.* 12.1 // Eph. 4:26; Pol. *Phil.* 1.3 // Eph 2:5, 8–9.

422 On the extensive parallels between Eph and the prescript of Ign. *Eph.*, see Schwindt 2002: 57–59. Other passages where Ignatius seems to use Eph are e.g. Ign. *Eph.* 1.1–2 // Eph 5:1–2; Ign. *Pol.* 6.2 // Eph 6:11–17.

423 See Zetterholm 2003: 203–216 for an analysis of Ignatius' role in the development of the early Christ-movement from a social scientific perspective.

believers in Asia Minor on many points and b) that the letter was accepted as authoritative by at least some of the recipients and consequently *influenced their cognition*. My working hypothesis—as uncertain as it is—will therefore be that the text both reflects and had an impact on the norms and the identity of Christ-believing communities in Asia Minor. I do not claim that there ever was a community whose shared cognition was a perfect carbon copy of the thoughts articulated in Ephesians. Such bold claims are beyond the evidence and contradict the normal patterns of intra-cultural variation.[424] It is, however, likely that there were communities that had similar shared perceptions. Assuming this as a working hypothesis makes it a worthwhile historical task to ask questions not only about the text itself, but also about how the practical behavior norms expressed in the text would have functioned as part of the identity in a group. Such a discussion about potential group dynamic effects of the imagination expressed by Ephesians is not history *wie es eigentlich gewesen*, but history as it typically could have been. Such history writing is hypothetical but it still has its value, since our limited sources, both Ephesians and other texts of the early Christ-movement, allow no safe way to approach the very relevant historical question of how the first Christ-believers interacted (see chapter 3.2).

---

[424] Cf. chapter 4.

15 The Structure, Rhetorical Strategy, and Purpose of the Letter

The main purpose of this study is not to scrutinize the structure and rhetorical strategy of Ephesians. Rather, the purpose is to reconstruct the the identity in Christ that the text expresses—the narrative rationale, the prototypical attributes, the prototypical behavior norms etc. Nevertheless, in order to analyze these matters it is necessary to have a grasp of the structure, rhetorical strategy, and purpose of the text, since the rhetorical strategy of the author influences the way in which the ingroup ideals are presented. The author does not just reflect cognitions, he presents them strategically in a way which he believes will achieve pragmatic goals such as changing the recipients' beliefs or inspiring them to take action.

The specific occasion of Ephesians is—and will probably always be—disputed, since the letter lacks explicit mention of specific circumstances. There has been no lack of innovative suggestions, but none of them have achieved much acceptance.[425] The scholarly efforts to mirror-read Ephesians have mainly produced the result that a search for a *specific* occasion (e.g. a historical crisis) of the letter is more or less futile.

A reasonable purpose of the letter does, however, appear possible to suggest. As I discussed in the introduction to this study, many scholars have recently suggested that the purpose of the letter is identity formation.[426] The purposes of the letter are a) reminding them of their privileged position in Christ (1:3-2:22), and b) exhorting them to "lead a life worthy of the calling to which you have been called" (4:1, 4:1-6:20). I

[425] See e.g. Lincoln 1990: lxxiv-lxxxiii for an overview of suggestions.

[426] See chapter 1.3, particularly note 39.

will accept identity formation as the purpose of the letter and use it as the point of departure for my analysis. One advantage of this understanding of the purpose of the letter is that it does not require a particular occasion, since preaching maturation and commitment to their identity in Christ was reasonably a frequently recurring topic in the Christ-movement.[427] Most importantly, however, we can shift our analytical focus from guessing a very particular occasion to discussing how the letter might have influenced everyday community life.

The structure and the rhetorical strategy of the letter needs more discussion, though. Most commentators agree that the body of the letter falls into two main parts, 1:3–3:21 with mainly theological content and 4:1–6:20 with mainly paraenetic content.[428] It is, however, difficult to determine how these two halves relate. Roy Jeal summarizes the problem well:[429] a) There is very little paraenetic concern in 1:3–3:21 while paraenesis is the main theme of 4:1–6:20, as opposed to what we find in the undisputed Pauline letters, where theology and exhortation tend to be more mixed in the text. b) The realized eschatology (2:1–10) with salvation expressed in the perfect (ἐστε σεσῳσμένοι, 2:6), especially the statement that the Christ-believers are "created in Christ Jesus for good works, which God prepared beforehand to (ἵνα) be our way of life" (2:10), makes it incomprehensible why they are in need of any exhortation at all.[430] The tension between indicative and imperative in the undisputed Pauline epistles seems to have turned from a tension to a gap. c) The paraenesis is not logically dependent on the theology, only thematically linked. What Jeal means by "logical" is, however, vague, although he probably means that the exhortations are not formally argued for on the basis of the theology found in the first half.

[427] Best 2004: 74 points out that if the purpose is identity formation, or "maturation" as he prefers to call it, then the letter needs no specific occasion, since maturation would always have been a relevant issue. See also Jeal 2000: 56–59; Lincoln 1990: lxxiv-lxxv who prefer to talk about the letter's "rhetorical situation" rather than its historical situation.

[428] For one example, see Lincoln 1990: xxxv-xlvi.

[429] Jeal 2000: 7–13.

[430] However, Jeal has not fully appreciated the ambiguous nature of the ἵνα-clauses in 2:10, see chapter 18.3.1 particularly n. 543.

The cognitive perspective of this analysis will, however, expose why the two halves were probably understood as a coherent whole, in spite of the lack of stringent argumentation.

In earlier attempts to understand the rhetorical structure of the letter, scholars have compared the letter to ancient epistolary and rhetorical conventions. Although Ephesians, unlike Paul's undisputed letters, does not seem to be occasioned by a particular situation, Ephesians is structured like a Pauline letter.[431]

1:1–2 Prescript
1:3–6:20 Body
- 1:3–22 Eulogy and prayer report
- 2:1-22 Errand: Reminder about their identity
- 3:2-13 Digression: Paul's ministry
- 3:1, 14–21 Prayer report[432]
- 4:1a Request formula, παρακαλῶ οὖν ἡμᾶς…[433]
- 4:1b-6:20 Errand: Exhortation to live according to their calling

6:21–24 Postscript

An epistolary analysis does give us some help to understand how the letter relates identity to behavior norms. The request formula in 4:1 was

[431] Cf. Lincoln 1990: xxxv-xlvii. There is no consensus as to the genre of letter. Aune 1987: 217–218 suggests that the letter should be categorized as a "general letter" since it lacks signs of a specific occasion. Jeal 2000: 24, n. 49, however, critically thinks that "[t]he category 'general letter' seems to be a catch bag for letters that do not lend themselves to clear epistolary analysis." Dahl 1987: 141 suggests "letter of reminder and congratulation." Lincoln 1990: xl-xli agrees with Dahl, but adds that the second half of the letter looks more like a "letter of advice", making the letter a mixture of two epistolary genres. Letters are, however, often difficult to classify, see Hoehner 2002: 69–77, Aune 1987: 199, 203.

[432] According to Bjerkelund 1967: 184-185, the double prayer reports make Eph close to 1 Thess in structure.

[433] This formula is quite common in Ancient letters, but not in oratory. "Als allgemeines Resultat haben wir feststellen können, dass Aufforderungen von der Art der *p*.-Sätze [παρακαλῶ-Aufforderungen] hauptsächlich in brieflichen und diplomatischen, nicht aber in rhetorischen und paränätischen Zusammenhängen vorkommen", Bjerkelund 1967: 109, 109–111. Cf. Thorsteinsson 2003: 47–54.

frequently used to signal the transition from "background information" that motivates the request to the request itself.[434] We can therefore assume that the first part of the letter is supposed to motivate the second part of the letter. However, an epistolary analysis does not help us with the most important question – *how* are the two halves connected? Moreover, the long elaboration in the first half of the letter seems to be an errand in its own right, not just a background for the second half.[435] We should therefore treat reminder in the first half (2:1-22) as av errand in its own right.[436]

Dissatisfied with the explanatory capacity of an epistolary analysis, Roy Jeal and (more briefly) Andrew Lincoln have analyzed the letter as speech, specifically as a written sermon, using rhetorical analysis.[437] Both Jeal and Lincoln argue that 1:3–3:21 should be understood as *narratio/exordium*, followed by *exhortatio* in 4:1–6:9.[438] Lincoln argues that the letter should therefore be seen as a mixture of epideictic speech in

---

[434] A letter of request typically had the following structure: "1) a background information of the request, sometimes implied by inferential conjunction, such as διό or οὖν, 2) a verb of request—typically ἀξιῶ, δέομαι, ἱκετεύω, ἐρωτῶ, παρακαλῶ, or the phrase καλῶς ἂν ποιήσαις—the choice of which often reveals the social relationship between the correspondents, and 3) the content of the request.", Thorsteinsson 2003: 47.

[435] Many have seen chapter 2 and the relation between Jews and gentiles as the main errand of the letter, see Best 2004: 68–69; Yee 2004: 3–17 for an overview. Best 2004: 75, while refuting the idea that chapter 2 is the main errand of Ephesians, concedes that one may call the relation to Israel a "subsidiary" reason to write the letter.

[436] διὸ μνημονεύετε ὅτι in 2:11 is the only imperative in the first half of the letter and therefore seems to stand out as the main point of his argument in the first half.

[437] Jeal 2000; Lincoln 1990: xli-xliv. Both Jeal and Lincoln discuss the structure of the letter from an epistolographic point of view, too. Lincoln cites the dissertation which is later published by Jeal and thus seems to be inspired by Jeal.

[438] Jeal 2000: 62–67. While Jeal thinks that the *exordium* and the *narratio* are intertwined in 1:3–3:21, Lincoln 1990: xliii labels 1:1–23 *exordium* and 2:1–3:21 *narratio*. Jeal's suggestion is more sensitive to the nature of 1:3–3:21.

the first half, followed by deliberative speech in the second half.[439] Jeal, however, concludes that Ephesians does not fit into the three classical genres of speech (judicial, deliberative and epideictic) and proposes that Ephesians belongs to a different genre, which he calls a "sermon," although no rhetorical handbook from antiquity mentions such a genre.[440]

Jeal's analytical category "sermon" gives us some help to see the nature of the letter. He defines a sermon as speech which is:

> … directed to an audience of θεωροί who, rather than acting as κριταί who make a decision on the basis of the argument presented to them, are encouraged to think and behave in accord with the speaker's or author's leading and persuasion. The speaker/author is concerned to stimulate the thoughts and the sentiments of the audience rather than argue critically, so as to persuade the audience to take the course of action seen to be appropriate.[441]

His main point, which is an important one, is that a characteristic of "sermons" is that the author does not formally *argue* for the norms in the *exhortatio*, based on the *narratio*.

If persuasion is not by argument, by what is it then? Jeal manages to capture the character of the persuasive strategy in Ephesians to a certain extent, when he argues that "identification" is the key.[442] This identification will "lead the recipients to accept and attempt to attain the goals that the author had in mind."[443] The first half of the letter functions to create identification and the second half is intended to use this identification in order to inspire action. However, Jeal has somewhat confusing ideas about what the recipients should identify with. Rather

---

439 Lincoln 1990: xli-xlii.

440 Jeal 2000: 49, 41–50.

441 Jeal 2000: 49.

442 Jeal 2000: 67–70. Cf. Lincoln 1990: xlii.

443 Jeal 2000: 70. Lincoln 1990: xlii argues similarly, although with less focus on identity, that "the epideictic first part of the letter leads well into the deliberative second part … The celebration, worship and prayer that precede the paraenesis are likely to move and inspire the readers to the action called for more effectively than if the letter had consisted primarily of a string of exhortations."

than arguing that they should identify with the author's vision of their identity in Christ he proposes that they should identify with the content of the statements in the text. Jeal largely fails to see that identification with statements—that is, the narratives in the text—is only a part of the identification with the social identity to which these narratives belong.[444]

While Jeal is on the right track, he is notoriously vague about what identification is and how identification is thought to imbue action. He just cannot describe the process which leads a person to go from identification to behavior with more precise terms than that the identification "draws them to assent" and makes them "inclined to become moved to."[445] Jeal has identified the problem of Ephesians well, but only provided part of the answer.

This is where the cognitive perspective of the present analysis can provide a way forward. By using cognitive psychology, we can discuss *how* the human mind takes the leap from identification to action. We can also discuss the relation between identity in Christ and embracement of ingroup narratives without confusing what the recipients are supposed to identify with. In this analysis we will be able to reconstruct the important elements of the ingroup prototype and ingroup narratives and analyze the causal beliefs held in these perceptions. We will then be able to examine how ordinary cognitive processes of, for instance, attribution make it possible for recipients to take the step from identity to behavior.

A cognitive perspective. Analyzing Ephesians with the aid of epistolographic and and rhetorical conventions has many merits, as we have just seen. However, these perspectives do not engage directly with how our minds handle social identities. Therefore I think it will be of better help if we try do describe the rhetorical strategy of Ephesians with the aid of the cognitive theories that we have explored in the previous chapters of this study. I will therefore proceed to using a social identity perspective on the rhetorical structure of the letter and argue that the

---

[444] To be fair, it should be said that Jeal occasionally uses expressions which reveal that he imagines that the recipient are supposed to identify with narratives "as Christians" (e.g. Jeal 2000: 73), i.e., as ingroup members.

[445] Jeal 2000: 69–70.

author uses the following strategies to persuade the recipients and thus inspire identity formation:

- The author makes the ingroup salient and valuable in the eyes of the recipients by referring to the ingroup narratives, which provide the rationale of the group. As we discussed in chapter 9.2, a social identity has to be salient in order to be the identity with which someone identifies. Reminding the recipients of the narratives about the value and meaning of the group is an efficient way to make that identity salient and to make the narrative resources that come with that identity easily accessible in the recipients' memory (cf. chapter 11).
- The author makes the identity distinct and meaningful by comparison with "the gentiles." As we saw in chapter 7, a group is experienced as more meaningful and valuable when it is contrasted with other groups. The contrast highlights why the group exists and why identification with the group can be a source of self-esteem and meaning.
- The author portrays the implied author Paul as prototypical in order to strengthen the credibility of the message. This rhetorical strategy works because the group experiences prototypical group members as embodying everything the group stands for, as we concluded in chaper 8.3. As such, the prototypical group member is experienced as someone who tells the truth.
- The author subtly suggests that although the recipients are in no way deviant, they are still not as prototypical as they should be, in order to create a need in the recipients to improve their prototypicality. Individuals generally prefer to see themselves in a positive light. When an individual identifies with a group, she wants to see herself as a good group member. If there is a tension between the ingroup prototype and her self-image, she experiences a cognitive dissonance, which she has to resolve (see chapter 6.1). Otherwise she will experience herself as deviant. As we saw in chapter 9.3, committed group members who feel that their prototypicality is questioned tend to go to great lengths in order to be accepted by the group again. Combining rhetorical strategies that increase the commitment and identification with strategies that subtly suggest that they are not fully prototypical

will therefore induce a longing to improve and become more prototypical.

- The author proposes causal connections between behaviors, prototypical attributes, and God's divine initiative, in order to induce beliefs that certain behaviors are caused by being prototypical and that others are caused by being deviant. We discussed in chapter 11.1 that causal beliefs were central to narrative thinking and in chapter 6 we explored attributions as a kind of causal beliefs. Ephesians is a text that masterfully interweaves the different aspects of the group's identity and norms with causal beliefs.

Prescript (1:1–2) – Evoke social identity as Christ-believers and establish the authority of the implied Paul: The implied author "Paul" mentions that he is "apostle by the will of God" and thus establishes his authority and prototypicality, and thereby his credibility. The recipients are greeted by two of their ingroup designations, "holy" and "believers in Christ Jesus," which serves to make the identity in Christ salient. The relevant self is the social identity in Christ.

Eulogy (1:3–14) – Make the ingroup identity salient and valuable and connect with the recipients: The author recounts important positive elements in the ingroup narrative and thus reminds the recipients of all the reasons to be a Christ-believer in congratulary tone.[446] As he recounts the narrative of all God's gifts to them, he establishes a relation of "asymmetrical

---

[446] Dahl 2000: 279–314 suggests that the eulogy in Ephesians might be seen as a "congratulary" or a "self-congratulary" benediction and shows numerous Jewish parallels to this genre. This description highlights the positive function of the text in making the ingroup identity salient and experienced as valuable. Caragounis 1977: 39–45 reviews various suggestions regarding the specific character of the eulogy and suggests that the eulogy has numerous parallels with Jewish traditions, but that no particular eulogy or hymn can be pointed out as its specific predecessor. See also Hoehner 2002: 153–161 for a thorough review of the various scholarly proposals on the subject of the genre of the eulogy.

reciprocity" between God and the Christ-believers.[447] God, "the patron," has bestowed gifts upon them which they cannot possibly match. As grateful "clients" they should, however, respond with gratitude and loyalty. The themes in the eulogy prepares for many, but not all, of the themes in the rest of the letter.[448] The mention of these positive and probably quite familiar themes makes the ingroup identity salient and hopefully increases the recipients' sense that their identity is important and valuable. It is worth noting that none of the sensitive errands of the letter (conduct and relation to Jews and gentiles) are touched upon in the eulogy. The author only advances themes which will be appreciated without objection. In this way he displays the implied author's prototypicality and increases group salience without risking to repulse the recipients. The author uses "we" throughout the eulogy, which signals that the author belongs to the same ingroup as the recipients. In v. 13 he does, however, use "you" when he talks about when they came to faith. This change has a double effect: a) He affirms that "also you" (καὶ ὑμεῖς) belong to the ingroup, while at the same time b) subtly reminding them that the author belonged to the ingroup before they did (and therefore knows better).[449]

---

447 By using the term "asymmetrical reciprocity" rather than "general reciprocity" to label exchange outside the family between agents with unequal power, I follow Crook 2005 in his modification of the term "generelle Reziprozität" suggested by Stegemann and Stegemann 1995: 43. Crook's term gives more correct associations.

448 Arnold 1989: 70–71.

449 Jeal 2000: 88–89 presses the including effect of καὶ ὑμεῖς too one-sidedly in an affirming direction. ἀκούσαντες in 1:13, an ingressive aorist, indicates that the recipients were not included until they "became faithful."

Recipients are placed firmly ingroup, but away from the prototypical centre of the ingroup category. The implied Paul is put at the prototypical centre.

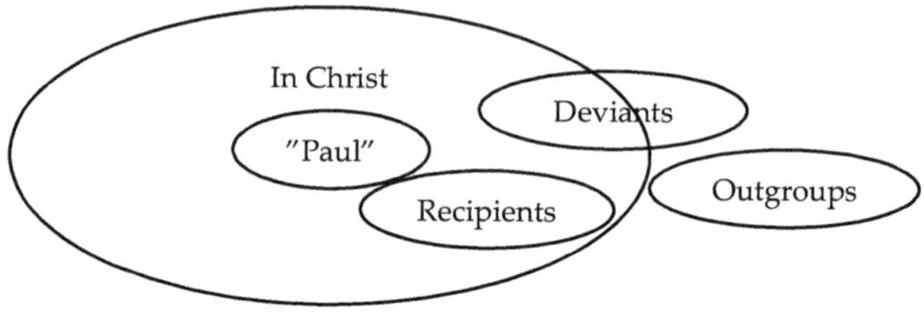

Prayer and thanksgiving (1:15–23) – Subtly suggest that the recipients need more prototypical knowledge: "I" (the prototypical author) pray for "you" (the less prototypical recipients) that the Spirit may give "you" knowledge. There is an important difference between praying and letting people know that you are praying. In the latter case you want them to *know* that you are trying to help them with something which is flawed in their lives. The form of prayer gives a sense that the author is benevolent and wishes to help them. The content of the prayer suggests that they are currently lacking in knowledge—knowledge which will be presented to them directly after the prayer. Since the implied Paul prays for them, this hints at him being superior to them, that he knows what knowledge they are missing and that he therefore is capable of telling them the truth. The recipients are ingroup but not fully prototypical and therefore they need to listen to the prototypical implied Paul in order to improve. The thanksgiving is also a further reminder of the great things God has done and partly fills the same identity-strengthening function as the eulogy. The double strategy is to a) include them, bond with them and make them appreciate their identity, but also b) to induce a feeling that they deviate from the prototype and need improvement.[450] As was discussed in chapter 8.2 and 9.3, if a group member is committed, yet feels that his or her status within the group is not what it should be, he or she will often go to great lengths in order to improve his or her ingroup status. If the author successfully makes the recipients

[450] Cf. Jeal 2000: 97–99.

committed yet insecure about their knowledge, they will be receptive to the knowledge which he presents in the next section.

Errand: reminder (2:1–22) – Urge the recipients to accept the author's specific interpretation of their identity: Now that the author has made the ingroup identity salient and suggested that they are lacking in prototypical knowledge, the recipients are hopefully in a mindset where they are willing to listen to the implied Paul's claimed knowledge about how they relate to their past as gentiles, to Israel and to Christ.

- *Background information (2:1–10) – Present the ingroup's history in a way that supports the author's claim:* The author recounts how they used to have a detestable life as non-believing gentiles, the major outgroup of the letter, and then were saved from their misery by Christ. Their past as non-believing gentiles contrasts with their new valuable identity in Christ. The description of their past highlights the value and meaning of their identity and prepares them for the coming reminder. Moreover, this passage, just like previous passages, holds references to what God has done for them, which hopefully increases the recipients' commitment.
- *Reminder (2:11–22) – Present the interpretation of their identity:* By now, the author has prepared them by a) making their ingroup identity salient, by b) reminding them of their deficiency and by c) recounting the ingroup narrative in a way which hopefully will make them feel that his interpretation is the correct one. Now he can tell them that they have been included in "Israel" through Christ and that this is infinitely better than their past. Their new existence is characterized by there being no opposition between "you," gentile Christ-believers, and Jewish Christ-believers. Their identity is, however, in sharp contrast to their past as non-believing gentiles. Also this passage holds references to what God has done for them, which hopefully increases the recipients' commitment. The passage therefore both functions to a) make a claim which is a concern in itself and b) increase commitment as a preparation for the hortatory half of the letter.

Digression (3:2–13) – Strengthen the credibility of the message by presenting the prototypical merits of the implied Paul: For seemingly no reason the implied Paul interrupts his prayer which he begins in 3:1.[451] In the digression he reminds them of a) his suffering (3:1, 13[452]) and b) his knowledge from God (3:2–4, 7–9), that is, his prototypical merits.[453] The recipients should understand that the message comes from someone who embodies truth and commitment.[454] Paul's suffering and imprisonment prove his commitment to group ideals, since he is willing to realize the ideals in practical action even when the cost is high. (As we discussed in chapter 9.3, commitment motivates costly behavior.) Moreover, Paul's divine revelation guarantees his capacity to disclose the truth. The content of the knowledge is that God has made the gentiles inheritors (v. 6), which supports the claim in 2:11–22. The passage also functions to assert the implied Paul's prototypicality as a preparation for the forthcoming exhortations in the rest of the letter. The digression is formally an interruption of the prayer which he starts in 3:1 and then continues in 3:14. Two of the themes of the prayer are growth in knowledge and power from God, both of which are attributed to Paul in the digression (3:4, 7). Paul is presented as someone who has achieved the qualities which he will soon pray that they achieve. The prayer prepares for the requests beginning in 4:1 (see below). In this way, the digression gives weight to the prayer and consequently indirectly to the request. Further, Paul emphasizes that he suffers *for their sake* (3:1, 13) and evangelizes *to them* (3:2, 8), emphasizing that their relation is an asymmetrical relation, similar to the relation between a benevolent

---

[451] *Digressio* was a conventional device in ancient rhetoric, often aiming to secure the favor of the audience, both towards the speaker and towards the subject, see Jeal 2000: 163–164.

[452] 3:1 is not formally part of the digression, but the theme of Paul's suffering 3:1 and 3:13 forms an *inclusio* which begins and ends the digression.

[453] Cf. Esler 2007; Shkul 2009: 142-172.

[454] Byrskog 2005: 117–118 points out that Paul exhorts the recipients as "prisoner in the Lord" in 4:1. The references to Paul's suffering therefore seem intended to improve his prototypicality and strengthen the force of the exhortations in the second half of the letter.

patron and a client.[455] In other words, Paul has in his prototypical position given them gifts they cannot return in any other way than by gratitude and loyalty to him—and to his message. In sum, the passage functions a) to show Paul's prototypicality, b) to create a bond of gratitude between the implied author and the audience, c) to give further weight to the previous message and d) to prepare for the forthcoming prayer and request. Also this passage holds references to what God has done for them, which hopefully increases the recipients' commitment.

Preparatory prayer and praise (3:1, 14–21) – Prepare for the hortatory half of the letter by subtly suggesting that the recipients need more prototypical inner qualities: "I" (the prototypical author) pray for "you" (the less prototypical recipients) that the Spirit will provide more of the prototypical qualities of power, knowledge and love so that "you" may grow and become better Christ-believers. The prayer, just like the prayer in 1:15–23, subtly suggests that the recipients are lacking in prototypicality, but also that they can attain more of these qualities. The prayer, together with the previous passages, has ideally (from the author's point of view) put them in a state of mind where they value their identity in Christ but realize their shortcomings and therefore long to become more prototypical. As a result, they are hopefully ready to listen to any suggestion about how they can become more prototypical in practice. As was discussed in chapter 6, people tend to assume that action is the result of attributed qualities and therefore this prayer about prototypical attributed qualities prepares for the explication in the second half of the letter of how they should "lead a life worthy of the calling" (4:1). As we will see, the prototypical behavior norms are presented as the manifestation of the attributed character traits, which are expressed in this prayer and elsewhere in the first half of the letter.

Main errand: request (4:1–6:9) – Urge the recipients to accept the practical solution as to how they may achieve the prototypicality, which they by now hopefully feel that they need: As will be detailed in the analysis below, this

---

[455] Cf. n. 447. Cf. also Jeal 2000: 111–112.

second half of the letter continuously resumes themes from the first half of the letter and uses the momentum that has been built up in the first half to give the exhortations authority and meaning. Samuel Byrskog shows that 4:1–16 functions as a bridge between the first and the second half of the letter, incorporating both paraenetical and non-paraenetical material.[456] Significantly, all gifts are presented as "given" by God (4:7, 11), envisioning a direct causal link between God's agency and prototypical behavior (cf. chapter 16). Most of the practical norms in the second half are presented as the visible expressions of prototypical attributed qualities, such as holiness, the Spirit, power, knowledge and love. Some of the practical norms in the text are these:[457]

- The recipients should strive for unity and appreciate the leaders (4:1–16)
- The recipients should live a life which is opposed to the outgroup, the gentiles, and instead act according to their identity in Christ (4:17–31)
- The recipients should speak and act in a way which is characterized by love and holiness (5:1–6)
- The recipients should not associate with deviants/outsiders but instead speak and act as people who live in the light, both in worship and in the household (5:7–6:9)

Final exhortation (6:10–20) – Paint a vivid picture which highlights the importance of commitment: In the armor-metaphor, several elements in the ingroup prototype are depicted as the causes behind continued commitment in difficult times. Through power from God they attain all sorts of prototypical virtues, giving them power to "stand against the wiles of the Devil" (6:11) rather than lose their commitment. Behavior and attributes are largely seen as the fruit of spiritual influence throughout the letter and therefore a fitting conclusion of the letter is the notion of a war against the influence of evil spirits through the empowerment of God.

---

[456] Byrskog 2005.

[457] The sections in the list are based on how the text signals a new section with οὖν + περιπατέω. Cf. the discussion in n. 475.

Postscript (6:21–24). The final words of the letter mainly reinforce the impression of a benevolent author who is dedicated to encourage the recipients in their identity in Christ.

This interpretation of the rhetorical strategy of the letter from a cognitive perspective will guide the exploration of identity and behavior norms in the following chapters of this study.

16 The Narrative Rationale of the Identity in Christ

Every group nourishes a narrative about who they are—why their group exists and has value (cf. chapter 11). These narratives hold causal beliefs that explain why things are the way they are (see chapter 11.1). The purpose of this chapter is to explore how the author of Ephesians weaves a narrative web of coherence by narrating a chain of causally related events, beginning with God's agency and ending in the identity of the group. In Ephesians, God is the original cause and fundamental rationale of their identity in Christ. The narrative rationale of the group is that God has chosen them and paved way for their identity through the Christ-event. Just like many spiritual entities across cultures (cf. chapter 6.4), God is an interested agent with intentions. A central aspect of our analysis of the narrative rationale expressed in Ephesians is therefore to ask what dispositions the author attributes to God as an explanation for his actions and how the author tells the narrative about the relation between God and the ingroup.

According to Ephesians, God has an eternal plan, which was hidden at first but now has been revealed (3:9). The fulfillment of this plan is the goal which the author attributes to God as the cause of God's actions in relation to the ingroup and the Christ-event. The "purpose" (πρόθεσις) is to reveal his wisdom to the spiritual world, and this purpose was fulfilled through the Christ-event and the *ekklēsia* (3:10–11).

The Christ-event is crucial in the fulfillment of his plan. The expressed content of the Christ-event is the cross (2:16), perhaps the descent to the underworld or to death (4:9),[458] the resurrection (1:20) and

---

[458] κατώτερα τῆς γῆς in 4:9 could be interpreted either as a) Hades, b) earth (as opposed to Heaven) or c) death/the grave, see Hoehner 2002: 533–536.

the ascension to the heavenly throne (1:20–21). All good things are achieved "through" or "in" Christ (ἐν Χριστῷ, e.g., 1:6, 10–11; 2:10, 18; 3:11–12). The author interprets the death of Christ as a sacrifice to God (1:7, 2:13, 5:2, 25). The function of the resurrection is less clear, but perhaps the author imagines some kind of victory where he "took captives" (4:8–10). Perhaps victory over death or spiritual powers is imagined (1:20–21; 2:4–6, cf. 1 Cor 15:26).[459] However, it is obvious that the author believes that the Christ-event is crucial to God's plan and has achieved great things for the ingroup. His plan from the beginning is to "sum up (ἀνακεφαλαιόω) everything in Christ" (1:9–10). The much discussed verb "sum up" holds connotations of a) bringing into a whole, b) renewal and c) summing up under a head, none of which are easily excluded.[460] Ernest Best rightly thinks that the summing up in 1:10 should be read together with the revealing of wisdom in 3:10, that is, God reveals his wisdom in order to "sum up" everything.[461] Best points out the ambiguity as to whether God wants to reconcile with or just triumph over the spiritual world as he reveals his wisdom to it.[462]

However, the Christ-event cannot reveal God's wisdom on it's own. Rather, the Christ-event needs to be complemented with the *ekklēsia*. As a part of God's plan, God has chosen the ingroup before the beginning of the world (1:4–5). God reveals his wisdom through Christ *and* the *ekklēsia* (3:10–11). That is, God seems to need the *ekklēsia* to fulfill his plan. In this narrative, the ingroup is not an end in its own right in God's grand plan, but an instrument to manifest his wisdom.

---

[459] Schwindt 2002: 399–430, having proposed a variety of intriguing possibilities, concludes that "Eph 4,8–10 beinhaltet ein complexes Traditionsgefüge, das eine Vielzahl von Assoziationen zulässt, wobei nicht leicht zu erkennen ist, welche davon der Deuteropauline bewusst aufgegriffen hat" (p. 429).

[460] Barth 1974: 90–92; Bieringer 2005; Hoehner 2002: 219–221 for summaries of the scholarly discussion.

[461] Best 2004: 322–327.

[462] Best correctly points out that both reconciliatory and triumphalistic eschatology existed in first century Judaism. Caragounis 1977: 143–146 suggests that the *anakefalaiōsis* is exaltation for the *ekklēsia* but submission for the opposing cosmic powers.

Attribution: God has a plan + God thinks that the ingroup is instrumental to fulfill this plan → God chooses the ingroup

Attribution: God has a plan + God thinks that the Christ-event is instrumental to fulfill this plan → God launches the Christ-event

The driving force of God's action is his "will" (θέλημα, 1:5, 9, 11); his "good pleasure" (εὐδοκία, 1:5, 9); his "decision" (βουλή, 1:11).

Causality: God's will → God has a plan to reveal his wisdom to the spiritual world and to sum up everything in Christ.

But why would God want to reveal his wisdom and sum up everything in Christ? The key passages 1:10, 20 and 3:10–11, where we are told of Christ's triumph over cosmic forces, are possible to associate to various myths and philosophies of Greek and Jewish origin. Since the author is most probably a Hellenized Jew, this should come as no surprise.[463] The Jewish apocalyptic myth of the fallen angels who will ultimately be judged (e.g., 1 Enoch 6–13) could do well as a background. So could the Jewish apocalyptic vision of the world recognizing God's sovereignty and submitting to God and Zion (e.g., Zech 14). The vocabulary in Ephesians (and Colossians) of Christ as the head over the body of the *ekklēsia* (4:7–16, cf. 2:20–22) and the cosmos (1:10, 1:20–23) can also easily be associated with Greek cosmologies such as the Stoic and Middle

[463] Schwindt 2002: 7–45, in his summary of the history of research about the cultural background to Ephesians, shows how scholarly interest has moved from theories about Gnostic and Hellenistic influence on Ephesians to theories about eschatological Jewish and Hellenized Jewish influence. After a thorough examination of possible cultural backgrounds, Schwindt concludes that Ephesians "verbindet das geschichtlich-apokalyptische mit einem zeitunabhängigen-gnoseologischen Heilsdenken, wie sie von dem alexandrinischen Judentum kategorial paradigmatisch entworfen worden ist" (p. 508). Schwindt suggests that Ephesians is predominantly influenced by Jewish strands of thought and that any influence from Greek philosophy comes mainly via Hellenized Jewish thought.

Platonist concept of the cosmos as a coherent body governed by *logos*.[464] The "summing up" of everything in Christ could also be associated with the Stoic doctrine of *ekpyrōsis*, that the emanated world will collapse back into the *logos* that has caused it.[465] George van Kooten has, however, correctly pointed out that the Greek philosophical thought of a *logos* which fully controls and harmonizes the world has been adapted to an eschatological framework in Ephesians, so that the cosmos is not yet harmonious and not all opposing powers are fully subdued (e.g., 6:10–18).[466] In the present, Christ is only head of the *ekklēsia* and the rest of the world still opposes his rightful lordship over the cosmos.

The myths and cosmologies which have been proposed as the historical background for Ephesians share the imagination of God as an agent who wishes to set right and harmonize a world out of order, either by triumph, by reconciliation or by unification. In a very general way

---

464 On the concept of cosmos as *sōma* in Greek philosophy compared to Colossians and Ephesians, see van Kooten 2003, especially pp. 17–58. The judgment of Fischer 1973: 57 that we can find only general similarities but "keine hinreichende Erklärung" in a comparison with the Stoics is sound. Fischer 1973: 76 suggests "das hellenistische Judentum mit seine Sophia- und Logosspekulationen" as the most probable background. Cf. also n. 463. Schnackenburg 1982: 59 sees Stoic pantheism, orphic mystic belief in a God to whom everything will return and possibly the Gnostic myth about the world as the result of a fallen *Sofia* as possible backgrounds for 1:10. Lincoln 1990: 31 notes regarding 1:10 that "[i]n the Greek world οἰκονομία was regularly used for God's ordering and administration of the universe."

465 On *ekpyrōsis*, see Boas 1973.

466 Van Kooten 2003 analyzes the background in Graeco-Roman philosophy to the cosmic Christology in Colossians, Ephesians and the undisputed Pauline writings. In his analysis of Ephesians (pp. 147–203), he recognizes that the Stoic and Middle Platonist influence has been transformed into a Jewish apocalyptic framework, where τὰ πάντα is not already fully held together by the cosmic Christ (cf. Col 1:17). As opposed to the Gods/*logos* who are imagined by Greek philosophers to be an omnipresent force in the cosmos, the author of Ephesians imagines that Christ's dominion has only begun to spread through the cosmos through the *ekklēsia*. According to van Kooten, Ephesians is positioned between the authentic Paul's acute eschatology and the cosmology in Colossians, where Christ's dominion over the cosmos is already a reality.

these thought patterns resemble how the author imagines that God wants to reveal himself and thus subdue the fallen world—including the spiritual world—to Christ. But why? We still have not answered how the author imagines God's motivation in anthropomorphic terms.

The text gives hints about what motivates God in the mind of the author. One important reason seems to be "glory" (δόξα), that is, recognition and honor.[467] The idea that God is motivated to act "for his name's sake" (Ps 23:3) was familiar in Jewish thought.[468] One of the central themes in the eulogy is that God aims at receiving praise and glory for his actions (1:6, 12, 14). Jerome Neyrey has shown that in Greco-Roman antiquity the only appropriate response to the unconditional gifts of the gods—the divine patrons—was commitment, that is, faithfulness, loyalty, gratitude, honor, etc.[469] In Ephesians, God, the patron, wants due honor from his clients, that is, from all humans and spirits. God has carried through his plan "in order to show" (ἵνα ἐνδείξηται) his goodness (2:7). His glory is "in/through" (ἐν) Christ and the *ekklēsia* (3:21). Either by reconciliation or by triumph, God will get due honor and Christ and the *ekklēsia* are God's instruments for achieving this honor.

Causality: God wants glory → God has a plan to achieve glory

Another reason for God to elect them is mercy and love, that is, his benevolent attitude towards them. God "is rich in mercy" and it is "because of (διά) his great love" that he has saved them, that is, launched the Christ-event and chosen them (2:4, cf. 5:1–2). Interestingly, the "us" who God loves does not seem to be primarily each individual, but the *ekklēsia* as a whole (5:25). This suggests that when the author talks about "us" as chosen "before the foundation of the world" (1:6), it

---

[467] Caragounis 1977: 137–139 rightly suggests that God's aim for glory is the ultimate end of his actions in Ephesians. Dahl 2000: 120 observes the striking similarity between Qumran and Ephesians in that both seem to reflect groups who see themselves as instruments for God's glory.

[468] Glatt-Gilad 2002.

[469] Neyrey 2005: 485–489.

does not mean that God has chosen each individual, but the ingroup as a whole. They are chosen "in Christ."

The attribution of mercy and love to God makes the ingroup an end in itself. A God who both sees his group as an instrument of glory and actually cares about the group is obviously quite easy to imagine for the author, just as is frequently the case in Jewish traditions (e.g., Ps 23).

> *Attribution:* God loves the ingroup → God launches the Christ-event + God chooses the ingroup

The author has a very rich vocabulary for the privileged status before God which they have received in and through Christ::

- chosen (1:4)
- adoption as children (1:5)
- in Christ (e.g., 1:5, 7)
- grace (1:6–7; 2:5, 7–8; 4:7; 6:24)
- redemption (1:7, 14)
- forgiveness (1:7)
- inheritance (1:11, 14, 18; 3:6; 5:5)
- salvation, saved (1:13; 2:5, 8; 6:17)
- sealed with the Spirit (1:13; 4:30)
- God's possession (1:14)
- hope (1:18; 2:12; 4:4)
- called (1:18; 4:1, 4)
- body of Christ (1:23; 2:16; 3:6; 4:4, 12–16; 5:23, 30)
- loved (2:4; 5:2, 25)
- made alive (2:5)
- raised with Christ and seated in heaven in Christ (2:6)
- God's workmanship, created in Christ (2:10)
- citizens (2:12, 19)
- partakers in the covenant of promise (2:12; 3:6)
- close (to God) (2:13, 17)
- access to God (2:18; 3:12)
- God's household members (2:19)
- built upon … Christ (2:20–22)
- dwelling-place for God (2:22)
- Christ in their hearts (3:17)
- filled with the fullness of God (3:19)

- new man, created to be like God (4:24)
- children of light (5:8–9)
- having a Lord in Heaven (6:9)

This multitude of expressions gives associations to all kinds of life spheres, for instance the household, the body, the patron-client system, God's covenant with Israel, etc. They all express the same basic point: The ingroup has a privileged status in relation to God. Some of the metaphors suggest not only privileged status, but also a belief in some kind of mystical or spiritual unity with God, for instance the frequent expression "in Christ" and the recurring body metaphor. They are in Christ and God, and Christ lives in them. The sum of the narrative is that they are chosen by God and that through the Christ-event they can gain privileged status.

Causality: The Christ-event + Chosen by God → Privileged status in relation to God

The narratives explored in this section are the fundaments of the rationale for the existence of the group. They tell the story of why belonging to the group is valuable (cf. chapter 11). As we will explore in chapter 18, these narratives also motivate ingroup norms in various ways and are therefore important for our understanding of the behavior norms in Ephesians. The causal flow in the narratives about the rationale of the group can be summarized like this:

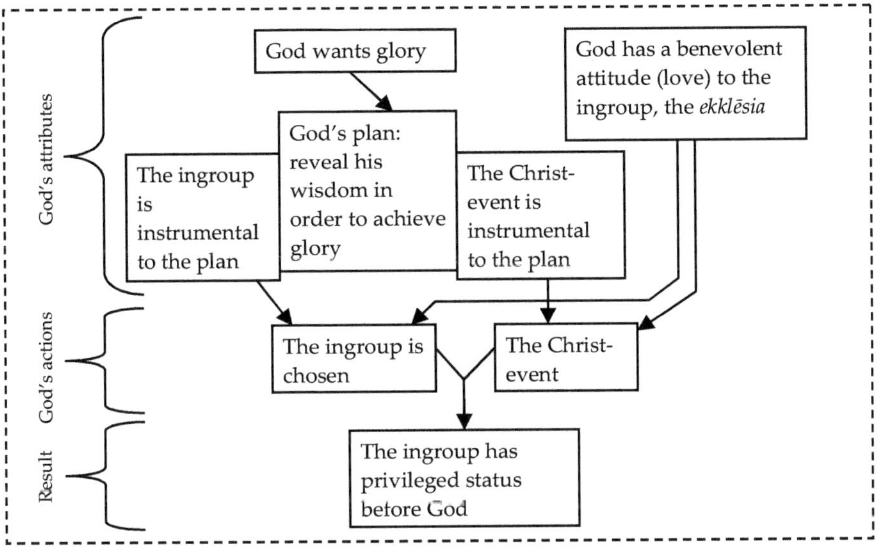

In the forthcoming chapters, particularly chapter 18, we will see that this narrative is important for the ingroup prototype, both a) since God, their patron, has set the standards for who they should be, and b) since God has provided them with (i.e. caused) the Spirit and other ingroup traits, such as power and love.[470]

[470] Cf. chapter 18.3. Both of the thought patterns a) and b) have been discussed in chapter 6.4, where a) is treated in category a1 and b) in category b1.

17 Narratives About Social Categories in Ephesians

How does ethnicity—being Jewish and gentile—relate to the identity in Christ? How do household identities relate to the identity in Christ? How does the category of the leaders relate to the identity in Christ? These questions are an important part of our understanding of identity and behavior norms in Ephesians, since the ingroup prototype is always formulated in relation to other possible social identities.

The social and narrative world of Ephesians is populated with people belonging to several categories and subcategories. As we discussed in chapters 7.1–7.2, groups tend to form their ingroup prototype in relation to relevant outgroups in a way that maximizes the distinctiveness and value of the ingroup. A good rhetorician can use this and portray certain ideals as the opposite of the attitudes and behaviors of the outgroups. Moreover, as we discussed in chapter 9.1, groups can relate to each other either as distinct groups, as subgroups to a common ingroup or in a relation where one group is a subgroup to the other. It is therefore necessary to understand how the author relates the group cognitively to various groups, in order to understand how the ingroup prototype is presented in Ephesians.

17.1 The Non-Believing Gentiles

There are strong dichotomies in Ephesians between non-believing gentiles and "Israel" (2:11–12), and between the non-believing gentiles and the *ekklēsia* (4:17–24). Being a Christ-believer is portrayed as the antithesis of the non-believing gentiles, the major contrasting outgroup of the *ekklēsia*. Yet the recipients of Ephesians are portrayed as former non-believing gentiles.

17.1.1 The Past of the Gentiles (and Israel)

The recipients' past as non-believing gentiles. In Ephesians, the past, "then" (ποτέ, 2:2f, 11, 13; 5:8), is depicted as a situation where the recipients belonged to the outgroup, the gentiles. In their past, they were in the worst possible situation, dominated by evil spiritual forces (2:2). They, as gentiles, "were—at that time without Christ[471]—aliens from the commonwealth of Israel, and strangers from the covenants of promise, having no hope, and without God in the world" (2:11–12, NRSV modified). They were "strangers and aliens" (2:19).

The many descriptions of the different ways in which the gentiles were outsiders suggest an exclusive self-understanding of Israel as God's chosen people. No doubt there were several views among Second Temple Jews regarding the position of the gentiles,[472] but the author chooses to describe the past in a very dichotomous way as a state when there was a "dividing wall" and "enmity" between Jews and gentiles (2:14, 16). The gentiles were the contrasting outgroup of Israel.

This kind of description of the recipients' past has several rhetorical effects. First, it maximizes the contrast between their valuable present and their past lives and motivates them not to return to their previous lives. We could say that their past selves becomes an constrasting outgroup, which highlights the value of their identity in Christ (cf. chapter 7). Swaying commitment to the group would always have been a potential danger from the perspective of the group (see chapter 9.3). Moreover, the description of their past is also indirectly a description of the current non-believing gentiles. Therefore, the description of the past maximizes the value and distinctiveness of the group, not only in relation to the recipients' past, but also in relation to the present outgroup of non-believing gentiles.

Israel's past as sinful covenant partners. In the past, the Jews had the covenant and the citizenship in Israel. But even so, they had—at least to some extent—forfeited their advantage in the past, according to the author. He contrasts "you" with "we" in 2:1–3, saying this:

---

471 I agree with Yee 2004: 97–99 that ἦτε ... ἀπηλλοτριωμένοι forms a periphrasis around τῷ καιρῷ ἐκείνῳ χωρὶς Χριστοῦ.

472 E.g. Lieu, North and Rajak 1992; Smith 1987.

> You [i.e., the gentiles] were dead through the trespasses and sins, in which you once lived, following the course of this world … also we all (καὶ ἡμεῖς πάντες) [i.e., the Jews too] lived in the passions of our flesh, following the desires of flesh and senses, and we were by nature children of wrath, like everyone else (ὡς καὶ οἱ λοιποί)
> (2:1–3, NRSV modified)

By stressing "also we all … like everyone else" the author concedes that the Jews had no more control over their destructive desires than the gentiles had. According to conventional Hellenistic wisdom, destructive desires by necessity caused vicious behavior (see chapters 6.3 and 18.3.7). This viciousness, in turn, caused God's wrath. The Jews were "near" (ἐγγύς) and the gentiles were "afar" (μακράν), but both had to get their "peace" through Christ (2:17, cf. 2:12). These thoughts are in line with Paul's statement in Romans, where he writes that the Jews have a principal advantage but that they have lost that advantage through their way of life (Rom 1:18–3:19). It is, however, important to note that while the author attacks the sinfulness of the gentiles fiercely, he mentions the sinfulness of the Jews just in passing, as if he has no interest in a major attack on the Jews.

In short, it is better to be a Jew than a gentile, but it is even better to be a Christ-believer. This value hierarchy is part of the problem, which has brought about extensive scholarly debate about the exact relation between Israel and the *ekklēsia* in Ephesians. We will return to this problem in chapter 17.2, but first we should examine the group's relation to non-believing gentiles in the narrative present.

17.1.2 The Non-Believing Gentiles as the Major Outgroup of the *Ekklēsia*

The non-believing gentiles are depicted as the outgroup, which the Christ-believers distance themselves from, also in their present situation (4:17–24). "Therefore I say and testify in the Lord, no more do/should you walk like the gentiles walk … put away your former way of life, your old self" (4:17, 22, my translation). The infinitive clause can be interpreted both as an exhortation and as a statement about who they are,[473] which is typical of this kind of identity rhetoric. As we discussed in chapter 6.1, the tension between indicative and imperative is typical of any ingroup prototype. The Christ-believers are distinct, yet they must ensure that they remain distinct.

The gentile stereotype is the contrasting background against which the author portrays the ideal life in Christ also in the paraenetic passages after 4:17–24, where no outgroup is explicitly mentioned, as Daniel Darko aptly demonstrates.[474] The most telling passage is 5:1–6,[475] where the attributed trait "holy" is contrasted with stereotypical gentile behavior. There it is stated that "it is becoming for holy ones" (πρέπει ἁγίοις) to avoid "fornication (πορνεία) and every impurity (ἀκαθαρσία) or greed (πλεονεξία)" (5:3). Further, "it is not proper" (οὐκ ἀνῆκεν) with "shameful behavior" (αἰσχρότης), "foolish talk" (μωρολογία) and "sarcasm" (εὐτραπελία[476]) (5:4). Then fornication, impurity and greed are repeated and greed is equated with idolatry (5:5). The mention of fornication (5:3, 5), impurity (5:3, 5) and idolatry

[473] *Accusative + infinitive clauses*. Verbs in the infinitive can introduce both final, subjective, objective, and occasionally also consecutive dependent clauses, see Blass and Debrunner 1961: §390–393; Blomqvist and Jastrup 1996: §268–270. But most importantly, infinitive clauses, just like ἵνα-clauses, may be interpreted as having either imperative or indicative function. For example, the phrase "He chose us … in order that you would/might/should be holy (εἶναι ἡμᾶς ἁγίους) …" (1:4) may be interpreted as fact, potentiality and duty.

[474] Darko 2008: 31–71.

[475] Lincoln 1990: 294 thinks that the content of 5:1–2 fits better with the preceding section (4:25–32) than with the following verses (5:3–7). However, as Hoehner 2002: 643 rightly points out, the second half of the letter has a recurring pattern, where the author uses οὖν + περιπατέω to signal the progression to a new section (4:1, 17; 5:1–2, 7–8, 15). Although it might appear that love (the theme of 5:1–2) fits better with compassion and forgiveness (the theme of 4:32) than with the injunction against impurity and fornication (5:3), we should respect the formal signals of the text. These signals help us understand how the author probably perceived the relation between different concepts. This will be important in chapter 18.3.5, where I discuss love as an attributed character trait.

[476] εὐτραπελία, "sarcasm" had the positive connotation of "wittiness" in Attic Greek, but here holds the connotation of humor that works in negative ways, see Hoehner 2002: 655–656.

(5:5) (and before this passage also stealing, 4:28) is most easily understood as a stereotype of gentiles by a Jewish Christ-believing writer.[477] The enumeration of deviant behaviors and vices in 5:1–6 has extensive similarities with the description of the gentiles in 4:17–22:

- "fornication" (πορνεία), 5:3 – "licentiousness" (ἀσέλγεια[478]), 4:19
- "fornication" (πορνεία), 5:3 – "deceitful desire" (ἐπιθυμίαι τῆς ἀπάτης), 4:22
- "impurity" (ἀκαθαρσία), 5:3 – "impurity" (ἀκαθαρσία), 4:19
- "greed" (πλεονεξία), 5:3 – "greed" (πλεονεξία), 4:19
- "shameful behavior" (αἰσχρότης), 5:4 – "licentiousness" (ἀσέλγεια), 4:19
- "foolish talk" (μωρολογία[479]), 5:4 – "futility of mind" (ματαιότης τοῦ νοός), 4:18–19

"Impurity" and "greed" are verbatim similarities while the other words cover similar content. The ingroup's identity as "holy" is put in stark contrast to the conduct of the gentiles. The gentiles are the major outgroup, the inverse of the life in Christ.[480]

The passage is followed by another two contrastive passages. First, walking in the light is contrasted with walking in the dark (5:7–14). Second, walking in wisdom is contrasted with foolishness (5:15–20). Just like in 5:1–6, it is not explicated whether the one who walks in the dark and the one who is a fool is an outsider or a deviant within the group. Since the passage plays on the contrast between a prototype and an outgroup stereotype, this vagueness is probably intended. As discussed in chapter 8.2, deviants are a threat to the group since they are perceived

---

[477] *T. Reub.* 1.6; 3.3; 4.6–8; Wis 2:16; *1 Enoch* 10.11; *T. Jud.* 14.5; *Arist.* 152. Cf. Goodman 1992: 72–74; Yee 2004: 53–56. See also chapter 18.4.6.

[478] ἀσέλγεια, with the basic connotation of boundary-free sensual appetite, is sometimes used in association with improper sexual lust, see Hoehner 2002: 590.

[479] μωρολογία can be seen as a practical behavior indicating a mind without knowledge and insight.

[480] Cf. Shkul 2009: 216-237.

as similar to the outgroup stereotype and thus undermine the ingroup distinctiveness.

This contrastive description fits the meta-contrast principle from social identity theory, which predicts that the group will tend to describe the outgroup as the opposite of itself, since the ingroup is experienced as maximally valuable if it is perceived as maximally contrasting to outgroups as possible (see chapter 7.2). The description of the gentiles also fits the self-esteem hypothesis, which predicts that the group seeks to describe outgroups in a way that enhances the self-esteem of the ingroup (see chapter 7.1).

This absolute contrast is not necessarily the response to external threats. Rather, if anything, it may represent that the author believes that the relations to the outsiders are becoming too benevolent and that the social borders are not distinct enough. The author might be creating opposition as much as he is responding to it, in order to increase commitment.[481] As we discussed in chapter 8.2, labelling certain behaviors and individuals deviant can reinforce the sense of meaning and value in the group. Therefore, rhetorics of contrast may mean that that the author feels that some group members are acting in a way that dissolves the sense that the group is distinct and valuable.

In sum, the non-believing gentiles make up the major outgroup of the letter. The author's thrust against the gentiles functions to a) increase the distinctiveness and the self-esteem of the group, b) form the ideals and norms of the group (the ingroup prototype) and c) inspire the recipients not to feel committed to non-believing gentiles but rather to the identity in Christ.

---

[481] E.g. Arnold 1989; MacDonald 2004 assumes external threats to be behind Ephesians, while Shkul 2009: 216-237 suggests that the author constructs opposition. A fair historical guess would be that the truth is somewhere in between—there are real social problems, perhaps weak boundaries, perhaps harassments, perhaps both, but the author responds to the social situation by exaggerating the difference between ingroup and outgroup.

17.1.3 Evangelization as an Aspect of the Relation to the Gentiles?

The gentiles are considered to be the major outgroup of the *ekklēsia* in Ephesians, as discussed in the previous section. They are described in starkly negative terms as the opposite of the Christ-believers. But does Ephesians reflect an introversionist or conversionist attitude? Is the author of Ephesians only interested in keeping the recipient group "holy and blameless" (1:4) or does he imagine that evangelization is integral to their identity in Christ? This question is difficult to answer, but nevertheless important for this study, since if evangelization is normative, then it is a behavior norm strongly associated with the group's identity. The principal attitude to non-believers will be discussed in this section, and the result of this discussion will be used in chapter 18.4.2 when we discuss evangelizing speech as a behavior norm.

Margaret MacDonald uses Bryan Wilson's often employed sect typology in order to classify the sectarian outlook of Colossians and Ephesians, respectively.[482] First she categorises the Colossian community as a conversionist sect, based on Col 4:2–6:

> Colossians combines strong mission motifs with a certain caution with respect to outsiders. The reference to "outsiders" offers an especially strong indication of the "sectarian" tendencies of the Pauline churches. ... In one type of sect labelled "conversionist" sect by sociologist Bryan Wilson there is a particularly strong tension between the desire to remain distinct from the outside world and the goal of mission. ... This is in contrast with more "introversionist" sects that often physically separate themselves from the rest of society in hope of guaranteeing isolation from the evil world ...[483]

I could not agree more on this analysis of Colossians. However, when she considers Ephesians, she argues that Ephesians corresponds to a community with a largely introversionist attitude, that is, a sect with a

[482] MacDonald 2000; Wilson 1970. See Holmberg 1990: 77-177 for an overview of how sect typologies have been used in New Testament studies.

[483] MacDonald 2000: 174, cf. 56.

very weak interest in converting new members, and a strong interest in maintaining their own holiness:

> Recent highlighting of the extensive parallels between Ephesians and the QL [Qumran Literature] ... has drawn my attention to the fact that Ephesians reveals a stronger introversionist sectarian response than the other Pauline epistles ... Community members feel threatened by spiritual powers that shape the outside world (e.g., 1:21; 2:2; 6:10–20). These spiritual powers are understood as inseparably linked to the evil that believers witness in their everyday lives (2:2). Believers are urged to set themselves apart from those around them as saints (holy ones)—in essence to turn into the church and away from the non-believing world. ... Ephesians displays very little interest in dialogue between believers and non-believers.[484]

I agree with MacDonald that Ephesians sets the ingroup strongly apart from the outgroup (e.g., 4:17–24, cf. chapter 17.1.2 above). However, as MacDonald rightly notes in her analysis of Colossians, also conversionist groups distinguish themselves strongly from the surrounding world. Therefore, the strong dichotomy between "us" and "the gentiles" in Ephesians cannot be taken as an argument for an introversionist outlook. Further, I agree with her that Ephesians is quite (but not entirely) silent about missionary activity, but I think she overstates the implications of this silence. After all, not even all undisputed Pauline letters stress evangelization, simply because it is not the purpose of the letters, and Paul can certainly not be accused of having an introversionist rather than a conversionist attitude.

MacDonald compares Ephesians to the Qumran literature and concludes that although Qumran is certainly stronger in its introversionist tendency, both share the same basic attitude.[485] Later on in her commentary, she does, however, modify her standpoint and acknowledges that Ephesians "holds some of the tendencies which are typical of a conversionist response," referring to 3:8–13; 6:19–20.[486] She

---

[484] MacDonald 2000: 21. In an earlier work she maintained that Ephesians represents a non-introversionist attitude, see MacDonald 1988: 102.

[485] MacDonald 2000: 211–212.

[486] MacDonald 2000: 237–238, cf. 321–322.

also recognizes that the household code (5:21–6:9) shows that the group did not withdraw physically from society. Nevertheless, she minimizes the importance of these passages and maintains that Ephesians expresses a withdrawing attitude.

I agree with MacDonald that Ephesians is somewhere in between the introversionist and the conversionist attitude, but would like to give more credit to the conversionist tendency than MacDonald does. I would like to argue that the analogy with Qumran is misleading, since the difference between the Qumran literature (specifically the sectarian documents) and Ephesians is greater than MacDonald acknowledges.

First, the Qumranite *Damascus Document* reflects a community that thinks of themselves as a group who withdrew because they were already seeking God more sincerely than others, a "remnant" (CD I.1–5; II.11–13). They remember their past as a state where they were admittedly sinful (I.9) but at least better than others since they were the only ones who "sought for him [i.e., God] with a perfect heart" (I.10). Because of their effort, God sent them the Teacher of Righteousness (I.10–11). The author of Ephesians, on the other hand, describes the recipients as a group created out of the worst kind of sinful people—gentiles under the influence of evil spirits (2:1–10). As opposed to the Qumranites, they remember their past as a state where they were in no way better than others. Their identity is that they are converted from their major outgroup—conversion is fundamental to who they are.

Second, the Qumranite *Rule of the Community* displays a different attitude than Ephesians towards new members. The *Rule of the Community* is a document that has been redacted many times and reflects a group having gone through different phases through history. In one phase, new members were seen as (fairly) righteous people who needed to be tested rather than converted (1QS VI.8–22); in another phase, new members were seen as converts from a sinful life who needed to confess their sins (1QS I-II).[487] The latter attitude is more conversionist and the former introversionist, but not even in the more conversionist phase do

---

[487] Pouilly 1976 (reviewed in Gagnon 1992) considers columns I-IV to be the latest redactional layer and a result of a revitalization of the community, while VI.8b-VII.25 is the result of an earlier wave of new members. Metso 1997 reaffirms that I-IV is the fruit of a late stage of redaction.

we get close to the attitude of Ephesians. Not even in this phase do we find any traces of missionary activity or a self-identification of the group as a whole as converted sinners. In Ephesians, on the other hand, it is assumed that all members, both old and new, were converted from a sinful life (2:1–10). Moreover, we get no hints of rigorous testing in Ephesians, but only of education for the newly converted (4:20–21).

Third, the attitude in the *War Scroll* of Qumran is triumphalistic, imagining the destruction of all people under the dominion of the evil spiritual realm (e.g., 1QM I.5–17). There is no hope for outsiders, only doom. Nils Ahlstrup Dahl argues that there is a great difference between the Qumranite and the Ephesian dualism:

> The Qumran sectarian looks back to Moses and beyond him to the predetermination of the cosmos in creation in a spirit of unbroken continuity ... the two camps of which the world consists have existed from time immemorial, and nothing has changed since the primordial situation ... For the writer to the Ephesians the whole situation has been completely transformed by a radical break in the continuity—the event of Jesus Christ.[488]

MacDonald is quite right that Ephesians shares the view of the Qumranites that the "world" is helplessly under the control of the evil spirits, but does not take into account that Ephesians differentiates strongly between the people in the world and the spiritual forces who dominate them. Their identity is that they are people who used to be under the dominion of the evil spirits, but have now been freed through the Christ-event, followed by their conversion response—faith (2:1–10).[489] The author is careful to emphasize that their war is "not against blood and flesh" but against evil spirits (6:12). God triumphs over the evil spirits by saving people through Christ (3:10–12). This imagination is a conversionist imagination, where people can be liberated from the dominion of evil through evangelizing efforts. As opposed to the

---

[488] Dahl 2000: 117.

[489] Dahl 2000: 122–123 suggests that although Ephesians uses predestination language just like the Qumran literature, it acknowledges the free response of humans to God's calling. I will argue below in chapter 18.1 that the author sees no opposition between predestination of the *ekklēsia* and the initiative of the individual.

imagination of the *War Scroll*, there is still hope for those under the dominion of evil.

In short, Ephesians differs from the sectarian Qumran texts as to how the letter narrates a) the memory of the group's past, b) the group's method of handling new members and c) the imagination of whether there is any hope for the outgroup. These very important differences suggest that using the Qumran community heuristically in order to capture the character of Ephesians easily leads to a somewhat distorted characterization of Ephesians.

In sum, although I agree with MacDonald that the conversionist stance is not as salient in Ephesians as in Colossians, I do think, however, that she overestimates the introversionist attitude in Ephesians. First, strong differentiation from outsiders is typical for both introversionist and conversionist sects. Second, the text identifies the members of the group as converted sinful people, including the first members. Third, the introduction of recipients into the group is not described as a test, but as a conversion followed by education. Fourth, the group may be "at war" with an evil world dominated by evil spirits, but they imagine that the non-believing gentiles can be rescued from the dominion of evil. The conversionist attitude is more than a "tendency"; it is an integral part of their identity. Current circumstances (persecution, harassment) may have caused them to focus on defense, but the conversionist imagination is still well integrated into their ingroup identity.

Since this study analyses the relation between identity and behavior norms, the conclusion reached here is important. If we assume a more positive attitude to conversion, imagined as spiritual victory, it will have effect on how some of the vague expression in the armor-metaphor (6:10–20) should be translated into behavior norms. This will be discussed in chapter 18.4.2.

17.2 Israel and the *Ekklēsia*

What is the relation between Israel and the *ekklēsia* after the Christ-event (2:11–22)? According to Ephesians, the recipients used to be outside the "commonwealth of Israel" (2:12), but have now been included (2:13, 19). The new category of Christ-believers may or may not be called "Israel," since the text does not explicitly spell out "Israel" in the verses where the author talks about their inclusion (2:13, 19), but this new category does, nevertheless, have all the advantages of the covenant. The relation between Israel and the *ekklēsia* is not very easy to determine from these verses. We should recognize that we ask the wrong question when we try to determine the exact relation between the two, since the author's main intention is not to discuss their exact relation to "Israel" but to remind the recipients of how valuable their current situation is compared to their past. Nevertheless, "Israel" seems to be part of the author's narrative and scholars have therefore tried to determine how the author understands the relation between Israel and the *ekklēsia*. The scholarly discussion has mainly produced three kinds of interpretations:

The first interpretation is that the *ekklēsia* is a new category which either replaces or duplicates Israel after the Christ-event, so that all Christ-believers, both Jews and gentiles, belong to a new category.[490] All the positive aspects of Israel are taken over by the Christ-believers and non-believing Jews are implicitly not included in the new category:

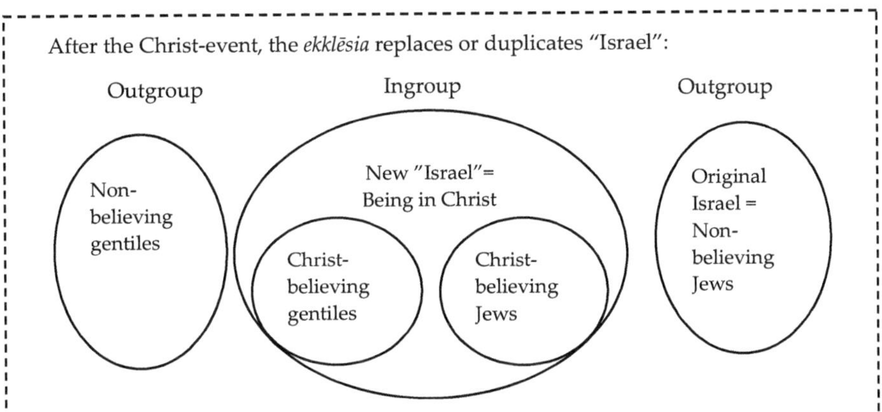

The second interpretation is that being in Christ means incorporation into Israel.[491] Israel is reformed and expanded in a way that allows the inclusion of Christ-believing gentiles, but all Jews are implicitly still part of Israel:

[490] Hoehner 2002: 395–396; Lincoln 1990: 134; Merklein 1973: 72–76.

[491] Barth 1974: 269–270; Yee 2004. On Yee's position, see also n. 518.

Christ-believing gentiles included into the expanded "Israel" through the Christ-event:

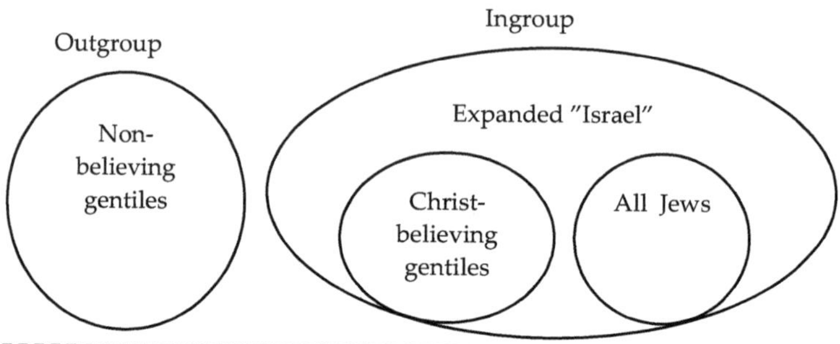

The third interpretation is that the relation between the *ekklēsia* and Israel is ambiguous or in a process of change.[492] The reason that the author is silent about non-believing Jews and expresses the inclusion of the gentiles in such an open-ended way is that the *ekklēsia* is in a situation where they are undecided about their relation to their Jewish heritage:

The relation between being in Christ and being in Israel is ambiguous and still under negotiation: (The partial overlap is intended to illustrate an ambiguous relation.)

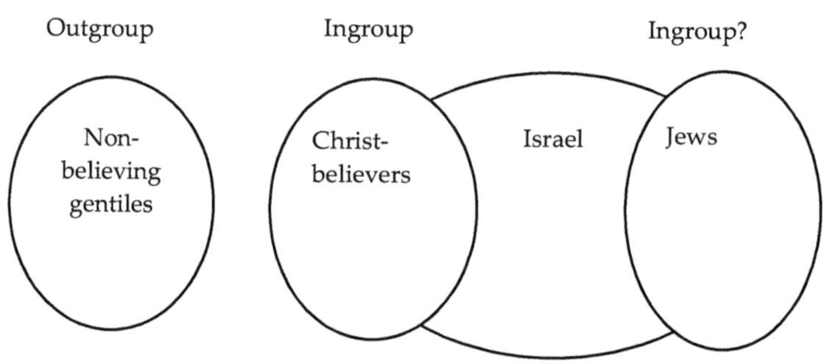

492 MacDonald 2004; Shkul 2009: 79-141. MacDonald emphasizes how external pressure may have made their relation to "Israel" ambiguous, while Shkul analyzes the author of Ephesians as an "entrepreneur of identity" who only partly moves the identity in Christ from the second interpretation mentioned above towards the first interpretation mentioned above.

Self-categorization theory states that identities can be cognitively ordered into hierarchies in our brains, where some identities are sub-categories to other identities (see chapters 5.1 and 9.1). I intend to show that the key to understandning the cognition of the author is that being in Christ is a sub-category to being a member of Israel. Being in Christ is neither just inclusion into Israel, nor a replacement for or a parallel to Israel, but a sub-category.

The author of Ephesians does not use the ethnic designation "Jew" (Ἰουδαῖος); instead he uses "Israel" (Ἰσραήλ, 2:12).[493] Ἰουδαῖος, "Jew", was a usually an ethnic designation; "Israel," on the other hand, was often understood more in terms of a covenant.[494] Therefore one can find texts which do not equal "Israel" with the group of the Jews.[495] Since

[493] The literature on Ἰουδαῖος and Ἰσραήλ/ישראל is extensive. See e.g. Cohen 1999: 11-106; Kuhn 1967; Tomson 1986; Ulfgard 1998: 31–34; Yee 2004: 89–91 for overviews.

[494] Tomson 1986 suggests that "Israel" is often used in intra-Israelite debates, while "Jew" is used inter-ethnic contexts. The usage of "Israel" would therefore suggest that the author considers this to be an intra-Israelite matter. Tomson discusses whether the usage of "Israel" in Eph 2:12 is potentially anomalous, since one could claim that the issue in Eph 2 is not intra-Jewish. He then concludes (rightly) that the author wants the gentiles to consider themselves part of Israel (pp. 285–288).

[495] As Elliott 2000 has shown, the Qumran texts and the Pseudepigrapha indicate that some Jewish groups did not equal Israel with the ethnic Jewish people. Elliott's account partly challenges Sanders 1977; 1992, who claims that the main stream of first century Judaism had a very inclusive attitude towards all ethnic Jews. At least some groups did not equate Israel with all ethnic Jews. Paul uses "Israel" in two ways in his letter to the Romans 9–11. Almost consistently, Israel equals all ethnic Jews (9:27, 31; 10:19, 21; 11:2, 7, 25–26). In these passages he emphasises their failure before God, but that they will be saved in the end. On one occasion, however, Paul writes that "not all who are of Israel are Israel" (9:6) and opens up for the possibility that "Israel" does not necessarily equal ethnic descent, cf. Dunn 1998: 504–509. He also states that the gentiles have been added to the "olive tree" (11:17–24) and that the gentiles are partakers of Abraham's covenant (4:1–25), thus including gentiles into the covenant of Israel. Paul does, however, refrain from explicitly calling the gentiles "Israel." (Paul might, however, call all the Christ-believers ὁ Ἰσραὴλ τοῦ Θεοῦ in

there was a tendency not to use "Israel" as a solely ethnic term, we are therefore justified in suspecting that the author of Ephesians has a covenantal rather than an ethnic understanding of "Israel."

The key passage is 2:11–12. In 2:11 the author uses expressions explicitly pointing to the ethnic roots of the Jews and gentiles, but in 2:12 he uses expressions pointing to the special covenantal status of the Jews before God. The two statements in 2:11–12, both beginning with ὅτι, become complementary:

> Therefore, remember that (ὅτι) then,
> you gentiles in the flesh (ἐν σαρκί)
> (the ones called (οἱ λεγόμενοι) the uncircumcision
> by the ones called (οἱ λεγόμενοι)
> the handmade (χειροποίητος) circumcision in the flesh)
> that (ὅτι[496]) you were—at that time without Christ[497]—
> aliens from the commonwealth of Israel,
> and strangers to the covenants of promise,
> having no hope and without God in the world.
> (2:11–12, my translation)

In this way, the author differentiates between two aspects of their outsidership. The first aspect is ethnic descent; the other is their lack of status before God.

In the first statement (2:11), the author reiterates their status as gentiles "in the flesh." They lack circumcision, the established ethnic boundary marker between Jews and gentiles.[498] Twice he writes "the ones called" (οἱ λεγόμενοι) to signal that it is a process of labeling. With a distancing language, he recounts the opinion of a stereotypical Jew, hinting that this distinction is not the important one. Moreover, he adds the adjective "handmade" (χειροποίητος), probably as an allusion to the Pauline tradition, which contrasts circumcision of the heart with

---

Gal 6:16 if the preceding καί is interpreted as an epexegetic καί, cf. Blass and Debrunner 1961: §442.9.)

[496] The second ὅτι resumes the sentence after the parenthetical explanation of "gentiles in the flesh", see Lincoln 1990: 124.

[497] See n. 471.

[498] MacDonald 2000: 241.

circumcision of the flesh (e.g., Rom 2:28–29; Phil 3:2–3; Col 2:11).[499] Altogether we get the impression that the author wants to signal that ethnicity is not the relevant distinction. Rather, it is the exclusion from the covenant that matters.

"Israel" in the second statement (2:12) is associated with the special status that the Jews as citizens of Israel and covenant partners have before God, as we discussed above. The phrase "covenants of promise" further strengthens the interpretation that it is the covenantal aspect of Israel that the author has in mind. As opposed to the first statement about ethnic descent, the author does not distance himself from this description of their past, but considers this to be their past status in relation to God.[500]

The recipients used to be without this status when they were not in Christ. But now, when they are in Christ, they have this status before God, according to 2:19–22. They used to be "strangers" but are now "co-citizens" (συμπολῖται, 2:19), referring back to 2:12 where it was stated that they used to be excluded from the "citizenship (πολιτεία) of Israel." They used to be "aliens" (παροίκοι) but now they are "household

---

499 Hoehner 2002: 354–355; Lohse 1964.

500 Yee 2004: 71–125 argues that 2:11–12 is entirely a "straight reportage" of the attitude of a "typical" ethnocentric Jew and that the author himself reports this attitude mainly in order to dispute such an attitude in the remainder of Eph 2. "The point is *not* the Gentiles' existence as being separated from the 'theocratically constituted nation' prior to their conversion ... Still less was the author referring to the Gentiles as being estranged from God. Rather, it is human hostility, in particular it is the alienation between two ethnic groups prior to their reconciliation, that is in view" (p. 100). While I agree that the author signals distance from the ethnic description in 2:11, nothing indicates that 2:12 is a "straight reportage" of someone else's attitude. Rather, the descriptions in 2:12 are picked up in 2:19 as the author declares that their past condition has changed. 2:12 is therefore most probably the author's own opinion about their actual status before God, rather than just the opinion of the "typical" Jew. While I agree with Yee that the author is trying to redefine the covenant in non-ethnic terms, Yee's analysis of 2:12 is too much of an attempt to rescue the author, who obviously shares the opinion of the "typical" Jew that gentiles (unless they are in Christ) are estranged from God (cf. 4:17–19).

members (οἰκεῖοι) of God" (2:19).[501] In 3:6, the Christ-believing gentiles are again described as partakers of the covenant in several ways through a range of συν-constructs. They are "co-heirs and co-body and co-sharers of the promise in Christ Jesus."[502] The author thus distinguishes the concept of Israel from its content of ethnic descent.

Does this mean that being in Christ equals being in Israel? Both the interpretation that Israel is expanded and that "Israel" is reformed or duplicated into something new (see above) suggest, in one way or another, that being in Christ is equivalent to the status of being in Israel (although one may hesitate to use the label "Israel"). I think these interpretations are mistaken.

The first interpretation above, that the author reforms the idea of Israel and appropriates the heritage of Israel in a way which excludes non-believing Jews from the new category, cannot explain the lack of attack against non-believing Jews. Nowhere is there the slightest suggestion that some Jews, the "circumcision in the flesh" who had "citizenship of Israel" (2:11–12) even before Christ, could be excluded from Israel. We could, however, consider Nils Alstrup Dahl's proposal that the author does not care about real non-believing Jews, just about

---

[501] The last term, "household members", could be taken to mean they have become blood relatives to the Jewish people, since that is the most common use of the word in the LXX, see Hoehner 2002: 394. But the text says that they are "household members *of God*" (cf. 2:22). The building-metaphor in the subsequent verses (2:20–22), using a number of words based on the οἰκ-stem, makes it clear that the household metaphor is intended to refer to the special status before God gained in Christ, rather than blood relations to the Jewish people. Since the author is writing in the Pauline tradition, it is worth noting that in Gal. 6:10 Paul talks about the "household (οἰκεῖος) of faith", which is not an ethnic use of the metaphor of οἰκεῖος.

[502] "Co-heirs" (συγκληρονόμοι) (cf. 1:14, 18) and "co-sharers (συμμέτοχοι) of the promise" (cf. 1:13; 2:12) are designations referring to how they share the special covenantal status which the Jews have before God (Hoehner 2002: 441–448), but does not include "fleshly" ethnic descent. "Co-body" (σύσσωμα), however, probably refers to the body of Christ, and neither to the status of being Israelites, nor to ethnic descent, since the author uses σῶμα to refer to the body of Christ in 4:1–16. σῶμα should not be interpreted as ethnic descent, since the author uses σάρξ to refer to ethnic descent in 2:11.

the cultural heritage.[503] Dahl notices the total lack of explicit distinction between Christ-believing Jews and other Jews and then concludes that the author is just interested in the Jewish roots of the Christ-movement, but not in contemporary Jews. Shkul argues similarly that the author is mainly interested in the ideological resources of Israel in his building of Christian identity.[504] It may seem reasonable to assume that real non-believing Jews have fallen out of the author's social and cognitive world, since he does not discuss them. However, such an assumption fails to explain how the author, who most certainly is a Jew,[505] so easily uses a "we" which refers to those in Christ (most instances of ἡμεῖς refer to the Christ-believers), and at the same time uses a "you" which refers to the gentile Christ-believers (e.g., 2:11–22), only to occasionally change what "we" refers to, contrasting a Jewish "we" to a gentile "you" (2:1–3, cf. 1:11–13). An author who writes like this obviously thinks of himself as both a Jew and a Christ-believer and sees no contradiction between these two social identities. The author can therefore scarcely be indifferent to the Jews, his own ethnic group. Moreover, there is not a single attempt to distance himself from the category of the Jews. Had he seen the identity in Christ as something different from both, he probably would have contrasted both of them, according to the meta-contrast principle (see chapter 7.2). Only someone who still sees himself as a Jew and does not have a problem with that would write in this way. As we concluded in chapter 17.1.1, the force of the attack on the shortcomings of the gentiles is much stronger than that on the Jews, which suggests that the author does not want the recipients to increase their social distance to the Jews as much as their distance to the gentiles. Since the author himself is a Jew, it would be wrong to assume that he is unknowing of or uninterested in there being non-believing Jews. But what would be reasonable to assume is that he avoids discussing non-believing Jews in this text since the addressees are gentile. He wants the gentile recipients

---

[503] Dahl 2000: 444–447.

[504] Shkul 2009: 79-141.

[505] See Best 2004: 8; Yee 2004: 35–45 for arguments that the author is a Jew who identifies himself as a Jew and who knows the Jewish cultural matrix. (Perhaps someone who very cleverly imagines himself to be a Jew could manage to write a text like Ephesians, but such a hypothesis seems quite far-fetched.)

to understand that the non-believing gentiles are the outgroup, which they should not identify with (4:17–19). The non-believing Jews are not the subject of the letter; they are not the outgroup, which the author aims to contrast. If he had mentioned that some Jews were not Christ-believers, he might even have undermined his own rhetorical strategy, giving the recipients a reason to question their relation to Israel.

On the other hand, the interpretation that the author expands the concept of Israel to include both Jews and Christ-believing gentiles cannot explain other aspects of the text. First, the author very clearly states that the criterion for being in Christ is faith in him (1:13; 2:8, 18; 3:12), which is not a criterion for belonging to Israel. Second, many advantages in relation to God are expressed in a way indicating that they are not available for all Jews but only for those who are in Christ, for instance adoption as sons (1:5), redemption and forgiveness (1:6–7), salvation (2:5–6) and the Spirit (1:13; 2:18).[506] Being in Christ is a category associated with more privileges than the category of Israel. Those who are in Christ have everything that those who are in Israel have—and more.

In sum, what we have seen so far is this:

- The author thinks of himself as a Jew and never distances himself from this identity. He can therefore scarcely be indifferent and unknowing about non-believing Jews.
- The author assumes that the major outgroup both in the past and the present are the gentiles and attacks non-believing gentiles with much more force than he does non-believing Jews
- The author never excludes non-believing Jews from Israel
- The author includes the Christ-believing gentiles in the covenant and the commonwealth.
- Being in Christ has all the advantages of being in Israel as well as advantages that non-believing Jews do not have.

---

[506] Note that the author uses "we" in all these passages, which means not only the Christ-believing gentiles receive these gifts in Christ, but also the Christ-believing Jews. (Had the Jewish author thought that only the gentiles were previously without these gifts he had used "you" instead.) This implies that non-believing Jews do not have the gifts mentioned in these passages.

- The criterion for being in Christ is faith in him, which is not described as a criterion for being in Israel. To be in Christ is a more exclusive category.
- The author avoids saying that the Christ-believing gentiles are ethnically one with the Jews; rather they are one in Christ as Jews and gentiles.

All these seemingly irreconcilable observations have prompted the third kind of interpretation mentioned above—that the relation to Israel and non-believing Jews is ambiguous and still under construction. Margaret MacDonald describes the relation to the Jews in Ephesians as "ambiguous."[507] She proposes that the text reflects the political situation under Domitian, when he imposed the *fiscus judaicus*. The historian Suetonius (c:a 69–130 C.E.) writes:

> Besides other taxes, that on the Jews was levied with the utmost rigor, and those were prosecuted who, without publicly acknowledging that faith, yet lived as Jews, as well as those who concealed their origin and did not pay the tribute levied upon their people. (Suetonius, *Dom.* 12.2)

MacDonald follows Stephen Wilson in assuming that the reference to those who "lived as Jews" might include Christ-believers.[508] A Jewish umbrella would both have advantages (the right to gather as a synagogue, exemption from the official cult) and disadvantages (*fiscus judaicus,* marginalization, occasional persecution), which could very possibly give rise to an ambiguous attitude towards Israel among gentile Christ-believers.[509] MacDonald's historical reconstruction certainly assumes more than can be read out of the text (which she acknowledges), but pinpoints something important. She argues that gentile Christ-believers would feel ambiguous about what relation they had to the Jews and that the "ambiguous use of labels is tied to ambiguity in the boundaries of the community itself and points to a period of fluctuation between Jewish and distinctly 'Christian' identity.

---

[507] MacDonald 2004.

[508] Wilson 1995.

[509] Cf. Zetterholm 2003: 178–224. See also chapter 14.1 above.

[...] The permeable boundaries and ambiguous categories probably reflect concrete experiences in the *ekklēsia* of shifting identity."[510]

MacDonald's description of the situation is better than Ernst Käsemann's proposal that the author is a defensive Jew who writes into a situation where the gentiles had already marginalized the Jews in the *ekklēsia*.[511] Käsemann's proposal fails to explain why the author does not actively defend the position of Jewish Christ-believers. MacDonald's description is also better than the proposal by Tet-Lim Yee that the author, a confident but benevolent Jew wrestling with the ethnocentrism of certain other (Christ-believing) Jews, is writing in order to make Israel more inclusive for the gentiles.[512] His interpretation stumbles on 2:12, which he argues is the opinion of a "typical" Jew, rather than the ethnocentric opinion of the author himself.[513] Moreover, Yee's proposal does not explain why an author would try to convince gentiles, who are the recipients of the letter rather than Jews, that Jews should discard ethnocentrism. The author is neither defensive, nor worried about Jewish ethnocentrism, but nevertheless eager to remind them that being in Christ somehow has included them into Israel (2:12). To imagine a confident Christ-believing Jew writing to gentile recipients who are confused and have ambiguous perceptions about their relation to Israel would indeed make sense of the author's confident, yet apparently urgent reminder in 2:11–22.

MacDonald's theory does, however, have problems. First, there is no absolute need to assume very specific external threats or pressure in order to make sense of 2:1–22 (cf. chapter 18.4.3). Internal tensions within the group could equally well have occasioned the text, even if there were no particular problems arising from the outside. In the passage in 2:14–18 which celebrates that gentiles and Jews can be unified in Christ, the

---

510 MacDonald 2004: 433, 422.

511 Käsemann 1980. Fischer 1973: 76–94 similarly suggests a historical situation where "die Entfremdung zwischen Juden und Christen sich so rasch vollzog, daß ein jüdisches Eigenleben innerhalb der christlichen Gemeinde der Mehrheit als völlig untragbar erschien" (p. 93). Käsemann's suggestion has been criticized as speculative by e.g. Lincoln 1990: lxxx; Yee 2004: 4–5.

512 Yee 2004.

513 See n. 500.

author uses ἵνα + subjunctive mode for "create" (κτίζω, 2:15) and "reconcile" (ἀποκαταλλάσσω, 2:16), which makes it possible to interpret the vision of unity both as a fact and as an ideal goal of the *ekklēsia*.[514] ἵνα + subjunctive can introduce both consequence, "so that he" and purpose, "in order that he might."[515] This might suggest that the author has yet to see the peace fully realized even in Christ. Exactly what these tensions could be about is impossible to guess, except that there might have been friction between gentiles and Torah-practicing Jews (2:15, cf. discussion in chapter 18.4.1).

A more important problem with MacDonald's theory is that she does not distinguish between the cognition of the author and the cognition of the recipients. MacDonald assumes that the author shares the cognition of the recipients, when she claims that the text expresses an ambiguous relation to Israel. It might indeed be probable that the boundaries were experienced as ambiguous for a gentile Christ-believer in the post-Apostolic era, for instance due to external pressure or internal conflict, as we discussed above. I accept MacDonald's idea that the *recipients* may have experienced the boundaries as ambiguous. But that does not mean the categories were ambiguous in the same way for the *author*, who is a Jew, not a gentile, and who still without any demarcation from his ethnic roots implicitly considers himself to be a Jew. We must understand the text as reflecting the cognition of the author, which in this case might be opposed to the cognition of the recipients. The strong emphasis in passages dealing with ethnicity, for instance 2:11 (the only imperative in

---

[514] ἵνα + aorist subjunctive does not necessarily have a temporal past meaning. "In Greek the temporal significance of the corresponding indicatives has been carried over to a much smaller degree to the moods (subjunctive and optative, also to the infinitive and participle) … the temporal relationship is determined by something else appearing in the speech or the narrative" (Blass and Debrunner 1961: §318). E.g. Eph 1:17; 2:7, 9; 3:16, 18, 19; 4:10 show that the author of Ephesians uses ἵνα + aorist subjunctive without past meaning. Lincoln 1990: 133 is therefore wrong in claiming that 2:14–18 solely describes something that has already taken place. He does so in order to dismiss the theory that tensions between Jewish Christians and gentile Christians may have occasioned the text.

[515] See n. 543 for further discussion about ἵνα + subjunctive.

the first half of the letter) and 4:17 (double verbs in the first person singular), suggests that the author expects the recipients not to agree with him entirely and that he believes he will have to convince them. In the following I will argue that it is most reasonable to assume that the author has a clear perception of the social identities, including the relation to Israel, in his own mind. For strategic reasons (see below), however, the author does not use expressions that make his perception easily accessible to us.

Having tested the three kinds of proposals which previous scholarship has put forward, it is time to test a fourth, novel, interpretation of the relation between Israel and the *ekklēsia* in Ephesians—that the identity in Christ is cognitively organized as a subcategory to Israel, inheriting all the attractive properties of Israel and adding further properties to the subcategory. The statements of the author become quite consistent if we imagine that the cognitive hierarchy of social identities in his mind looks like this:

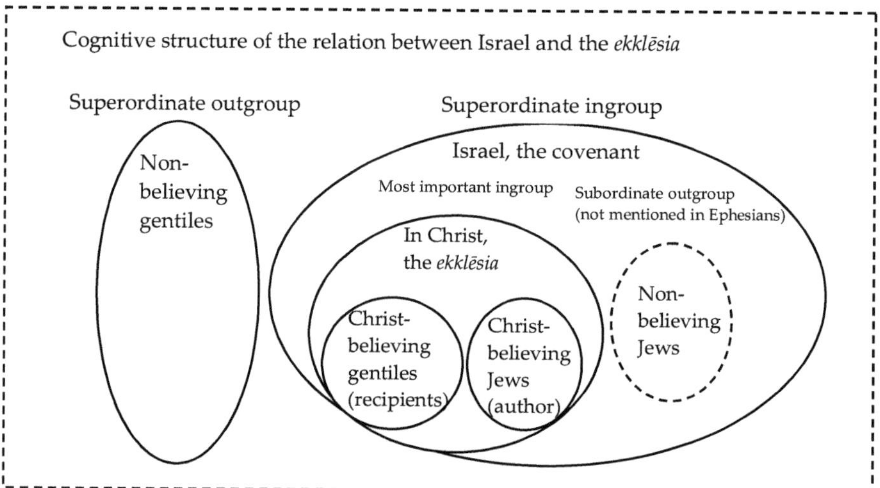

Through the Christ-event, those who believe in Christ have formed an exclusive subcategory in Israel. Only in this subcategory is there salvation. Other Jews are still in the covenant and therefore "close"

(2:13),[516] but just like "then" they are still "by nature the children of wrath, like everyone else" (2:3).[517]

This understanding of the hierarchy of social categories is more coherent with all the observations we made above compared to the suggestions of previous scholarship.[518] It explains why it is better to be a Jew than to be a gentile, but better still to be in Christ. It explains why the category of Christ-believers inherits all the valuable characteristics of Israel, but yet adds more exclusive valuable characteristics to the category. At the same time, it explains why the author sees no contradiction or tension between his identity as a Jew and his identity as a Christ-believer, but yet sees a strong contradiction between being in Christ and being a gentile.

One could object that the category of Christ-believers has some characteristics that are the opposite of the category of Israel. Torah observance, particularly circumcision, is "invalidated" in Christ (2:11, 15, cf. the discussion in chapter 18.4.1). In contrast, for most other Jews, practicing the Torah is central to their interpretation of what it means to be a member of Israel. It is, however, quite common that a subcategory modifies some of the prototypical characteristics of a superordinate

---

[516] Since it is the gentiles who used to be "afar" (μακρὰν) but "have been brought near" in 2:13, it is implicit that the Jews were "near" all the time.

[517] In 2:2 the author writes about "you", i.e., the gentile recipients, but in 2:3, he changes the subject to "we all" and includes the Jews among those who are "by nature the children of wrath."

[518] For a while, Yee 2004 seems to come close to my suggestion. He suggests that the author does not have any interest in replacing ethnic Israel or creating something new parallel to Israel, but to create a place for the gentiles within God's covenant. Yee is careful to point out that this place is not identical to Israel. In the end, however, Yee comes close to the solution of Barth 1974: 269–270 as he imagines that being in Christ is not a sub-category to being in Israel but that the covenant has been expanded and made inclusive and therefore no longer should be called "Israel" (pp. 176, 190–198). Yee's theory that the author is trying to cleanse the covenant from ethnic exclusivism does not explain what advantage a Jew would have from becoming a Christ-believer (besides reconciliation with gentiles), while the solution above suggests that there is something more exclusive and valuable in Christ even for a Jew (cf. 2:3, 5).

category.[519] The author of Ephesians obviously thinks that the modifications of the category of Israel in the subcategory of the *ekklēsia* are improvements. Although non-believing Jews would consider the Christ-believers to be deviant, the author constructs the *ekklēsia* as the most prototypical subcategory of Israel, those who fulfill God's plan.

In what hypothetical historical situation would the author want to a) discredit the recipients' gentile past and stress their distinction from non-believing gentiles, b) imply that the *ekklēsia* is a sub-category to Israel, and c) avoid the subject of non-believing Jews? A hypothetical history reconstruction, where the gentile Christ-believing recipients a) tend to adapt to their gentile environment and not maintain the boundaries towards the non-believing gentiles as strictly as the author envisions, and/or b) are ambivalent in their perception about whether the *ekklēsia* is part of Israel, would fit quite well into the rhetorical strategy of the letter. If increased social distance to the non-believing gentiles and decreased cognitive distance to the covenant of Israel are the goals of the author, it is perfectly understandable that he avoids the subject of non-believing Jews. This also means that MacDonald's theory about hostility from the gentile surrounding seems overstated, since the author would not have spent so much energy reinforcing the boundaries if there already was a conflict situation that created strong boundaries.[520] Rather, as we will discuss further in 18.4.3, a hypothetical historical background which would explain the text better is that the recipients have too benevolent relations to their gentile surroundings (in the author's opinion) and that the author aims to create an imagination of opposition and conflict with the surrounding world. In order to achieve this goal, the author refers to memories of suffering (which are probably real memories, not just fictional ones) and creates an atmosphere of potential hostility in relation to the gentiles.

---

[519] For instance, various subgroups of scholars (e.g. postcolonial, feminist, Marxist scholars) can sometimes identify themselves as a subcategory of scholars who modify some aspect of scholarly ideals among "mainstream" scholars in order to fulfill other scholarly ideals and goals better than previous scholarship.

[520] Cf. Shkul 2009: 175-239.

17.3 Household Identities and the Identity in Christ

The most striking feature of the household code in Ephesians (5:21–6:9) is that it says absolutely nothing extraordinary about practical behavior norms. The widely spread patriarchal ideals of the ancient Mediterranean world in general are reproduced: the submissive household categories, women, children and slaves should be respectful and obedient, and the dominant husbands, fathers and masters (who are ideally one and the same husband-father-master) should be benevolent towards those he is in charge of.[521] Some have claimed that Ephesians partly reforms conventional ethics, for instance by introducing the passage with an exhortation of mutual submission and by demanding selfless love from the dominant part.[522] While it is certainly true that the author demands a giving, caring and benevolent attitude from the dominant household members, it would be quite unfair to the surrounding society to claim that the household ethics of other groups was typically characterized by a morality that promoted ungiving, uncaring and malevolent attitudes towards women, children and slaves.[523] "Love-patriarchalism"[524] as a cultural pattern was spread in much wider circles than just the early Christ-movement. Moreover, Ephesians does not seem to be interested in resolving any of the problems we may reasonably assume were part of the social life of the intended recipients. He does not confront individuals who in a Pauline vein wish to withdraw from the household structure (cf. 1 Cor 7 in contrast to 1 Tim 2:15; 4:3; 5:3–16; 6:1–2) and he does not negotiate the situation of those who do not live in wholly Christ-believing households

---

521 Osiek and Balch 1997: 118–121; Schüssler Fiorenza 1994: 251–284.

522 E.g. Mollenkott 2003. See Dawes 1998: 6–8 for an overview of similar suggestions. Osiek 2002 makes a more interesting observation when she argues that although the patriarchal patterns remain, at least the author makes women, children and slaves visible by addressing them as morally responsible subjects.

523 E.g. Veyne 1987: 36–50 argues that loving harmony between spouses was a common ideal in the Roman era. According to Osiek and MacDonald 2005: 120, Ephesians "is infused with notions of affection and unity that have points in common with the most sentimental ideals of the Roman family."

524 The term "love-patriarchalism" was coined by Theissen 1982: 107.

(cf. 1 Cor 7; 1 Pet 2:18–3:7; 1 Tim 6:1–2).[525] In short, reformation or negotiation of the practical content of household behavior seems to be of little interest to Ephesians.

Ephesians and other deutero-Pauline texts do, however, modify Paul in a very profound way, if we look at the relation between household identities and the identity in Christ from a socio-cognitive perspective.[526] In 1 Cor 7 and Philem, there is a tension between household identities and the identity as a Christ-believer, which indicates that Paul sees the identity in Christ as a social category separate from the household identities (cf. Gal 3:28). Since the individuals who joined the Christ-movement typically belonged to households as well, Paul feels necessitated to negotiate between these identities in areas where these identities might cause loyalty conflicts (cf. chapter 9.1). In Paul's view, household identities were bound to compromise one's commitment to the identity in Christ (1 Cor 7).

Identity in Christ and household identities as different and potentially conflicting social categories, according to Paul

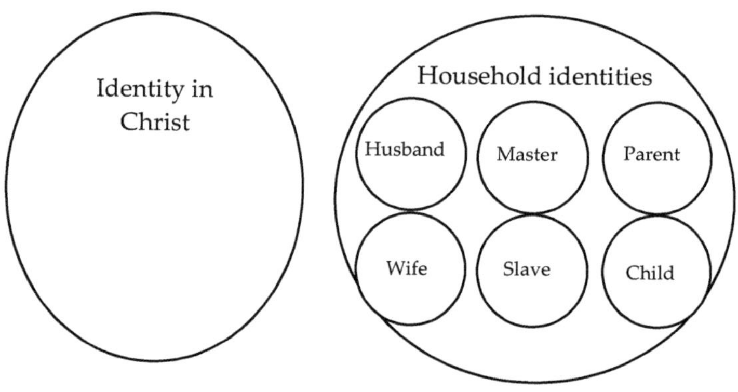

In the household code of Ephesians, as well as in other deutero-Pauline texts (Col 3:18–4:1; Eph 5:21–6:9; 1 Tim 3:1–13; Tit 2:1–10), however, the

525 Cf. Osiek and MacDonald 2005: 124.

526 The following overview of the relation between Paul and the deutero-Pauline authors is based on Roitto 2008.

tension between household identities and the identity in Christ is gone. Being a good household member is just part of being a Christ-believer.

Household identities as subcategories to the identity in Christ, according to deutero-Pauline authors

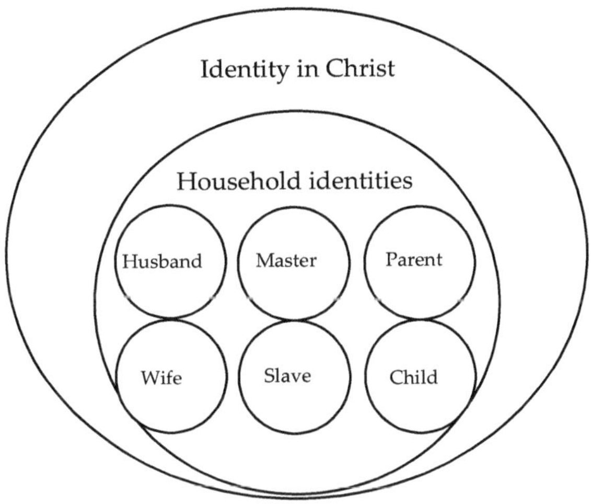

As we discussed in chapter 11.2, narratives can be used to motivate behavior through analogy. In the following I will argue that the author of Ephesians creates selective analogical transfers of themes from the Christ-narrative to the narrative about household norms, in order to integrate household identities into the identity in Christ. In this way, household norms become something which is an expression of the identity in Christ (rather than a problem, which must be negotiated in relation to the identity in Christ).

Gregory Dawes analyses the metaphorical language of 5:21–33 extensively, using metaphor theory.[527] Throughout the study, he scrutinizes how the relation between Christ and the *ekklēsia* serves as an analogy for the relation between husband and wife. He argues that analogies are always intended to be partial and that we are not justified in thinking that everything the author says about the relation between

[527] Dawes 1998.

Christ and the *ekklēsia* is intended to be transferred into the relation between husband and wife.[528] More specifically, the pattern of submission on behalf of the *ekklēsia* is intended to be transferred to the wife and the pattern of love on behalf of Christ is intended to be transferred to the husband. However, the author does not intend to say, for instance, that the husband "saves" the wife if she is submissive (5:23b) or that the husband's love "sanctifies" the wife (5:26–27). (Nevertheless, metaphor language is creative and there is nothing in the text to stop the reader from drawing a variety of conclusions.[529])

Dawes' analysis fits very well with the discussion in chapter 11.2 about how narrative themes could be transferred from one context to another through analogical thinking and thus motivate behavior. Dawes does, however, focus entirely on the analysis of the metaphors and does not ask what social impact the author aims to achieve when he makes such a massive effort to create analogies between the narrative about Christ (the most central ingroup narrative), and household behavior. As we discussed initially, the author probably does not aim at reforming household behavior in any practical sense, since the love-patriarchalism was quite uncontroversial and since the text seems insensitive to the complexities of real social life.

If Ephesians seems to have nothing particular to add as regards practical household behavior, why does he elaborate these analogies? The rhetoric of Ephesians makes perfect sense if we assume that the author's goal is to integrate the household sphere as a subcategory to the identity in Christ in the shared cognition of the recipients. Daniel Darko points out that the household code should be seen as an extension of the theme of walking "as wise" (ὡς σοφοί), beginning in 5:15.[530] No new

---

[528] Dawes 1998: 81–109.

[529] The problematic generative force of the metaphorical language of Eph 5:21–33 has frequently been pointed out, see e.g. Osiek 2002. See also Dawes 1998: 51–64 on the generally generative force of metaphorical language.

[530] Darko 2008: 83–85. Darko argues that the purpose of the household code is neither apologetic nor assimilationist, i.e. not written in response to external threats or pressure (pp. 69–108). Darko observes the lack of apologetic features in the text and suggests that the purpose of the code is simply to encourage harmonious relations within the households of the *ekklēsia*. My hypothesis,

sentence begins in 5:21 or 5:22, but one long sentence starts in 5:18 and ends in 5:24. Analyzing the household code as a separate unit ignores the linguistic signals of the author, who rather signals the beginning of a new section in 5:15 with the phrase "then (οὖν) ... walk (περιπατέω) ... as wise."[531] The household code should therefore be seen as an integral part of how they "walk"—how they manifest their identity in Christ in their behavior.

Why does the author dwell so extensively on aspects of the Christ-event, even aspects that are probably not intended to be transferred into the household sphere? There are strong thematic links in the household code to the rest of the letter: submission under Christ (5:21, 24 // 1:22), the head-body-imagery (5:23, 28–33 // 1:10[532], 22; 4:15–16) Christ's sacrificial death out of love (5:25–27 // 5:2) and sanctification and purification of the group (5:26–27 // 1:4, 2:21) are all themes that have been developed earlier in the letter.[533] All these intratextual thematic cross-references induce the impression that household behavior has to do with the identity in Christ. Many of the references are not intended to translate into household behavior, but only to add to the impression that the household should be understood as an aspect of the identity in Christ. By acting conventionally in the household in the light of the Christ-narrative, Christ-believers fulfill their purpose and become more prototypical.

In addition to the transfer of narrative patterns, the text probably also transfers emotions between the Christ-narrative and the household. The references to the Christ-narrative bring to the fore the emotions that the deeds of Christ are immensely important. As we discussed in chapter 11.2, analogies can transfer not only intellectual patterns but also emotions from one sphere to another. Therefore, when the author mentions how Christ died for the recipients and that their belief in him

---

however, is not only that but also that the author aims to *integrate* household identities into the identity in Christ.

[531] Cf. n. 475 pointing out that οὖν + περιπατέω is used in Ephesians to signal new sections.

[532] Bieringer 2005 argues that in the context of Ephesisans, ἀνακεφαλαιόω in 1:10 may very well be connected to the image of Christ as the head.

[533] Cf. Dawes 1998: 122–194; Osiek and MacDonald 2005: 127–131.

saves them and makes them holy, he creates the emotion that the behavior of Christ is immensely noble. These emotions can then be transferred into the household sphere through the analogies and thus induce a feeling that household morality is a noble aspect of their valuable identity in Christ.

These analogical associative processes are, of course, not very rational and stringent and do not hold up to critical analysis, but nevertheless probably had an intuitive and emotional effect on the recipients. In the words of Leslie Mitton:

> It is true that this is a passage which many have felt to be extremely impressive and it has certainly excercised a considerable influence upon doctrine. But if it is studied in detail, it is found to be lacking in systematic construction and in strong internal connexions. If it is read in public with oratory skill, it can sound most impressive. If it is studied item by item and analysed in detail, it is less satisfactory.[534]

Mitton's critique is by all means correct. It is, however, not very meaningful to accuse the author of logical flaws, as Mitton does, since the rhetorical effort is entirely associative, as I have argued above.

Another feature in 5:21–33, which becomes understandable if the author's main intention is to transform household identities into an aspect of the identity in Christ, is the lack of originality and detail in the practical exhortations. As we discussed above, the author does not argue for anything very particular in practical terms. He repeats conventional norms and does not seem to target any particular intragroup problems. Instead, he puts effort into giving conventional morality new narrative motivations. This is his strategy to expand the applicability of the identity in Christ into new life spheres. When the recipients behave conventionally in the household, they should think of themselves as Christ-believers.

When the author continues to the relation between parents and children (6:1–4), the idea that the household is a subcategory to the identity in Christ is already established. He therefore gives briefer motivations. The short phrases "for the sake of the Lord" (6:1) and

---

[534] Mitton 1981: 210.

"according to the Lord's will" (6:4) signal that these household identities should also be considered to be part of the identity in Christ. The author also narrates the causal rationale to act according to the norms by quoting the promise of long life in the Decalogue (6:2–3; Exod 20:12).

Next, in the passage about the relation between masters and slaves (6:5–9), the rhetoric of analogy returns. Slaves should obey their masters in analogy with their obedience to Christ. Then both slaves and masters are reminded of the narrative about the (future) judgment of God as a motivation to act according to household norms. The masters are reminded that they "have the same Master in Heaven" (6:9) as their slaves; that is, they belong to the same ingroup and will be judged by the same standards. Again, the rhetorical effect is that household identities and household behavior should be seen in the light of their identity in Christ.

The social effect of a successful integration of household identities into the identity in Christ would be that the identity in Christ expands its sphere of salience into everyday life in a very profound way. As we discussed in chapter 9.1, different social situations fit different social identities. The household identities were the most important identities for many people in everyday life and we can, without becoming too speculative, assume that household identities were the identities that were salient for the longest time per day in an average person's life. If household identities are subordinate to the identity in Christ, then the identity in Christ is salient every time a household identity is salient. The identity in Christ is lifted to a hegemonic position in the cognitive setup of any group whose cognition is like that of the author of Ephesians.

The hegemonic position of the identity in Christ would have made it possible to live conventional lives in the midst of non-believing gentiles and yet to have a frame of mind, which made it possible to think of oneself as different and distinct.[535] Carolyn Osiek and Margaret MacDonald argue that this is a defensive strategy, tailored to make the Christ-believers invisible in the surrounding society while they at the same time considered themselves distinct and separate.[536] While

---

535 Cf. Darko 2008: 130–131.

536 Osiek and MacDonald 2005: 122–123.

cognitive separation from the world is certainly an important aspect of the socio-cognitive effect of the household code in Ephesians, it must also be emphasized that it is a form of mental separation, which at the same time enables the group to be present among non-believing gentiles. The household code has no evangelizing ambition, but is nevertheless a necessary condition to remain in interaction with the surrounding society. If the identity as Christ-believers was salient in their household dealings with the surrounding society, this had at least the potential of fulfilling their purpose "that through the *ekklēsia* the wisdom of God in its rich variety might now be made known to the rulers and authorities in the heavenly places" (3:10, NRSV modified, cf. the discussions in chapters 17 and 18.1.3).

We may also consider another social consequence of integration of household identities into the identity in Christ. If we assume an increasing number of households where all or at least most of the household members were Christ-believers in the deutero-Pauline era, then it would have been increasingly awkward to treat household identities and the identity in Christ as separate social identities in the way Paul did.[537] We need not assume the idealized situation depicted in the household code of Ephesians, just that entirely Christ-believing households had an increasing influence over the negotiated consensus of the *ekklēsia*. In such a situation, the author could have utilized the model of the Greco-Roman household cult and made their identity in Christ a sub-category to the household identity. Instead he takes over the Jewish covenant model and makes the household identities subcategories to their identity in Christ, just like the Jewish household was frequently considered a subcategory to the covenant people of Israel.[538] We can reasonably assume that this view of the household resolved some of the ambiguities as to whether the members of entirely Christ-believing households should interact as Christ-believers or as household members in a given situation. The answer is that they should interact as Christ-believing household members in the household.

---

[537] I argue for this historical development in Roitto 2008.

[538] Cf. Josephus, *C. Ap.*, 2.157, 199–201. 2.157 is quoted above in chapter 6.4.

In sum, Ephesians integrates household identities into the identity in Christ and makes them subcategories to the identity in Christ through analogical transfers between the Christ-narrative and the household sphere. Assuming that the recipients accepted the author's rhetoric, the identity in Christ became salient in many everyday life situations.

17.4 The Leadership as a Prototypical Subcategory

The leaders form an exclusive subcategory to the identity in Christ.[539] The author claims a gate-keeper position for the leaders in relation to those who wish to become prototypical.[540] In one long sentence in 4:11–16, we are told about role of the leaders:

> And he [i.e., Christ] gave [that some would be][541]
> apostles,
> prophets,
> evangelists
> and pastors and teachers,
> to (πρός) equip the saints,
> for (εἰς) the work of ministry,
> for (εἰς) building up the body of Christ,[542]

---

539 One could also consider analyzing the leadership as roles in a social network of dyadic relations within the community (see chapter 5.3). However, since the text does not differentiate between unique roles among the leaders, but rather enumerates them together as a collective of leaders and gives them all the same function within the group, it is better to analyze them as a subcategory.

540 I will argue here, together with Gosnell 2000; Shkul 2009: 190–204, that the author aims to position the leaders in a way that makes the recipients dependent on them if they are to become prototypical group members.

541 Lincoln 1990: 249 argues that τοὺς μεν ... τοὺς δὲ simply implies a list of what Christ gave. In the context of 4:7, however, the author might mean that Christ gives the commission of the enumerated ministries to certain individuals, see Hoehner 2002: 540–541.

542 The three tasks, "equip the saints", "work of ministry", "building up the body of Christ" could be interpreted in two ways: All three tasks could be read as referring to the commission of the leaders. Another possibility is that the first task is the commission of the leaders and that the subsequent tasks are the duties of every Christ-believer, which the leaders should "equip" them for. See e.g.

until (μέχρι) all of us come
to the *unity*
of the *faith*
and of the *knowledge* of the Son of God,
to maturity, to the measure of the full stature of Christ.
so that (ἵνα)
we no longer would/should be (subjunctive[543])
children,
tossed to and fro and blown about
by every wind of doctrine,
by people's trickery,
by their craftiness in deceitful scheming
but *speaking the truth* in *love,*
we would/should *grow up* (subjunctive)
in every way into him who is the head, Christ
from whom the whole body,
joined and knit together

Lincoln 1990: 253, who argues for the former position. However, both interpretations are possible.

543 *ἵνα + subjunctive clauses.* ἵνα can introduce both final ("in order that"/"with the purpose of"), consecutive ("so that"/"with the consequence that") and subjective and objective ("to"/"that") dependent clauses in Koine Greek. (Consecutive, subjective and objective usage of ἵνα + subjunctive is absent in Attic Greek but becomes common in Koine Greek.) See Blass and Debrunner 1961:§369, §378, §390-§393; Blomqvist and Jastrup 1996:§296.4. Another, more important, problem with ἵνα + subjunctive is that it is sometimes problematic to discern whether the dependent clause expresses a duty or a consequence. "As a substitute for the imperative ... ἵνα with the subjunctive is occasionally employed", Blass and Debrunner 1961:§387. When we read "so that/ in order that (ἵνα) we would/should no longer be children" (4:14, my translation) or "we are his workmanship, created ... for good works... so that/in order that we would/should walk in them (ἵνα ἐν αὐτοῖς περιπατήσωμεν)" (2:10, my translation), this phrase could either express the belief that a Christ-believer does or a belief that a Christ-believer should. This kind of vague double meaning is, however, not only inherent in the syntactic construct, but also in the perception of the ingroup prototype, as we discussed in chapter 6.1. The prototype both tells the group who they are and who they should be. We should therefore assume that these kinds of linguistic expressions reproduce—willingly or intuitively—the functional duplicity of the ingroup prototype.

by every ligament
with which it is equipped,
as each part is working properly,
promotes the body's *growth*
in *building* itself up in *love*.
(4:11–16, NRSV modified)

The author does not differentiate the commission of the five different ministries he enumerates. Rather, he puts them all in one category, which we may call "the leaders." Apostles and prophets have been mentioned twice earlier in the text. In 2:20 they are the foundation of the *ekklēsia* and in 3:5 they are the mediators of knowledge about the "mystery." They are exemplars of the global Christ-movement with unique access to knowledge. In 4:11, three other leadership titles, probably the local leaders,[544] are associated with the apostles and prophets as they are enumerated in the same category. The rhetorical effect is that the prototypical properties of apostles and prophets are also properties of the local leaders, since they belong to the same category, which gives the impression that they are similar.[545] The local leaders are mediators of divine knowledge, just like their predecessors, the apostles and the prophets.

The leaders are singled out in the context of 4:7–16, which begins with the statement that Christ has given grace to everyone "according to the measure (κατὰ τὸ μέτρον) of the gift of Christ" (4:7). The leaders are not the only ones who have been given gifts and have a task (4:7, 16), but

[544] Ephesians does not reveal much about the details of the local leadership structure so we can only guess that they are *local* leaders. The titles do not match the offices in e.g. 1 Tim. Therefore, we cannot know very much about the content of their commission, except what the titles themselves suggest. εὐαγγελισταί somehow preach the gospel, but we cannot know whether they preach to outsiders or within the group. The context suggests intragroup preaching, but the word itself suggests evangelization directed towards outsiders (cf. chapters 18.1.3 and 19.4.2). If the latter is intended the office may either be local (cf. 2 Tim 4:5) or itinerant (cf. Acts 21:8). ποιμένες and διδάσκαλοι may be closely related, since there is no definite article in front of the latter. ποιμήν suggests a general leadership function and διδάσκαλος suggests a teaching function, see e.g. Lincoln 1990: 250–253.

[545] On perceived intragroup similarity, see chapter 5.2.

different people have been given different amounts of "grace," which should probably be interpreted as different roles within the group. Since Christ, God and the Spirit are depicted as givers of all prototypical characteristics throughout the letter (see chapter 18.3.1), it is reasonable to infer that the author aims to suggest that the leaders have been given more prototypical qualities than other members. This assumption is strengthened by the author's claim that the special gifts of the leaders are intended to help the rest of the group become prototypical (4:12–16). Only someone who embodies the prototype can teach others.

> *Causality:* Christ has given special "gifts" to the leaders → The leaders are particularly prototypical

As we discussed in chapter 8.3, a leader must be thought of as prototypical by the other group members in order to be able to influence others. The author makes an effort here to associate the leaders with prototypicality, both by associating them with the apostles and the prophets and by suggesting that they have been given a greater measure of gifts from Christ. The statements about the leaders' gifts should be seen in contrast to the prayer in 3:14–19, which suggests that the recipients are not yet fully prototypical (cf. the discussion in chapter 15). The leaders are positioned closer to the prototypical center than ordinary group members are.

The author then narrates that the purpose of the leaders is to enhance all kinds of prototypical characteristics in the group: love, knowledge, unity, faith and maturity. (These characteristics have been italicized in the quotation above.) The purpose of the leadership is signaled by "until" (μέχρι) and "so that" (ἵνα) followed by descriptions of increasing prototypicality in the group. We will go through the different prototypical properties in chapter 18.3 below, but for now we can just note that the author narrates a causal connection with the implication that ordinary group members should respect and listen to the leaders:

> *Causality:* The prototypical leaders equip ordinary group members with prototypical charateristics → The group becomes more prototypical → *Duty:* One should accept and follow the teaching of the leaders

Peter Gosnell has analyzed Eph 4:7–16 as an attempt to give the local leaders a position where they can control information.[546] He argues that although the description of false teachings in 4:14 (cf. 5:6) probably does not reflect a particular crisis, there is almost always a continuous inflow of alternative information into any group unless they live in complete isolation. The text is intended to give the leaders a position where they can fend off potential competitors and potential alternative teachings, which could be presented to the group either from within the group or from members of other parts of the Christ-movement. I agree. Alternative teachings are depicted as deviant and destructive and those who teach them are attributed with a will to deceive. As we discussed in chapter 8.2, deviants are often perceived as a threat to the sense of distinction and to the self-esteem of the group and this fear of the deviant can be used rhetorically to marginalize competitors. In Ephesians, anyone who listens to alternative teachings is considered to be immature and unstable, like a child, risking to become as deviant as the teacher to whom he or she listens. The typical reactions towards a deviant is reproach, marginalization and eventually even exclusion (see chapter 8.2). If the leaders and other group members were convinced about the protective function of the leaders, it is reasonable to imagine that the leaders felt obliged and justified to instigate such measures against those who questioned their teaching. In contrast to the threat of becoming deviant by listening to alternative teaching, Ephesians narrates that those who listen to the leaders become prototypical. This is the positive side of the narrative, which promises gain to those who respect the leaders.

Causality: A group member embraces the teaching of the leaders → The member becomes more prototypical

Causality: A group member embraces alternative teachings → The member becomes deviant → *Duty:* The member should be reproached, marginalized or, in a worst case scenario, even excluded

---

[546] Gosnell 2000.

In this way, the author provides a narrative giving the leaders control over what information is reliable. The social effect of this narrative, assuming that the group believed in it, is that the information flow in the group will become more coherent and consequently that cognitive dissonance will decrease.[547] As we discussed in chapter 8.1, group members tend to need affirmation from each other in order to maintain their group beliefs. Especially religious groups, who consider doctrine (narrative truth) to be important, tend to need affirmation that their beliefs are correct. The narrative about the leadership is formulated in a way that gives the leaders moral ground to fend off alternative teachings and thus maintain stronger cognitive conformity within the group. This, in turn, makes it easier for the members to remain committed to the group, since the meaning of the group is experienced as comprehensible and clear (cf. chapter 9.3). As authoritarian as this may be, it was probably an efficient method to maintain cognitive certainty and thereby the sense of meaning, which in turn increased commitment.

[547] Cf. Shkul 2009: 190-206.

18 A Reconstruction of the Ingroup Prototype

We have now outlined the strategy and purpose of Ephesians (chapter 15), explored the narrative rationale of the identity in Christ according to the text (chapter 16) and mapped all the social categories that the author handles within his cognitive universe (chapter 17). We are well prepared to reconstruct the ingroup prototype and ask how it motivates behavior norms and guides group dynamics. Why does it follow from being a Christ-believer to do what Ephesians prescribes? How does the author create a sense that these behaviors are expressions of the identity in Christ?

The method of this chapter is to search the text thematically for expressed causal links between different attributes and behaviors and then analyze these patterns with the help of the theories that were explored in chapters 5 to 11. We should not interpret the result as the sum of the author's entire cognition of the ingroup prototype, since the purpose of Ephesians is not to catalogue every detail of the ingroup ideals. Rather, the author selects certain aspects of his ideals and presents them in a way he hopes will have an impact on his recipients (cf. chapter 15). Therefore, we will not get a complete picture of the author's imagination of the ingroup prototype. Nevertheless, the text is rich enough to give us a fair idea of the major aspects of the author's cognition of the prototype.

With this method we will be able to analyse Ephesians in a new way that allows us to understand better how Ephesians creates a well integrated imagination of the identity in Christ. We will discover a mutally reinforcing relation between the Spirit, attributed characteristics, and behavior that can potentially function both encouraging and judging within the group. We will see how the author encourages behaviors that reinforce the sense of cognitive certainty in the group and discourages behaviors that might cause doubt among group members. We will also see how the attributions are interwoven with the narrative rationale of the group in a way that justifies processes of intra-group status differentiation, inclusion and exclusion. In short, we will have a new understanding of the relation between identity and behavior norms in Ephesians.

18.1 Entrance Criteria: The Necessary Conditions for the Individual's Identity in Christ

We begin by looking at the borders of the identity in Christ according to Ephesians. What seems to be the minimal criteria for being a group member?

Many categories, including social categories, have a number of minimal criteria which must be fulfilled in order for a category member to belong to that category (see chapter 5.1). These minimal criteria do not equal the full ingroup prototype, but are part of it. Being an ideal group member demands more than just being ingroup. Nevertheless, by looking at these minimal criteria, we discover important basic aspects of the category. Therefore we begin our reconstruction of the ingroup prototype of Ephesians with an examination of the minimal entrance criteria for belonging to the group. God's initiative is the primary cause of the ingroup's current position (see chapter 16). However, there are also references to human agency as the cause of the individual's belonging to the group. These glimpses of the narrative about entrance into the group implicitly reveal the border criteria for belonging to the group.

First, a certain amount of *knowledge*, that is, getting to know and learn about Christ (4:20–21), is seen as something which has lead to the recipients' identity in Christ: "After they had heard (ἀκούσαντες) the word of truth" they received ingroup status (1:13).

We can notice that the author ties Paul's agency to their knowledge. It is due to Paul's mission they have achieved the knowledge that they are invited into the community of Christ-believers (3:2, 6–9). Since the implied Paul is presented as the intermediary between God and the recipients in the narrative about how they achieved the knowledge necessary to become part of the group (cf. chapter 18.3.3 below), his credibility is strengthened.

Second, knowledge ideally leads to *faith* (πίστις, "faith, faithfulness, loyalty," cf. the discussion in chapter 18.3.4), which is the most prominent theme in the narrative about the individual's way into the group. In the introduction, having emphasized God's initiative (1:3–11), the author makes use of an aorist participle with the function of temporal order, "after you had come to believe" (πιστεύσαντες, 1:13), to articulate that faith in Christ is a precondition for belonging to the ingroup.[548] The same pattern can be seen in the narrative about how the Christ-event brought salvation in 2:4–8. Having emphasized that they themselves have done nothing to deserve this, he writes at end of the passage that they have been saved "through (διά) faith" (2:8, cf. 3:12, 17).

The relation between God's agency and human agency seems to be modeled on the pattern of asymmetrical reciprocity typical of the patron-client system.[549] The gift of the patron (God) consists of all those things which he can bestow upon the client (the ingroup) in his position of power. All that is demanded of the clients, who could not possibly return equally valuable gifts, is that they are loyal (πιστός) and that they acknowledge the honor (e.g., 1:12) of the patron.[550] In other words, the cultural narrative about the prototypical patron is used analogically to characterize the relation between God's and the Christ-believers' agency (cf. chapter 11.2). Later generations would problematize the relation between human and divine agency, but for the author of Ephesians this is not a problem. God is the powerful patron who has made their identity possible and then it is up to the individuals to become grateful clients who gladly accept the conditions of God's patronage.

Some passing references are also made to *baptism* (4:5, 5:26), which is thought to have a cleansing function which "makes [the *ekklēsia*] holy" (ἁγιάζω, 5:26).

The author does not say anything about the sequential order between knowledge, faith and baptism. However, 1:13 indicates that faith is the initial reaction to having heard the gospel (i.e., getting knowledge).

---

[548] Although the aorist participle does not necessarily denote the past, "the idea of relative past time came to be associated with the aorist participle", cf. Blass and Debrunner 1961: §339.

[549] Cf. n. 447.

[550] Cf. chapter 16 on how God is motivated by his will to get due honor.

Therefore, the author seems to imagine a narrative about the individual's entrance into the group where knowledge leads to faith, which in turn leads to baptism.

Causality: Knowledge → Faith → Baptism → Being in Christ

The letter expresses some quite basic beliefs about what is required in order to belong to the ingroup. A group member has to a) have basic knowledge of the identity and rationale of the group (get to know Christ), b) be committed to God and thus to the group (faith, faithfulness) and c) go through the required rite of initiation (baptism).

Initial knowledge about Christ, faith and baptism are of course parts of the ingroup prototype. They are, however, just minimal conditions for belonging to the group of Christ-believers and not a full description of the ideal Christ-believer. As our discussion in chapter 18.3 will show, these characteristics are not at the center of the rhetoric of the author, but rather just assumed and mentioned in passing in order to make other points. (The theme of knowledge is central to the author, see chapter 18.3.3, but then he talks about deeper knowledge than just initial knowledge about Christ.) We can therefore assume that the conditions for entrance into the group were well established and uncontested in the shared cognition of the author and the recipients at the time of writing.

18.2 Self-Designation as "Holy Ones"

In the prescript of the letter, the recipients are greeted as "the holy ones" or "the Saints" (οἱ ἅγιοι) and as "faithful/believing" (πιστοί) in Christ Jesus" (1:1). Of these two designations, "the holy ones" (1:1, 15, 18; 2:19; 3:5, 8, 18; 4:12; 6:18) occurs much more frequently in the letter than "the faithful/believers" (1:1, 19). "The holy ones" is clearly the preferred ingroup designation and at the core of their identity in Christ according to Ephesians.

Holiness is the quality of the divine, God himself, and therefore a human group who wants to be appropriate for approaching the divine must be holy too.[551] "For I am the LORD your God; sanctify yourselves

[551] E.g. Hoehner 2002: 137–140.

therefore, and be holy, for I am holy" (Lev 11:44). The holiness logic of Leviticus applies to Ephesians too.[552] The recipients of Ephesians should strive to be "created alike God in true righteousness and holiness (ὁσιότης)" (4:24, NRSV modified).[553] God's plan with the ingroup and the Christ-event is both a) to save them and b) to reveal his wisdom through them and in this way achieve glory (see chapter 16). Therefore the ingroup has to be suitable for God and express God's character to the world, that is, they have to be holy.

The first statement about the recipients' identity in the letter is that God has chosen them "to be (εἶναι) holy (ἅγιος) and blameless (ἄμωμος) before him in love" (1:4). "Holy and blameless" occurs again when the author describes the effect of baptism (5:27). The Christ-event together with baptism "sanctifies" (ἁγιάζω) the ingroup so that the *ekklēsia* can be "without a spot or wrinkle or anything of the kind, but that she may be (ἵνα ᾖ) holy and blameless" (5:27, NRSV modified). It is interesting that the author uses ambiguous syntactic constructs in both cases where he makes use of this phrase. In 1:4 he employs an infinitive, which could be understood as both final and consecutive and thus both denote cause and duty: "so that we are," "so that we may be" or "in order that we should be." In 5:27 he uses ἵνα + subjunctive mood, which can also be understood as "so that we are," "so that we may be" or "in order that we should be."[554] These syntactic constructs are as ambiguous as the functions of the identity prototype they describe—both descriptive and prescriptive. As discussed in chapter 6.1, the ingroup prototype of any group holds a tension between indicative and imperative that allows a great flexibility in how it is used within the group. In the case of holiness, the attributed state of holiness is both a) a causal consequence of God having chosen them and b) a duty which

---

[552] Cf. Lyons 2007.

[553] ὁσιότης is similar to ἅγιος, but while ἅγιος is a state before God, ὁσιότης is a virtue, a disposition to piety. See Hoehner 2002: 612; Lincoln 1990: 288.

[554] See discussion in nn. 473 and 543. Many scholars ignore the possibility that these phrases are intended to be vague and open to double interpretations and deem εἶναι in 1:4 to be an infinitive of purpose and ἵνα ᾖ in 5:27 to be a ἵνα-clause of purpose, e.g. Hoehner 2002: 178, 760; Jeal 2000: 86; Schnackenburg 1982: 44.

follows from being chosen by God. In the following, we will discuss how this tension might have created group dynamic effects.

Causality/duty: In Christ → Holy, blameless

Holiness and behavior. Holiness is a *state* before God more than a *disposition*. The Christ-believers are (or should be) "holy and blameless *before him* [i.e., God]" (1:4). As we discussed in chapter 6, attributed dispositions are often considered to cause behavior. Holiness, however, is a state rather than a disposition. We should therefore not assume that holiness is considered to *cause* behavior in the same way as the attributed character traits power, knowledge, love, faith and righteousness, which we will discuss below. Nevertheless, "holy and blameless" is modified with "in/through (ἐν) love" in 1:4, which tells us that the author associates holiness with the disposition love. We should interpret the preposition ἐν as signaling instrument or quality,[555] which

[555] *ἐν*. The preposition ἐν is the favorite preposition of Ephesians, occurring no less than 122 times. It has a wide range of usages, but for the discussion about causality we should concentrate on cases where ἐν could be considered to express a causal belief. The problem is that ἐν can often be interpreted as expressing both instrument and agency ("through/by"); place and sphere ("in (the sphere of)") and manner and quality ("as characterized by"), see Blass and Debrunner 1961: §218–219. Sometimes ἐν is used together with a spiritual agent, the Spirit or Christ. "In Christ" (ἐν Χριστῷ) frequently denotes the spiritual sphere in which the Christ-believers are, but it can at the same time be interpreted as having an instrumental sense; for example, they have been given grace "in/through (ἐν) the beloved one" (1:6). Throughout the letter, the Spirit is seen as the agent who gives them power, knowledge, etc. Whenever we have the expression "in/through (ἐν) the Spirit" (2:18, 22; 3:5; 4:30; 5:18; 6:18) it is therefore generally wise to assume that the author uses ἐν to articulate that the Spirit is an agent. The imagination to be in the sphere of a spiritual agent often holds a causal belief in itself, as was discussed in chapter 6.4. We should therefore see no contradiction between a local and an instrumental understanding of ἐν, since both make sense only if we assume the belief that spiritual agents cause things to those who are in their sphere. ἐν is also used together with various attributed character traits, most frequently together with "love" in the phrase "in love" (ἐν αγάπῃ, 1:4; 3:17; 4:2, 15–16, 5:2). In these instances we can either understand the phrase to mean "caused by the character trait of love" or "characterized by the

would mean that the author thinks love causes holiness or at least that without love there is no holiness. Love and holiness are also associated in 5:1–6.[556] God grants the status of holiness to those who love, but not to those who lack love.

Causality: Love → Holiness

Being holy is connected directly to practical behavior norms in 5:1–6. There it is stated that "it is becoming for holy ones" (πρέπει ἁγίοις) to avoid "fornication" (πορνεία), "impurity" (ἀκαθαρσία), and "greed" (πλεονεξία) (5:3). Further, "it is not proper" (οὐκ ἀνῆκεν) with "shameful [speech] behavior" (αἰσχρότης), "foolish talk" (μωρολογία) and "sarcasm" (εὐτραπελία[557])" (5:4). Then fornication, impurity and greed is repeated and greed is equated with being an "idolater" (εἰδωλολάτρης, 5:5). The enumerations in 5:3–5 hold both behavior (fornication, shameful behavior, foolish talk, sarcasm, idolatry) and vices (impurity, greed). MacDonald points out that what comes in and out of the mouth is a frequent purity concern in Jewish tradition and that this sometimes also includes the words that come out of the mouth.[558] It is therefore not surprising that speech—words that come out of the mouth—are associated with impurity and are therefore seen as opposed to holiness.

---

quality of love." The second sense does not formally have a causal meaning, but only makes sense if we assume that the author believes that virtues, such as love, are what cause people to act. Therefore both interpretations of the meaning of ἐν hold a causal belief that love causes people to act in the cases where "in love" qualifies a behavior. However, sometimes the phrase qualifies other attributed character traits; for instance, "holy and unblemished in love." In these cases it is preferable to leave open the possibility that the author uses ἐν in the qualitative sense, since he understands love as the overarching super-virtue which defines the other characteristics.

[556] Cf. n. 475.

[557] εὐτραπελία, "sarcasm" had the positive connotation of "wittiness" in Attic Greek, but here holds the connotation of humor that works in negative ways, see Hoehner 2002: 655–656.

[558] MacDonald 2000: 308, 311–312.

The author claims, without further explanation, that there is a correlation between belonging to the category of holy ones and not behaving in certain ways. Far from functional arguments about good or bad consequences certain behaviors may have, the argument is simply that these behaviors and vices are not fitting for someone who is holy, that is, they indicate that one is not prototypical. Certain dispositions and behaviors are necessary in order to remain holy, but holiness does not necessarily cause these characteristics. However, when we discuss the group dynamic effect of this correlation, we can still assume that group members can *attribute* the status of holiness or impurity to each other depending on how they see each other behave, just like they attribute dispositions. Since holiness, just like many other attributed characteristics, is morally loaded, people will be able to claim and give ingroup status as prototypical holy group members, depending on behavior.

> *Causality:* No impurity or greed → Holy
>
> *Attribution:* No fornication, idolatry, shameful (speech) behavior, foolish talk or sarcasm → Holy → *Duty:* Give status and appreciation to those who avoid these behaviors.

The argument is framed a) by the admonition to become "imitators" of God (5:1), an analogy argument (see chapter 11.2) which makes God himself, the holy one, their ultimate exemplar, and b) by a threat that these behaviors will cause God's wrath and exclusion from the kingdom of God and Christ (5:5–6). The argument about what is fitting thus appeals to the basic rationale of the group—being God's favored clients (cf. chapter 16). In other words, the implicit agent who gives and takes away the status of holiness is God.

Holy behavior, distinction from the gentiles and marginalization of deviants. In chapter 17.1.2 we discussed how the deviant behaviors in 5:1–6 are very similar to the description of the gentiles in 4:17–24. A group tends to form its identity in relation to outgroups in a way which maximizes the distinctiveness and self-esteem of the ingroup (see chapters 7.1 and 7.2). Deviant behavior that obscures the distinction between ingroup and outgroup is usually less tolerated than other deviances (see chapter 8.2).

By associating certain behaviors with the outgroup, the author makes them more intolerable than they would otherwise have been and thus justifies reproach, marginalization and perhaps even exclusion of those who behave in this way. As one might expect, the author threatens those who behave in a deviant manner with exclusion (5:5–6) and concludes with the advice that the ingroup members should "have no association with them [i.e., the deviants]" (5:7).

> *Causality:* Fornication, shameful behavior, foolish talk or sarcasm → Not holy → *Duty:* Reproach, marginalize and, if nothing else helps, exclude those who practice these behaviors from the *ekklēsia*

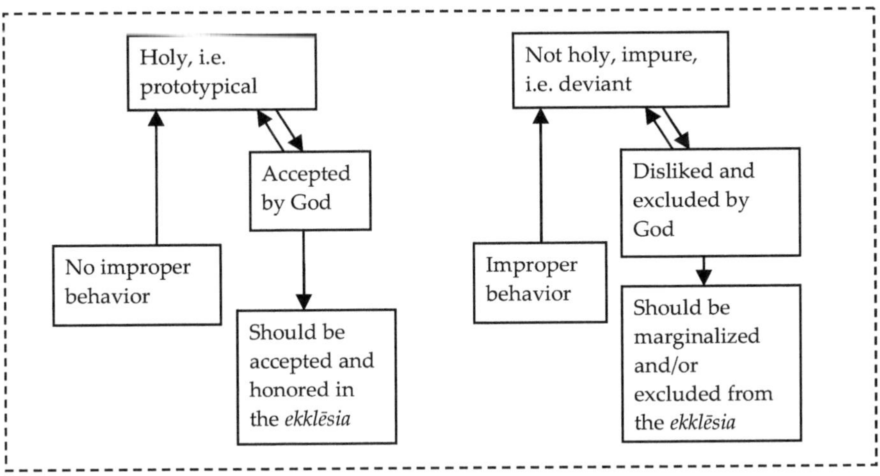

In short, by looking at behavior one can attribute holiness or impurity to members and thus draw conclusions about whether one should honor them or reproach and marginalize, perhaps even exclude them. The identity as holy can therefore motivate people to behave according to group norms in order to achieve the status of holiness in the eyes of oneself, of the group and of God. Regarding exclusion, Ephesians does not give us reason to believe that the group excluded deviant members very frequently. In many groups, exclusion is a possible end station in unresolvable conflicts within a group (see chapter 8.2). The possibility of exclusion, of not having "any inheritance in the kingdom of Christ and of God" (5:5), lurks as a threatening possibility in the cognitive world of

Ephesians. However, exclusion was probably more effective as a potential threat than as a real event in motivating conduct. Normally, the positive effects—status within the group and in the face of God, a positive self-image—were probably more important motivators.

Summary. Being holy is a central ingroup designation and an attribute which is closely associated with the narrative about a privileged position before God. Holiness equals being fitting for and accepted by God. Because of their privileged position, the Christ-believers should behave accordingly in order to remain in this position. Holiness is therefore an attribute which motivates both behaviors and the social dynamics of giving status and marginalization, inclusion and exclusion. Moreover, holy behaviors are contrasted with the behavior of the gentiles, their major outgroup, which further motivates proper behavior and also increases the self-esteem and distinctiveness of the group. The narrative about their holiness thus has a wide range of psychological and group dynamic effects (cf. chapter 10).

18.3 Ingroup Attributes and the Behavior Norms Associated with Them

Having explored the minimal criteria for belonging to the group and the group's self-designation as holy ones, it is now time to explore the attributed character traits of the prototypical Christ-believer and the behaviors associated with these traits. As we discussed in chapter 6.1, the ingroup prototype is typically characterized by an attributed and a visible behavioral side where the attributes are believed to cause the behavior. We also saw that there was typically a tension between indicative and imperative, causality and duty, in these attributions. This tension was necessary, since the ingroup prototype could have a great variety of psychological and group dynamic functions (see the summary in chapter 10). In the analysis of Ephesians we will discover an intricate network of attributions and causal beliefs that has the potential to guide group dynamics in many different ways.

18.3.1 The Spirit

In Ephesians the Spirit is believed to be an agent who causes character traits and behavior. God may (potentially) "grant that you may be strengthened (κραταιόω) in your inner being with power (δύναμις) through his Spirit (διὰ τοῦ πνεύματος αὐτοῦ)" (3:16). In chapter 6.4 we explored the cultural pattern in the ancient Mediterranean world to attribute the cause of virtue and action to spiritual agents (gods, angels, demons, etc.). The letter to the Ephesians shares the imagination of for instance Paul, Philo and Epictetus (see subsection b2 in chapter 6.4) that the divine agent inspires morality from inside the minds and bodies of the believer. In our exploration of this kind of imagination we concluded that the tension between indicative and imperative was effective in inspiring and judging behavior and in guiding group dynamics. In this section we will explore how the author imagines that the empowering Spirit is or should be the cause of both behavior and virtue.

Having the Spirit is a central part of the attributed side of the ingroup prototype. The recipients have been "sealed" with the Holy Spirit (1:13–14). "Through/in (ἐν) one Spirit" the Christ-believers have access to God (2:18). The author emphasizes that the Spirit is one (2:18; 4:3–4), so we should assume that the author refers to one and the same spirit, whether the label of the Spirit is "the holy Spirit" (1:13; 4:30), "the Spirit of wisdom and revelation" (1:17), or simply "the Spirit" (2:18, 22; 3:5, 16; 4:3–4; 5:18; 6:17–18).[559]

---

[559] A possible exception is the phrase "be renewed regarding the Spirit of the mind" (ἀνανεοῦσθαι ... τῷ πνεύματι τοῦ νοός) in 4:23, where "the Spirit" might refer either to the human spirit or to the divine Spirit. Since Ephesians refers to extra-human spiritual agents in all other cases where πηεῦμα is mentioned and since the Spirit is thought to empower the "inner man" (3:16), there is reason to think that the phrase refers to the divine Spirit, see Schnackenburg 1982: 204. However, since the Spirit is nowhere else referred to as "of your mind" but rather as "of God", etc., (Rom 8:9) and since the phrase occurs in a context where the recipients are exhorted to "put on the new man" (4:24), there is also reason to consider the phrase to be a reference to the spirit of man, see Lincoln 1990: 286–287. However, although the reference is unclear, it is clear that any renewal of the spirit of man is considered to occur through the

Prayer for the Spirit. The implied Paul reports twice in Ephesians that he prays for the recipient (1:16–19a; 3:14-19, cf. discussion in chapter 15). These two prayers are key elements in our understanding of the ingroup prototype, particularly the role of the Spirit. As I suggested in chapter 15, these prayers introduce the attributed character traits which are considered to be most central to the ingroup prototype. We will therefore begin our investigation of the imagination of the Spirit with a discussion about the structure of these prayers and what causal beliefs they express.

The first prayer report in 1:16–19a has the following structure:

I do not cease to give thanks … in my prayers… (1:16)
  that (ἵνα) God … will give you (1:17a)
    the Spirit[560] of wisdom and revelation (1:17b)
      in/through/regarding (ἐν) knowledge of him (1:17c)
  so that you
    - [since you have] the eyes of your hearts enlightened -
  may know (εἰς τὸ εἰδέναι)… (1:18b)
    what is … the inheritance … (1:18c)
    and what is … his power toward us … (1:19a)
(my translation)

The genitive construct "the Spirit of wisdom…" indicates that the Spirit causes knowledge in those under its influence.[561] The prepositional

---

agency of the divine Spirit (3:16; 6:18), see Arnold 1989: 88–89; Hoehner 2002: 608–609.

[560] I agree with Fee 1994: 674–676 that it makes more sense to interpret πνεῦμα σοφίας καὶ ἀποκαλύψεως as the divine Spirit than as the human spirit, in spite of the absence of a definite article. A Spirit "of revelation" most probably refers to the divine Spirit. Cf. πνεύματι Θεοῦ without definite article in Rom 8:14 and πνεῦμα τοῦ Θεοῦ πνεῦμα σοφίας (etc.) without definite article in Isa 11:2, LXX.

[561] The author of Ephesians is infamous for his love of genitive constructs. These constructs are often imprecise and aim more at aesthetical effect than pedagogical clarity. There is no such thing as final or consecutive genitive, but nevertheless many kinds of genitive constructs presuppose a causal belief. For example, qualitative genitives express the quality of something, and sometimes

phrase "in/through (ἐν) knowledge" could either signal that knowledge is an *instrument* to get the Spirit or the *sphere* of knowledge.[562] While both are possible, the former possibility is intriguing, since it would indicate a mutually reinforcing causal chain between the Spirit and knowledge, where knowledge renders the Spirit and the Spirit gives knowledge. The perfect tense of the participle "enlightened" (πεφωτίσμενος) also suggests that a certain amount of knowledge is a precondition for the "the Spirit of wisdom," if we assume that it refers to enlightenment that preceded the entire prayer. [563] Again, knowledge gives the Spirit, which in turn gives more knowledge. (This will be discussed further in chapter 18.3.1.) The consecutive infinitive "so that you may know (εἰς τὸ εἰδέναι) ..." indicates that the Spirit causes insight into a) the group's privileged position and b) that God gives them power. The center of the prayer is increased knowledge, which fits the rhetorical agenda of the author. As I argued in chapter 15, the prayer for knowledge prepares for

---

this quality is causal. The phrase "the unity of the Spirit" (ἑνότης τοῦ πνεύματος, 4:3) may be understood as "the unity which is characterized by the Spirit," that is, the Spirit has some kind of influence which causes unity.

562 See the discussion about ἐν in n. 555.

563 πεφωτισμένους τοὺς ὀφθαλμούς ... (1:18a) floats free between the ἵνα-phrase in 1:17 and the εἰς τὸ-phrase in 1:18b. The phrase could therefore be interpreted in many ways, see Hoehner 2002: 261–262 for an overview. It could be seen a) as referring back to δώῃ, ὑμῖν or πνεῦμα in 1:17, b) as a circumstantial participle, c) as an absolute accusative, or d) as referring forward to ὑμᾶς. Hoehner prefers c) in spite of absolute accusatives being rare in Koine Greek. However, Hoehner ignores the fact that accusative absolute is almost always neuter (not masculine) and singular (not plural), see Blomqvist and Jastrup 1996: §278. Even more problematic is the interpretation of Lincoln 1990: 46–47 that it is a description of ὑμῖν that has been influenced by the following ὑμᾶς and thus changed case from dative to accusative. The grammatically least problematic solution is d), that it is a description of ὑμᾶς. It has, however, probably been placed before εἰς τὸ in order to form a bridge between the first and the second half of the prayer. This solution also makes the phrase functionally analogous to the perfect participle "rooted and founded in love" (3:17) in the second prayer in Ephesians (see discussion in n. 564 below). The perfect tense suggests that the entire phrase is a prerequisite to either the entire prayer or the second half of the prayer.

the presentation of knowledge in chapter 2 of Ephesians. We will return to the connection between the Spirit and knowledge below, but for now we summarize the causal beliefs that the prayer expresses:

> *Causality:* Prayer + Spirit (+ Previous knowledge) → Knowledge about God → Knowledge about ingroup value and empowerment

The second prayer report in 3:14–19 is structured like this:

I bow my knees to the father … (3:14–15)
a. that (ἵνα) he will give you … (3:16a)
b1. to be strengthened (infinitive) … (3:16b)
through (διά) the Spirit …(3:16c)
b2. so that Christ dwells (infinitive) (3:17a)
through (διά) faith … (3:17b)
c. [in order that you may become (ἵνα ἦτε)]
rooted and founded in love (3:17c)
a′. in order that (ἵνα)
[having become rooted and founded in love]
you will be strong/able (3:18a)
b1′. to comprehend (infinitive)… (3:18b)
what is the breadth and the height … (3:18c)
b2.′ so that [you] know (infinitive) … (3:19a)
the love of Christ (3:19b)
c′. in order that (ἵνα) you will be filled … (3:19c)
(my translation)

In short, the imagination of the prayer is as follows: God gives (*a*) power by means of the Spirit (*b1*) (i.e., the Spirit causes power). This causes Christ to dwell in them (*b2*), which causes them to be founded in love (*c*). To be founded in love (*c*) is necessary if they are to have the capacity (*a′*) to comprehend (*b1′*), which causes them to know the love of Christ (*b2′*). As the final result of the process imagined in the prayer they will become filled with the fullness of God, that is, fully prototypical (*c′*).[564]

[564] The prayer is built around two ἵνα-clauses (*a, a′*) with two infinitive clauses under each ἵνα-clause (*b1, b2, b1′, b2′*), followed by a third ἵνα-clause (*c′*). *c′* might be seen as a summarizing request, depicting the result of the first two ἵνα-clauses (*a, a′*), see g.g. Arnold 1989: 86–87; Hoehner 2002: 490;

Schnackenburg 1982: 147. The infinitives under the first two ἵνα-clauses could either be seen as parallel (*b1* parallels *b2*, *b1'* parallels *b2'*) or sequential (*b1* causes *b2*, *b1'* causes *b2'*). Although there is really no way of knowing what the author intended, I will treat them as sequential, that is, as expressing a causal relationship. We have the same problem with the relation between *a* and *a'*, which too could be both parallel and sequential. I will treat them as sequential as well, since the difficult phrase *c* seems to serve a connective function between the first and the second half of the prayer. There is also a shift from God's initiative in *a* to human response in *a'*, which indicates that *a'* should be seen as the effect of *a*.

The phrase in *c and a*, "in/through love rooted and founded" (ἐν ἀγάπῃ ἐρριζωμένοι καὶ τεθεμελιωμένοι), has puzzled commentators. "Rooted and founded" are perfect participles, referring to something which is completed. Furthermore, as the participles are in the plural, they cannot describe God, who is the giving subject in *a*. Rather, they must describe the recipients. Since the phrase is written in the nominative case, it should, if grammatically correct, refer to something which is either a subject or a nominal predicative. It is grammatically least problematic to see the phrase as an introduction to the second ἵνα-clause, *a'*, rendering the translation "in order that (ἵνα), being rooted and founded in love, you may…", see Hoehner 2002: 482–484. This solution is grammatically correct, but frankly aesthetically disruptive in an otherwise quite symmetrically built prayer, unless the author has a good reason to do so. Why would the author want to obscure his structure of ἵνα-clauses and infinitive clauses in *a* and *a'* by putting a lengthy nominal phrase (*c*) before the ἵνα in *a'*? Another solution is that the phrase in *c* is a prayer-wish parallel to the two previous infinitive clauses (*b1, b2*), see Lincoln 1990: 197. This is possible, but confusing when the two first sub-clauses to a are infinitives and since the solution destroys the symmetry between *a* and *a'*. A third solution is that the phrase is an irregular nominative, referring to the subjects in *b1* and *b2*, and therefore should be seen as the result of the two preceding infinitive clauses (*c* is the result of *b1* and *b2*, and thus the result of *a*), see Arnold 1989: 87; Caragounis 1977: 75. The phrase in *c* would then become parallel to the ἵνα-clause in *c'* in the manner sketched above and the prayer would have a symmetrical structure. The weakness of this solution is that the participles in *c* are in the perfect, that is, expressing something already completed, which seems somewhat strange if they are supposed to express a future result, see Hoehner 2002: 483. I would like to propose that a combination of the first and the third solution is the best. Just in order to show the symmetry with the ἵνα-clause in *c'*, I have extrapolated ἵνα ἦτε in the structure above, which would make the phrase a nominal predicative.

Causality: Paul prays + Spirit → God gives → Power → Christ in them → Love → Capacity (i.e., power) → (Knowledge of) love → Filled (i.e., perfected and prototypical)

This prayer links many of the most fundamental attributed character traits of the ingroup prototype in a mutually reinforcing network of causality, revealing a belief in a dynamic interplay between the Spirit, power, knowledge, love and being in Christ, where these elements can potentially strengthen each other (and manifest in behavior).[565] This prayer, together with the first prayer, will therefore be most important in our discussion below.

The believer can be more or less influenced by the Spirit. The author's imagination is not just a static belief that the Spirit works in those who are Christ-believers. Although the letter starts with a declaration that "in Christ" (1:10) they have the Spirit (1:13–14), the implied author's next step is to pray that God "may give them the Spirit of wisdom and revelation" (1:17). They should be "renewed" in the Spirit (4:23). The message is clear enough: although they have the Spirit, they do not yet have it fully.

Those who have to faith in Christ receive the Spirit (1:13–14) and are "a dwelling-place for God through/in (ἐν) the Spirit" (2:22, my translation). The preposition ἐν in 2:22 could denote both causality and position.[566] If we assume that it denotes causality, then the Spirit somehow causes them to become a dwelling-place for God. In the prayer in 3:16–17 we find a parallel chain of thought, where the author prays that they may be empowered "through the Spirit" (διὰ τοῦ πνεύματος) so that "Christ may live in your hearts through faith" (cf. discussion

---

Surely, *c* should be linked grammatically with *a′*, but the reason for the author to put *c* before the ἵνα in *a′* is that he sees *c* as a bridge between *a* and *a′*. The solution is then to see *c* as both the result of *a* and as a precondition for *a′*. The phrase in *c* should then be translated twice: "[*a*] may God give … [*c*] in order that you become rooted and founded in love, [*a′*] so that, [*c*] having been rooted and founded in love, [a′] you will be able …"

[565] Cf. chapter 6.2.

[566] See n. 555.

above). The phrase "through the Spirit" suggests that the Spirit is God's agent, who causes them to become empowered, which consequently causes Christ to live in them.[567] The expressions "in Christ," "dwelling place for God" (2:22), and "Christ lives in your hearts" (3:17) basically refer to the same belief—the spiritual closeness between God/Christ and the ingroup. If we put all these observations together, we discover a mutually reinforcing (circular) chain of causality in the cognition of the author, where being in Christ means having the Spirit, which empowers the believer, which, in turn, causes the Christ-believer to be even closer to Christ:

> *Mutually reinforcing causality:* In Christ → Has the Spirit → Empowered by the Spirit → God/Christ being in you (which equals being in Christ) even more

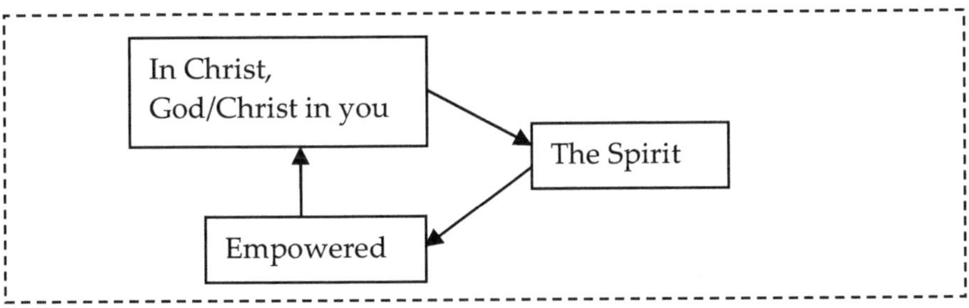

We should not assume that this circular thinking is somehow flawed, but rather interpret the circularity as a mutually reinforcing spiral. The

---

[567] The parallel phrase "through faithfulness" (διὰ τῆς πίστεως) in 3:17 may also be read a causal middle step between the empowerment and Christ living in them, parallel to how διά functions in 3:16. The causal belief expressed in 3:17 would then be that the Spirit gives them powers, which strengthen their faithfulness, which in turn renders Christ to live in them. The alternative that faithfulness should be understood as something which is a prerequisite and works synchronically with the Spirit is, however, more reasonable, since Ephesians does not consider faithfulness to be something which should grow (see chapter 18.3.4 below) but rather as something which is a trait of a Christ-believer from the very beginning (1:13, see chapter 18.1 above), cf. Arnold 1989: 89.

author imagines that the state of being in Christ is in need of continuous renewal and growth. Although they are in Christ, they are not yet in a state where they are "filled with all the fullness of God" (3:19). Clinton Arnold recognizes the tension between "already" and "not yet" in this imagination, but does not discuss the social implication of such imagination.[568] The implication is of course that the ingroup members must never just sit back and relax, but must continue to live in a way which causes this reinforcing circle to continue. Although the recipients are already in Christ and have the Spirit, the process is still incomplete and they still need to "walk worthy of the calling to which you were called" (4:1) if they want to remain in Christ and take part of his power. (The power theme will be explored further in chapter 18.3.2.) Such an imagination inspires prototypical behavior.

The mutual interaction between behavior, emotions and spiritual influence. The Spirit is considered to inspire behavior in Ephesians. The most straightforward passage is the long sentence in 5:18–24.[569] The sentence begins with an exhortation to "be filled with the Spirit" followed by a number of participles referring to prototypical behavior:

> ...but be filled with the Spirit,
> singing psalms and hymns and spiritual songs among yourselves,
> singing and
> making melody to the Lord in your hearts,
> giving thanks to God the Father at all times and for everything...
> subjecting to one another out of reverence for Christ...
> (5:18b-21, NRSV modified)

The author clearly believes that the Spirit inspires these behaviors (which will be further discussed in chapter 18.4.2.) However, we should not assume that the author thinks the inspiration is automatic and infallible. The participle construct is vague and could also be interpreted in the opposite way—that the behaviors are the means by which one becomes filled with the Spirit. We may even suspect that the vague participle construct is intended, since—as we shall see below—the

[568] Arnold 1989: 97.

[569] Cf. Darko 2008: 83–85.

author seems to imagine a mutual causal relationship between the Spirit and behavior.

Since the author thinks of influence from the Spirit as a process, it is not surprising that he thinks there are behaviors and emotions which give "the Devil a place/chance (τόπος)" (4:27) and "grieves the Holy Spirit" (4:30). 4:25–32 has a loose but repetitive structure:

a. Speech behaviors—exhortation to speak the truth (4:25)
b. Emotions and spiritual hazard—excessive anger gives the Devil a chance (4:26–27)
c. Intragroup care—stealing versus helping the needy (4:28)
a′. Speech behaviors—corrupt words versus building up (4:29)
b′. Emotions and spiritual hazard—emotional outbursts grieve the Spirit (4:30–31)
c′. Intragroup care—kindness and forgiving (4:32)

Both in b and b′, emotions are associated with spiritual influence. If one feels destructive emotions, there is a danger that one behaves improperly and thus loses the Spirit and instead becomes influenced by the Devil. The different elements in the sentence in 4:26–27 are loosely interconnected.[570] Literally, the text says "Be angry (ὀργίζω) and do not sin (ἁμαρτάνω)!—the sun should not set on your excessive anger (παροργισμός)!—and do not give the Devil a place/chance!" The sentence does not specify the relation between anger, sin and influence from the Devil. However, it is reasonable to assume the author believes that controlled anger is allowed, but not prolonged excessive anger that leads to sin and strife (cf. 4:31). Somehow, this lets the Devil influence the Christ-believer (and perhaps also the whole group). As discussed in chapter 6.3, anger was considered the worst of all emotions by Stoics such as Seneca, while others, such as Aristotle believed that a controlled amount of anger was intrinsic to the virtue of courage. The author of Ephesians seems to be closer to Aristotle, as he thinks that a certain amount of anger is acceptable, perhaps even appropriate, but that too much anger can lead to sin. The reason for thinking that excessive anger

[570] E.g. Hoehner 2002: 618–623.

might lead to sin is probably that it can lead to loss of self-control. Elsewhere the author urges them not to "get drunk with wine, in which is dissipation (ἀσωτία), but be filled in Spirit" (5:18). In this passage, the author sees an opposition between the Spirit and "dissipation/incorrigibility" (ἀσωτία), the tendency for destructive life without self-control.[571] In sum, Ephesians expresses a conviction that excessive and prolonged emotions will lead to sin:

Causality: Excessive prolonged emotions → Sin

Three verses after 4:26–27 the author warns them not to "grieve the Holy Spirit of God, with which you were marked with a seal for the day of redemption" (4:30). By mentioning the seal and the day of redemption, the author alludes to the eulogy in the introduction of the letter where it is stated that the Spirit is their seal (1:13–14), that is, their guarantee to be saved. The recipients are thus indirectly told that there is a potential risk to lose the seal, of being excluded from the ingroup and the salvation, if they do not behave properly. (Indeed, there is a risk that the entire group comes under the influence of the Devil if some behave wrongly.) It is not clear if it is the speech behaviors in 4:29, the emotions in 4:31 or perhaps every negative behavior and emotion mentioned in 4:25–32 which grieve the Spirit.[572] The καί in the beginning of 4:30 points back to the speech behavior in 4:29, but since destructive emotions give the Devil a chance in 4:27, there is reason to think that the grief of the Spirit is also associated with the emotions in 4:31. Deeming from the general impression of the letter where the author preaches that the recipients should be holy and blameless, it would be reasonable to assume that the author thinks any kind of improper behavior or emotion grieves the Spirit.

In 4:31 the author enumerates three aggressive emotions, "bitterness (πικρία) and wrath (θυμός) and anger (ὀργή)" followed by two speech behaviors, "screaming (κραυγή) and malice/slander (βλασφημία)," which are probably considered to be the effect of the emotions. The passage is parallel to 4:27, where sin is seen as the effect of excessive

[571] Hoehner 2002: 701.

[572] Lincoln 1990: 307.

anger. Only in 4:31 and in 1:13—the two places where the Spirit is described as a seal—is the Spirit described with the epithet "holy." The function of "holy" is perhaps to suggest that the believer can become impure through excessive emotions, that is, improper for God, and this is what grieves the Spirit.[573]

In sum, the author believes that improper behavior, inaugurated by emotions, can remove the Spirit as the inspiring spiritual agent and give "place" (τόπος) for the Devil as the inspiring spiritual agent (cf. Matt 12:43–45). The positive reinforcing circle of causality sketched above can be broken: people have to act according to ingroup norms and avoid deviance in order to remain under the influence of the Spirit.

> *Causality:* Improper behavior and emotions → The Spirit is grieved → The Spirit potentially leaves → The "seal," that is, the status before God is lost + The Devil gets a place → *Attribution:* No longer holy and under the Spirit → *Duty:* Should be reproached, marginalized and as a last resort, excluded

This imagination that the character of man—virtues, spiritual status, and so on—can only stay intact if one behaves accordingly is in no way unique to Ephesians. On the contrary, it was quite a common understanding of the relation between behavior and attributed traits. Both the wisdom tradition and the Greco-Roman philosophical traditions frequently exhorted people to reinforce their virtue through their daily conduct, as we have already discussed in chapter 6.3. The Pharisees (as described by Josephus), Paul, Philo and Epictetus all express views that do not resolve the tension between human moral choice and spiritual influence, just like Ephesians (see chapter 6.4). This broader pattern, in turn, fits well into the inherent tension between indicative and imperative that seems to exist in all prototypes (see chapter 6.1). The Christ-believer both do and should be influenced by the Spirit in his or her behavior. The imagination of the spiritual dynamics of a Christ-believer in Ephesians could be sketched like this:

---

573 Elsewhere the author says that certain impure behaviors are improper for holy ones and lead to being outside the kingdom (5:1–6, see chapter 18.2).

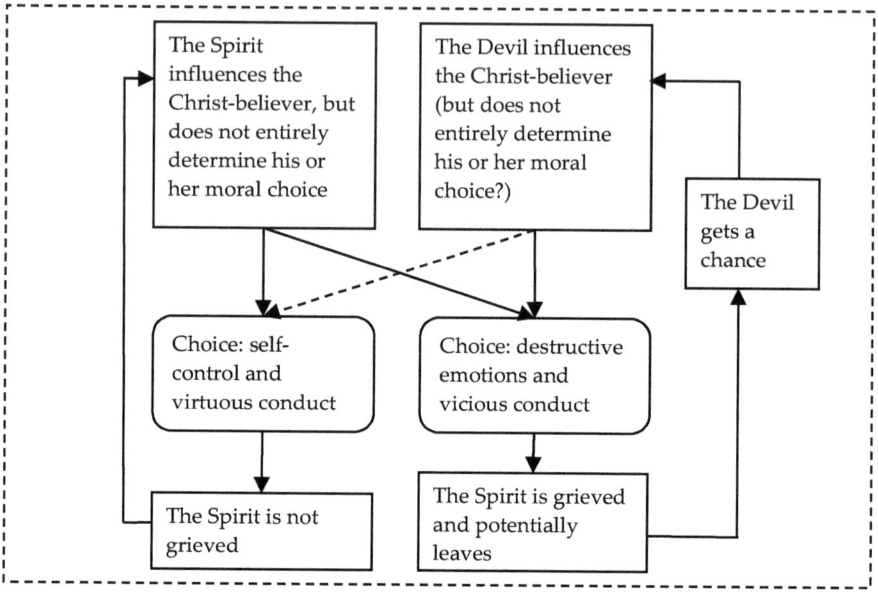

In the chart above I have chosen to draw a dashed causal arrow from the influence of the Devil to virtuous moral conduct, since Ephesians does not express explicitly that a Christ-believer who has gone partially astray in his/her moral conduct could come back under the influence of the Spirit. But if we allow ourselves a bit of historical speculation, it is quite reasonable to imagine that ingroup members who were accused of a conduct that gave the Devil a chance thought that they could gradually improve their spiritual status and come back under the influence of the Spirit, for instance by prayer, by repentance and by improving their character and moral conduct (cf. chapters 6.3 and 6.4). (The scheme is only valid for a Christ-believer. For a person who does not belong to the group, moral conduct is considered impossible in Ephesians, since that person is so strongly under the influence of evil spirits that only belief in Christ can help; cf. chapter 17.1 and the discussion below.)

This imagination has obvious group dynamic effects, if we assume that it became the shared cognition of a group of Christ-believers. The group members would then believe that one can draw conclusions about people's spiritual status from their visible behavior. Such a belief certainly has the potential to function in the social dynamics of the ingroup to regulate behavior (see chapter 6.1). The individual, who is motivated to avoid cognitive dissonance between behavior and his/her spiritual standing, would make an effort to behave in a way that allows him or her to think of him-/herself as someone under the influence of the Spirit. The imagination is encouraging, since it promises continued and perhaps even deepened presence of the Sprit for those who behave according to group norms. It is also demanding, perhaps even frightening, since the Spirit might leave those who do not behave properly. In the group, people would feel justified to make judgments about prototypicality and deviance; status and marginalization; inclusion and exclusion, based on other group members' behavior. (Cf. the social patterns which we discussed in relation to holiness in chapter 18.2) These social processes could most likely be both encouraging (5:18-24) and condemning (4:25-32), depending on the situation.

The Spirit and ingroup distinctiveness. Having the Spirit also distinguishes the ingroup from the outgroup. Those who do not belong to the ingroup, "the children of disobedience," are characterized by being under the influence of evil spiritual forces (2:2). These evil spirits also influenced the recipients in their past (2:2), but thanks to Christ they can now be under the same positive spiritual influence as the first Jewish holy ones (2:18). The ingroup is at war with these evil spiritual forces (6:10–18). Their weapon in this war is "the sword of the Spirit" (6:17) and they become empowered for this battle "in/through the Lord" (6:10). This imagination of different spiritual domains creates a sense of cognitive distinctiveness and positive self-evaluation in relation to the outgroup (see chapters 7.1, 7.2 and 17.1.2).

> *Causality:* Belonging to the ingroup → Under the influence of the Holy Spirit

> *Causality:* Belonging to the outgroup → Under the influence of evil spiritual agents

What social situation might be the background of this dichotomous imagination of the relation between spiritual influence and behavior? The main thesis of Clinton Arnold's book, *Ephesians: Power and Magic,* is that the author wants to comfort and inspire the recipients to have confidence that Christ is stronger than the evil spirits whose power they fear.[574] While I appreciate his recognition of the importance of spiritual powers, he partly misreads the rhetorical thrust in the description of the gentiles. An alternative reading, proposed by Minna Shkul, is that the author thinks the recipients *should* be more cautious in relation the outside world, that is, he aims to reinforce the distinction between the recipients and "the gentiles" by contrasting the two spheres of spiritual dominion.[575] The image of "us" under influence of a positive spiritual force, contrasted with "them" under the influence of negative spiritual forces, makes anyone who obscures the distinction between the ingroup and "the gentiles" deviant. The phrase "I say and testify that you no longer are/should be like the gentiles" (4:17, my translation) signals that one of the urgent errands in the letter is to convince the recipients that it is the gentiles who are their outgroup. The author might think that their social distinction is currently not clear enough. As I will discuss further in chapter 18.4.3, it is quite reasonable to assume that there is some truth in both Arnold's and Shkul's arguments. The recipients probably experienced at least potential threats from their surroundings, but the author most likely exaggerates the threats in order to reinforce a sense of social distance and distinctiveness.

The Spirit causes knowledge, love and unity. Three more threads need to be touched upon briefly in relation to the subject of the Spirit and then left for further discussion in sections below: a) that the Spirit causes knowledge, b) that the Spirit causes love, and c) that the Spirit causes unity.

Knowledge. As discussed above in chapter 18.1, the author imagines that getting to know Christ is one of the causes which lead the individual into Christ. Nevertheless, this initial knowledge is in no way complete, since the author prays that God may give the recipients "the Spirit of wisdom and revelation, in/through (ἐν) knowledge of him, so that you—[since you have] the eyes of your hearts enlightened—may know…" (1:17–18a, my translation; cf. the discussion about the structure

[574] Arnold 1989.

[575] Shkul 2009: 216-237.

of the prayer reports above). The preposition ἐν in the phrase "in/through (ἐν) knowledge of him" could be understood instrumentally, that is, as meaning that "by means of" knowledge of God, you get the Spirit of knowledge and wisdom. Initial knowledge grants the Spirit, which causes further knowledge. The grammatical construct is, however, vague and ἐν could also be interpreted as a marker of the sphere of knowledge; that is, the knowledge is *about* him.[576] The perfect tense of "enlighten" (φωτίζω) is a better indication that the author imagines the recipients as already having knowledge that precedes the influence of "Spirit of knowledge and wisdom," something that the prayer will hopefully result in.[577] A positive reinforcing circle of causality between knowledge and Spirit seems to be imagined.

In the prayer in 3:14–19, knowledge is indirectly associated with the Spirit via the power theme. Having prayed that the Spirit may give them power (3:16), the implied Paul picks up the power theme again in the second clause of the prayer: "...in order that you may have strength/capacity (ἐξισχύω) to comprehend..." (3:18). The Spirit has empowered them, which (potentially) causes them to be characterized by "strength" (ἰσχύς), which in turn enables them to achieve knowledge and insight. This insight thereafter makes them "filled with the fullness of God," that is, they are more fully in Christ (3:19). This is another mutually reinforcing causality. Both the prayer in 1:16–19 and the prayer in 3:14–19 reflect a conviction that divine knowledge and having the Spirit reinforce each other mutually:

> *Mutually reinforcing causality:* (Initial) knowledge → In Christ → The Spirit → Power → (More) knowledge → (More fully) in Christ

---

[576] E.g. Hoehner 2002: 258–259.

[577] Cf. the discussion about the grammatical structure of the prayer report above.

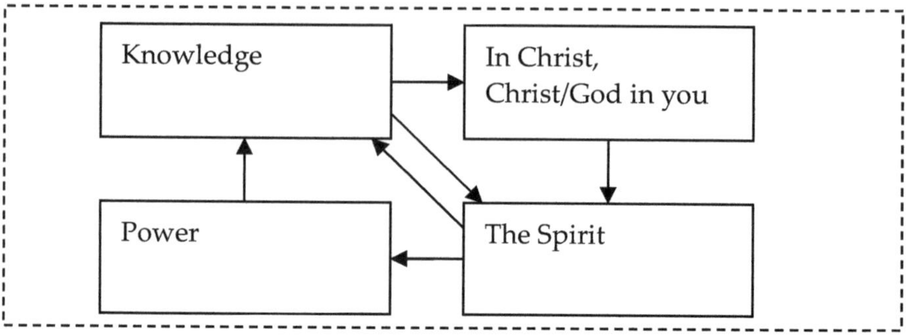

The potential group dynamic of this causal belief is similar to the belief that power and the Spirit reinforce each other mutually. The recipients are told that they have to keep working in order to grow in knowledge. However, since knowledge is a part of the mutually reinforcing dynamics, the beliefs relate more directly to speaking "the truth." If one speaks "truth", that is, according to group conventions, then one is acclaimed as inspired by the Spirit. On the other hand, if one can suspect someone to articulate unacceptable claims of truth, the group is justified to think that this person is not under the influence of the Spirit. Once this conclusion is drawn, it might become a duty to reproach, marginalize and in the end perhaps even exclude that person from the ingroup. (The relation between knowledge and behavior will be elaborated further in chapter 18.3.3. Speech behaviors will be further discussed in chapter 18.4.2.)

Love. The Spirit is also the force behind the attributed character trait "love" in the prayer in 3:14–19. Being empowered by the Spirit, so that Christ dwells in them, they will be "rooted and founded in love" (3:17; cf. the discussion about the structure of the prayer report above). In the second half of the prayer, the author starts from this rootedness in love and sees it as the basis for "knowing the love of Christ, which surpasses all knowledge" (3:19), that is, an even greater love than the one in 3:17. (The details of the love theme will be discussed in chapter 18.3.5 below.)

> *Causality:* Spirit → Power → Love → Knowledge → (Even more) love

Unity. The Spirit is also somehow the agent behind the unity of the group. They are "built together … through/in (ἐν) the Spirit." (2:22).

They should "keep the unity of the Spirit" (4:3). Success in bringing unity to the group can therefore be considered a sign that the Spirit is effective within the group and, conversely, a lack of unity is a sign that the Spirit does not work in them. (The theme of unity will be elaborated further below in chapter 18.4.1.)

Attribution: Influence from the Spirit → Unity

Summary. The Spirit holds a very central position within the cognitive structure of the prototypical Christ-believer. The Spirit is the generative force causing a great number of other characteristics: power, knowledge, love, unity. However, the chain of causality is not unidirectional but bidirectional. The Spirit causes virtues and virtuous behavior, and virtue and virtuous behavior cause the presence of the divine to grow stronger in the believer. Vicious behavior and destructive emotions can, however, cause the Spirit to draw back, giving the Devil a chance to influence the believer. Life in Christ is imagined as an ongoing process, where the Christ-believers must reinforce the presence of the Spirit by the way they conduct their lives.

Since a central aspect the group rationale in Ephesians is that they are under the dominion of God (in contrast to the gentiles), the causal beliefs about the relation between behavior, virtue and spiritual influence has both self-regulatory and group dynamic effects. The committed individual who identifies with being a Christ-believer is motivated to act in a way that allows a positive self-image as someone who is under the Spirit. If the committed individual experiences herself to be successful in her efforts, her identity in Christ may become a source of self-esteem. The group can make judgments about the spiritual status of one another by attributing certain spiritual influence to certain behaviors. This can be used to regulate behavior, to encourage and oblige each other, and to justify inclusion and exclusion as well as giving status and marginalization.

18.3.2 Power

In the previous section we concluded that the Spirit imbues the ingroup with power, according to Ephesians. This section explores how this power relates to other ingroup traits and behavior norms.

The author is convinced that there is a "surpassing greatness of his power (δύναμις) toward us who believe in accordance with (κατά) the working (ἐνέργεια) of the dominion (κράτος) of his strength (ἰσχύς)" (1:19, my translation). God is "able to do exceedingly more than we can ask and understand, in accordance with (κατά) the power (δύναμις) which works (ἐνεργέω) in us" (3:20, my translation). The recipients should "be empowered (ἐνδυναμόω) in Christ and in the dominion (κράτος) of his strength (ἰσχύς)" (6:10, my translation).

Clinton Arnold argues that the multitude of vocabulary for power in Ephesians is mainly pleonastic.[578] The function of the variety of synonyms, piled upon each other, is to emphasize God's power. According to Arnold's analysis, "working" (ἐνέργεια, also ἐνεργέω) is distinct from "power" (δυναμίς), "dominion" (κράτος) and "strength" (ἰσχύς) in the sense that "working" denotes the realization of power, while the other words denote potentiality. In terms of this study, "power," "dominion" and "strength" are God's attributed character traits while "working" is a summarizing word for the actions that come as a result of the attributed character traits. The genitive phrase "the working of the dominion of his strength" (1:19) would then consist of a genitive of origin followed by a genitive that is mainly pleonastic (cf. 6:10). In other words, the origin of the "working" is "dominion" and "strength." The same pattern is seen in the phrase "power (δύναμις) which works (ἐνεργέω) in us" (3:20), where "power" is the basis of the activity to "work" (cf. 3:7).

Empowered to act prototypically. Ephesians suggests that the recipients may become increasingly empowered to act for the goals of the *ekklēsia*. In the prayer in 3:14–19, the author first uses a passive power verb, "to become strengthened" (κραταιωθῆναι) (3:16), in the first ἵνα-clause of

---

[578] Arnold 1989: 73–75.

the prayer (cf. the discussion about the prayer report in chapter 18.3.1). However, in the second ἵνα-clause he uses an active power verb about the recipients, "be able/be strong" (ἐξισχύσητε) (3:18, cf. 3:20). The prayer reflects a belief that one can go from being strengthened to being strong, "through (διά) the Spirit" (3:16). In the same manner, the concluding passage about spiritual warfare (6:10–20) is introduced by the exhortation to be "empowered (ἐνδυναμόω) in the Lord and in the dominion (κράτος) of his strength (ἰσχύς)" (6:10, my translation). God's power is channeled into the believers by the Spirit. In this way, the ingroup members are given power from God.

> *Causality:* God canalizes his power to the ingroup (through the Spirit) → The ingroup members become empowered

The author believes that the ingroup has powers that derive directly from God. Anyone who holds such beliefs considers him-/herself to be capable of things beyond normal human capacity. This belief can have a self-fulfilling capacity, since the believer will have motivation to act in an "empowered" manner in order to avoid cognitive dissonance between the identity prototype and behavior (see chapter 6.1).[579] The prayer in 3:14–19 is followed by praise to God (3:20–21), who is able to "do exceedingly more than we can ask and understand, in accordance with (κατά) the power that works in us" (3:20). The κατά in 3:20 could be understood as "to the same extent as," which then would mean that God can only intervene in their lives to the extent that the Spirit works in them. Therefore, the same social dynamics as we saw in relation to holiness and the Spirit can be imagined in relation to the power theme too:

> *Attribution:* The power of God works in the ingroup member → Visible good behavior → *Duty:* Give status and include this ingroup member

[579] This is not intended to be a statement about whether spiritual influence is something more than a belief or not. It is, however, beyond the scope of historical investigation to say anything about whether supernatural agents actually interfere with human behavior.

Attribution: The power of God does not work in the ingroup member → Lack of visible good behavior → *Duty:* Reproach, marginalize and perhaps even exclude this ingroup member

Empowered virtues and behaviors. What character traits and behaviors, then, are associated with empowerment from God? In the prayer in 3:14–19, the author states that being empowered leads to the following dispositions:[580]

- "love" (ἀγάπη)
- "understanding" (καταλαμβάνω), "knowledge" (γνῶσις)

In 6:10–20 the empowerment from God is likened to putting on God's armor. It is therefore justified to interpret this passage as an expansion of the consequences of the empowerment. By "putting on" God's power, the Christ-believers get:

- power to "stand" (ἵστημι) in the battle against evil spiritual forces
- "truth" (ἀλήθεια) (which belongs to the knowledge theme)
- "righteousness" (δικαιοσύνη)
- "faith" (πίστις)
- "salvation" (σωτήριον) (which equals belonging to the ingroup)
- "readiness (ἑτοιμασία) of the gospel of peace" and "speech (ῥῆμα) of God" from the Spirit, probably evangelizing speech (see chapter 18.4.2 for a detailed discussion)

Causality: Empowered → Love, faith, righteousness, knowledge, salvation, resistance against evil spiritual forces, evangelizing capacity

These character traits and behaviors will be treated more fully in the sections below, but here we can just reaffirm the conclusion from the investigation of the Spirit (see chapter 18.3.1) that power from God through the Spirit is the cause of all virtues and proper attitudes.

---

580 Cf. the discussion about the causal structure of the prayer in chapter 18.3.1.

Prayer, the prototypical behavior of empowerment. In the final verses of the armor-metaphor (6:10–20), the author lets the recipients know that the method for putting on the armor—that is, God's power—is prayer "at all times in/through the Spirit" for all the holy ones (6:18), especially for "Paul" (6:19–20). Prayers for Paul will give him "boldness" to evangelize. Prayer "in the Spirit" (6:18) is a practical, visible behavior considered to have consequences for how much power one has. The passage is a glimpse of how the author imagines that the causal circle between the Spirit and power (see chapter 18.3.1 above) can be reinforced through practical behavior.[581]

We can imagine how this belief about the effect of prayer would have functioned in a community of Christ-believers. While praying alone reinforces the individual's sense of empowerment, praying together has group dynamic effects which achieve more than that. Praying together is a practical manifestation of the group's identity, since the group has beliefs about prayer "in the Spirit" (6:18) as both expressing and enhancing prototypicality. When the implied Paul prays for the ingroup (1:15–23; 3:14–21) and mentions that he regularly prays for them (1:15–16) he reminds them of his own prototypicality. He is a praying person, that is, a person of power and Spirit, and his prayers help them to grow and become as prototypical as he himself is.

Attribution: Has the Spirit → Prayer in the Spirit → *Causality:* Empowerment a) of oneself and b) of the *ekklēsia*

Continuing our historical imagination, the author seems to assume that the recipients prayed in their gatherings (5:19, 6:18–20). We can therefore safely assume that they did pray together. When they did so, they demonstrated to each other that they belonged together and were all committed and prototypical. The prayers gave a sense that they, as a group, were empowered by God. Perhaps some of the leaders, just like the implied Paul (1:15–23; 3:14–21), took the lead in these prayers. This would then reinforce their leadership roles. In any group, leader credibility comes from the leader's capacity to be appreciated as prototypical - more prototypical than the others and therefore capable of

[581] Cf. Arnold 1989: 112.

showing the way (see chapter 8.3). To take the lead in common prayers would then be a visible way for leaders to manifest their prototypicality. As we discussed in chapter 17.4, the leaders are described in 4:7–16 as central to the process of building up the body of Christ and making it perfect. God's "working" (ἐνέργεια) is different in each member (4:16), and the leaders have been given especially much of God's gifts (4:7, 11). It is therefore reasonable to think that not only the author but also the recipients thought that the leaders were generally more empowered than the average member was. Leading prayers would then reinforce this image of the leaders.

Summary. In Ephesians, God is depicted as a powerful divine agent, who gives his power to the Christ-believers. The survey of the power theme affirms the conclusion from the previous section (chapter 18.3.1) that the Spirit empowers the recipients to become more prototypical in virtue and action. Prayer is considered to induce God's power and is therefore a very important behavior in the group. It is a way to manifest their identity and commitment before each other.

18.3.3 Knowledge

Unique knowledge is a central ingroup characteristic according to Ephesians. God has "made known (γνωρίζω) the mystery of his will" (1:9) to them. Claiming superior knowledge was a common phenomenon in the cultural matrix surrounding the early Christ-movement. Those who were educated scorned those who were not; philosophers idealized the rational man, capable of understanding each situation correctly in harmony with the *logos;* prophets, seers and apocalyptic writers claimed unique knowledge directly from the divine sphere. Claiming superior knowledge and insight was a source of self-esteem and status (just like it is today).

The source of the ingroup's knowledge is God himself through the Spirit (cf. chapter 18.3.1 above). The Spirit is "a Spirit of wisdom and revelation" (1:17) who "enlightens" (φωτίζω) them (1:18). God himself is characterized by "wisdom (σοφία) and understanding (φρόνησις)" (1:8, cf. 3:10). God has always known the "mystery/secret" (μυστήριον) of the gospel, but has now revealed it to them (1:9; 3:3, 5, 9).

Causality: God reveals knowledge to the ingroup (through the Spirit) → The ingroup has knowledge

The superior knowledge of Paul and the leaders. As outlined in chapter 15, the implied Paul narrates his unique revelation in the digression in 3:2–13. God has "made known (γνωρίζω) the mystery through a revelation (ἀποκάλυψις)" to Paul (3:3–4) and his mission is to let the recipients understand this mystery (3:8–9). Paul is the human key mediator of God's knowledge to the recipients (3:2, 8–9). This description of Paul makes him influential in many ways. First, he is prototypical, because a) God has chosen him (that is, he is in God's favor), and because b) he has direct access to the knowledge a prototypical group member should have. Second, his unique position gives him informational power; that is, he has knowledge that they need but which only he can provide. The presentation of Paul as someone with superior knowledge therefore gives the message of the letter increased rhetorical power.

Necessity/duty: God has given Paul unique knowledge → The recipients must/should listen to the message of the letter in order to become prototypical

As we have already discussed in chapter 17.4, the leaders are associated with the authority of Paul and the other apostles in 4:7–16 in a way that suggests that the leaders possess unique knowledge, which the group members must listen to. The claim that the leaders have superior knowledge probably had the effect that they could increase their control over the evaluation of the information flow in the group. Therefore, the leaders had influence they could employ to decrease cognitive uncertainty within the group.

The imperfect knowledge of the recipients. While the implied Paul is simply just said to have knowledge, Ephesians emphasizes that the average group member still needs to be improved. The appropriation of knowledge on behalf of the recipients is seen as a process which started in the past but is yet to be finished. As discussed in chapter 18.1, a certain amount of knowledge about Christ seems to be seen as prior to their conversion. Knowledge about Christ is a necessary condition for the individual's incorporation into Christ (1:13). However, the letter assumes that the recipients have learned more after their conversion. The phrases "That is not the way you learned (μανθάνω) Christ" (4:20) and "For surely you have heard about him and were taught (διδάσκω) in him" (4:21) echo some kind of educational situation in the past, perhaps the education they received when they were newly converted. In other words, the author acknowledges that the recipients have learned at least enough to be decent Christ-believers.

When the author talks about the present situation, however, he very rarely says that the recipients actually know something in the indicative, and these few places are meant as reminders rather than affirmations (5:5, 6:8).[582] Rather, the author describes the current situation almost entirely in terms of knowledge they should have but still do not have, at least not fully. He prays that they may have "the Spirit of wisdom and revelation" who will help them understand their privileged position before God (1:17–19). Later he prays again that they "may know Christ's love" (3:19). He has written to them in order to enable them "to perceive my [i.e., the implied Paul's] understanding" (3:4) and leaders are to give them "the knowledge of the son of God" (4:13, cf. chapter 17.4). They should take care that "no one deceive" them "with empty words" (5:6) and "try to find out what is pleasing to the Lord" (5:10). They must live "not as unwise people but as wise" (5:15) and "not be foolish, but understand what the will of the Lord is" (5:17). The message is clear—their knowledge and wisdom is far from perfect, and they must keep striving for better knowledge if they ever would like to become prototypical. Implicitly, this message puts them in a position of dependence in relation to those who know more than they do; that is, the implied author and the leaders.[583] Moreover, as we already have discussed in chapter 15, the subtle suggestion that although they are ingroup they are not yet fully prototypical in their knowledge induces a will to improve their knowledge.

---

[582] οἶδα in 5:5 and 6:8 is formally in the perfect tense, but has the function of the present tense.

[583] Cf. the discussion in chapter 17.4 about how the leaders are in a position where their control over the information flow in the group increases.

The content of the knowledge. The content of this ingroup knowledge consists of a) narrative knowledge about what God and Christ have done and will do, b) knowledge about right and wrong and c) experiential knowledge of God and Christ, that is, divine mystical insight.

Narrative knowledge. The author refers to the ingroup narratives throughout the letter and expects his readers to be familiar with these beliefs.[584] (As we discussed in chapter 15, it is probably a part of the author's rhetorical strategy to refer to these well known narratives in order to make the ingroup identity salient and build the image of a prototypical implied author.) Occasionally he even mentions explicitly that they have or ought to have narrative knowledge about their position and God's actions: a) They have heard the gospel that they have been saved (1:13). Paul prays b) that they may know their "hope" and their "riches," that is, their privileged position, (1:18) and c) that they may know that God's power works in them (1:19). Moreover, d) Paul has taught them the mystery that the gentiles are "fellow-heirs" (3:6).

Narrative knowledge forms the rationale for the existence of the group and therefore it is prototypical to know and accept these narratives. It is important that they are not "tossed to and fro and blown about by every wind of doctrine" (4:14, cf. 5:6). "False" teachings are possible threats to the identity in Christ (cf. discussion in chapter 17.4).

Knowledge about right and wrong. Ephesians portrays the prototypical Christ-believer as someone who has moral knowledge. The lengthy section where practical behavior norms are the main issue (4:17–6:9) is framed by knowledge argumentation. If we focus on the theme of knowledge and truth, the passage can be summarized like this:

4:17–19	The gentiles lack knowledge, and therefore act shamefully and are "alienated."
4:20–21	The ingroup, however, has learned "the truth in Christ."
4:22	They should therefore not act as they used to, that is, like the gentiles.

[584] Cf. nn. 417 and 419.

4:23–24a	Rather, they should "renew the Spirit of your minds," that is, learn even more,
4:24b	for with "truth" (i.e., knowledge) come righteousness and holiness.
4:25–5:7	"Therefore" (διό) practice all kinds of moral behavior; the passage contains occasional references to knowledge and truth: 4:25 Speak the truth rather than lies! 5:5 You know which behaviors exclude you from the Kingdom. 5:6 Do not be deceived!
5:8–9	Live in the light! (Truth is one of the fruits of being in the light.)
5:10	"Examine what is pleasing to the Lord!" That is, know God's will!
5:11–14	Expose evil deeds, for all will be revealed in the light!
5:15–16	Be wise rather than unwise! Time is short.
5:17	Therefore avoid foolishness! Understand God's will!
5:18–6:9	More behavior norms; the passage contains occasional references to knowledge: 5:32 "Mystery," that is, secret God-given knowledge (cf. 3:3–9). 6:8 Slaves know they will be rewarded for good deeds. 6:9 Masters know they share the Lord in Heaven with the slaves.

In short, moral knowledge is a theme that penetrates the rhetoric about morality in Ephesians. The recipients should always strive to understand what God wants them to do (5:10, 17) and they should know they must avoid false teachings which lead to immorality (4:14; 5:6). To know what is right is (or should be) to do what is right. In other words, knowledge is a prototypical attributed character trait that can be used to explain and evaluate behavior. (The rhetoric on the topic of God-inspired moral knowledge presupposes the belief that God has a will regarding their behavior. As we discussed in chapter 6.4, the imagination of God or other spiritual agents as interested agents with opinions about human conduct is a frequent imagination across cultures.)

If knowledge about God's moral will is prototypical, then attribution of moral knowledge as an explanation and evaluation of behavior has the same group dynamic effect as other kinds of attributes: Knowledge makes them distinct and superior in relation to the gentiles, their outgroup, at least in their own eyes (4:17–21; 5:8; see chapters 7.1 and 7.2). Therefore, if someone does not act in accordance with his or her knowledge about God's will, he or she is like the outgroup and will be disliked by God, which means that the group is right to consider him or her deviant (4:22; 5:7, 11; see chapter 8.2). God might even exclude from the Kingdom those who act contrary to their knowledge about God's will (5:5), which implies that the group should reproach, marginalize and possibly even exclude those people from the *ekklēsia* in order to keep the *ekklēsia* holy.

> *Causality/duty:* God has a will regarding behavior → It is prototypical to know God's will and act accordingly

> *Attribution:* Knows God's will → Acts according to group norms → *Causality:* Is liked by God → *Duty:* The ingroup should give status to such a person

> *Attribution*: Does not know God's will → Does not act according to group norms → *Causality*: Is disliked by God → God might exclude that person from the Kingdom →*Duty*: The ingroup should reproach, marginalize and even exclude such a person

Religious insight. The letter refers to experiential knowledge about God on a number of occasions. What the author means by this kind of knowledge is vague, as is often the case with religious experience.[585]

---

[585] Much has been written to analyse the content of the μυστήριον and the meaning of ἐπίγνωσις, e.g. Caragounis 1977, Dahl 2000: 349–388. For further references, see footnotes in Hoehner 2002: 214, 258–259, 428–434, 488–489. I will not add to this discussion, but just acknowledge the vague and indeterminate character of this knowledge. As we discussed in chapter 8.1, religious "truth" is often vague.

Knowledge is "insight (ἐπίγνωσις) about him," that is, about God himself (1:17). They should "apprehend (καταλαμβάνω) ... what is the breadth and the length and the height and the depth [of an unspecified object], and know (γινώσκω) the love of Christ which surpasses knowledge (γνῶσις), in order that" they "may become filled with all the fullness of God" (3:18–19, my translation). These passages refer to knowledge which is some kind of profound experience of God, rather than narrative knowledge or knowledge about right and wrong. This "insight" (ἐπίγνωσις) is contrasted with being an "infant" who can be lead astray (4:13–14), that is, the more mystical and experiential aspects of knowledge are seen as prototypical maturity.

Harvey Whitehouse argues in his theory about modes of religiosity that "doctrinal" religions emphasize narrative truth, which is stored in semantic memory, while "imagistic" religions emphasize religious experience, which is stored in episodic memory.[586] As his theory has been tested on real religious contexts, Whitehouse has increasingly recognized that also doctrinal religion is dependent on episodic religious experience for motivation.[587] Ephesians, just like large portions of the early Christ-movement, could be categorized as expressing doctrinal religion, since narrative truth is considered to be important (see discussion above and in chapter 8.1). Nevertheless, Ephesians also expresses the importance of profound experiences of the divine. We cannot grasp exactly what Ephesians has in mind, but we can observe that the author refers to knowledge which seems to be something other than narrative doctrinal knowledge.

It is very likely that religious experiences occurred in the recipient communities, but not once does the author acknowledge that the

---

[586] Whitehouse 2004. See Ketola 2007 for an evaluation of Whitehouse's theory. Whitehouse's theory is based on the idea that "semantic memories" (i.e. memories of semantic expressions such as narrative utterances) are handled by the brain in a different way than "episodic memories" (memories of direct experiences such as an emotionally intense ritual). Semantic memories are more systematic and logical while episodic memories are more emotionally engaging.

[587] Whitehouse has recognized the importance of religious experience even in doctrinal religion all along, but emphasizes this dependence in e.g. Whitehouse and Martin 2004.

recipients have the profound insight considered to be the route to prototypicality. Rather, the author prays twice that they may reach this knowledge (1:17; 3:18–19) and tells them once that their leaders will help them reach it (4:11–14). No matter what this kind of profound knowledge might have been, we can notice that the author presents an undefined kind of knowledge as something they do not have but that they should strive for under the guidance of their leaders (cf. chapter 17.4).

If we are to imagine the effects of such a thought figure in a group, it clearly puts the average ingroup member in a position where his or her prototypicality is easily questioned. Since the insight about God is described in such elusive terms, there is no way to demonstrate beyond doubt to oneself or to others that one has achieved such insight. Therefore the individual is always dependent on the affirmation of those who are supposed to have insight, that is, the leaders (cf. chapter 17.4). The leaders can always claim that this or that behavior is the result of lacking profound insight. It is significant that the leaders are said to help them reach "the unity (ἑνότης) of faith and of insight about God" (4:13) and perhaps also that a "perfected" group member will be able to do "work of service" (4:12).[588] Unity and willingness to serve, two evident interests of the leaders, are presented as prime signs of this deeper knowledge and maturity. I have no doubt that people actually had profound religious experiences, but having an experience and claiming that the outer signs of such an experience is cohesion and cooperation are two quite different things. In harmonious circumstances with no intragroup conflict, unity and willingness to serve is of course beneficial for the entire group, not just for the leaders. I do not suggest that the leaders sought to oppress. Nevertheless, the rhetoric of cooperation as a sign of knowledge together with the rhetoric of superior religious insight on behalf of the leaders would certainly give the leaders a position where they could define what "unity" meant in a situation of disagreement.

---

[588] The phrase "work of service/ministry" in 4:12 can be interpreted either as something the leaders should do or as something every group member should do, see n. 542.

As we have seen, both in the discussion about moral knowledge and in the discussion about profound religious insight, the recipients are put in a position where they are acknowledged as having a certain amount of knowledge, but the focus is, nevertheless, on their improvement in knowledge. The rhetorical strategy of depicting the recipients as firmly ingroup but yet far away from the prototypical ideal (cf. chapter 15) is evident in our survey of the knowledge theme. The purpose of such rhetoric is to create cognitive dissonance between the perception of the prototypical ideal and the perception of the self in the recipients, which inspires a subjective need to improve oneself. A group member who experiences him-/herself to be questioned by the group tends to either affirm his or her commitment through prototypical action or distance him-/herself from the group in order to maintain self-esteem (cf. chapter 9.3). The aim of the author is no doubt that the recipients take the former route.

Summary. Knowledge, both narrative knowledge, moral knowledge and profound experiential knowledge, is considered to be prototypical in Ephesians. Lack of knowledge *does* explain the amoral behavior of the gentiles and deviants, while, in contrast, moral knowledge *should* cause the recipients to behave prototypically. Although the author affirms a certain amount of God-given knowledge on behalf of the recipients, his main focus is on the knowledge they should strive for, both moral knowledge and religious insight. The rhetorical strategy is to create a need among the recipients to improve one's prototypicality, before oneself, before God and before the group. This strategy is combined with a strategy to claim superior knowledge on behalf of the implied Paul and the leaders in order to strengthen both the message of the letter and the credibility of the local leaders.

18.3.4 Faith

Being "faithful/believing/trusting/loyal" (πιστός) is certainly a part of the identity in Christ according to Ephesians. In chapter 16 we discussed how Ephesians models the relation to God in analogy with a patron-client relation. The appropriate response to the divine patron's initiative and gifts is gratefulness and loyalty. The different aspects of the term "faith" fit well into the expectations of the patron-client relationship between God and the Christ-believers. πίστις and its cognates could be consistently translated with "faithfulness", "commitment" and "loyalty" throughout the letter, that is, the word refers to the commitment to Christ, and thereby to the *ekklēsia*.[589] As long as the individual is faithful, God, the patron, will accept him/her as his client and bestow his generous gifts upon him/her.

The recipients are called "faithful/believing" (πιστοί) in the greeting of the letter (1:1). The implied Paul is delighted over their faith and that it gives him reason to pray for them unceasingly (1:15–16). Faith is the quality that gives them access to God and salvation (2:8; 3:12, 17). "Having come to faith" (πιστεύσαντες, ingressive aorist), is a precondition for the "seal" of the Spirit (1:13), that is, for being ingroup. Moreover, faith is considered to be "a shield" that protects from attacks from evil spiritual forces (6:16). Faith in God makes the believer remain under the dominion of God's power (1:13, 19). In other words, faith is an entrance criterion for being in Christ, for entering (and remaining) in the patron-client relationship to God.

> *Causality:* Faith → The Spirit, salvation, access to God (that is, belonging to the ingroup), protection from evil spiritual agents under the dominion of God

Faith is not described as a characteristic that develops and grows dynamically in the same way as power, love or being filled with God

---

[589] I am aware that although πιστός can be translated "faithful/loyal/committed" and πίστις "faithfulness/loyalty/commitment", the standard lectionaries do not mention "be faithful/loyal/committed" as a possible translation of πιστεύω. However, since πιστεύω is a cognate of the other two words and since πιστεύω is used to describe how the Christ-believer became group members, I still find "be faithful" a proper translation of πιστεύω in the case of Ephesians. Such a translation would do justice to the insights of the new perspective on Paul, where the πίστ-stem is connected to covenant theology, e.g. Dunn 1990: 340-346, 371-379. If Ephesians is written in Pauline tradition, it is reasonable to think that also Ephesians uses the πίστ-stem, including the verb πιστεύω, to express a covenant relation, i.e. being faithful. However, I will not insist on this translation, but translate πιστεύω with the the more general phrases "have faith"and "believe".

does.[590] Rather, faith is described as a border criterion in order to belong to the group and to be in God's favor (1:13; 2:8; 3:12; see chapter 18.1) Faith is rhetorically used as a static attribute, which the author never argues they need more of. It is considered to be a necessary condition for the process whereby Christ lives in them increasingly (3:17), but does itself seem to be constant rather than growing.[591]

Faith and behavior. Faith is not used directly to motivate behavior norms, even though the author thinks that faith is important. Attribution of behavior to faith is suspiciously absent in the more practical sections of the letter. Since the author has not argued that their faith needs improvement in the first half of the letter, the recipients have not been motivated to strive to improve their faith. Attribution to faith therefore makes a poor argument for behavior compared to attribution to other character traits. The closest we come to behavior norms is that faith, together with knowledge, is associated with unity (4:13), which in turn is associated with various behaviors (see chapter 18.4.1).

Attribution: Faith + Knowledge → Unity

Summary. Faith is a border criterion for the ingroup category rather than something that grows and develops in Ephesians. Therefore it is not used to explain and moralize about prototypical behavior. Rather, faith is used to describe the Christ-believers' attitude towards God, their divine patron.

18.3.5 Love

"Love" (ἀγάπη) is the virtue of selfless benevolence and affection,[592] but in the context of Ephesians we get the impression that the author uses "love" in a much wider sense to describe general perfection in virtue.

[590] In other texts, faith is something that one can have more or less of, e.g. Mark 16:17–18, John 14:12, Rom 12:6. Ephesians, however, focuses its rhetoric on other attributed characteristics.

[591] Cf. n. 567.

[592] Hoehner 2002: 180–182.

Love is the super-virtue, the basis for all other virtues. When the ingroup member is characterized by love, he or she is God-like (5:1–2), holy (1:4) and entirely filled with the fullness of God (3:14–19).

"Love" is one of God's and Christ's characteristics in Ephesians.[593] It is because of "the great love with which he loved us" that God is "rich in mercy" and decides to save the *ekklēsia* in spite of their sin (2:4–8). (Cf. the discussion about God's motivations in chapter 16.) Christ was driven by love when he sacrificed himself for their sake (5:2). Moreover, God relates to the ingroup as to "beloved children" (5:1). Finally, the relation between God (the father) and Christ is that Christ is his "beloved" (1:6). God's and Christ's love is transferred into an ideal for the group through analogy (see chapter 11.2). The ingroup should be "imitators" of God and "walk in love" (5:1–2). Their love should be similar to Christ's love (5:1–2). Moreover, the ingroup should strive to "know Christ's love" (3:19). The most extensive analogical transfer of divine love, however, is that husbands should love their wives in analogy with Christ's love (5:25–27, see chapter 17.3).

Love, the super-virtue. Love gives the impression of being a super-virtue when we examine the relation between love and other attributed virtues and states. In 1:4 and 4:2 we have enumerations of desirable characteristics, which are modified by "in/through (ἐν) love." The group's purpose is to be "holy and blameless in/through love" (1:4) and they should "walk worthy of the calling ... with all humility (ταπεινοφροσύνη) and gentleness (πραΰτης), with patience (μακροθυμία), forbearing each other in/through love" (4:2). ἐν in the phrase "in/through love" could either be understood as "by means of" (instrument) or "as characterised by" (manner).[594] Love is the umbrella virtue, which either causes or sets the standards for other virtues—or

[593] If we take ἐν ἀγάπη in 1:4 to describe God's action in 1:5, rather than to describe how the ingroup should be "holy and blameless", then God has "predestined" them "in love." ἐν ἀγάπη in 1:4 would then be the first mention of love as God's motivation in the letter. I do, however, agree with Hoehner 2002: 182–185; Lincoln 1990: 17 that the latter interpretation of ἐν ἀγάπη as defining "holy and blameless", is more probable.

[594] See n. 555.

both, which is quite probable if we consider the centrality of love in the prayer in 3:14–19 (see discussion below). Love is also associated with the state of holiness, as was discussed in chapter 18.2. To "walk in love" means doing what is "fitting for holy ones" (5:2–3, cf. 1:4).

> *Causality/characterization:* Love → Other virtues and the state of holiness

Love in the mutually reinforcing process of growth. What makes the virtue of love grow in the Christ-believers and how does love cause growth? The phrase "rooted and founded in love" in 3:17 may be understood in several ways in the context of 3:14–19. I have given my position on how the statement about being "rooted and founded in love" should be interpreted in relation to other elements in the prayer in chapter 18.3.1: The first half of the prayer starts with the Spirit and ends with love. Being empowered by the Spirit, so that Christ dwells in them, they will be "rooted and founded in love" (3:17). In the second half of the prayer, the author starts from this rootedness in love and sees it as the basis for knowing "the love of Christ that surpasses knowledge" (3:19), that is, an even greater love than the love in 3:17. Knowing Christ's love in 3:19 is probably not just meant to be a passive intellectual insight about love, but a transformation of themselves into loving people (cf. 5:1–2).[595] If they know this divine love, they will be "filled with all the fullness of God" (3:19), that is, perfect prototypical Christ-believers. In 4:15–16 the author argues that the ingroup, "speaking the truth in love, ... must grow up in every way into ... Christ." Love is again the virtue that causes growth. In short, love partakes in the mutually reinforcing dynamics of growth (just like knowledge does):

> *Causality:* In Christ → Spirit → Power → Love → Filled, grown up, etc., that is, fully in Christ, or in other words, perfection

[595] In chapter 18.3.3 I argued that in Ephesians knowing means doing. In this case, knowing love means living it.

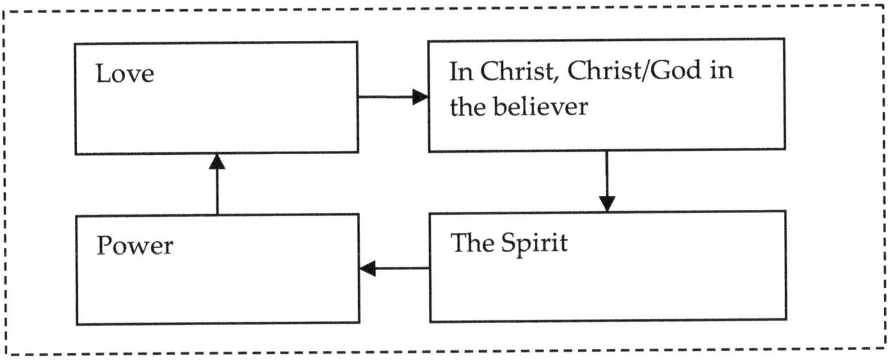

The author progresses from the indicative to the imperative in his rhetorical use of the love theme throughout the letter. In the beginning of the letter he commends them for their "love for all the holy ones" (1:15), but later on prays that they may become "rooted and founded in love" (3:17) and "know Christ's love" (3:19). He then commands them to "walk worthy of their calling … in love" (4:1–2; cf. 4:15, 17) and to "walk in love, as Christ has loved you" (5:2). Love is yet another of these prototypical qualities which the author gives them some credit for but then urges them to improve. (Cf. the discussions about the Spirit in chapter 18.3.1 and the discussion about knowledge in chapter 18.3.3 for the group dynamic effects of this rhetoric.)

Loving behavior. Not very surprisingly, love is associated with several behaviors. (The surprise, however, is *what* behaviors are associated with love.) The hortatory section 5:1–6 begins with an exhortation to exercise Christ-like self-sacrificing love (5:1–2).[596] He then enumerates several behaviors which are improper if they are to live in love. These behaviors have already been partly discussed in the section about holiness (19.2), since the author more or less equals holiness and love in this passage. It is striking, though, that none of the behaviors he mentions are about care, which we perhaps would have expected as the practical implication of love. This affirms the thesis that love is a general super-virtue in Ephesians, which leads to just about every desirable behavior.

---

[596] See n. 556 on why 5:1–2 should be read as an introduction to 5:1–6 rather than as a conclusion to 4:25–5:2.

Speech. Speech behavior and truth are the most urgent expressions of love in 5:1–6. The rhetorical construction of the passage gives us reason to believe that the author is not primarily worried about "fornication," "impurity," "greed" and "idolatry" (5:3, 5). These are stereotypical traits of the gentiles, as discussed in chapter 17.1.2. Mentioning these overtly deviant behaviors rather functions to frame the speech behaviors in 5:4 and smear them with undesirable associations. The exhortation in 5:3 is not that the stereotypically gentile behaviors should not be practiced, but that they "should not even be *spoken of*." This is a first indication that the real worry here is speech. In 5:6–7 it becomes apparent that it is speech behaviors which the author is really worried about as he writes "let no one deceive you with *empty words* (κενοὶ λόγοι)." Those who speak those "empty words" are "the sons of disobedience," that is, deviants, whom the Christ-believers should not be "partakers" with. The focus of the passage is that if one walks in love one does not practice "shameful [speech] behavior" (αἰσχρότης),[597] "foolish talk" (μωρολογία) and "sarcasm" (εὐτραπελία), but rather "thanksgiving" (εὐχαριστία) (5:4). Three undesirable speech behaviors are contrasted with one desirable speech behavior.

The association between love and proper speech in 5:1–6 should be read together with the usage of love in 4:14–15. There they are exhorted to avoid "every wind of [false] teachings" and instead "grow, speaking the truth (ἀληθεύω) in/through *love,* into ... Christ" (my translation). Love is imagined in both these passages to result in avoidance of deviant speech (4:14; 5:6). Instead they are urged to adhere to the truth which their leaders provide (4:15; cf. the discussion in chapter 17.4) and to give thanks (5:4). Surprisingly, then, love is more strongly associated with conventional speech behavior than with practical care in Ephesians.

"Thanksgiving" (5:4) might refer to loyal partaking in the common prayers. This gives us reason to think that "shameful [speech] behavior," "foolish talk" and "sarcasm"—the words that contrast "thanksgiving"—also refer to speech behavior when the group gathers. Lincoln thinks that these speech behaviors refer to talk about sexual

---

[597] Since αἰσχρότης is enumerated together with other speech behaviors, and since the parallel section in Col 3:5–8 uses αἰσχρολογία, the author probably has shameful speech behaviors in mind, see Lincoln 1990: 323.

immorality, since he thinks that the sins in 5:3, 5 all refer to sexual sin, while Hoehner is rightly more skeptical to the idea that "impurity" should be narrowed down to just sexual impurity and that "greed" should necessarily refer to sexual greed.[598] Hoehner argues that we should interpret the vocabulary as speech which is hurtful to other individual ingroup members, since the passage is introduced with an exhortation to love.[599] However, although "love" normally is associated with care, nothing in this passage or in the content of the words indicates that this is the case here. Just as in 4:14–15, the author uses the positive connotations of love to achieve other goals. Since the speech behaviors are framed by stereotypical gentile behavior, the text probably refers to speech that undermines the group's internal unity and obscures the distinctiveness towards the gentiles. "Shameful [speech] behavior," "foolish talk" and "sarcasm" are probably challenges to the cohesion of the group.

The implication of 4:14–15 and 5:1–6 is that anyone who speaks conventionally is considered to be loving, that is prototypical, but anyone who listens to other teachings or questions the truth and norms, which are group consensus, is probably without the virtue of love, that is, deviant rather than prototypical. Such a person is without love and therefore probably disliked by God and should be reproached, marginalized, and possibly even excluded (cf. chapter 18.2). In sum, the author effectively turns the attributed virtue of love into a rhetorical tool to control speech behavior. The most loving act is to not undermine other group members' beliefs.

Attribution: Love → Speaks in conventional manner (and takes part in the common prayers) → *Causality:* Liked by God → *Duty:* Give status and honor

Attribution: Lack of love → Speaks deviantly and challenges the ingroup order → *Causality:* Disliked by God → *Duty:* Reproach, marginalize and, if necessary, exclude

---

598 Hoehner 2002: 652–653; Lincoln 1990: 322–323.

599 Hoehner 2002: 655–656.

Beside the dynamics of inclusion and exclusion, the social dynamics of speaking conventionally is a sense of cognitive certainty, as we have already discussed in the analysis of the knowledge theme (see chapters 8.1 and 18.3.3). Speech norms are the most important way to safeguard cognitive certainty and thereby the sense that the meaning and value of the group is comprehensible.

Unity. The author also associates love with unity in 4:1–6, in a way that confirms the analysis above, namely that the author uses the virtue of love in order to inspire ingroup cohesiveness:

> I urge (παρακαλῶ) you to walk worthy of the calling…
> [enumeration of virtues]
> forbearing (participle) each other
> *in love*
> making every effort (participle) to keep the unity…
> [enumeration of things that are "one"] (my translation)

The passage centers on the two participle phrases about unity and forbearing. The phrase "in love" can be understood as belonging to both participles and thus forms a bridge between the first half (virtues) and the second half (unity). The virtues mentioned before "in love" in this passage remain quite unspecific, but as the analysis below in chapter 18.4.1 about unity will argue, they have an anti-competitive edge. Love is placed as the summarizing super-virtue which characterizes these other virtues and the act of "forbearing." The sentence in 4:1–6 implies that people who have these prototypical virtues—love being the most important one—make every effort to keep the unity. Conversely, people who do not strive for unity lack love. We are going to explore the theme of unity below in chapter 18.4.1, but for now we can just tentatively conclude that love is also in this passage used to stress conformity.

> *Attribution:* Love → Anti-competitive virtues → Forbearance (and other actions) stimulating unity → *Causality:* Unity

Care. The love theme returns again in the instructions to husbands how they should treat their wives with Christ-like love (5:25–33). Although the author's main purpose is to integrate the household into the identity in Christ rather than to reform household behavior (see chapter 17.3), he gives us a glimpse of information about how he imagines that the husband's love to his wife should be expressed in practice. The husband should "nourish and care" for his wife as he does for his own body (5:29). In this passage the virtue of love has retained its typical connotation within the Christ-movement of selfless care and affection.

Summary. Love is a super-virtue in Ephesians, causing and characterizing all other virtues. The author does not, however, use attribution to love primarily in order to inspire selfless care of other group members, but to inspire unity and conformity in speech. Just like many other attributed character traits in Ephesians, love is construed as something that can grow and develop in mutually reinforcing causal interaction with the Spirit.

18.3.6 Righteousness

"Righteousness" (δικαιοσύνη) is not the most prominent attributed character trait in Ephesians, but it is worth touching upon briefly since the author uses the term three times (4:24; 5:9; 6:14) and the related term "righteous/right" (δίκαιος) once (6:1). The term δικαιοσύνη, which translates צדקה in the Septuagint, denotes generally praiseworthy and good behavior and attitudes towards God and humans. The term is used for those who behave according to the requirements of the covenant.[600] Righteousness could therefore be analyzed both as a character trait and as a term for covenantal status. However, as Hoehner points out, "righteousness" is complemented with "holiness/piety" (ὁσιότης) in 4:24, a word commonly used for a proper attitude towards God, so at least in this case "righteousness" seems to primarily mean good behavior and attitudes towards humans.[601] Therefore it seems like the author uses the term "righteousness" as a character trait.

The usage of the virtue of righteousness in Ephesians is quite sweeping and difficult to connect to specific behavior norms. In 4:23–24 "righteousness" is part of a sentence that describes "the new man (ὁ

[600] Dunn 1998: 334–346.

[601] Hoehner 2002: 612. Hoehner notes that Philo, *De Abr.* 37.208 differentiates the terms in this way.

καινὸς ἄνθρωπος), created according to the likeness of God" (NRSV modified). The sentence is a bridge between the renunciation of the gentile lifestyle in 4:17–22 and the practical exhortations in 4:25–32. The passage in 4:17–22 about the gentiles emphasizes their lack of knowledge. Moreover, the first exhortation in 4:25–32 is to speak the truth. Therefore it is significant that "the new man" is characterized by "righteousness and holiness/piety *of truth*" (4:24). The genitive "of truth" is probably either a genitive of quality or a genitive of origin, that is, "truth" is what characterizes or causes righteousness. A similar association between truth and righteousness is made in 5:9, where the identity in Christ as "children of light" is characterized by "every goodness, righteousness and *truth*." The author's imagination therefore seems to be that the "new man" has knowledge of the truth, which makes him righteous, and therefore he speaks the truth (cf. chapter 18.3.3 above about knowledge).

Causality: In Christ → New man → Knowledge of the truth → Righteous → *Attribution:* Speaks the truth

The third mention of righteousness is in the armor-metaphor (6:10–20), where righteousness is a "breastplate" (6:14). A breastplate has a defensive function, but the metaphor is not elaborated further. Perhaps the idea that sinful behavior "gives the Devil a place" (4:27) is behind the metaphor. Righteous behavior would then protect against giving the Devil a chance.

18.3.7 Emotions

Emotions (πάθη) play an important role as the cause of action in Ephesians. As was discussed in chapter 6.3, some, like Aristotle, considered moderate and adequate emotions to be intrinsic to virtue. Others, like the Stoic Seneca, primarily discussed how emotions could undermine virtue. (The Stoics did, however, allow for *eupatheia*, benevolent emotions.)

The author of Ephesians seems to think that moderate emotions are allowed, but that excessive emotions are dangerous (4:25–32, especially v. 27, see the discussion above in chapter 18.3.1). Therefore, we can reasonably assume that he imagines that some emotions can be intrinsic to virtue. As a consequence, it is not always easy to distinguish words for emotions from words for virtues and vices. Some positive words have an emotional content, while at the same time being virtues. For example, "tenderhearted" (εὔσπλαγχνος) (4:32) literally means "with benevolent intestines" and the intestines were often considered to be the seat of emotions.[602] These positive emotions which lead to good, however, do not occupy the thought of Ephesians as much as potentially destructive emotions do. The focus in this section will therefore be the emotions that the author considers to be a potential threat to the group.

The destructive emotions of the gentiles. The fundamental problem of the gentiles is their lack of knowledge about God (4:17–18). This lack of knowledge is "due to (διά) the hardening of their heart" (4:18). The gentiles, "having ceased to feel (ἀπαλγέω), have given themselves over to licentiousness (ἀσέλγεια) into practice of every impurity in greediness (πλεονεξία)" (4:19, my translation). ἀπαλγέω literally means "having ceased to feel pain" but in the context it has the meaning of "having ceased to feel morally obliging emotions."[603] Their old (gentile) selves are "corrupted according to the desires (ἐπιθυμία) of deceit" (4:22). The imagination here is that the lack of good emotions leads to a) lack of insight about God (4:17–18) and to b) the replacement of these good emotions with destructive ones, such as "licentiousness," "greediness" and "desire." These destructive emotions then cause people to "practice every impurity."

> *Causality:* Loss of good, morally obliging, emotions → Loss of knowledge about God + destructive emotions → *Attribution*: impure (i.e., vicious) actions

The emotions of Christ-believers. The author worries about what behavior the wrong kinds of emotions within the group can cause. In the discussion about the Spirit (chapter 18.3.1), we concluded that negative aggressive emotions, which lead to the loss of self-control, were considered to cause people to sin (4:25–32). This sin in turn could

---

602 Hammett 2000.

603 Lincoln 1990: 278.

potentially cause the Spirit to leave them and give the Devil a chance to influence them instead. Elsewhere, wine is considered to cause loss of self-control and sin, which is opposed to being filled with the Spirit (5:18). The negative emotions in Ephesians can be categorized into two groups: a) emotions that disturb the ingroup unity, and b) emotions that decrease commitment to Christ. As we have repeatedly concluded in this study, ingroup cohesion and commitment is of great concern to the author.

Some emotions are potentially dangerous, since they disturb the ingroup unity. The aggressive emotions in 4:25–32 are considered to cause people saying abusive things to each other, which of course would decrease the sense of unity in the group. These emotions are also indirectly opposed to caring actions in this passage. Since aggressive emotions undermine care they are dangerous for the unity of the group.

Other emotions might decrease commitment. Having told them about his heroic mission to evangelize, the implied Paul asks the recipients not to "lose heart (ἐγκακέω) over my sufferings for you; they are your glory" (3:13). The subject of suffering will be discussed in chapter 18.4.3 below, but here we can just notice that the author sees a danger that hardships might decrease the emotional sense of commitment.

Conclusion. The author of Ephesians probably evaluates proper emotions as being morally good, even morally inspiring, but his greatest worry is how destructive emotions might be a danger to the group. People driven by desire will probably commit all kinds of deviant deeds. Aggressive emotions will cause ingroup strife. Emotions of despair might decrease commitment. The author therefore motivates people to control their emotions in several ways. One strategy is to use the outgroup as a stereotype of what happens to people with destructive emotions. Another strategy is to connect emotions to narratives about spiritual influence. Moreover, he tells them that they should feel pride rather than despair when someone in the group ("Paul") is threatened. If accepted by the recipients, these narratives may function to guide emotions (and thus behaviors) in a direction which increases cohesion and commitment.

18.3.8 Summary

An answer to the important question about the relation between theology and ethics in Ephesians is apparent—the relation is causal. Ephesians narrates a rich network of causal beliefs that make behavior norms feel as an integral outcome of being a Christ-believer.

The sum of the investigation so far is a reconstruction of a complex of narratives about how different agents, both human and divine, with different characteristics, act according to their character and according to the spiritual agents influencing them. These narratives are used in the letter to guide judgments about prototypicality and deviance and thus form the group rationale for ingroup dynamics such as behavior norms, cognitive certainty, self-esteem, a sense of purpose, leadership, cohesion, giving status and marginalization, inclusion and exclusion.

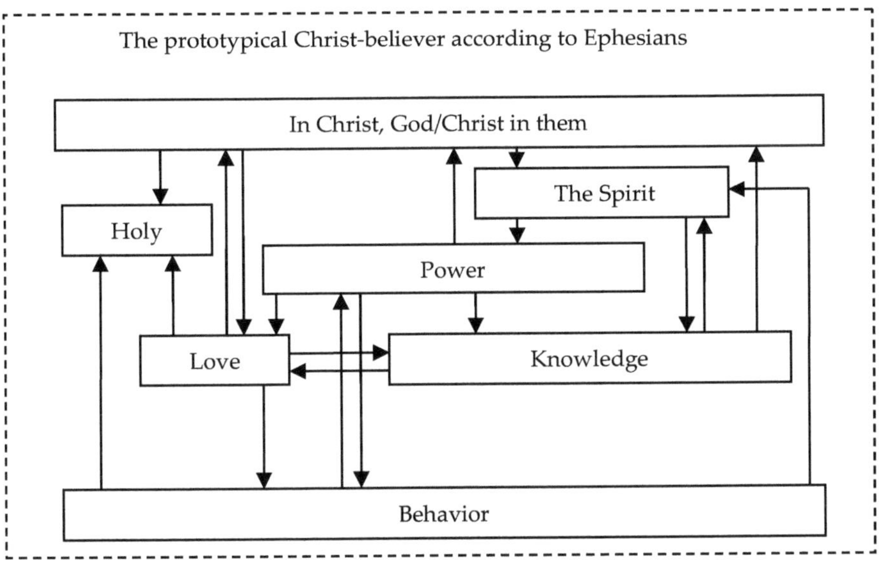

This (perhaps somewhat impenetrable) image summarizes all expressed causal connections that Ephesians makes between being in Christ, holiness, the Spirit, power, love, knowledge and behavior. Dense as the figure is, I have nevertheless excluded faith and righteousness from the picture and withheld from diversifying behavior into different kinds of behavior, in order to make the picture a bit less complex. The image should not be interpreted as a summary of every aspect of the prototypical Christ-believer that the historical author of Ephesians had in his mind, but as a summary of the aspects of the Christ-believer which the author of Ephesians has cared to express in his letter. As we have emphasized all along, the author articulates a vision of the prototypical Christ-believer in order to influence the recipients. From this we can make a partial reconstruction of the prototype the author maintains and promotes.This study has brought to light that the prototype is structured in a way which encourages certain group dynamic effects if it is embraced by a local community of Christ-believers. In the discussions above, we found several causal beliefs, which we could describe as "mutually reinforcing" (or "intertwined," "circular," "dialectical," etc.), all interwoven into a self-reinforcing network. Life in Christ is imagined as a continuous process of either improvement or deterioration. The process of growth can potentially lead to perfection (e.g., 3:19; 4:12–13), but it is in continuous need of reinforcement through prototypical behavior in order to avoid falling out of the dominion of the Spirit and the Kingdom of Christ and God (4:27, 30; 5:5).

The attribution processes, which are integrated into the ingroup prototype, facilitate the dynamics of inclusion and exclusion, giving status and marginalization. As we have been able to conclude repeatedly in our analysis, there is a tension between indicative and imperative in the prototype, which the letter makes use of very efficiently. In order to promote certain behaviors and beliefs, the author narrates causal connections between behavior, attributes and status before God, which justify the reproach and marginalization of deviants and the praise of those who conform to the behavior norms of the group. At the same time, the recipients are told that although they are without doubt ingroup, they are still lacking in prototypical qualities. This rhetoric is intended to create a need to act in a way which hopefully increases their prototypicality.

The dynamic of the ingroup prototype is clarified by contrasting it with the gentiles (their former identity), who are characterized by destructive attributes, such as evil spiritual influence, lack of knowledge and vicious desires. The contrasting rhetoric strengthens their sense of distinctiveness and superiority, which increases cognitive clarity, self-esteem and social distance from outsiders.

Many of the behaviors the letter promotes as expressions of prototypical attributes are focused on group cohesion. The norms of speaking in a way that confirms ingroup consensus and of avoiding alternative teachings bolster a sense of cognitive certainty in the group, since such behavior reinforces the group's shared cognition. The imagination of the leadership as uniquely gifted with knowledge creates a group dynamic where the leaders can dissuade the group from accepting alternative interpretations and thus increases cognitive certainty. Under the theme of "unity" the author encourages the recipients to avoid contest and conflict, which increases the possibility to cooperate and creates a climate where the individual is affirmed by the group (as long as he or she behaves according to group norms).

18.4 Spheres of Behavior Norms

Up to this point, the analysis has started from the most prominent aspects of the attributed side of the ingroup prototype in Ephesians—being in Christ, holiness, Spirit, power, knowledge, faith, love and righteousness—and traced how these attributed characteristics are considered to both cause and require behavior. From this point, the investigation of the prototype will use a different perspective and start from different spheres of behavior norms—unity, speech, suffering, intragroup care, household behavior and deviant behavior. The function of this new perspective is partly to summarize the findings from a different point of view, but most importantly the change of view will help us discuss new aspects of the ingroup prototype and of how the recognition of these ideals might have functioned to form group dynamics.

18.4.1 Unity

Being united is clearly a very central aspect of the identity in Christ. The ideal of unity is motivated by the narrative about what we might call "spiritual" or "mystical" unity "in Christ," about being "a holy temple in the Lord" (2:21) and partaking in "the body of Christ" (3:12). The narrative about the Christ-believers' spiritual status becomes the rationale for the argument that they should become in practice what they are by their new nature (4:1–16).

This unity is stressed on two levels: a) the intergroup level, where the author emphasizes that the two subgroups of Jewish and gentile Christ-believers are united in Christ, and b) the inter-individual level, where he exhorts them to strive for unity. The first discussion occurs in the first half of the letter (2:1–3:13) while the second discussion occurs in the second half (4:1–6:9). There is a thematic continuity between these two levels of unity, but the content of the exhortations in the second half does not justify the claim that the second half of the letter merely develops the unity between Jews and gentiles in practical terms. Rather, the exhortations show a shift in focus from the unity of ethnic subgroups to the unity of all group members. Although many norms in the hortatory half of the letter are presented in contrast to gentile stereotypes (4:17–6:9), there is no such contrast in 4:1–16, which is the passage that deals most extensively with unity. We should therefore analyze these two aspects of unity as two distinguishable (although not entirely separable) sets of practical problems within a community.

Practical unity between Jews and gentiles. The intergroup relation between the two subgroups of Jewish and gentile Christ-believers is intriguing, and has already been discussed in chapter 17.2. As was concluded above, this unity in Christ is an exclusive subcategory to the covenant of Israel, including both Jews and gentiles. The main argument in 2:11–22 is that the gentiles "have been brought near" (2:13) through Christ. A consequence of this (but not the main point of the passage) is that Jews and gentiles have been united (vv. 14–16).

The author does not explicate the practical conditions for this inter-ethnic unity in very clear terms. All he writes is that "the law of commandments in/regarding regulations" (ὁ νόμος τῶν ἐντολῶν ἐν δόγμασιν) is "invalidated/cancelled/rendered inoperative/abolished" (καταργέω)[604] in this new unity between Jews and gentiles in Christ (2:15). How can we best understand this phrase? It is reasonable to

[604] Although many modern translations, e.g. NRSV, NIV, NAS, translate καταργέω with "abolish", I will avoid that translation, since "abolish" has connotations of "destroy entirely." There is no reason to think that the author, who probably borrowed the term from Paul (e.g. Rom 3:31; 7:6) means more than "nullify" or "render inoperative", cf. Hoehner 2002: 375.

assume that the phrase refers to the Torah in one way or another, but exactly how? In what way and for whom is the Torah invalidated? The interpretation of the phrase depends entirely on how one understands the letter's imagination of the relation between Israel and the *ekklēsia* (see chapter 17.2).

Lincoln and Hoehner, who think of the *ekklēsia* in Ephesians as a new covenant different from the old covenant, argue that the author has nullified the validity of the Torah entirely, for Jews and gentiles alike.[605] Such an interpretation is quite plausible if one thinks of the *ekklēsia* as something outside ethnic Israel. After all, the plain meaning of the phrase seems to be that the commandments of the Torah have been invalidated.

However, the interpretation that the practice of the Torah is entirely invalidated for both Jews and gentiles becomes less self evident if we conceive of the *ekklēsia* as a subcategory to Israel, which I argued in chapter 17.2. Also the interpretation that the *ekklēsia* is a widening of Israel makes the interpretation above problematic. Paul was not entirely prepared to "invalidate" the Torah (Rom 3:31; 7:6).[606] Although Paul demands that gentiles should not practice the Torah, he does not seem to object to Christ-believing Jews who continue their practice.[607] Why would the deutero-Pauline author of Ephesians, who is also a Jew, be prepared to demand that Christ-believing Jews should not practice the Torah, especially if he imagines that the *ekklēsia* does not substitute or parallel Israel?

---

605 Hoehner 2002: 374–377; Lincoln 1990: 141–143.

606 The usage of καταργέω in Rom 3:31; 7:6 is that God has not invalidated the Torah (3:31), but that the Christ-believers have been "invalidated/discharged from" (κατηργήθημεν ἀπό) the Torah in Christ (7:6). Ephesians, on the contrary, claims that it is the Torah that has been invalidated. Yet Ephesians is at least partly congruent with Romans, since the text claims that the law has been "invalidated" (2:15) "in Christ" (2:13). Both Romans and Ephesians describe the sphere of being in Christ as a state where one is exempted from the Torah. The question which both texts do not answer explicitly is whether Jewish Christ-believers should stop practicing the Torah or not.

607 Tomson 1990, summarized in Zetterholm 2009: 134-139.

Barth and Yee, who emphasize that the author of Ephesians is a Jew who thinks of the gentile converts as "co-citizens" (συμπολῖται, 2:19) of a widened "Israel," are more reluctant to think that the Torah itself is under attack.[608] Rather, it is its divisive effect which is criticized. The phrase about invalidating the Torah appears in a sentence which describes how the Christ-event "breaks down the dividing wall, the enmity" between Jews and gentile in order to "create in himself one new man" (2:14–16). Moreover, the specification that the Torah has been invalidated "in/regarding regulations" (ἐν δόγμασιν) suggests that the problem concerns concrete halakhic commandments. Yee rightly points out how the Torah could become both a practical and symbolical divider between Jew and gentile in the *ekklēsia,* which would have made unity difficult.[609] He argues extensively for the interpretation that the author does not really attack the Torah itself as something evil (just like Paul did not in Rom 7:7); he just considers it to be a hindrance to unity in the Christ-believing group. Besides, the author cites the Torah as an authority in the household code (5:31; 6:2–3).

If we assume that the author primarily opposes the divisive effect of the halakhic practice of the law, how does he imagine that Jews and gentiles should get along practically? What practical norms could be implied in 2:15? We can only guess. Perhaps the author imagines that practical life in Christ should be free from the halakhic employment of the Torah, for Jew and gentile alike. This is not entirely unproblematic, since the author appeals to the Torah in the household code (5:31; 6:2–3; see also 5:3, 5). The Torah is used as an authority, at least selectively. Perhaps he envisioned that Jews (and gentiles) only needed to give up the belief in the salvatory function of practicing the Torah and rid themselves of the pride of having the Torah (cf. 2:8–9), but not actually

---

608 Barth 1974: 287–291; Yee 2004: 152–161.

609 Yee 2004: 154–161. Similarly, Zetterholm 2003: 156–164 in his analysis of the Antioch incident (Gal 2:11–14) suggests that the Jewish *halakha* regulating table fellowship with gentiles was interpreted differently by James and Paul, respectively. While Paul embraced the gentiles as covenant partners, James saw them as god-fearers, with whom full table fellowship was improper. The practical social effect of the Torah was an issue from the very beginning of the Christ-movement.

change their behavior. This is possible, but not entirely unproblematic, since the ethnically significant practices of the Torah, if interpreted in an excluding way, could have caused social division inside the group, as Yee argues. A third possibility is that the author has divisive food regulations in mind. We know that table fellowship between Jews and gentiles was an issue in previous generations (Gal 2:11–14) and this passage might reflect the solution to this issue. Nothing in the text does, however, reveal that the author has table fellowship in mind. We have to admit that the letter fits into a wide range of possible hypothetical historical reconstructions on this point.

Although it is difficult to interpret the exact practical intention of the author, there is a change in attitude in Ephesians compared to Paul and the Apostolic decree. While Paul insists that Christ-believing gentiles should not practice the Torah, he still urges them to be considerate and not practice certain behaviors which may be interpreted as idolatry (Rom 14:1–15:13; 1 Cor 8, 10).[610] At least in Romans the admonitions seem to be prompted by care for Jewish believers (Rom 14:2, 5, 20). The Apostolic decree in the same vein urges the Christ-believing gentiles not to practice a handful of behaviors which would offend their Jewish fellow believers (Acts 15:1–31). In contrast to this, the author of Ephesians seems to imagine that pressure is on the Jews not to cause division by practicing the the Torah—or certain aspects of the Torah. Since the entire letter is mainly written to gentiles, Eph 2:15a should, however, not be interpreted as an appeal to Jewish Christ-believers, but rather an acknowledgement that the gentiles can (or should be able to) expect their Jewish co-believers to be flexible in order to avoid social division.[611] Thus, the text seems to reflect the consensus that it is not the

---

[610] Nanos 1996: 52 argues that Paul taught the Apostolic decree and that this decree is one variation of the Jewish *halakha* regulating the intercourse with god-fearers, similar in function to the Noachide laws (*t. ʿAbod. Zar.* 8:4). Paul does, however, also put pressure on the Christ-believing Jews to allow table-fellowship between Jews and gentiles (Gal 2:11–14), cf. n. 609 above.

[611] *Contra* Yee 2004: 71–125, who in his analysis of Eph 2:11–13 assumes that the author fights Jewish ethnocentrism. Yee's interpretation entirely neglects that the implied audience is not Jewish but gentile. The author's aim can scarcely be to correct a Jewish attitude if the implied recipients are gentiles.

gentiles who are to be considerate, but the Jews.[612] (The gentiles, on the other hand, should gratefully remember that they have been incorporated into the covenant in Christ, 2:11–22.) Unfortunately, the practical implication of 2:15 can never become more than speculation.

> *Causality:* Christ-event → The Torah is "invalidated" → *Duty:* A Christ-believer, either Jew or gentile, should relate to the Torah in a non-divisive manner (which is not detailed in the text)

We must recognize that, since the short phrase simply says too little, it is open for several readings.[613] As I argued above, there is reason to believe that the Jewish author did not intend to argue for a total abandonment of all Torah practice for all Christ-believers, including Jews.[614] However, no matter what the author intended, the gentile Christ-believing readers, who most likely belonged to the Pauline tradition just like the author did, in all probability had no interest in practicing the Torah. Therefore, they probably interpreted the phrase as meaning total rejection of all Torah practice, especially in Christ-believing communities that contained no Jewish Christ-believers. In that case, Shkul argues, Ephesians failed to communicate its intentions with this vague phrase.[615] The imperative in 2:11, which is the only imperative in the first half of

---

[612] If the author, who is probably a Jew (cf. n. 505), concedes that the Jews have a responsibility to modify their behavior, then it might reflect a social situation where the gentile believers have more influence over the behavior norms of the group than they had in previous generations.

[613] Shkul 2009: 135 rightly recognizes that the text means different things to different readers, depending on presuppositions brought to the text.

[614] Although it is not entirely likely that a Jewish author who thinks that being in Christ means inclusion into Israel would abandon the Torah without qualification, it is of course not inconceivable. The representation of being in Christ as a subgroup to Israel, not just an expansion of Israel, makes it possible to think that the subgroup modifies the characteristics of the superordinate group (see discussion in chapter 17.2). I.e., being in Christ could be seen as a special subcategory that is exempted from the Torah. Such an exemption could be imagined to extend to the Christ-believing Jews, too.

[615] Shkul 2009: 140.

the letter, seems to indicate that the author feels he has to convince his gentile recipients about his position (see also chapter 17.2). The earliest known user of Ephesians is Ignatius of Antioch (see chapter 14.2), who certainly subscribes to an interpretation of "Christianity" as something outside "Judaism." Ignatius thinks that "it is outlandish (ἄτοπόν ἐστιν) to proclaim Christ and practice Judaism (ἰουδαΐζω)" (Ign. *Magn.* 10:3). Since Ignatius readily uses Ephesians, he could not have interpreted Ephesians as arguing for only a partial abandonment of the Torah. Unfortunately the phrase in Eph 2:15 is so brief that we simply do not know if the author intended something less radical.

Unity between group members. Unity on the inter-individual level is the first exhortation in the hortatory half of the letter (4:1–6). As we have discussed in the different sections above, many of the prototypical character traits of a Christ-believer are supposed to result in unity: The Spirit inspires unity (2:22; 4:2). Love makes one strive for unity (4:1–6, 15–16). Faith (4:13) and knowledge (4:13–16) result in unity. To reach unity is to become "a perfect man," that is, fully prototypical (4:13). If the group reaches unity it embodies all the desirable characteristics of a Christ-believing community. The author emphasizes unity strongly and seems to think that this is the most central practical expression of the identity in Christ.

> *Attribution:* Being in Christ → Spirit + Love + Knowledge + Faith → Unity

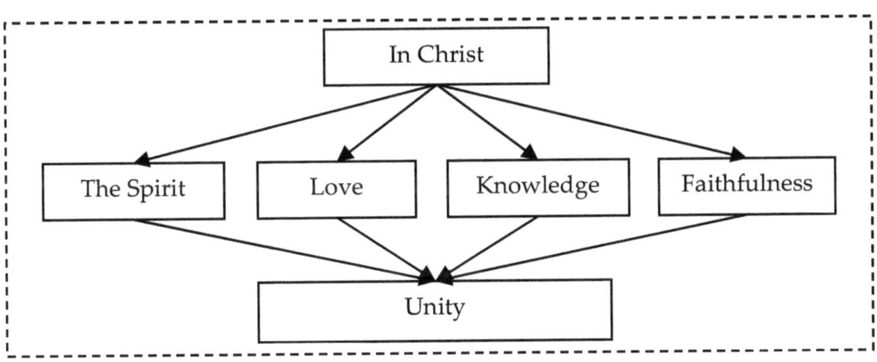

What, then, are the practical implications of unity, according to the imagination of the author? What behaviors and attitudes are expected? The discussion about unity on the inter-individual level in Ephesians contains more detailed practical exhortations than the discussion about unity between Jews and gentiles does.

Cooperation above competition. The introduction of the hortatory half of the letter starts with an enumeration of a number of anti-competitive character traits, which are imagined to lead to unity. The recipients should live "with all humility (ταπεινοφροσύνη) and gentleness (πραΰτης), with patience (μακροθυμία)" (4:2, cf. 4:32). "Humility" (ταπεινοφροσύνη) was generally considered a negative trait in the Greco-Roman world, but it was considered to be a positive characteristic in the Jewish prophetic literature.[616] For the Greeks and the Romans "humility" meant weakness and servility, but for the prophets it was the positive opposite of the arrogance of those who did not value and respect God and neighbours. "Gentleness" (πραΰτης) is the willingness to "waive one's rights that come from seeking the common good without being concerned for personal reputation or gain."[617] "Patience/long-temperedness" (μακροθυμία) is a non-aggressive attitude, tolerant of shortcomings.[618] These three traits should be accompanied with the attitude of "forbearing each other in love" (4:2). As discussed in chapter 6.3, the often competitive honor and shame paradigm and the duty-driven paradigm of *homonoia* balanced each other in the collective culture of the Mediterranean world. By introducing the hortatory half of the letter with these virtues, the author of Ephesians aims to suppress the competitive aspects of interaction, at least within the group.[619] (On the intergroup level, on the other hand, the author readily shames the gentiles.) Rather than intragroup competition, he wants people to see their part in the *homonoia* of the body of Christ (4:7–16). Exactly what actions the author has in mind when he talks about "forbearance" is of course impossible to guess, but we can at least

---

[616] Lincoln 1990: 235–236.

[617] Lincoln 1990: 236.

[618] Lincoln 1990: 236.

[619] Theissen 2007: 420–433 suggests that "Aggressionsverminderung" was a common theme in early Christ-movement.

conclude that the author thinks the recipients should seek for non-competitive, forgiving relations within the group.

Attribution: Humility + Gentleness + Patience → Non-competitive, cooperative, forgiving relations → *Causality:* Unity

Role differentiation. Unity does not mean that everyone is the same. Within the ingroup, the author imagines different subgroups and roles with partly different duties (cf. chapter 5.3). Everyone has a distinct role to fulfill, which helps to build up the community (4:16). If the recipients are to reach unity, they must respect the leadership (4:11–14), especially the leaders' superior knowledge about the truth (4:14–15; see discussion in chapters 17.4 and 18.3.3). When the identity in Christ expands into the household sphere, unity is expressed in terms of harmonious relations between individuals with different roles (5:21–6:9; see discussion in chapter 17.3). Although the author begins the household code by exhorting all household members to subject themselves to each other (5:21), he has no symmetrical subjection in mind. This pattern of different and unequal roles both in the community and in the household is quite in harmony with the *homonoia*-ideal—an ideal which was frequently expressed with body metaphors just as in Ephesians.[620] *Homonoia* is reached when everyone realizes his or her role in the group and fulfills the obligations that come with that role. How one should contribute to the manifestation of unity therefore depends on what subgroup one is considered to belong to. A leader should teach, a newcomer should learn; an inferior household member should be submissive, a superior one should be benevolent. The unity theme therefore functions to legitimize hierarchies in the community. The perfect body of Christ can only be accomplished if differences in status and duty within the group are accepted.

Causality: Everybody does his/her part → Unity → Perfection of the *ekklēsia*

---

[620] See n. 197.

Speech. Finally, the unity theme is associated with teaching and ingroup speech (see chapters 18.3.3 and 18.3.5). Unity is reached whenever the ingroup accepts and speaks the teachings of the group and avoids alternative teachings (4:13–15, cf. 5:6). The author exhorts them to "putting away falsehood, let all of us speak the truth" since they are "members of one another" (4:25). They should not speak any "corrupt word" (λόγος σαπρός) but only speak that which is "good for building up" (4:27). In short, the "building up" (4:12) of the body of Christ is imagined to be dependent on a shared teaching. As has been discussed earlier in for instance chapters 8.1 and 18.3.3, religious knowledge is by its largely non-empirical nature cognitively uncertain, which potentially increases the need for ingroup affirmation in order to maintain the beliefs. The author seems to realize the social turbulence which may arise when people disagree, since he believes that unity is achieved through a culture where people are only given honor and acceptance if they say certain things and speak in a certain manner. The sectarian rationality of this thinking—unity through conformity—probably helped to maintain the ingroup.

Summary. Ephesians presents unity as a highly important norm, both unity between Jew and gentile and unity between individual members. Both aspects of this unity are motivated by the narrative about their spiritual unity in Christ. Moreover, just about every prototypical character trait is associated with unity. Regarding the unity between Jew and gentile, it is not easy to determine to what extent Jewish Christ-believers should stop practicing the Torah, but I concluded that the author thinks the halakhic practice of the Torah at least needs to be modified so that it does not cause division. When the author explicates the practical expressions of unity on the inter-individual level, he emphasizes anti-competitive attitudes, role differentiation and conventional non-divisive speech—behaviors which all would have increased the sense of unity within the group.

18.4.2 Speech

We have already had ample reason to examine speech as prototypical behavior in Ephesians. This section will summarize these discussions and fill in gaps in areas that have not been adequately covered previously. Speech norms go in three directions in Ephesians: a) intragroup interaction, b) evangelizing speech, and c) prayer and thanksgiving to God.

Intragroup interaction. Intragroup speech norms are associated with just about every attributed character trait found in Ephesians. As the analyses above have already shown, correct speech is particularly associated with holiness, knowledge, love and proper emotions (see chapters 18.2, 18.3.3, 18.3.5 and 18.3.7). Speech norms appear in virtually every section of the hortatory half of the letter. In 4:1–16, where unity and spiritual growth is the main concern, the ideal of "speaking the truth/being truthful" (ἀληθεύω) is seen as the practical expression of spiritual perfection, contrasted with destructive teachings (4:12–15). In 4:17–31, which is introduced by the contrast between a gentile lifestyle and being in Christ, the author exhorts the recipients that they should "[while] putting away the lie, speak the truth" (4:25), to "let no corrupt word come out of your mouth, but [rather] that which [is] good for building up" (4:29), and to avoid "evil-speaking" (4:31). In 5:1–6, which is introduced by the exhortation to be like God and live in love, the author forbids them to speak in a disruptive way, followed by a threat of exclusion. In 5:7–14, under the heading of being children of light, the exhortation not even to speak about "the unfruitful works of darkness" is repeated (5:11–12).

As we have already discussed in chapter 18.3.3, the group dynamic effect of these norms, if they are practiced, is a climate which enhances commitment and decreases cognitive uncertainty. I have also discussed that speech was a way to present oneself as prototypical before the group (see e.g., chapter 18.2). I will therefore not repeat these arguments again, but rather discuss other potential group dynamic effects of speech behavior in Ephesians.

First, to "speak the truth" (4:25) is probably a general exhortation not to lie and not just a prohibition of advocating false teachings. Such a norm, if it was efficiently internalized, would have increased the mutual intragroup honesty and control, which would have made it more socially costly to be deviant and more rewarding to be prototypical. The taboo against even speaking about what is considered to be deviant behavior (5:3) probably also decreased the possibility to question group norms.

Second, the feeling of being a superior group would have increased if the group members managed to control their speech, since they would then only have heard each other speaking prototypically and in this way would have been mutually ignorant of any deviant thoughts that might have haunted certain individuals.

Third, we may imagine that there was an encouraging aspect of speech behavior norms. As discussed above in chapter 18.4.1, the emphasis on unity probably had an anti-competitive edge. Everyone should act in a way that is good for the entire group. Speech was the key behavior for "building up" (4:29). However, it would be wrong to argue that the author promotes some kind of generally affirmative speech behavior ("You are loved as you are"). Rather, the emphasis of the letter is spiritual growth, which makes it more reasonable to imagine that encouragement meant they should try to convince each other to reach for perfection.

In sum, conformist intragroup speech is frequently emphasized in Ephesians. It is central to group dynamics, since the norms are very central to cognitive certainty, self-esteem in relation to other groups, intragroup honesty, intragroup conformity and encouragement to become more prototypical. Speech is also the key behavior when it comes to displaying prototypicality within the group.

Evangelizing speech. In the discussion in chapter 17.1.3 about what kind of attitude Ephesians has towards evangelization, I concluded that the author probably considered evangelization to be a relevant part of the group's identity, since they remembered themselves as converted (2:1–22). This evangelization was part of God's triumph over evil spiritual agents (2:2; 3:10; 6:12). Although this aspect of their identity might be suppressed, perhaps due to external pressure, it is, nevertheless, an integral part of their identity.

In this light, some of the elements of the armor-metaphor (6:10–20) may be fruitfully understood as evangelizing. The introduction to the armor-metaphor is clearly defensive (6:11, 13), but the specification in 6:14–17 of the six pieces of the metaphorical equipment which the Christ-believers are to "put on" (6:11) can be seen as holding both defensive and attacking elements. Just like any conversionist sect, they both want to keep themselves holy (defense) and convert people (attack). The first, the third and the last element of the equipment have been interpreted as potentially referring to evangelization. We should therefore evaluate whether we have sufficient reason to interpret these elements as evangelizing activities which liberate people of flesh and blood from the dominion of the evil spiritual realm and bring them into the dominion of Christ. The vague and inconclusive language in the description of these pieces of equipment makes several interpretations possible.

The first piece of equipment, "girding your loins in truth" (περιζωσάμενοι τὴν ὀσφὺν ὑμῶν ἐν ἀληθείᾳ, 6:14, my translation), could possibly be evangelizing. Arnold points out that "truth" is a description of the gospel in 1:13, and discusses the possibility that the girding of the loins might be interpreted as a readiness to proclaim.[621] Arnold does, however, acknowledge that "truth" is more likely a general reference to living truthfully and speaking the truth (4:25; 5:9). In the wider interpretation of "truth," the girding of the loins becomes a defensive metaphor where holding on to the truth gives protection against attacks from the evil spiritual realm. This wider understanding is preferable, since it does not press a too specific meaning onto the concept of "truth."

The third piece of equipment, "shodding the feet in the preparation of the gospel (ἑτοιμασία τοῦ εὐαγγελίου) of peace" (6:15, my translation), can more easily be argued to have evangelizing content. The key word "preparation" (ἑτοιμασία) has connotations of both "readiness" and "steadfastness."[622] The genitive construct "preparation of the gospel" could be understood either defensively or as evangelizing. The defensive interpretation, argued for by Hoehner, is "the steadfastness [to stand, cf. 6:14] which comes from [holding on to] the gospel," that is, a genitive of origin, where the gospel is the origin of the steadfastness.[623] The believer is enabled to stand firm as a result of holding on to the gospel. The evangelizing interpretation, argued for by Rudolf Schnackenburg, is "readiness for the gospel," that is, an objective genitive, where the object of the readiness is the gospel.[624] The believer is

621 Arnold 1989: 110.

622 Barth 1974: 770–771, 797–799; Lincoln 1990: 448–449.

623 Hoehner 2002: 843.

624 Gnilka 1971: 311–312; Schnackenburg 1982: 284–285.

ready to act for the sake of the gospel, that is, to evangelize. Hoehner argues that the phrase cannot be seen as evangelizing, since the emphasis of the armor-metaphor is defensive (6:11, 13).[625] Attack can, however, be seen as the best defense in a world view where victory over evil spirits is at hand whenever someone is converted. All other usages of "gospel" (εὐαγγέλιον) and "evangelize" (εὐαγγελίζομαι) in Ephesians refer to the process of evangelizing, not just to the content of the gospel (1:13; 2:17; 3:6, 8; 6:19).[626] There is a scholarly discussion whether the phrase is inspired by the wording in LXX, Isa 52:7, πόδες εὐαγγελιζομένου ἀκοὴν εἰρήνης—a passage which clearly is about preaching good news and where the "feet of the one who evangelizes" are mentioned. Barth argues that since the entire metaphor in Ephesians 6:10–20 is about a soldier, the footwear should be imagined to be the stable shoes of a soldier (*caligula*) as opposed to the bare feet which swift messengers had.[627] Consequently, he argues that Isa 52:7 did not inspire the phrase in 6:15 and that the feet are meant to stand fast rather than to bring forth the gospel. Lincoln counters that argument by noting that 6:15 does not mention the shoes, only the feet, which indicates that the inspiration is Isa 52:7 rather than the correct footwear of a Roman soldier.[628] In sum, in the light of Isa 52:7 and the use of "gospel" and "evangelize" in Ephesians, it is quite plausible that the feet are meant to be ready to bring forth the gospel. Attack is the best defense.

The sixth piece of equipment, "the sword of the Spirit, which is the word (ῥῆμα) of God" (6:17), can easily be interpreted as evangelizing. The genitive phrase "the word (ῥῆμα) of God" could be understood in

[625] Hoehner 2002: 844.

[626] In 1:13 the hearing of the gospel leads to faithfulness. In 2:17 the evangelizing results in the group being saved. In 3:6 the gentiles are fellow-heirs "through" (διά) the gospel. In 3:8 we told that Paul has "evangelized" the message in 3:6 to the gentiles. In 6:19 Paul wants to make the gospel known. In sum, the author of Ephesians uses the εὐαγγελ-stem to signal the process of spreading the gospel. The content of the gospel is often referred to with the word μυστήριον. The use of εὐαγγέλιον/εὐαγγελίζομαι and μυστήριον, respectively, becomes clear especially in 3:2–13.

[627] Barth 1974: 798–799.

[628] Lincoln 1990: 448. Cf Schnackenburg 1982: 284–285.

two ways. The defensive interpretation is "the word which comes from God," that is, a genitive of origin (or "the word spoken by God," a subjective genitive), where God gives the words necessary for defense.[629] The evangelizing interpretation is "the word about God," that is, an objective genitive, where the word tells the gospel about God's magnificent plan.[630] Also the interpretation "the word which comes from God" could be taken as evangelizing, that is, as evangelizing words inspired by God.[631] Hoehner, who understands the entire metaphor as defensive, emphasizes that ῥῆμα often carries a more confronting and judging connotation than λόγος and draws the conclusion that the word is apologetic rather than evangelizing.[632] This use of ῥῆμα may be the case in many texts, but certainly not in Paul's letter to the Romans, a text which clearly has inspired Ephesians.[633] There ῥῆμα is used about the preached word and the word of Christ through which preaching comes about (Rom 10:8, 17–18).[634] Moreover, the only other use of ῥῆμα in Ephesians is 5:27. Here the ῥῆμα has a cleansing and sanctifying effect, associated with baptism, which makes ῥῆμα a word that is effective in the process of conversion. (This converting understanding of ῥῆμα does not necessarily exclude the apologetic or judging connotation. We can certainly imagine conversion through apologia and reproach.) Besides, the metaphor of a sword implies more than defense. Evangelizing "attacks" with the word of God defeat the evil spirits whenever they succeed in their mission and this helps the ingroup to stand firm.

Assuming that the third and the sixth piece of the armor are offensive and evangelizing, we discern a repetitive structure:

---

[629] Hoehner 2002: 852–854.

[630] Schnackenburg 1982: 286.

[631] Lincoln 1990: 450–451.

[632] Hoehner 2002: 853; MacDonald 2004: 346.

[633] See n. 417.

[634] Cf. Lincoln 1990: 451. Paul also uses ῥῆμα in 2 Cor 12:4 with no judging connotation, and in 2 Cor 13:1 with a connotation of judging testimony.

a. Girding loins in truth (6:14a)—defense
b. Breastplate of righteousness (6:14b) — defense
c. Shodding the feet in readiness for the gospel of peace (6:15) — attack
a′. Shield of faith (6:16) — defense
b′. Helmet of salvation (6:17a) — defense
c′. Sword of the Spirit, which is the word of God (6:17b) — attack

In short, although the interpretation of the diffent elements in the armor-metaphor will always be difficult due to the brevity and vagueness of the metaphor, there is sufficient reason to believe that the armor-metaphor implies an exhortation to be ready to evangelize as a part of the war against the evil spiritual realm. The evangelizing interpretation is supported by the analysis in chapter 17.1.3 that the author of Ephesians imagines the ingroup to have a conversionist identity.

The act of evangelization is seen as primarily consisting of speech. The recipients came to believe "having heard the word of truth, the gospel of your salvation" (1:13). Paul's task is to "evangelize ... and to make everyone see what is the plan of the mystery" (3:8–9, NRSV modified). The ideal of the implied Paul is that "whenever I open my mouth, words may be given me so that I will fearlessly make known the mystery of the gospel" (6:19, NIV).

The consistent emphasis on speech is a change in the evangelizing strategy from Paul's mission in Corinth. Paul claims in his correspondence with the Corinthians that "My speech and my proclamation were not with plausible words of wisdom, but with a demonstration of the Spirit and of power" (1 Cor 2:4). In spite of the strong belief in the power of the Spirit in Ephesians, evangelization is a matter of "making known" rather than of demonstrating God's power. Speech and wisdom are, however, caused by the power of the Spirit (cf. chapter 18.3.1). In this way, the evangelizing word in Ephesians is equivalent to the power demonstrations in 1 Corinthians, since the evangelizing words ultimately derive from God's power (6:10). The practical strategy is, nevertheless, no longer demonstration of supernatural power (miracles, prophecy, etc.) but rather evangelizing speech which informs the outsiders of "the mystery."

In sum, since conversion is a part of the identity in Christ in Ephesians, we have reason to believe that some of the elements of the armor-metaphor (6:10–20) should be interpreted as "attack," that is, evangelization. Conversion of new members was a victory against evil spiritual forces. As opposed to Paul, Ephesians only emphasizes speech as the method of evangelization.

Prayer and thanksgiving to God. The most fundamental rationale for the existence of the group is that they are chosen by God (see chapter 16 above). God is their patron and they are his faithful and loyal clients. Therefore it is obviously very important to have a practical expression for communion with God—prayer. The intragroup dynamics of prayer was discussed in the section about power (see chapter 18.3.2) and it was concluded that prayer is considered to be the practical catalyst that stimulates the positive mutually reinforcing causal circle in which the Spirit empowers the believer. Prayer is thus both an expression of prototypicality and something which causes prototypicality.

The thanksgiving aspect of prayer has not been covered above, however. In the hortatory half of the letter, "thanksgiving" is contrasted with destructive speech (5:4). In contrast to being drunk with wine, the recipients are exhorted to "be filled with the Spirit, as you sing psalms and hymns and spiritual songs among yourselves, singing and making melody to the Lord in your hearts, giving thanks to God the Father at all times and for everything" (5:18–20). An attitude of thankfulness to God is considered prototypical and its practical expressions are different kinds of praise in the form of thanksgiving prayers and songs.[635] Since the very existence of the group is a result of God's working, it is almost self-evident that expressions of gratitude and emotional attachment to God are important.

Besides a sense of closeness to God, praise in a group also has group-dynamic effects. The praising activity should be directed not only to God, but also "to each other" (ἑαυτοῖς) (5:19). The thanksgiving prayers

[635] Neyrey 2005 remarks that thankfulness was generally considered to be one of the most important aspects of a proper attitude to the gods.

and the songs most probably had a narrative content,[636] which functioned to remind the participants of the rationale and value of their identity (cf. chapters 2.1 and 11). Moreover, seeing and hearing each other sing and praise probably increased the sense that their belonging to Christ was worth appreciating (cf. chapter 8.1).

In sum, prayer and praise to God is a speech behavior that may express gratitude, increase the sense of being empowered under the Spirit, remind of the narrative rationale of the Christ-believers' identity, and nurture the feeling that they belonged to a community of committed believers.

18.4.3 Endurance and Suffering

The digression on Paul's ministry in 3:2–13 is framed by the statements that Paul is a prisoner (3:1) and that he is suffering (3:13). The presentation of Paul is introduced by an emphatic "*I* Paul" (ἐγὼ Παῦλος) followed by "prisoner of the Lord" (3:1). It seems that this is the most impressive start of the presentation of Paul that the author can imagine. In the end of the letter he also portrays Paul as an "ambassador in chains" (6:20). The willingness to suffer for the Lord seems to have been an increasingly powerful way to be accredited with prototypicality in the first post-apostolic generations. The deutero-Pauline authors emphasize Paul's imprisonment with admiration (Col 4:18; 1 Tim. 1:8; 2:9).[637] According to 1 Peter, suffering "as a Christian" is very honorable (1 Pet. 4:12–19). Ignatius of Antioch gets charismatic authority from his imprisonment and impending martyrdom. He even compares his imprisonment to that of Paul's (Ign. *Eph.* 11–12), which indicates that he thinks of Paul as being the exemplar of a suffering Christian. The Shepherd of Hermas reserves the right side of the throne in heaven for those who have suffered for Christ (Herm. *Vis.* 3.1.9). We can therefore assume that the emphasis on Paul's imprisonment in Ephesians is

---

[636] We do not know this for sure, but it is hard to imagine that the hymns did not hold references to the ingroup narratives, especially since the hymnal passages in Ephesians, e.g. 1:3–14; 2:14–18, recount narratives about God's initiative.

[637] Esler 2007.

intended to remind the recipient of what a committed and therefore prototypical person the implied Paul is.[638] (Being prepared to identify with a group even when the cost is very high, for instance when you have to suffer for it, is a sign of high commitment, as we discussed in chapter 9.3) The rhetorical force which has been created through the references to Paul's suffering is then used in the beginning of the hortatory half of the letter to give weight to the exhortations: "Therefore, I, the prisoner in the Lord, urge you…" (4:1, my translation).[639]

Narrating Paul's suffering in the past does not only function to legitimize Paul's authority, but also as an example for others to follow. Intriguingly, there are no explicit references to actual persecution of the recipients in the letter.[640] Nevertheless, the author seems to imagine that being a Christ-believer potentially leads to difficulties. In the passage on preparation for spiritual warfare (6:10–20) the recipients are encouraged to endure "the schemes of the Devil" (6:11) and "extinguish all the flaming arrows of the evil one" (6:16). A good Christ-believer is someone who manages to "stand" (6:13), that is, to stay committed, in spite of all hardships. The attribute that will help them to endure is power from the Lord (6:10). (Ephesians also refers in passing to the suffering of Christ as a prototypical expression of love (5:2, 25), but these passages do not develop the theme of suffering further.)

> *Attribution:* Power (+ Love) → Endures suffering, that is, stays committed

The greatness of Paul's imprisonment and suffering is that these hardships have come upon him for the sake of the gospel to the gentiles (3:1, 13, 6:20). As was discussed in chapters 17.1.3 and 18.4.2,

---

638 Fischer 1973: 95–108 shows that Paul's suffering for the sake of the gentiles was a standard component of the portrait of Paul in deutero-Pauline literature.

639 Cf. Byrskog 2005: 117–119.

640 Best 2004: 647 finds this surprising in the light of other post-70 texts from Asia Minor (especially 1 Pet, Rev). However, if the letter was written in a situation where persecution was currently not very intense, it is not very surprising that the author puts more focus on the memory of suffering in the past and on potential suffering, but less on current suffering.

evangelizing activity is considered to be a part of the war against the evil forces (6:15, 17). This may be understood to mean that the recipients are not only supposed to keep committed in spite of suffering; they are also supposed to be prepared to suffer as a result of their evangelizing activity. It is not enough to save themselves by staying holy (introversionist attitude) but they should also evangelize, even if it means suffering (conversionist attitude, cf. chapter 17.1.3 above).

When a group experiences a threat, the individuals who belong to the group tend to diverge in opposite directions, depending on their commitment (see chapter 9.3). Those who are strongly committed become even more dedicated, trying to affirm the value of the group when they have to suffer for their identity, but those who have weaker commitment tend to slip out of the group in order to save their own interests and self-esteem. In Ephesians, the threat seems more potential than actual, since there are no clear references to actual suffering on behalf of the recipients. Nevertheless, the author prepares them for the potential threat (6:10–20). He conceives of the potential threat as a source of pride and claims that every time Paul suffers (and presumably also every time any individual suffers) it increases the honor of the entire group (3:13). On the other hand, if they are not committed enough and encounter hardships, they might fall into the grip of the Devil (6:11–13). In short, the author argues that if they endure suffering their status will increase. This narrative probably had an impact that motivated them to endure sufferings if necessary. More importantly, however, it had an effect in times when they did not actually need to suffer—the identity as a group prepared to suffer and an atmosphere of potential threats from other groups might have inspired commitment and a sense of superiority.

We may therefore assume that the author invents potential threats just as much as he warns for them. Shkul criticizes MacDonald and Esler for reading the suffering passages in Ephesians as reflections of real threats, although Ephesians lacks references to actual threats.[641] Instead she argues that Ephesians constructs a threat for strategic reasons. By insinuating a threat from the surrounding world, the author creates

---

[641] Shkul 2009: e.g. 142-145, 149 n. 13, 180-182 criticizing Esler 2007; MacDonald 2004.

social distance to outgroups and an obligation to be loyal to the ingroup in the face of this threatening situation. It is likely that the theme of suffering creates commitment, as argued above. However, in the context of a large number of other texts from the early Christ-movement that discuss suffering,[642] it is probably an overstatement to claim that the author constructs a threat out of thin air, which does not reflect any real experience. A rhetorician who does not start from the experiences of the audience would probably not be very convincing, since new information more easily feels true if it fits what one already knows.[643] Although we do not know for sure, it is quite likely that the author and the recipients have memories of real threats (harassment, marginalization, persecution, etc.) in mind when he exhorts them to "stand" (6:10–20). It is also quite probable that the author himself saw potential threats from other groups and from the spiritual world. Nevertheless, we should acknowledge that there were strategic reasons to exaggerate these potential threats.

Summary. There is no reference to actual threats to the group in Ephesians, but readiness to suffer and endurance are nevertheless described as prototypical ideals. The author emphasizes Paul's suffering in order to give the message in the letter credibility and in order to give an example for others to follow. When the author emphasizes suffering as an ideal, it probably increases the commitment of the committed but repulses those who are not that committed. At the same time, the imagination of a potential threat increases the social distinction and distance to the non-believing gentiles and a sense of obligation to be loyal to the group.

18.4.4 Practical Intragroup Care

We have already seen in chapter 18.4.1 that the ideal of unity in Ephesians was promoted as an anti-competitive attitude of kindness, forgiving and tolerance for minor flaws (4:2–3, 32). Moreover, people were encouraged to do their part in the building of the body of Christ

---

[642] Cf. n. 640.

[643] See n. 135.

(4:17). In spite of this, the author has surprisingly little to say about practical ingroup care, in the sense of material, practical or juridical help to the needy. The most important observation is therefore the relative lack of attention to this subject compared to for instance the speech norms.

There is, however, one short passage that promotes intragroup care. In the middle of a discussion which is dominated by discourse about emotions and speech behaviors (4:25–32; cf. chapter 18.3.7), the author makes an abrupt break in his discussion and writes: "Thieves must give up stealing; rather let them labor and work honestly with their own hands, so as to have something to share with the needy" (4:28). There is, however, not much more we can do with this passage than to notice that if the group members indeed gave to the needy, it probably would have increased the sense of unity and belonging.[644] The author does not argue directly for this norm with reference to the metaphor of the *ekklēsia* as a body, but the metaphor of the body is used as an argument for the first exhortation in the passage (4:25) and it is not unreasonable to imagine that the author thinks the idea of parts of a body helping each other is relevant to the behavior norm of helping the needy, too (cf. 4:16). For some reason—maybe because he thinks that the norm is plainly obvious—the author does not feel the need to motivate this norm explicitly with reference to ingroup narratives or to attributed traits.

18.4.5 Household Behavior

The practical exhortations in the household code (5:21–6:9) do not need to be repeated here, as they have already been discussed in chapter 17.3. There it was concluded that the practical exhortations in the household code are unspecific, conventional and do not wrestle with any of the dilemmas that probably would have arisen in the real social settings of the recipient communities. The rhetorical effort of Ephesians aims at integrating the household and the *ekklēsia,* so that the household becomes a subcategory to the identity in Christ. Therefore, the text does not say anything particularly interesting about practical household

[644] On the contrasting behavior of "stealing", see chapter 18.4.6.

behavior. The dominant part (husband, parent, master) should be benevolent towards the submissive part (wife, child, slave) and the submissive part should be obedient—as Christ-believers, for Christ's sake and in a Christ-like manner.

18.4.6 Exceedingly Deviant Behaviors

There are a few behaviors mentioned in Ephesians that are considered to be so deviant that the author barely feels the need to explain why they are deviant. He probably expects the recipients to recognize these behaviors as deviant without further argument.

First, we have the norm "He who has been stealing (ὁ κλέπτων) must steal no longer," which functions as a contrast to the norm that one should work in order to be able to share with the needy (4:28, NIV). The author obviously feels no need to motivate this norm, but rather uses it as an opposite to honest work (cf. chapter 18.4.4). Some commentators think that the exhortation might reflect a real problem of day workers who stole when they were unemployed,[645] or slaves who stole from their masters.[646] A better explanation, however, is that "stealing" is a standard stereotype of the old sinful (gentile) self (cf. Rom 2:21; 1 Cor 6:10; 1 Pet 4:14).[647] Stealing is here simply used as a stereotyped opposite of the desired ideal that they should do decent work and share with the needy. Hence, we should be hesitant to read this norm as mirroring a real problem. As was discussed in chapter 7.2, the experience of being distinct from the outgroups makes the ingroup meaningful. Therefore it is efficient to use contrasting stereotypes of the outgroup to argue for ingroup behavior norms, in this case honest work.

Second, we have the deviant behaviors "fornication" and "idolatry" accompanied by the state "impurity" and the attributed disposition "greed" in the passage about walking in love (5:3, 5). These behaviors have been discussed above in the sections about gentiles, holiness and love (see chapters 17.1.2, 18.2 and 18.3.5). I concluded that these

---

645 Best 1992; Hoehner 2002: 624–625.

646 Gnilka 1971: 271.

647 Lincoln 1990: 303.

behaviors are very similar to the stereotypical Jewish description of the gentiles and that the author is not really worried about these behaviors but rather about speech. The argumentation he uses against these behaviors does not really explain why they are wrong. Rather he just says that "it is fitting" not to even talk about these behaviors and that anyone who carries them out does not have "any inheritance in the kingdom of Christ and of God" (5:5). The argument is simply that the behaviors are deviant and that those who perform them will be excluded, but no explanation as to why they are wrong is given. This indicates that the author expects his recipients to understand without explanation. These stereotypical behaviors are similar in function to the norm of not stealing in that they are not mentioned for their own sake but in order to back up another argument.

In sum, both "stealing," "fornication" and "idolatry" are deviant behaviors, associated with the gentiles, which the author does not mention for their own sake but in order to promote or discourage other behaviors.

With this section, the analysis of the ingroup prototype in Ephesians has come to an end. It is now time to summarize and evaluate the results.

Conclusion and Prospects for Further Research

In the theoretical part of this study, I argued that the cognitive sciences, particularly different branches of cognitive psychology, may improve our understanding of the early Christ-movement. I argued that there are basic innate cognitive patterns in the human mind—categorization, causal thinking, attribution, analogical thinking and narrative comprehension—that provide a good hermeneutical starting point for historians who aim to understand the cognitive constructs that governed the experience of past subjects in cross-culturally valid categories. Has this shown to be true? I think the text study of Ephesians has made a case that cognitive psychology can help the historian produce novel and well-founded interpretations of an already well explored text. A systematic application of the insight from cognitive psychology has helped us to better understand the imagination of Ephesians. Using cross-culturally valid cognitive patterns, this study has been able to bridge the gap between 21st century scholars and the first recipients of Ephesians in a new way. The result of the investigation is a systematic comprehension of the relation between identity and behavior norms in Ephesians described in categories common to us and to the first Christ-believers.

This study has utilized a number of cognitive perspectives. The most important of these are a) social identity theory (see chapters 5 to 10), b) attribution theory (see chapter 6), and c) basic insights about narrative comprehension (see chapter 11). A few scholars have analyzed Ephesians using social identity theory before this study (see chapter 1.3), but not to the same extent as this study does. No study before this one has combined social identity theory with attribution theory (and other cognitive theories). Therefore, this study has been able to systematically work through the cognitive structure of the ingroup prototype in a new way. The cognitive perspective of this study has also facilitated a discussion about the potential cognitive and group dynamic effects of the ingroup prototype and the narratives that are expressed in Ephesians. Furthermore, the author's rhetorical strategy to influence the cognition of the recipients has been analysed with a cognitive approach. In this conclusion I will focus on the innovative results of the study.

The heart of this analysis of Ephesians is the reconstruction of how the author presents the ingroup prototype together with reflections about what social effects this prototype could have if it became the shared cognition of the group. We will soon return to the results of the analysis of the ingroup prototype, but first I would like to highlight a number of results in the sections that paved the way for the analysis of the prototype:

First, social identity theory and other cognitive theories helped to estimate the probability that the norms of Ephesians were approximately accepted by contemporary communities of Christ-believers (see chapter 14.2). In a situation where we have no record of the immediate reception of the text we can only speculate hypothetically about to what extent Ephesians reflects and/or successfully constructs the shared cognition of the intended recipient communities. A cognitive perspective provides a way to conceptualize such hypothetical estimation. Ephesians gives voice to traditions and norms that are present in many other texts from the early Christ-movement. This suggests that Ephesians to a large degree appeals to already shared cognition. Therefore, since the text to a large extent reiterates what the recipients already experience as true, the implied author gains credibility as a good prototypical ingroup member. Moreover, Ephesians takes advantage of the prototypical image of Paul in the deutero-Pauline era in order to give weight to its message. These factors, together with the observation that the letter seems to have been positively received by Ignatius of Antioch (and others) a few decades later, gave us reason to conclude that it is a reasonable hypothesis that the letter both reflects and successfully constructs the shared cognition of the recipient communities to some degree.

Second, social identity theory together with attribution theory provided a new perspective on the rhetorical strategy of the letter (see chapter 15). I argued that the rhetorical strategy has several components.

The basic strategy is to make the identity in Christ salient and valuable by actualizing the narrative rationale of the group so that they feel motivated to become prototypical group members. This strategy is combined with the rhetorical strategy to subtly suggest that although the recipients are certainly ingroup, they are still lacking in prototypical qualities and need to improve. At the same time, the author positions the implied Paul as a very prototypical exemplar with superior knowledge and commitment. While making their identity in Christ salient and valuable and creating a need to improve, the author narrates their relation to different social categories and the connection between prototypical attributes and behaviors. Throughout the letter he narrates the prototypical attitude towards a number of social categories: the gentiles, Israel, the leaders and the household. The most important narratives for this study are, however, the attributions between behaviors and prototypical dispositions and spiritual states. The rhetorical strategy of Ephesians is to narrate the causes of different behaviors and evaluate these causes as either prototypical or deviant. The author aims to induce the belief that certain behaviors are caused by certain prototypical attributes while other behaviors are caused by deviant attributes. As recent attribution research predicts, there is a tension between the indicative and the imperative (causal effect and duty) in the rhetoric of Ephesians. They are holy and they should do what is fitting for holy ones. They do have the Spirit and they should beware not to grieve the Spirit. They are loving and they should act in a loving manner to remain in the Kingdom. Et cetera. If the recipients accept the causal connections that the letter suggests, they will have motivation to act according to the behavior norms of the letter in order to be prototypical—both in their own eyes, in the eyes of God and in the eyes of other group members. In short, cognitive psychology can help us understand why the rhetorical strategy of Ephesians works. The rhetoric about the relation between identity in Christ and norms (often called "theology and ethics") can be fruitfully analyzed in terms of cognitive patterns that are common to us and to the recipients.

Third, this study has explored the narrative about God's agency as the rationale of the group and concluded that God is portrayed as an anthropomorphic agent with motivations. These motivations explain why God has chosen the group. God has the typical attributed character traits of a patron: he wants recognition (glory, honor) and he has a benevolent (loving) attitude toward his subjects. These are the reasons why God bestows gifts upon the group. Among these gifts is the Spirit, which empowers them and gives them prototypical character traits. In this way, their behavior and behavior norms are constructed as both caused and demanded by God, which gives particular weight to the norms. The narrative chains of causality go all the way from the narrative about God's agency to their behavior (norms) and form a coherent narrative whole between identity and behavior norms.

Fourth, this study has used self-categorization theory to discuss hierarchies of identities in a new way. I argued that although the non-believing gentiles are definitely the Christ-believers' major outgroup (the group in relation to which they maximize their distinctiveness and value), conversion and evangelization towards the gentiles is still part of the identity in Christ according to Ephesians. Further, I argued for a novel solution to the long-standing scholarly debate about the relation between the *ekklēsia* and Israel in Ephesians. I introduced the possibility that one social category can be a subcategory to another social category and argued that the *ekklēsia* is neither just an expansion of Israel, nor a new or parallel "Israel" but rather a subcategory to Israel. This would explain a number of features in Ephesians, such as a) that there is a strong front towards non-believing gentiles but not towards non-believing Jews, b) that the *ekklēsia* inherits most of the characteristics of Israel, modifies a few of these characteristics and adds a number of exclusive features, and c) that although non-believing Jews are implicitly in a position more "close" to God than non-believing gentiles, it is still an advantage for Jews to become Christ-believers according to Ephesians. The insight about hierarchies of identities was also used to understand the rhetorical effort of the household code. The author aims at making household identities into subcategories of the identity in Christ and his rhetorical method to achieve this is to imbue conventional household norms with motivations from the Christ-narrative through analogical transfers. Finally, the position of the leaders was analyzed as a prototypical subcategory of Christ-believers, whose teaching other believers should listen to. The most important insight about the leadership was, however, that they are put in a position where they have legitimacy to control the information flow in the community and thus to increase the cognitive certainty within the group.

Most importantly, however, this study has scrutinized in detail how the author presents the ingroup prototype. Here I will highlight the most central results of the reconstruction of the prototype:

First, we found repeatedly that the chains of causality between different attributes (dispositions and spiritual states) and behaviors are believed to be mutually reinforcing. The author imagines that the status before God as holy, influence from the Spirit, power, knowledge, love, etc., can increase or decrease through their way of life. Perhaps surprisingly, faith is an exception; it is considered to be a minimal criterion for being in Christ, but not a character trait that should grow and develop. For the other attributes, however, the imagination is that they must be reinforced through continuous prototypical behavior. If the recipients behave properly and strive to have virtuous attitudes, they can potentially become perfectly prototypical and "be filled with all the fullness of God" (3:19) through the reinforcing power of the Spirit, but if they behave in a deviant manner they can potentially break the positive reinforcing dynamics towards perfection and instead "give the Devil a chance" (4:27), that is, come under the influence of evil spiritual forces, lose the favor of God and eventually be rejected from the Kingdom (5:5). There is a tension between causality and duty in this imagination, just as could be expected from the theoretical discussions in chapter 6.1. This tension has multiple group dynamic effects. It makes the group members feel "empowered," that is, they become confident that they can do better than others thanks to the Spirit. At the same time, the prototype is formulated in a way that never allows certainty about one's prototypicality. Especially the analysis of the knowledge theme highlighted that the content of the profound knowledge of God and Christ, which is a part of the goal of perfection for a Christ-believer, is formulated in such a vague manner that one can never be confident that one has reached such insight. This leads to a situation where the striving for prototypicality must continue every day and where one's prototypicality can potentially be questioned by those in leading positions if one behaves in an unconventional manner. Therefore the recipients get motivation to continuously act in line with the concrete behavioral expressions of prototypicality in order to avoid cognitive dissonance between attributed characteristics and actual behavior, both in their own eyes and in the eyes of other group members. Moreover, the imagination legitimates group processes of giving status and marginalization; inclusion and exclusion, since group members find it legitimate to make judgments about status before God depending on behavior.

Second, this study has discussed the potential group dynamic effects that arise as the prototype is depicted in contrast to the non-believing gentiles. Deviant behavior is described as gentile-like behavior. This rhetoric describes the deviant as someone who undermines the group's distinctiveness and superiority in relation to the gentiles. If the rhetoric is successful, it creates a perception which typically creates a will to reproach, marginalize and finally perhaps even exclude the deviant, since the cognitive distinctiveness and self-esteem of the group potentially decreases due to the deviant. The threat of being disliked by God and other group members and, in contrast, the promise of perfection and appreciation by God and others, potentially motivates committed group members to embrace and practice group norms.

Third, this study has scrutinized how the author aims at creating a group climate which increases cognitive certainty and thereby commitment to the group. The most extensively discussed behavior norm in Ephesians is how they should speak to each other within the group, with the advice that they should only articulate the accepted teaching and avoid alternative teachings. Instead of foolish talk they should praise and worship—behaviors that certainly would increase the cognitive certainty about the rationale of the group and deepen the emotional attachment to Christ. The social and cognitive effect of this norm is that group members get their beliefs confirmed by other group members and do not have to experience cognitive uncertainty about their beliefs. This, in turn, makes it easier to value their identity in Christ and stay committed. The author associates proper speech strongly with prototypical attributes. The perhaps most surprising result of the analysis was that the virtue of love was more strongly associated with conventional speech than with practical care. Love is to speak in a way that does not undermine the cognitive certainty of the group. Less surprising is that the gifts of the leaders are idealized in way which gives the leaders control over the teaching in the group. Group members need to listen to the teaching of the leaders in order to gain the knowledge that leads to prototypicality. The leaders therefore have legitimacy to marginalize alternative teachings and teachers and thus to control the information flow in the group.

Fourth, this study has showed that Ephesians describes the ingroup prototype in way that promotes cooperation. Unity is not just about doctrinal cohesion but also about cooperative, anti-competitive, encouraging and anti-aggressive interaction; *homonoia* above agonistic competition and strife. The cooperation is, however, not egalitarian but rather hierarchically differentiated, both within the body of Christ and within the household. Good ingroup members know their respective roles in the greater whole and are prepared to put their own interests and impulses aside in order to do their part.

There is good reason to believe that cognitive psychology increasingly will contribute to the humanities, including biblical scholarship. Since the goal of historians, literary theorists, anthropologists, etc., is *understanding,* the increasing amount of insight produced by the cognitive sciences about how the human brain understands, feels and evaluates is highly relevant. As early as 1998 Alan Richardson predicted this development in a review of Mark Turner's book, *The Literary Mind*:

> When the intellectual history of the late twentieth century is written, Anglophone literary theory and criticism will probably come in for a wry footnote or two. Scholars of the future age may well find amusement in the pretensions of one English professor after another to solve the riddles of human agency, subject formation, language acquisition, and consciousness, with little or no awareness of the spectacular developments in psychology, linguistics, philosophy of mind, and neuroscience that form the central story of Anglo-American intellectual life from the 1950s to the present. These fields, which have been converging (along with artificial intelligence) under the rubric of "cognitive science" or "the cognitive neurosciences," have largely abandoned the Saussurean and Freudian approaches to language and mind that still set the terms for most literary theory—however dated within the disciplines from which they were originally borrowed. An entire new set of frameworks and paradigms, inspired by advances in neurobiology and computer science that were nearly unimaginable a half century ago, has proliferated in their stead, and the cognitive neurosciences have emerged as [the] most exciting and rapidly developing interdisciplinary venture of our era. That this remains news to many working in literature departments has already

> become something of an embarrassment; it will steadily prove more so.[648]

Richardson gets a bit too excited when he gives all other literary research the verdict "dated" and "an embarrassment" but he certainly has a point that the humanities have a lot to learn from what cognitive sciences have discovered about the human capacity for understanding. I reckon that this is happening now and will continue to do so in the forthcoming decades. The results produced by the cognitive sciences are, however, not a ready-made dictionary that the humanities can lean on without caution. There are still many unresolved issues regarding the capacities and restraints of the human mind. Anyone who wishes to use the insights of cognitive psychology must therefore first scrutinize the state of the debate within the community of cognitive scholars.

Within biblical studies, there is a small but growing number of scholars who explore what can be done with the aid of the cognitive sciences (see chapter 1.2). The cognitive approach will never become a hegemonic research paradigm, since it is no universal solution to all historical problems. I do, however, hope that more biblical scholars will discover the hermeneutical potential in exploring the structures of the human mind. Since the use of cognitive sciences demands double cross-disciplinary competence, many biblical scholars will remain uninterested in, perhaps even disapproving of, the use of cognitive psychology in historical research. Nevertheless, cognitive psychology increasingly influences many of the hermeneutical disciplines that biblical scholars are dependent upon. Biblical scholarship is therefore bound to feel its influence.

The specific framework that has been developed in this study has the potential to be used to analyze the relation between identity and behavior norms in just about any text of the early Christ-movement (as well as other contexts). The analysis of Ephesians is just a beginning.

---

[648] Richardson 1998: 168 reviewing Turner 1996.

Literature

Primary Sources and Translations

The Ante-Nicene Fathers: Translation of the Writings of the Fathers Down to A.D. 325. 1956. Translated by A. Roberts and J. Donaldson. Revised by A. C. Coxe. 10 vols. Grand Rapids, Mich.: Eerdmans.

Apostolic Fathers. 2003. Translated by B. D. Ehrman. Loeb Classical Library. Cambridge, Mass.: Harvard University Press.

Aristotle. *The Nicomachean Ethics.* 1947. Translated by H. Rackham. Rev. ed. Loeb Classical Library. London: Heinemann.

Aristotle. *Art of Rhetoric.* 1926. Translated by J. H. Freese. Loeb Classical Library. London: Heinemann.

Aristotle. *Athenian Constitution. Eudemian Ethics. Virtues and Vices.* 1952. Translated by H. Rackham. Loeb Classical Library. Rev. ed. Cambridge, Mass.: Harvard University Press.

Aristotle. *Politics.* 1932. Translated by H. Rackham. Loeb Classical Library. London: Heinemann.

Cicero, Marcus Tullius. *Letters to Atticus.* 1999. Translated by D. R. Shackleton Bailey. 3 vols. Loeb Classical Library. Cambridge, Mass.: Harvard University Press.

Cicero, Marcus Tullius. *On Duties.* Translated by W. Miller. Loeb Classical Library. Cambridge, Mass.: Harvard University Press.

Cicero, Marcus Tullius. *On the Nature of the Gods. Academics.* 1933. Translated by H. Rackham. Loeb Classical Library. London: Heinemann.

The Dead Sea Scrolls: Study Edition. 1997–1998. Edited by F. García Martínez and, E. J. C. Tigchelaar. 2 vols. Leiden: Brill.

The Epic of Gilgamesh: the Babylonian Epic Poem and Other Texts in Akkadian and Sumerian. 2003. Translated by A. George. London: Penguin.

Epictetus. *Discourses, Books III-IV. Fragments. The Encheiridion.* 1928. Translated by W. A. Oldfather. Loeb Classical Library. Cambridge, Mass.: Harvard University Press.

The Holy Bible … New Revised Standard Version. 1973. New York: Collins.

The Holy Bible. New American Standard Bible. 1995. Updated ed. Grand Rapids, Mich.: Zondervan.

The Holy Bible. English Standard Version. 2002. London: Collins.

The Holy Bible. New International Version. 1984. London: Hodder and Stoughton.

Josephus. *Jewish Antiquities*. 1930–1965. Translated by H. St. J. Thackeray et al. 9 vols. Loeb Classical Library. Cambridge, Mass.: Harvard University Press.

Josephus. *The Jewish War*. 1927–1928. Translated by H. St. J. Thackeray. 3 vols. Loeb Classical Library. Cambridge, Mass.: Harvard University Press.

Josephus. *The Life. Against Apion*. 1956. Translated by H. St. J. Thackeray. Loeb Classical Library. Cambridge, Mass.: Harvard University Press.

The Nag Hammadi Library in English: Translated and Introduced by Members of the Coptic Gnostic Library Project of the Institute for Antiquity and Christianity, Claremont, California. 1988. General editor: J. M. Robinson. 3rd completely revised edition. San Francisco: Harper & Row.

Novum Testamentum Graece… 1993. Edited by E. Nestle et al. 27th ed. Stuttgart: Deutsche Bibelgesellschaft.

Malherbe, Abraham J. 1986. *Moral Exhortation: A Greco-Roman Sourcebook*. Philadelphia: Westminster Press.

The Old Testament Pseudepigrapha. 1983–1985. Edited by J. H. Charlesworth. 2 vols. Garden City, N.Y.: Doubleday.

Philo. *On Abraham. On Joseph. On Moses*. 1935. Translated by F. H. Colson. Loeb Classical Library. London: Heinemann.

Philo. *On the Creation. Allegorical Interpretation of Genesis 2 and 3*. 1929. Translated by F. H. Colson and G. H. Whitaker. Loeb Classical Library. London: Heinemann.

Plato. *Laches. Protagoras. Meno. Euthydemus*. 1924. Translated by W. R. M. Lamb. Loeb Classical Library. London: Heinemann.

Plato. *Laws*. 1926. Translated by R.G. Bury. 2 vols. Loeb Classical Library. London: Heinemann.

Plato. *Republic*. 1930. Translated by P. Shorey. Loeb Classical Library. London: Heinemann.

Plutarch. *Moralia*. 1927–1969. Translated by F. C. Babbitt et al. 15 vols. Loeb Classical Library. Cambridge, Mass.: Harvard University Press.

Quintilian. *The Orator's Education*. 2001. Translated by D. A. Russell. 5 vols. Loeb Classical Library. Cambridge, Mass.: Harvard University Press.

Seneca, Lucius Annaeus. *Epistles*. 1917–1925. Translated by R. M. Gummere. Loeb Classical Library. London: Heinemann.

Seneca, Lucius Annaeus. *Moral Essays*. 1928–1935. Translated by J. W. Basore. 3 vols. Loeb Classical Library. London: Heinemann.

Septuaginta: id est Vetus Testamentum graece iuxta LXX interpretes. 1979. Edited by A. Rahlfs. Stuttgart: Deutsche Bibelgesellschaft.

Suetonius. *Lives of the Caesars*. 1914. Translated by J. C. Rolfe. 2 vols. Loeb Classical Library. Cambridge, Mass.: Harvard University Press.

The Tosefta: Translated from the Hebrew, with a New Introduction. 2002. Translated by J. Neusner. 2 vols. Peabody, Mass.: Hendrickson Publishers.

Software

BibleWorks 7. 2006. Norfolk, Va.: BibleWorks, LLC.

Secondary Literature

Abrams, Dominic. 1999. Social Identity, Social Cognition and the Self. Pages 197–229 in *Social Identity and Social Cognition*. Edited by Dominic Abrams, and Michael A. Hogg. Oxford: Blackwell.

Abrams, Dominic, and Michael A. Hogg. 1990. *Social Identity Theory: Constructive and Critical Advances*. London: Harvester Wheatsheaf.

Abrams, Dominic, Georgina Randsley de Moura, Paul Hutchison, and Tendayi Viki. 2005. When Bad Becomes Good (and Vice Versa): Why Social Exclusion Is Not Based on Difference. Pages 161–190 in *The Social Psychology of Inclusion and Exclusion*. Edited by Dominic Abrams, Michael A. Hogg, and José M. Marques. New York: Psychology Press.

Abrams, Dominic, Georgina Randsli de Moura, José M. Marques, and Paul Hutchison. 2008. Innovation Credit: When Can Leaders Oppose Their Group's Norms? *Journal of Personality and Social Psychology* 95:662–678.

Alexander, Philips. 2006. Predestination and Free Will in the Theology of the Dead Sea Scrolls. Pages 27–49 in *Divine and Human Agency in Paul and His Cultural Environment*. Edited by John M. G. Barclay, and Simon J. Gathercole. Library of New Testament Studies 335. London: T & T Clark.

Alford, Fred C. 1985. Is Jurgen Habermas's Reconstructive Science Really Science? *Theory and Society* 14:321–340.

Arnold, Clinton E. 1989. *Ephesians – Power and Magic: The Concept of Power in Ephesians in Light of Its Historical Setting*. Society for New Testament Studies Monograph Series 63. Cambridge: Cambridge University Press.

Atran, Scott. 1989. *Cognitive Foundations of Natural History: Towards an Anthropology of Science*. Cambridge: Cambridge University Press.

—. 2002. *In Gods We Trust: The Evolutionary Landscape of Religion*. Evolution and Cognition. Oxford; New York: Oxford University Press.

Augoustinos, Martha, Ngaire Donaghue, and Ian Walker. 2006. *Social Cognition: An Integrated Introduction*. 2nd ed. Thousand Oaks, Calif.: SAGE.

Aune, David E. 1987. *The New Testament in Its Literary Environment*. Library of Early Christianity 8. Philadelphia: Westminster Press.

—. 1994. Mastery of the Passions: Philo, 4 Maccabees and Earliest Christianity. Pages 125–158 in *Hellenization Revisited: Shaping a Christian Response within the Greco-Roman World*. Edited by Wendy E. Helleman. Lanham: University Presses of America.

Avemarie, Friedrich. 2006. The Tension between God's Command and Israel's Obedience as Reflected in Early Rabbinic Literature. Pages 50–70 in *Divine and Human Agency in Paul and His Cultural Environment*. Edited by John M. G. Barclay, and Simon J. Gathercole. Library of New Testament Studies 335. London: T & T Clark.

Baars, Bernard J. 2003. How Brain Reveals Mind: Neural Studies Support the Fundamental Role of Conscious Experience. *Journal of Consciousness Studies* 10:100–114.

Bar-Tal, Daniel. 1990. *Group Beliefs: A Conception for Analyzing Group Structure, Processes, and Behavior*. Springer Series in Social Psychology. Berlin: Springer.

—. 1998. Group Beliefs as an Expression of Social Identity. Pages 93–113 in *Social Identity: International Perspectives*. Edited by Stephen Worchel et al. London: SAGE.

Barclay, John M. G. 2006. "By the Grace of God I Am What I Am": Grace and Agency in Philo and Paul. Pages 140–157 in *Divine and Human Agency in Paul and His Cultural Environment*. Edited by John M. G. Barclay, and Simon J. Gathercole. Library of New Testament Studies 335. London: T & T Clark.

—. 2006. Introduction. Pages 1–8 in *Divine and Human Agency in Paul and His Cultural Environment*. Edited by John M. G. Barclay, and Simon J. Gathercole. Library of New Testament Studies; 335. London: T & T Clark.

Barclay, John M. G., and Simon J. Gathercole, eds. 2006. *Divine and Human Agency in Paul and His Cultural Environment*. Library of New Testament Studies 335. London: T & T Clark.

Barrett, Justin L., and Frank C. Keil. 1996. Conceptualizing a Nonnatural Entity: Anthropomorphism in God Concepts. *Cognitive Psychology* 31:219–247.

Barth, Markus. 1974. *Ephesians*. 2 vols. The Anchor Bible 34. Garden City, N.Y.: Doubleday.

Barton, Carlin A. 2001. *Roman Honor: The Fire in the Bones*. Berkeley, Calif.: University of California Press.

Bauer, Walter. 1934. *Rechtgläubigkeit und Ketzerei im Ältesten Christentum*. Beiträge zur Historischen Theologie 10. Tübingen: Mohr.

Bem, Daryl J. 1967. Self-Perception: And Alternative Interpretation of Cognitive Dissonance Phenomena. *Psychological Review* 74:183–200.

—. 1972. Self-Perception Theory. Pages 1–62 in *Advances in Experimentals Social Psychology*. Edited by L. Berkowitz. New York: Academic press.

Berger, Klaus. 2003. *Identity and Experience in the New Testament*. Minneapolis: Fortress Press.

Berger, Peter L., and Thomas Luckmann. 1966. *The Social Construction of Reality: A Treatise in the Sociology of Knowledge*. London: Penguin.

Best, Ernest. 1992. Ephesians 4:25: Thieves in the Church. *Irish Biblical Studies* 14:2–9.

—. 2004. *A Critical and Exegetical Commentary on Ephesians*. International Critical Commentary on the Holy Scriptures of the Old and New Testaments. London: T & T Clark.

Bieringer, Reimund. 2005. "...was im Welt im innersten zusammenhält": Eine exegetische Untersuchung zu ἀνακεφαλαιώσασθαι in Eph 1,10. Pages 3–36 in *Ethik als angewandte Ekklesiologie: Der Brief an die Epheser*. Edited by Michael Wolter. Serie Monografica di "Benedictina". Sezione biblico-ecumenica 17. Roma: Abbazia di San Paolo fuori le mura.

Bjerkelund, Carl J. 1967. *Parakalô: Form, Funktion und Sinn ser Parakalô-Sätze in den paulinischen Briefen*. Bibliotheca Theologica Norvegica 1. Oslo: Universitetsforlaget.

Black, Edwin. 1965. *Rhetorical Criticism; a Study in Method*. New York: Macmillan.

Blanz, Mathias. 1999. Accessibility and Fit as Determinants of the Salience of Social Categorizations. *European Journal of Social Psychology* 29:43–74.

Blasi, Anthony J., Jean Duhaime, and Paul-André Turcotte, eds. 2002. *Handbook of Early Christianity: Social Science Approaches*. Walnut Creek, Calif.: AltaMira Press.

Blass, Friedrich, and Albert Debrunner. 1961. *A Greek Grammar of the New Testament and Other Early Christian Literature*. Translated and edited by by Robert W. Funk. Chicago: University of Chicago Press.

Bloch, Maurice. 1998. *How We Think They Think: Anthropological Approaches to Cognition, Memory, and Literacy*. Boulder, Colo.; Oxford: Westview.

Blomqvist, Jerker, and Poul Ole Jastrup. 1996. *Grekisk Grammatik: Graesk Grammatik*. 2nd ed. København: Akademisk Forlag.

Boas, George. 1973. Cycles. Pages 621–627 in vol. 1 of *Dictionary of the History of Ideas: Studies of Selected Pivotal Ideas*. Edited by Ragnar Höistad et al. New York.

Boccaccini, Gabriele. 2006. Inner-Jewish Debate on the Tension between Divine and Human Agency in Second Temple Judaism. Pages 9–26 in *Divine and Human Agency in Paul and His Cultural Environment*. Edited by John M. G. Barclay, and Simon J. Gathercole. Library of New Testament Studies 335. London: T & T Clark.

de Boer, Martinus C. 1980. Images of Paul in the Post-Apostolic Period. *Catholic Biblical Quarterly* 42:359–380.

Bown, Nicola J., and Dominic Abrams. 2003. Despicability in the Workplace: Effects of Behavioral Deviance and Unlikeability on the Evaluation of in-Group and Members. *Journal of Applied Social Psychology* 33:2413–2426.

Boyer, Pascal. 1993. *Cognitive Aspects of Religious Symbolism*. Cambridge: Cambridge University Press.

—. 1995. Causal Understandings in Cultural Representations: Cognitive Constraints on Inferences from Cultural Input. Pages 615–644 in *Causal Cognition: A Multidisciplinary Debate*. Edited by Dan Sperber, David Premack, and Ann James Premack. Oxford: Clarendon Press.

—. 2001. *Religion Explained: The Human Instincts That Fashion Gods, Spirits and Ancestors*. London: Heinemann.

Brennan, Tad. 1998. The Old Stoic Theory of Emotions. Pages 21–70 in *The Emotions in Hellenistic Philosophy*. Edited by Juha Sihvola, and Troels Engberg-Pedersen. New Synthese Historical Library 46. Dordrecht: Kluwer Academic Publishers.

Brewer, Marilynn B., and Rupert J. Brown. 1998. Intergroup Relations. Pages 99–142 in *The Handbook of Social Psychology*. Edited by Daniel T. Gilbert, Susan T. Fiske, and Gardner Lindzey. 4th ed. Boston, Mass.: McGraw-Hill.

Brewer, Marilynn B., and Wendi Gardner. 1996. Who Is This "We"? Levels of Collective Identity and Self-Representation. *Journal of Personality and Social Psychology* 71:83–93.

Brower, Aaron M., and Judith L. Nye, eds. 1996. *What's Social About Social Cognition? Research on Socially Shared Cognition in Small Groups*. Thousand Oaks, Calif.: SAGE.

Brown, Rupert. 1988. *Group Processes: Dynamics within and between Groups*. Oxford: Basil Blackwell.

—. 2000. *Group Processes: Dynamics within and between Groups*. 2nd ed. Malden, Mass.: Blackwell Publishers.

Brown, William P. 1996. *Character in Crisis: A Fresh Approach to the Wisdom Literature of the Old Testament*. Grand Rapids, Mich.: Eerdmans.

Bruner, Jerome S. 1990. *Acts of Meaning*. Cambridge, Mass.: Harvard University Press.

Burris, Christopher T., and Lynne M. Jackson. 2000. Social Identity and the True Believer: Responses to Threatened Self-Stereotypes among the Intrinsically Religious. *British Journal of Social Psychology* 39:257–278.

Byrskog, Samuel. 2005. Ephesians 4:1–16 – Paraenesis and Identity Formation. Pages 109–138 in *Ethik als angewandte Ekklesiologie: Der Brief an die Epheser*. Edited by Michael Wolter. Serie Monografica di "Benedictina". Sezione biblico-ecumenico 17. Roma: Abbazia di San Paolo fuori le mura.

—. 2008. Memory and Identity in the Gospels: A New Perspective. Pages 33–57 in *Exploring Early Christian Identity*. Edited by Bengt Holmberg. Wissenschaftliche Untersuchungen zum Neuen Testament 226. Tübingen: Mohr Siebeck.

Cairns, Douglas L. 1993. *Aidos: The Psychology and Ethics of Honour and Shame in Ancient Greek Literature*. Oxford: Clarendon Press.

Callahan, Allan Dwight, and Richard A. Horsley. 1998. Slave Resistance in Classic Antiquity. *Semeia* 83/84:133–152.
Caragounis, Chrys C. 1977. *The Ephesian Mysterion: Meaning and Content.* Coniectanea Biblica. New Testament Series 8. Lund: LiberLäromedel/Gleerup.
Carr, Edward Hallett. 1961. *What Is History? The George Macaulay Trevelyan Lectures Delivered in the University of Cambridge January-March 1961.* London: Macmillan.
Carrithers, Michael, Steven Collins, and Steven Lukes, eds. 1985. *The Category of the Person: Anthropology, Philosophy, History*. Cambridge: Cambridge University Press.
Carruthers, Peter, Stephen Laurence, and Stephen Stich, eds. 2005–2008. *The Innate Mind*. 3 vols. New York: Oxford University Press.
Chaiken, Shelly, and Yaacov Trope, eds. 1999. *Dual-Process Theories in Social Psychology*. New York: Guilford Press.
Choi, Incheol, Richard E. Nisbett, and Ara Norenzayan. 1999. Causal Attribution across Cultures: Variation and Universality. *Psychological Bulletin* 125:47–63.
Chomsky, Noam. 1957. *Syntactic Structures*. Janua Linguarum Series Minor 4. The Hague: Mouton.
—. 1965. *Aspects of the Theory of Syntax*. Special Technical Report (Massachusetts Institute of Technology. Research Laboratory of Electronics) 11. Cambridge, Mass.: MIT Press.
Cialdini, Robert B., and Noah J. Goldstein. 2004. Social Influence: Compliance and Conformity. *Annual Review of Psychology* 55:591–621.
Clark, Elizabeth A. 2004. *History, Theory, Text: Historians and the Linguistic Turn*. Cambridge, Mass.: Harvard University Press.
Cohen, Shaye, J. D. 1999. *The Beginnings of Jewishness: Boundaries, Varieties, Uncertainties*. Berkeley, Calif.: University of California Press.
Collingwood, Robin George. 1946. *The Idea of History*. Oxford: Clarendon.
—. 1999. *The Principles of History and Other Writings in Philosophy of History*. Oxford: University Press.
Cooper, John M. 1998. Posidonius. Pages 71–112 in *The Emotions in Hellenistic Philosophy*. Edited by Juha Sihvola, and Troels Engberg-Pedersen. New Synthese Historical Library 46. Dordrecht: Kluwer Academic Publishers.
Cosmides, Leda, John Tooby, and Robert Kurzban. 2003. Perceptions of Race. *Trends in Cognitive Science* 7:173–179.
Costarelli, Sandro. 2005. Short Communication Affective Responces to Own Violations of Ingroup Norms: The Moderating Role of Norm Salience. *European Journal of Social Psychology* 35:425–435.

Crook, Zeba A. 2005. Reciprocity – Covenantal Exchange as a Testcase. Pages 78–91 in *Ancient Israel: The Old Testament in Its Social Context*. Edited by Philip F. Esler. London: SCM Press.

Cushman, Fiery, Joshua Knobe, and Walter Sinnott-Armstrong. 2008. Moral Appraisals Affect Doing/Allowing Judgments. *Cognition* 108:281–289.

Czachesz, István. 2007a. The Emergence of Early Christian Religion: A Naturalistic Approach. Pages 72–94 in *Explaining Christian Origins and Early Judaism: Contributions from Cognitive and Social Science*. Edited by Petri Luomanen, Ilkka Pyysiäinen, and Risto Uro. Biblical Interpretation Series 89. Leiden: Brill.

—. 2007b. The Transmission of Early Christian Thought: Toward a Cognitive Psychological Model. *Studies in Religion* 36:65–84.

D'Oro, Giuseppina. 2006. *Robin George Collingwood (Stanford Encyclopedia of Philosophy)* [URL]. http://plato.stanford.edu/entries/collingwood/ (cited 7 April 2008).

Dahl, Nils Alstrup. 1987. Interpreting Ephesians: Then and Now. *Currents in Theology and mission* 5:133–143.

—. 2000. *Studies in Ephesians: Introductory Questions, Text- and Edition-Critical Issues, Interpretation of Texts and Themes*. Edited by David Hellholm, Vemund Blomkvist, and Tord Fornberg. Wissenschaftliche Untersuchungen zum Neuen Testament 131. Tübingen: Mohr Siebeck.

Darko, Daniel K. 2008. *No Longer Living as the Gentiles: Differentation and Shared Ethical Values in Ephesians 4.17–6.9*. Library of New Testament Studies 375. London: T&T Clark.

Dawes, Gregory W. 1998. *The Body in Question: Metaphor and Meaning in the Interpretation of Ephesians 5:21–33*. Biblical Interpretation Series 30. Leiden: Brill.

Day, Matthew. 2007. Let's Be Realistic: Evolutionary Complexity, Epistemic Probabilism, and the Cognitive Science of Religion. *Harvard Theological Review* 100:47–64.

De Pierris, Graciela, and Michael Friedman. 2008. *Kant and Hume on Causality (Stanford Encyclopedia of Philosophy)* [URL]. http://plato.stanford.edu/entries/kant-hume-causality/ (cited 7 Nov 2008).

Deacon, Terrence William. 1997. *The Symbolic Species: The Co-Evolution of Language and the Brain*. New York: W.W. Norton.

Deaux, Kay, and Daniela Martin. 2003. Interpersonal Networks and Social Categories: Specifying Levels of Context in Identity Formation. *Social Psychology Quarterly* 66:101–117.

Decety, Jean, and Jessica A. Sommerwille. 2003. Shared Representations between Self and Other: A Social Cognitive Neuroscience View. *Trends in Cognitive Science* 7:527–533.

Deconchy, Jean-Pierre. 1984. Rationality and Controll in Orthodox Systems. Pages 425–445 in *The Social Dimension: European Developments in Social Psychology*. Edited by Henri Tajfel. European Studies in Social Psychology. Cambridge: Cambridge University Press.

DeSilva, David Arthur. 1995. *Despising Shame: Honor Discourse and Community Maintenance in the Epistle to the Hebrews*. Atlanta: Scholars Press.

Dillon, John M. 1986. Plutarch and Second Century Platonism. Pages 214–229 in *Classical Mediterranean Spirituality: Egyptian, Greek, Roman*. Edited by A. H. Armstrong. World Spirituality. London: Routledge.

Doojse, Bertjan, Naomi Ellemers, and Russell Spears. 1999. Commitment and Intergroup Behaviour. Pages 84–106 in *Social Identity: Context, Commitment, Content*. Edited by Naomi Ellemers, Russell Spears, and Bertjan Doojse. Oxford: Blackwell.

Doty, William G. 1973. *Letters in Primitive Christianity*. Guides to Biblical Scholarship. New Testament Series. Philadelphia: Fortress Press.

Dunbar, Robin. 1996. *Grooming, Gossip and the Evolution of Language*. London: Faber and Faber.

Dunn, James D. G. 1975. *Jesus and the Spirit: A Study of the Religious and Charismatic Experience of Jesus and the First Christians as Reflected in the New Testament*. London: SCM Press.

—. 1998. *The Theology of Paul the Apostle*. Edinburgh: T&T Clark.

Edwards, Derek, and Jonathan Potter. 1992. *Discursive Psychology*. Inquiries in Social Construction. London: SAGE.

Ellemers, Naomi, Russell Spears, and Bertjan Doosje. 2002. Self and Social Identity. *Annual Review of Psychology* 26:161–186.

Ellemers, Naomi, Wendy van Risjwijk, Jan Bruins, and Jan de Gilder. 2005. Group Commitment as a Moderator of Attributional and Behavioural Responses to Power Use. *European Journal of Social Psychology* 28:555–572.

Ellens, J. Harold, and Wayne G. Rollins, eds. 2004. *Psychology and the Bible: A New Way to Read the Scriptures*. 4 vols. Psychology, Religion, and Spirituality Series. Westport, Conn.: Praeger.

Elliott, Mark Adam. 2000. *The Survivors of Israel: A Reconsideration of the Theology of Pre-Christian Judaism*. Grand Rapids, Mich.: Eerdmans.

Engberg-Pedersen, Troels. 2006. Self-Sufficuency and Power: Divine and Human Agency in Paul and Epictetus. Pages 117–139 in *Divine and Human Agency in Paul and His Cultural Environment*. Edited by John M. G. Barclay, and Simon J. Gathercole. Library of New Testament Studies 335. London: T & T Clark.

Esler, Philip F. 1998. *Galatians*. New Testament Readings. New York: Routledge.

—. 2000. Models in New Testament Interpretation: A Reply to David Horrell. *Journal for the Study of the New Testament* 78:107–113.

—. 2003. *Conflict and Identity in Romans: The Social Setting of Paul's Letter*. Minneapolis: Fortress Press.
—, ed. 2005. *Ancient Israel: The Old Testament in Its Social Context*. London: SCM Press.
—. 2005. Social-Scientific Models in Biblical Interpretation. Pages 3–14 in *Ancient Israel: The Old Testament in Its Social Context*. Edited by Philip F. Esler. London: SCM Press.
—. 2007. "Remember My Fetters": Memorialisation of Paul's Imprisonment. Pages 231–258 in *Explaining Christian Origins and Early Judaism: Contributions from Cognitive and Social Science*. Edited by Petri Luomanen, Ilkka Pyysiäinen, and Risto Uro. Biblical Interpretation Series 89. Leiden: Brill.
—. Forthcoming. Prototypes, Antitypes and Social Identity in First Clement: Outlining a New Interpretative Model. In *Construction of Christian Identities [Preliminary Title]*. Edited by Edmondo Lupieri, and Mauro Pesce. Vigiliae Christianae Supplements. Leiden: Brill.
Evans, Richard J. 1997. *In Defence of History*. London: Granta.
Farnham, Shelly D., Anthony D. Greenwald, and Mahzarin R. Banaji. 1999. Implicit Self-Esteem. Pages 230–248 in *Social Identity and Social Cognition*. Edited by Dominic Abrams, and Michael A. Hogg. Oxford: Blackwell.
Fauconnier, Gilles, and Mark Turner. 2002. *The Way We Think: Conceptual Blending and the Mind's Hidden Complexities*. New York: Basic Books.
Fee, Gordon D. 1994. *God's Empowering Presence: The Holy Spirit in the Letters of Paul*. Peabody, Mass.: Hendrickson.
Festinger, Leon. 1957. *A Theory of Cognitive Dissonance*. Evanston, Ill: Row Peterson.
Festinger, Leon, Stanley Schachter, and Kurt Back. 1950. *Social Pressures in Informal Groups: A Study of Human Factors in Housing*. New York.
Fischer, Karl Martin. 1973. *Tendenz und Absicht des Epheserbriefes*. Forschungen zur Religion und Literatur des Alten und Neuen Testaments 111. Göttingen: Vandenhoeck & Ruprecht.
Fiske, Alan Page, Shinobu Kitayama, Rose Hazel, and Richard E. Nisbett. 1998. The Cultural Matrix of Social Psychology. Pages 915–981 in *The Handbook of Social Psychology*. Edited by Daniel T. Gilbert, and Susan T. Fiske. 4th ed. New York: McGraw-Hill.
Fiske, Susan T., and Shelley E. Taylor. 1984. *Social Cognition*. Topics in Social Psychology. New York: Random house.
Freund, Richard A. 1997. Individual vs. Collective Responsibility: From the Ancient Near East and the Bible to the Graeco-Roman World. *Scandinavian Journal of the Old Testament* 11:279–304.
Frick, Peter. 1999. *Divine Providence in Philo of Alexandria*. Texte und Studien zum Antiken Judentum. Tübingen: Mohr Siebeck.

Fuller, J. Bryan, Tim Barnett, Kim Hester, and Clint Relyea. 2003. A Social Identity Perspective on the Relationship between Perceived Organizational Support and Organizational Commitment. *Journal of Social Psychology* 143:789–791.

Furnish, Victor Paul. 1984. *2 Corinthians*. The Anchor Bible 32a. Garden City, N.Y.: Doubleday.

Gadamer, Hans-Georg. 1975. *Truth and Method*. London: Sheed & Ward.

—. 1989. Hermeneutics and Logocentrism. Pages 114–128 in *Dialogue and Deconstruction: The Gadamer-Derrida Encounter*. Edited by Diane P. Michelfelder, and Richard E. Palmer. Suny Series in Contemporary Continental Philosophy. Albany: State University of New York Press.

Gaddis, John Lewis. 2002. *The Landscape of History: How Historians Map the Past*. Oxford: Oxford University Press.

Gagnon, Robert A. J. 1992. How Did the Rule of the Community Obtain Its Final Shape? A Review of Scholarly Research. *Journal for the Study of the Pseudepigrapha*. 10:61–79.

Geertz, Clifford. 1973. Anthropological Approaches to the Study of Religion. Pages 87–125 in *The Interpretation of Cultures*. Edited by Clifford Geertz. New York: Basic Books.

von Gemünden, Petra. 2007. Affekte Und Affektekontrolle Im Antiken Judentum Und Urchristentum. Pages 249–270 in *Erkennen und Erleben: Beiträge zur Psychologischen Erforschung des frühen Christentums*. Edited by Gerd Theissen, and Petra von Gemünden. Gütersloh: Gütersloher Verlags-Haus.

Gentner, Dedre, Boicho N. Kokinov, and Keith James Holyoak, eds. 2001. *The Analogical Mind: Perspectives from Cognitive Science*. Cambridge, Mass.: MIT Press.

Gesenius, Wilhelm. 1910. *Gesenius' Hebrew Grammar*. Edited and enlarged by E. Kautzsch. Translated by A. E. Cowley. 2nd ed. Oxford: Clarendon Press.

Gill, Christopher. 1988. Personhood and Personality: The Four-Personae Theory of Cicero, De Officiis I. *Oxford Studies in Ancient Philosophy* 6:169–199.

Glatt-Gilad, David A. 2002. Yahweh's Honor at Stake: A Divine Conundrum. *Journal for the Study of the Old Testament* 98:63–74.

Gleason, Jean Berko. 2000. *The Development of Language*. 5th ed. Boston: Allyn and Bacon.

Gnilka, Joachim. 1971. *Der Epheserbrief*. Herders theologischer Kommentar zum Neuen Testament 10:2. Freiburg: Herder.

Goleman, Daniel. 1995. *Emotional Intelligence*. New York: Bantam Books.

Goodman, Martin. 1992. Jewish Proselytizing in the First Century. Pages 53–78 in *The Jews among Pagans and Christians in the Roman Empire*. Edited by Judith Lieu, John North, and Tessa Rajak. London: Routledge.

Gosnell, Peter. 2000. Networks and Exchanges: Ephesians 4:7–16 and the Community Function of Teachers. *Biblical Theology Bulletin* 30:135–143.

Goswami, Usha. 1998. *Cognition in Children*. Developmental Psychology. Hove: Psychology.

Gould, John. 1996. Tragedy and Collective Experience. Pages 217–243 in *Tragedy and the Tragic: Greek Theatre and Beyond*. Edited by M. S. Silk. Oxford: Clarendon Press.

Graesser, Arthur C., Brent Olde, and Bianca Klettke. 2002. How Does the Mind Construct and Represent Stories? Pages 229–262 in *Narrative Impact: Social and Cognitive Foundations*. Edited by Jeffrey J. Strange, Timothy C. Brock, and Melanie C. Green. Mahwah, N.J.: Lawrence Erlbaum Associates.

Griffiths, Paul E. 2002. What Is Innateness? *The Monist* 85:70–85.

Habermas, Jürgen. 1984. *The Theory of Communicative Action*. 2 vols. Cambridge: Polity Press.

—. 1990. *Moral Consciousness and Communicative Action*. Studies in Contemporary German Social Thought. Cambridge, Mass.: MIT Press.

Hakola, Raimo. 2007. Social Identities and Group Phenomena in Second Temple Judaism. Pages 259–276 in *Explaining Christian Origins and Early Judaism: Contributions from Cognitive and Social Science*. Edited by Petri Luomanen, Ilkka Pyysiäinen, and Risto Uro. Biblical Interpretation Series 89. Leiden: Brill.

Halperin, David J. 1993. *Seeking Ezekiel: Text and Psychology*. University Park, Pa.: Pennsylvania State University Press.

Hammett, John S. 2000. Stomach. Page 1253 in *Eerdmans Dictionary of the Bible*. Edited by David Noel Freedman, Astrid B. Beck, and Allen C. Myers. Grand Rapids, Mich.: Eerdman.

Haslam, S. Alexander. 2001. *Psychology in Organizations: The Social Identity Approach*. London: SAGE.

Haslam, S. Alexander, Penelope J. Oakes, McGarty Craig, John C. Turner, and Rina S. Onorato. 1995. Contextual Changes in the Prototypicality of Extreme and Moderate Outgroup Members. *European Journal of Social Psychology* 25:509–529.

Haslam, S. Alexander, and Michael J. Platow. 2001. Your Wish Is Our Command: The Role of Shared Social Identity in Translating a Leader's Vision into Followers' Action. Pages 213–228 in *Social Identity Processes in Organizational Contexts*. Edited by Michael A. Hogg, and Deborah J. Terry. New York: Psychology Press.

Haslam, S. Alexander, John C. Turner, Penelope J. Oakes, Craig McGarty, and Katherine J. Reynolds. 1998. The Group as a Basis for Emergent Stereotype Consensus. *European Review of Social Psychology* 8:203–239.

Heine, Steven J., and Darrin R. Lehman. 1997. The Cultural Construction of Self-Enhancement: An Examination of Group-Serving Biases. *Journal of Personality & Social Psychology* 72:1268–1283.

Hewstone, Miles. 1989. *Causal Attribution: From Cognitive Processes to Collective Beliefs*. Oxford: Basil Blackwell.

Hirschfeld, Lawrence A. 1995. Anthropology, Psychology and the Meaning of Social Causality. Pages 313–344 in *Causal Cognition: A Multidisciplinary Debate*. Edited by Dan Sperber, David Premack, and Ann James Premack. Oxford: Clarendon Press.

Hirschfeld, Lawrence A., and Susan A. Gelman, eds. 1994. *Mapping the Mind: Domain Specificity in Cognition and Culture*. Cambridge: Cambridge University Press.

Hoehner, Harold W. 2002. *Ephesians: An Exegetical Commentary*. Grand Rapids, Mich.: Baker Academic.

Hofstede, Geert. 2001. *Culture's Consequences: Comparing Values, Behaviors, Institutions, and Organizations across Nations*. 2nd ed. Thousand Oaks, Calif.: SAGE.

Hogan, Patrick Colm. 2003. *The Mind and Its Stories: Narrative Universals and Human Emotion*. Studies in Emotion and Social Interaction. Second Series. Cambridge: Cambridge University Press.

Hogg, Michael A. 2001. Social Categorization, Depersonalization, and Group Behavior. Pages 56–85 in *Blackwell Handbook of Social Psychology: Group Processes*. Edited by Michael A. Hogg, and R. Scott Tindale. Malden, Mass., Blackwell Publishers.

Hogg, Michael A., and Dominic Abrams. 1988. *Social Identifications: A Social Psychology of Intergroup Relations and Group Processes*. London: Routledge.

—. 1990. Social Motivation, Self-Esteem and Social Identity. Pages 28–47 in *Social Identity Theory: Constructive and Critical Advances*. Edited by Dominic Abrams, and Michael A. Hogg. London: Harvester Wheatsheaf.

—. 1999. Social Identity and Social Cognition. Pages 1–25 in *Social Identity and Social Cognition*. Edited by Dominic Abrams, and Michael A. Hogg. Oxford: Blackwell.

Hogg, Michael A., Kelly S. Fielding, and John Darley. 2005. Fringe Dwellers: Processes of Deviance and Marginalization in Groups. Pages 161–190 in *The Social Psychology of Inclusion and Exclusion*. Edited by Dominic Abrams, Michael A. Hogg, and José M. Marques. New York: Psychology Press.

Hogg, Michael A., and Barbara A. Mullin. 1999. Joining Groups to Reduce Uncertainty: Subjective Uncertainty Reduction and Group Identification. Pages 249–279 in *Social Identity and Social Cognition*. Edited by Dominic Abrams, and Michael A. Hogg. Oxford: Blackwell.

Holmberg, Bengt. 1978. *Paul and Power: The Structure of Authority in the Primitive Church as Reflected in the Pauline Epistles*. Coniectanea Biblica. New Testament Series 11. Lund: LiberLäromedel/Gleerup.

—. 1980. *Paul and Power: The Structure of Authority in the Primitive Church as Reflected in the Pauline Epistles*. Philadelphia: Fortress Press.

—. 1990. *Sociology and the New Testament: An Appraisal*. Minneapolis: Fortress Press.

—. 2008. Understanding the First Hundred Years of Christian Identity. Pages 1–32 in *Exploring Early Christian Identity*. Edited by Bengt Holmberg. Wissenschaftliche Untersuchungen zum Neuen Testament 226. Tübingen: Mohr Siebeck.

Horrell, David, ed. 1999a. *Social-Scientific Approaches to New Testament Interpretation*. Edinburgh: T & T Clark.

—. 1999b. Social-Scientific Interpretation of the New Testament: Retrospect and Prospect. Pages 3–28 in *Social-Scientific Approaches to New Testament Interpretation*. Edited by David Horrell. Edinburgh: T & T Clark.

—. 2000. Models and Methods in Social-Scientific Interpretation: A Response to Philip Esler. *Journal for the Study of the New Testament* 78:83–105.

—. 2005. *Solidarity and Difference: A Contemporary Reading of Paul's Ethics*. New York: T&T Clark International.

—. 2007a. The Designation Χριστιανός· 1 Peter 4:16 and the Formation of Christian Identity. *Journal of Biblical Literature* 126:361–381.

—. 2007b. Leiden als Diskriminierung und Martyrium: (Selbst-)Stigmatisierung und soziale Identität am Beispiel des ersten Petrusbriefes. Pages 119–132 in *Erkennen und Erleben: Beiträge zur psychologischen Erforschung des frühen Christentums*. Edited by Gerd Theissen, and Petra von Gemünden. Gütersloh: Gütersloher Verlags-Haus.

Hume, David. 1739. *A Treatise of Human Nature*. Oxford.

Hunter, John A., Sarah L. Cox, Kerry O'Brien, Maurice Stringer, Mike Boyes, Mike Banks, Gillian J. Hayhurst, and Maria Crawford. 2005. Threats to Group Value, Domain-Specific Self-Esteem and Intergroup Discrimination Amongst Minimal and National Groups. *British Journal of Social Psychology* 2005:329–353.

Irwin, Terence H. 1998. Stoic Inhumanity. Pages 219–242 in *The Emotions in Hellenistic Philosophy*. Edited by Juha Sihvola, and Troels Engberg-Pedersen. New Synthese Historical Library 46. Dordrecht: Kluwer Academic Publishers.

Jeal, Roy R. 2000. *Integrating Theology and Ethics in Ephesians: The Ethos of Communication*. Lewiston, N.Y.: Mellen.

Jenkins, Keith. 1991. *Re-Thinking History*. London: Routledge.

—. 1995. *On "What Is History?" From Carr and Elton to Rorty and White*. London: Routledge.

—. 2003. *Refiguring History: New Thoughts on an Old Discipline*. New York: Routledge.
Jokiranta, Jutta. 2005. *Identity on a Continuum: Constructing and Expressing Sectarian Social Identity in Qumran Serakhim and Pesharim*. Ph.D. Diss. University of Helsinki. Helsinki: Yliopistopaino.
—. 2007. Social Identity in the Qumran Movement: The Case of the Penal Code. Pages 277–298 in *Explaining Christian Origins and Early Judaism: Contributions from Cognitive and Social Science*. Edited by Petri Luomanen, Ilkka Pyysiäinen, and Risto Uro. Biblical Interpretation Series 89. Leiden: Brill.
Kant, Immanuel. 1787. *Kritik der reinen Vernunft*. 2nd revised ed. Leipzig: Philipp Reclam.
Kennedy, George Alexander. 1984. *New Testament Interpretation through Rhetorical Criticism*. Chapel Hill: University of North Carolina Press.
Ketola, Kimmo. 2007. A Cognitive Approach to Ritual Systems. Pages 95–114 in *Explaining Christian Origins and Early Judaism: Contributions from Cognitive and Social Science*. Edited by Petri Luomanen, Ilkka Pyysiäinen, and Risto Uro. Biblical Interpretation Series 89. Leiden: Brill.
Kille, D. Andrew. 2001. *Psychological Biblical Criticism*. Old Testament Series. Minneapolis: Fortress Press.
—. 2004. Reading the Bible in Three Dimensions: Psychological Biblical Interpretation. Pages 17–32 in *Psychology and the Bible: A New Way to Read the Scriptures*. Edited by J. Harold Ellens, and Wayne G. Rollins. Psychology, Religion, and Spirituality Series. Westport, Conn.: Praeger.
Kille, D. Andrew, and Wayne G. Rollins, eds. 2007. *Psychological Insight into the Bible: Texts and Readings*. Grand Rapids, Mich.: Eerdmans.
Klass, Morton. 2003. *Mind over Mind: The Anthropology and Psychology of Spirit Possession*. New York: Rowman & Littlefield Publishers.
Klauck, Hans-Josef. 2000. *The Religious Context of Early Christianity: A Guide to Graeco-Roman Religions*. Studies of the New Testament and Its World. Edinburgh: T & T Clark.
—. 2006. *Ancient Letters and the New Testament: A Guide to Context and Exegesis*. Waco, Tex.: Baylor University Press.
Knobe, Joshua. 2005. Theory of Mind and Moral Cognition: Exploring the Connections. *Trends in Cognitive Science* 9:357–359.
Knuuttila, Simo, and Juha Sihvola. 1998. How the Philosophical Analysis of Emotions Was Introduced. Pages 1–20 in *The Emotions in Hellenistic Philosophy*. Edited by Juha Sihvola, and Troels Engberg-Pedersen. New Synthese Historical Library 46. Dordrecht: Kluwer Academic Publishers.
van Kooten, Geurt Hendrik. 2003. *Cosmic Christology in Paul and the Pauline School: Colossians and Ephesians in the Context of Graeco-Roman Cosmology,*

with a New Synopsis of the Greek Texts. Wissenschaftliche Untersuchungen zum Neuen Testament 2. Reihe 171. Tübingen: Mohr Siebeck.

Kuhn, Karl Georg. 1967. Ἰσραήλ, Ἰουδαῖος, Ἑβραῖος in Jewish Literature after the OT. Pages 359–369 in vol. 10 of *Theological Dictionary of the New Testament*. Edited by Gerhard Kittel, and Gerhard Friedrich. Grand Rapids, Mich.: Eerdmans.

Kunda, Ziva. 1999. *Social Cognition: Making Sense of People*. Cambridge, Mass.; London: MIT Press.

Kurzban, R., and M. R. Leary. 2001. Evolutionary Origins of Stigmatization: The Functions of Social Exclusion. *Psychological Bulletin* 12:187–208.

Käsemann, Ernst. 1980. Ephesians and Acts. Pages 288–297 in *Studies in Luke-Acts*. Edited by Leander Earl Keck, and James Louis Martyn. New ed. Philadelphia: Fortress Press.

Lakoff, George. 1987. *Women, Fire, and Dangerous Things: What Categories Reveal About the Mind*. Chicago: University of Chicago Press.

Lakoff, George, and Mark Johnson. 1980. *Metaphors We Live By*. Chicago: University of Chicago Press.

—. 1999. *Philosophy in the Flesh: The Embodied Mind and Its Challenge to Western Thought*. New York: Basic Books.

Lawrence, Louise Joy. 2003. *An Ethnography of the Gospel of Matthew: A Critical Assessment of the Use of the Honour and Shame Model in New Testament Studies*. Wissenschaftliche Untersuchungen zum Neuen Testament 2. Reihe 165. Tübingen: Mohr Siebeck.

Le Bon, Gustave. 1896. *The Crowd: A Study of the Popular Mind*. London: Benn.

Leiner, Martin. 2007. Dem Evangelium die Seele wiedergeben? Grundsätzliche Fragen einer Psychologie des Urchristentums. Pages 29–58 in *Erkennen und Erleben: Beiträge zur psychologischen Erforschung des frühen Christentums*. Edited by Gerd Theissen, and Petra von Gemünden. Gütersloh: Gütersloher Verlags-Haus.

Leslie, Alan M. 1995. A Theory of Agency. Pages 121–141 in *Causal Cognition: A Multidisciplinary Debate*. Edited by Dan Sperber, David Premack, and Ann James Premack. Oxford: Clarendon Press.

Leslie, Alan M., Joshua Knobe, and Adam Cohen. 2006. Acting Intentionally and the Side-Effect Effect: Theory of Mind and Moral Judgment. *Psychological Science* 17:421–427.

Lieu, Judith. 1996. *Image and Reality: The Jews in the World of the Christians in the Second Century*. Edinburgh: T & T Clark.

—. 2004. *Christian Identity in the Jewish and Graeco-Roman World*. Oxford: Oxford University Press.

Lieu, Judith, John North, and Tessa Rajak, eds. 1992. *The Jews among Pagans and Christians in the Roman Empire*. London: Routledge.

Lincoln, Andrew T. 1990. *Ephesians*. Word Biblical Commentary 42. Waco, Tex.: Word Books.

Lindbeck, George Arthur. 1984. *The Nature of Doctrine: Religion and Theology in a Postliberal Age*. Philadelphia: Westminster Press.

Linde, Charlotte. 1993. *Life Stories: The Creation of Coherence*. New York: Oxford University Press.

Lloyd, Geoffrey. 1995. Ancient Greek Concepts of Causation Comparatist Perspective. Pages 536–556 in *Causal Cognition: A Multidisciplinary Debate*. Edited by Dan Sperber, David Premack, and Ann James Premack. Oxford: Clarendon Press.

Lohse, Eduard. 1964. Χειροποίητος, Ἀχειροποίητος. Page 436 in vol. 9 of *Theological Dictionary of the New Testament*. Edited by Gerhard Kittel, and Gerhard Friedrich. Grand Rapids, Mich.: Eerdmans.

Lundhaug, Hugo. 2007a. "In Her Nature She Is a Woman": Conceptual Blending in the Exegesis on the Soul (NHC II,6). Pages 141–160 in *Explaining Christian Origins and Early Judaism: Contributions from Cognitive and Social Science*. Edited by Petri Luomanen, Ilkka Pyysiäinen, and Risto Uro. Biblical Interpretation Series 89. Leiden: Brill.

—. 2007b. *"There Is a Rebirth and an Image of Rebirth": A Cognitive Poetic Analysis of Conceptual and Intertextual Blending in the Exegesis on the Soul (NHC II,6) and the Gospel of Philip (NHC II,3)*. Ph.D. diss., University of Bergen.

Luomanen, Petri. 2007. The Sociology of Knowledge, the Social Identity Approach and the Cognitive Science of Religion. Pages 199–230 in *Explaining Christian Origins and Early Judaism: Contributions from Cognitive and Social Science*. Edited by Petri Luomanen, Ilkka Pyysiäinen, and Risto Uro. Biblical Interpretation Series 89. Leiden: Brill.

Luomanen, Petri, Ilkka Pyysiäinen, and Risto Uro, eds. 2007a. *Explaining Christian Origins and Early Judaism: Contributions from Cognitive and Social Science*. Biblical Interpretation Series 89. Leiden: Brill.

—. 2007b. Introduction: Social and Cognitive Perspectives in the Study of Christian Origins and Early Judaism. Pages 1–36 in *Explaining Christian Origins and Early Judaism: Contributions from Cognitive and Social Science*. Edited by Petri Luomanen, Ilkka Pyysiäinen, and Risto Uro. Biblical Interpretation Series 89. Leiden: Brill.

Lyons, George. 2007. Church and Holiness in Ephesians. Pages 238–256 in *Holiness and Ecclesiology in the New Testament*. Edited by Kent E. Brower, and Andy Johnson. Grand Rapids, Mich.: Eerdmans.

Lyotard, Jean-François. 1984. *The Postmodern Condition: A Report on Knowledge*. Theory and History of Literature 10. Manchester: Manchester University Press.

MacDonald, Margaret Y. 1988. *The Pauline Churches: A Socio-Historical Study of Institutionalization in the Pauline and Deutero-Pauline Writings*. Society for

New Testament Studies Monograph Series 60. Cambridge: Cambridge University Press.
—. 2000. *Colossians and Ephesians*. Sacra Pagina Series 17. Collegeville, Minn.: Liturgical Press.
—. 2004. The Politics of Identity in Ephesians. *Journal for the Study of the New Testament* 26:419–444.
MacIntyre, Alasdair C. 1981. *After Virtue: A Study in Moral Theory*. London: Duckworth.
Malan, Francois. 2006. Identity, Ethics, and Ethos in Ephesians. Pages 257–287 in *Identity, Ethics, and Ethos in the New Testament*. Edited by Jan G. Van der Watt. Beihefte zur Zeitschrift für die neutestamentliche Wissenschaft und die Kunde der älteren Kirche 141. Berlin: Walter de Gruyter.
Malina, Bruce J. 1981. *The New Testament World: Insights from Cultural Anthropology*. Atlanta, Ga.: John Knox Press.
—. 2001. *The New Testament World: Insights from Cultural Anthropology*. 3rd ed. Louisville, Ky.: Westminster John Knox Press.
Malina, Bruce J., and Jerome H. Neyrey. 1996. *Portraits of Paul: An Archaeology of Ancient Personality*. Louisville, Ky.: Westminster John Knox Press.
Malle, Bertram F., and Sara D. Hodges, eds. 2005. *Other Minds: How Humans Bridge the Divide between Self and Others*. New York, NY.: Guilford Press.
Markus, Hazel R., and Shinobu Kitayama. 1991. Culture and Self: Implications for Cognition, Emotion and Motivation. *Psychological Review* 98:224–253.
—. 1994. A Collective Fear of the Collective: Implications for Selves and Theories of Selves. *Personality and Social Psychology Bulletin* 20:568–597.
Marohl, Matthew J. 2008. *Faithfulness and the Purpose of Hebrews: A Social Identity Approach*. Princeton Theological Monograph Series. Eugene: Pickwick Publications.
Marques, Jose M. 1990. The Black-Sheep Effect: Out-Group Homogenity in Social Comparison Settings. Pages 131–151 in *Social Identity Theory: Constructive and Critical Advances*. Edited by Dominic Abrams, and Michael A. Hogg. London: Harvester Wheatsheaf.
Marques, Jose M., Dominic Abrams, Dario Páez, and Michael A. Hogg. 2001. Social Categorization, Social Identification, and Rejection of Deviant Group Members. Pages 400–424 in *Blackwell Handbook of Social Psychology: Group Processes*. Edited by Michael A. Hogg, and R. Scott Tindale. Malden, Mass.: Blackwell Publishers.
Marques, Jose M., Dominic Abrams, Dario Paez, and Cristina Martinez-Taboada. 1998. The Role of Categorization and in-Group Norms in Judgments of Groups and Their Members. *Journal of Personality & Social Psychology* 75:976–988.
Marques, Jose M., Dominic Abrams, and R. G. Seredio. 2001. Being Better by Being Right: Subjective Group Dynamics and Derogation of Ingroup

Deviants When Generic Norms Are Undermined. *Journal of Personality and Social Psychology* 81:436–447.

Martin, Luther. 1981. Josephus' Use of Heimarmene in the Jewish Antiquities XIII, 171–3. *Numen* 28:127–137.

—. 2005. Towards a Cognitive History of Religions. *Revista de Estudos da Religião* 4:7–18.

—. 2007. The Promise of Cognitive Science for the Study of Early Christianity. Pages 37–56 in *Explaining Christian Origins and Early Judaism: Contributions from Cognitive and Social Science*. Edited by Petri Luomanen, Ilkka Pyysiäinen, and Risto Uro. Biblical Interpretation Series 89. Leiden: Brill.

Martin, Luther, and Jesper Sørensen, eds. 2009. *Past Minds: Studies in Cognitive Historiography*. London: Equinox.

Mauss, Marcel. 1985. A Category of the Human Mind: The Notion of the Person; the Notion of the Self. Pages 1–25 in *The Category of the Person: Anthropology, Philosophy, History*. Edited by Michael Carrithers, Steven Collins, and Steven Lukes. Cambridge: Cambridge University Press. Originally published in 1938. Une catégorie de l'esprit humain: La notion de personne. *Journal of the Royal Anthropological Institute* 68:263–281.

McCabe, Allyssa. 1997. Developmental and Cross-Cultural Aspects of Children's Narration. Pages 137–174 in *Narrative Development: Six Approaches*. Edited by Michael Bamberg. Mahwah, N.J.: Lawrence Erlbaum Associates.

Medin, Douglas L., Sarah J. Unsworth, and Lawrence Hirschfeld. 2007. Culture, Categorization and Reasoning. Pages 615–644 in *Handbook of Cultural Psychology*. Edited by Shinobu Kitayama, and Dov Cohen. New York: Guilford Press.

Meeks, Wayne A. 1983. *The First Urban Christians: The Social World of the Apostle Paul*. New Haven: Yale University Press.

—. 1986. *The Moral World of the First Christians*. Library of Early Christianity 6. Philadelphia: Westminster Press.

Megill, Allan. 2004. Coherence and Incoherence in Historical Studies: From the Annales School to the New Cultural History. *New Literary History* 35:207–231.

Mendelson, Jack. 1979. The Habermas-Gadamer Debate. *New German Critique* 18:44–73.

Menon, Tanya, Michael W. Morris, and Chi-yue Chiu. 1999. Culture and Construal of Agency: Attribution to Individual Versus Group Dispositions. *Journal of Personality and Social Psychology* 76:701–717.

Merklein, Helmut. 1973. *Christus und die Kirche: Die theologische Grundstruktur des Epheserbriefes nach Eph 2,11–18*. Stuttgarter Bibelstudien 66. Stuttgart: KBW-Verlag.

Metso, Sarianna. 1997. *The Textual Development of the Qumran Community Rule*. Studies on the Texts of the Desert of Judah 21. Leiden: Brill.

Meyers, J. L., and S. A. Duffy. 1990. Causal Inferences and Text Memory. Pages 35–52 in *Inferences and Text Comprehension*. Edited by A. C. Graesser, and G. H. Bower. The Psychology of Learning and Motivation 25. New York: Academic Press.

Michelfelder, Diane P., and Richard E. Palmer. 1989. *Dialogue and Deconstruction: The Gadamer-Derrida Encounter*. Suny Series in Contemporary Continental Philosophy. Albany: State University of New York Press.

Miller, Joan G. 1984. Culture and Development of Everyday Social Explanation. *Journal of Personality and Social Psychology* 46:961–978.

Mitternacht, Dieter. 1999. *Forum für Sprachlose: Eine kommunikationspsychologische und epistolärrhetorische Untersuchung des Galaterbriefs*. Coniectanea Biblica. New Testament Series 30. Stockholm: Almqvist & Wiksell International.

—. 2004. Theissen's Integration of Psychology and New Testament Studies: Learning Theory, Psychodynamics and Cognitive Psychology. Pages 17–32 in *Psychology and the Bible: A New Way to Read the Scriptures*. Edited by J. Harold Ellens, and Wayne G. Rollins. Psychology, Religion, and Spirituality Series. Westport, Conn.: Praeger.

—. 2007. A Structure of Persuasion in Galatians. Epistolary and Rhetorical Appeal in an Aural Setting. Pages 53–98 in *Exploring New Rhetorical Approaches to Galatians. Papers Presented at an International Conference at the University of the Free State, Bloemfontein March 13–14, 2006*. Edited by D. F. Tolmie. Acta Theologica Supplementum 9. Bloemfontein.

Mitton, Charles Leslie. 1981. *Ephesians*. New Century Bible. London: Marshall, Morgan and Scott.

Mollenkott, Virginia Ramey. 2003. Emancipative Elements in Ephesians 5.21–33: Why Feminist Scholarship Has (Often) Left Them Unmentioned, and Why They Should Be Emphasized. Pages 37–58 in *A Feminist Companion to the Deutero-Pauline Epistles*. Edited by Amy-Jill Levine, and Marianne Blickenstaff. Feminist Companion to the New Testament and Early Christian Writings 7. London: T & T Clark.

Moscovici, Serge. 1976. *Social Influence and Social Change*. European Monographs in Social Psychology 10. London: Academic Press.

Moxnes, Halvor. 1996. Honor and Shame. Pages 19–40 in *The Social Sciences and New Testament Interpretation*. Edited by Richard L. Rohrbaugh. Peabody, Mass.: Hendrickson Publishers.

Mulgan, C. F. 1968. Individual and Collective Virtue in the Republic. *Phronesis* 13:84–87.

Mullins, Terence Y. 1972. Formulas in New Testament Epistles. *Journal of Biblical Literature* 91:380–390.

Myth: Encyclopedia Britannica Online [URL]. http://search.eb.com/eb/article-9108748 (cited 4 January 2008).

Nanos, Mark D. 1996. *The Mystery of Romans: The Jewish Context of Paul's Letter*. Minneapolis: Fortress Press.

—, ed. 2002. *The Galatians Debate: Contemporary Issues in Rhetorical and Historical Interpretation*. Peabody, Mass.: Hendrickson Publ.

Neugebauer, Fritz. 1961. *In Christus: Eine Untersuchung zum paulinschen Glaubensverständnis*. Göttingen: Vandenhoeck & Ruprecht.

Neyrey, Jerome H. 1998. *Honor and Shame in the Gospel of Matthew*. Louisville, Ky: Westminster John Knox Press.

—. 2005. God, Benefactor and Patron: The Major Cultural Model for Interpreting the Deity in Greco-Roman Antiquity. *Journal for the Study of the New Testament* 27:465–492.

Nguyen, V. Henry T. 2008. *Christian Identity in Corinth: A Comparative Study of 2 Corinthians, Epictetus and Valerius Maximus*. Wissenschaftliche Untersuchungen zum Neuen Testament 2. Reihe 243. Tübingen: Mohr Siebeck.

Norenzayan, Ara, Incheol Choi, and Kaiping Peng. 2007. Perception and Cognition. Pages 569–594 in *Handbook of Cultural Psychology*. Edited by Shinobu Kitayama, and Dov Cohen. New York: Guilford Press.

O'Brien, Peter T. 1999. *The Letter to the Ephesians*. Pillar New Testament Commentary. Grand Rapids, Mich.: Eerdmans.

O'Keefe, Tim. 2006. *Epicurus [Internet Encyclopedia of Philosophy]* [URL]. http://www.iep.utm.edu/e/epicur.htm (cited 26 Aug. 2008).

Oakes, Penelope J. 1990. The Categorization Process: Cognition of the Group in the Social Psychology of Stereotyping. Pages 28–47 in *Social Identity Theory: Constructive and Critical Advances*. Edited by Dominic Abrams, and Michael A. Hogg. London: Harvester Wheatsheaf.

Oakes, Penelope J., Alexander S. Haslam, and Katherine J. Reynolds. 1999. Social Categorization and Social Context: Is Stereotype Change a Matter of Information or of Meaning? Pages 55–79 in *Social Identity and Social Cognition*. Edited by Dominic Abrams, and Michael A. Hogg. Oxford: Blackwell.

Oakes, Penelope J., John C. Turner, and Alexander S. Haslam. 1991. Percieving People as Group Members: The Role of Fit in the Salience of Social Categorisation. *British Journal of Social Psychology* 30:125–144.

Olson, Gary A., and Lester Faigley. 1991. Language, Politics, and Composition: A Conversation with Noam Chomsky. *Journal of Advanced Composition* 11:1–36.

Operario, Don, and Susan T. Fiske. 1999. Integrating Social Identity and Cognition: A Framework for Bridging Diverse Perspectives. Pages 26–54 in *Social Identity and Social Cognition*. Edited by Dominic Abrams, and Michael A. Hogg. Oxford: Blackwell.

Osiek, Carolyn. 2002. The Bride of Christ: A Problematic Wedding – Ephesians 5:22–33. *Biblical Theology Bulletin* 32:29–39.
Osiek, Carolyn, and David L. Balch. 1997. *Families in the New Testament World: Households and House Churches*. Family, Religion, and Culture. Louisville, Ky.: Westminster John Knox Press.
Osiek, Carolyn, and Margaret Y. MacDonald, with Janet H. Tulloch. 2005. *A Woman's Place: House Churches in Earliest Christianity*. Philadelphia: Fortress Press.
Palmer, Michael. 1997. *Freud and Jung on Religion*. London: Routledge.
Parsons, Michael. 1995. Being Precedes Act: Indicative and Imperative in Paul's Writing. Pages 217–247 in *Understanding Paul's Ethics: Twentieth Century Approaches*. Edited by Brian S. Rosner. Grand Rapids, Mich.: Eerdmans.
Patrick, Dale. 1995. The Rhetoric of Collective Responsibility in the Deuteronomic Law. Pages 421–436 in *Pomegranates and Golden Bells: Studies in Biblical, Jewish and near Eastern Ritual, Law, and Literature in Honor of Jacob Milgrom*. Edited by David P. Wright et al. Winona Lake, Ind.: Eisenbrauns.
Pearson, Birger Albert. 1997. *The Emergence of the Christian Religion: Essays on Early Christianity*. Harrisburg, Pa.: Trinity Press International.
Percy, Ernst. 1946. *Die Probleme der Kolosser- und Epheserbriefe*. Acta Regiae Societatis Humaniorum Litterarum Lundensis 39. Lund: Gleerup.
Pickett, Cynthia L., and Marilynn B. Brewer. 2005. The Role of Exclusion in Maintaining Ingroup Inclusion. Pages 89–112 in *The Social Psychology of Inclusion and Exclusion*. Edited by Dominic Abrams, Michael A. Hogg, and José M. Marques. New York: Psychology Press.
Pinker, Steven. 1994. *The Language Instinct: How the Mind Creates Language*. New York: W. Morrow and Co.
Polkinghorne, Donald E. 1988. *Narrative Knowing and the Human Sciences*. Suny Series in the Philosophy of the Social Sciences. Albany: State University of New York Press.
Porter, Joshua Roy. 1965. Legal Aspects of the Concept of "Corporate Personality" in the Old Testament. *Vetus Testamentus* 15:361–380.
Porter, Stanley E. 1990. Two Myths: Corporate Personality and Language Mentality Determinism. *Scottish Journal of Theology* 43:289–307.
Pouilly, Jean. 1976. *La Règle de la communauté de Qumrân*. Paris: J. Gabalda.
Praetorius, Nini. 2004. Intersubjectivity of Cognition and Language: Principled Reasons Why the Subject May Be Trusted. *Phenomenology and the Cognitive Sciences* 3:195–214.
Premack, David. 1990. The Infant's Theory of Self-Propelled Objects. *Cognition* 36:1–16.
Premack, David, and Ann James Premack. 1995. Intention as Psychological Cause. Pages 185–199 in *Causal Cognition: A Multidisciplinary Debate*.

Edited by Dan Sperber, David Premack, and Ann James Premack. Oxford: Clarendon Press.

Pyysiäinen, Ilkka. 2003. *How Religion Works: Towards a New Cognitive Science of Religion*. Leiden: Brill.

Rackham, Harris. 1952. Introduction [to On Virtues and Vices by Aristotle]. Pages 484–487 in *Aristotle XX: Athenian Constitution, Eudemian Ethics, Virtues and Vices*. Translated by Rackman H. Revised ed. Loeb Classical Library. Cambridge: Harvard University Press.

Räisänen, Heikki. 2000. *Beyond New Testament Theology: A Story and a Programme*. 2nd ed. London: SCM Press.

Rebell, Walter. 1986. *Gehorsam und Unabhängigkeit: Eine sozialpsychologische Studie zu Paulus*. München: Kaiser.

Reicher, Stephen, Russell Spears, and Tom Postmes. 1995. A Social Identity Model of Deindividuation Phenomena. *European Review of Social Psychology* 6:161–198.

Reicher, Stephen, and Nick Hopkins. 2001. *Self and Nation: Categorization, Contestation and Mobilization*. London: SAGE.

Richardson, Alan. 1998. Brains, Minds and Texts: A Review of Mark Turner's the Literary Mind. *Review* 20:39–48.

Richardson, Brian. 2000. Recent Concepts of Narrative and the Narratives of Narrative Theory. *Style* 34:168–175.

Riggsby, Andrew M. 1998. Self and Community in the Younger Pliny. *Arethusa* 31:75–97.

Robbins, Vernon. 2007. Conceptual Blending and Early Christian Imagination. Pages 161–195 in *Explaining Christian Origins and Early Judaism: Contributions from Cognitive and Social Science*. Edited by Petri Luomanen, Ilkka Pyysiäinen, and Risto Uro. Biblical Interpretation Series 89. Leiden: Brill.

Roberts, Johnnie. H. 1986. Transitional Techniques to the Letter Body in the Corpus Paulinum. Pages 187–201 in *A South African Perspective on the New Testament*. Edited by J. H. Petzer, and P. J. Hartin. Leiden: Brill.

Robinson, Henry Wheeler. 1911. *The Christian Doctrine of Man*. Edinburgh: T & T Clark.

—. 1964. *Corporate Personality in Ancient Israel*. Facet Books, Biblical Series 11. Philadelphia: Fortress.

Rogerson, John W. 1970. The Hebrew Conception of Corporate Personality: A Re-Examination. *Journal of Theological Studies* 21:1–16.

Rohrbaugh, Richard L., ed. 1996. *The Social Sciences and New Testament Interpretation*. Peabody, Mass.: Hendrickson Publishers.

Roitto, Rikard. 2008. Act as a Christ-Believer, as a Household Member or Both? A Cognitive Perspective on the Relation between the Social Identity in Christ and Household Identities in Pauline and Deutero-Pauline Texts.

Pages 141–162 in *Identity Formation in the New Testament*. Edited by Mikael Winninge, and Bengt Holmberg. Wissenschaftliche Untersuchungen zum Neuen Testament 227. Tübingen: Mohr Siebeck.

Rollins, Wayne G. 1999. *Soul and Psyche: The Bible in Psychological Perspective*. Minneapolis: Fortress Press.

Rosch, Eleanor. 1978. Principles of Categorization. Pages 27–48 in *Cognition and Categorization*. Edited by Eleanor Rosch, and Barbara B. Lloyd. Hillsdale, N.J.: Erlbaum.

Ross, Lee. 1977. The Intuitive Psychologist and His Shortcomings: Distortions in the Attribution Process. Pages 173–220 in *Advances in Experimental Social Psychology*. Edited by L. Berkowitz. New York: Academic Press.

Runesson, Anders. 2008. Inventing Christian Identity: Paul, Ignatius and Theodosius I. Pages 59–92 in *Exploring Early Christian Identity*. Edited by Bengt Holmberg. Wissenschaftliche Untersuchungen zum Neuen Testament 226. Tübingen: Mohr Siebeck.

Russell, Daniel C. 2004. Virtue as 'Likeness to God' in Plato and Seneca. *Journal of the History of Philosophy* 42:241–260.

Sampley, Paul J. 1993. Ephesians. In *The Deutero-Pauline Letters: Ephesians, Colossians, 2 Thessalonians, 1–2 Timothy, Titus*. Edited by J. Paul Sampley, and Gerhard Krodel. Proclamation Commentaries. Minneapolis: Fortress.

Sandbach, Francis Henry. 1989. *The Stoics*. 2nd ed. Bristol: Bristol Classical Press.

Sanders, Ed Parish. 1977. *Paul and Palestinian Judaism: A Comparison of Patterns of Religion*. Philadelphia: Fortress P.

—. 1992. *Judaism: Practice and Belief: 63 BCD-66 CE*. London: SCM Press.

Saussure, Ferdinand de. 1960. *Course in General Linguistics*. London: Owen.

Schachter, Stanley. 1951. Deviation, Rejection and Communication. *Journal of Abnormal and Social Psychology* 13:303–314.

Schank, Roger C. 1995. *Tell Me a Story: Narrative and Intelligence*. Rethinking Theory. Evanston, Ill.: Northwestern University Press.

Schank, Roger C., and Tamara R. Berman. 2002. The Persuasive Role of Stories in Knowledge and Action. Pages 287–313 in *Narrative Impact: Social and Cognitive Foundations*. Edited by Jeffrey J. Strange, Timothy C. Brock, and Melanie C. Green. Mahwah, N.J.: Lawrence Erlbaum Associates.

Schnackenburg, Rudolf. 1982. *Der Brief an der Epheser*. Evangelisch-Katholischer Kommentar zum Neuen Testament 10. Zürich: Benziger Verlag.

Schwindt, Rainer. 2002. *Das Weltbild des Epheserbriefes: Eine religionsgeschichtlich-exegetische Studie*. Wissenschaftliche Untersuchungen zum Neuen Testament 148. Tübingen: Mohr Siebeck.

Schüssler Fiorenza, Elisabeth. 1994. *In Memory of Her: A Feminist Theological Reconstruction of Christian Origins*. 2nd ed. New York: Crossroad.

Shaver, Kelly G. 1985. *The Attribution of Blame: Causality, Responsibility, and Blameworthiness*. Springer Series in Social Psychology. New York: Springer-Verlag.

Shelley, Cameron, and Paul Thagard. 1996. Mythology and Analogy. Pages 152–183 in *Modes of Thought: Explorations in Culture and Cognition*. Edited by David R. Olson, and Nancy Torrance. Cambridge: Cambridge University Press.

Shkul, Minna. 2009. *Reading Ephesians: Exploring Social Entrepreneurship in the Text*. Library of New Testament studies 408. London: T & T Clark.

Shore, Bradd. 1996. *Culture in Mind: Cognition, Culture and the Problem of Meaning*. New York: Oxford University Press.

Sihvola, Juha, and Troels Engberg-Pedersen, eds. 1998. *The Emotions in Hellenistic Philosophy*. New Synthese Historical Library 46. Dordrecht: Kluwer Academic Publishers.

Simpson, Tom, Peter Carruthers, Stephen Laurence, and Stephen Stich. 2005. Introduction: Nativism Past and Present. Pages 3–23 in *The Innate Mind: Structure and Contents*. Edited by Peter Carruthers, Stephen Laurence, and Stephen Stich. New York: Oxford University Press.

Smith, Morton. 1987. *Palestinian Parties and Politics That Shaped the Old Testament*. 2nd ed. London: SCM Press.

Snodgrass, Klyne. 1996. *Ephesians*. The NIV Application Commentary. Grand Rapids, Mich.: Zondervan.

Sorensen, Eric. 2001. *Possession and Exorcism in the New Testament and Early Christianity*. Wissenschaftliche Untersuchungen zum Neuen Testament 157. Tübingen: Mohr Siebeck.

Spears, Russell, Bertjan Doojse, and Naomi Ellemers. 1999. Commitment and the Context of Social Perception. Pages 59–83 in *Social Identity: Context, Commitment, Content*. Edited by Naomi Ellemers, Russell Spears, and Bertjan Doojse. Oxford: Blackwell.

Sperber, Dan. 1975. *Rethinking Symbolism*. Cambridge Studies in Social Anthropology 11. Cambridge: Cambridge University Press.

—. 1995. Introduction. Pages xv-xx in *Causal Cognition: A Multidisciplinary Debate*. Edited by Dan Sperber, David Premack, and Ann James Premack. Oxford: Clarendon Press.

—. 1996. *Explaining Culture: A Naturalistic Approach*. Cambridge: Blackwell.

Sperber, Dan, David Premack, and Ann James Premack, eds. 1995. *Causal Cognition: A Multidisciplinary Debate*. Oxford: Clarendon Press.

Stafford, Emma. 2000. *Worshipping Virtues: Personification and the Divine in Ancient Greece*. London: Duckworth.

Stegemann, Ekkehard W., and Wolfgang Stegemann. 1995. *Urchristliche Sozialgeschichte: Die Anfänge im Judentum und die Christusgemeinden in der mediterranen Welt*. Stuttgart: Kohlhammer.

Stein, Nancy L., and Elisabeth A. Albro. 1997. Building Complexity and Coherence: Children's Use of Goal-Structured Knowledge in Telling Stories. Pages 5–44 in *Narrative Development: Six Approaches*. Edited by Michael Bamberg. Mahwah, N.J.: Lawrence Erlbaum Associates.

Stephens, William O. 2006. *Stoic Ethics [Internet Encyclopedia of Philosophy]* [URL]. http://www.iep.utm.edu/s/StoicEth.htm (cited 26 Aug 2008).

Strange, Jeffrey J. 2002. How Fictional Tales Wag Real-World Beliefs: Models and Mechanisms of Narrative Influence. Pages 263–286 in *Narrative Impact: Social and Cognitive Foundations*. Edited by Jeffrey J. Strange, Timothy C. Brock, and Melanie C. Green. Mahwah, N.J.: Lawrence Erlbaum Associates.

Strathmann, Hermann. 1967. Μάρτυς κλτ. Pages 474–514 in vol. 4 of *Theological Dictionary of the New Testament*. Edited by Gerhard Kittel, and Gerhard Friedrich. Grand Rapids, Mich.: Eerdmans.

Strauss, Claudia, and Naomi Quinn. 1997. *A Cognitive Theory of Cultural Meaning*. Publications of the Society for Psychological Anthropology 9. Cambridge: Cambridge University Press.

Tajfel, Henri. 1972. La catégorisation sociale. Pages 272–302 in *Introduction à la psychologie sociale*. Edited by Serge Moscovici. Paris: Larousse.

—. 1974. Social Identity and Intergroup Behaviour. *Social Science Information* 13:65–93.

—. ed. 1978. *Differentiation between Social Groups: Studies in the Social Psychology of Intergroup Relations*. European Monographs in Social Psychology 14. London: Academic Press.

—. 1981. *Human Groups and Social Categories: Studies in Social Psychology*. Cambridge: Cambridge University Press.

—. ed. 1982. *Social Identity and Intergroup Relations*. European Studies in Social Psychology. Cambridge: Cambridge University Press.

Tajfel, Henri, C. Flament, M. G. Billib, and Bundy R. P. 1971. Social Categorization and Intergroup Behaviour. *European Journal of Social Psychology* 1:149–178.

Tajfel, Henri, and John C. Turner. 1979. An Integrative Theory of Intergroup Conflict. Pages 33–47 in *The Social Psychology of Intergroup Conflict*. Edited by William G. Austin, and Stephen Worchel. Monterey, Calif.: Brooks/Cole.

Takemura, Kosuke, and Masaki Yuki. 2007. Are Japanese Groups More Competitive Than Japanese Individuals? A Cross-Cultural Validation of the Interindividual-Intergroup Discontinuity Effect. *International Journal of Psychology* 42:27–35.

Talbert, Charles H. 2007. *Ephesians and Colossians*. Paideia: Commentaries on the New Testament. Grand Rapids, Mich.: Baker Academic.

Taylor, John R. 2003. *Linguistic Categorization*. 3., rev. ed. Oxford Textbooks in Linguistics. Oxford: Oxford University Press.

Tellbe, Mikael. 2008. The Prototypical Christ-Believer: Early Christian Identity Formation in Ephesus. Pages 115–138 in *Exploring Early Christian Identity*. Edited by Bengt Holmberg. Wissenschaftliche Untersuchungen zum Neuen Testament 226. Tübingen: Mohr Siebeck.

—. 2009. *Christ-Believers in Ephesus*. Wissenschaftliche Untersuchungen zum Neuen Testament 242. Tübingen: Mohr Siebeck.

Thagard, Paul. 2007. *Cognitive Science (Stanford Encyclopedia of Philosophy)* [URL]. http://plato.stanford.edu/entries/cognitive-science/ (cited 23 May 2008).

Thagard, Paul, and Cameron Shelley. 2001. Emotional Analogies and Analogical Inference. Pages 335–362 in *The Analogical Mind: Perspectives from Cognitive Science*. Edited by Dedre Gentner, Boicho N. Kokinov, and Keith James Holyoak. Cambridge, Mass.: MIT Press.

Theissen, Gerd. 1974. Theoretische Probleme religionssoziologischer Forschung und die Analyze des Urchristentums. *Neue Zeitschrift für systematische Theologie und Religionsphilosophie* 16:35–56.

—. 1978. *Sociology of Early Palestinian Christianity*. Philadelphia: Fortress Press.

—. 1982. *The Social Setting of Pauline Christianity: Essays on Corinth*. Philadelphia: Fortress Press.

—. 1983. *Psychologische Aspekte paulinischer Theologie*. Forschungen zur Religion und Literatur des Alten und Neuen Testaments, N.F. 131. Göttingen: Vandenhoeck & Ruprecht.

—. 1987. *Psychological Aspects of Pauline Theology*. Philadelphia: Fortress Press.

—. 1999. *The Religion of the Earliest Churches: Creating a Symbolic World*. Minneapolis, MN: Fortress Press.

—. 1999. *A Theory of Primitive Christian Religion*. London: SCM Press.

—. 2007. *Erleben und Verhalten der Ersten Christen: eine Psychologie des Urchristentums*. Gütersloh: Gütersloher Verlags-Haus.

Theissen, Gerd, and Petra von Gemünden, eds. 2007a. *Erkennen und Erleben: Beiträge zur psychologischen Erforschung des frühen Christentums*. Gütersloh: Gütersloher Verlags-Haus.

—. 2007b. Erkennen und Erleben im frühen Christentum: Einleitung und Einführung. Pages 9–28 in *Erkennen und Erleben: Beiträge zur psychologischen Erforschung des frühen Christentums*. Edited by Gerd Theissen, and Petra von Gemünden. Gütersloh: Gütersloher Verlags-Haus.

Thorsteinsson, Runar M. 2003. *Paul's Interlocutor in Romans 2: Function and Identity in the Context of Ancient Epistolography*. Coniectanea Biblica. New Testament Series 40. Stockholm: Almqvist & Wiksell International.

Thraede, Klaus. 1994. Homonoia (Eintracht). Pages 176–289 in *Reallexikon für Antike und Christentum*. Stuttgart: Hiersemann.

Tomasello, Michael. 1999. *The Cultural Origins of Human Cognition*. Cambridge, Mass.: Harvard University Press.

Tomson, Peter J. 1986. The Names Israel and Jew in Ancient Judaism and the New Testament. *Bijdragen, tijdschrift voor filosofie en theologie* 47:120–140, 266–289.

—, 1990. *Paul and the Jewish Law: Halakha in the Letters of the Apostle to the Gentiles*. Assen: van Gorcum.

Trebilco, Paul. 2006. Christian Communities in Western Asia Minor into the Early Second Century: Ignatius and Others as Witnesses against Bauer. *Journal of the Evangelical Theological Society* 49:17–44.

Tremlin, Todd. 2006. *Minds and Gods: The Cognitive Foundations of Religion*. Oxford: Oxford University Press.

Triandis, Harry C. 1989. The Self and Social Behavior in Different Cultural Contexts. *Psychological Review* 96:506–520.

Triandis, Harry C., Robert Bontempo, Marcelo J. Villareal, Masaaki Asai, and Nydia Lucca. 1988. Individualism and Collectivism: Cross-Cultural Perspectives on Self-Ingroup Relationships. *Journal of Personality and Social Psychology* 54:323–338.

Turner, John C. 1982. Toward a Cognitive Redefinition of the Social Group. Pages 15–40 in *Social Identity and Intergroup Relations*. Edited by Henri Tajfel. Oxford: Academic Press.

—. 1985. Social Categorization and the Self-Concept: A Social Cognitive Theory of Group Behaviour. Pages 77–122 in vol. 2 of *Advances in Group Processes*. Edited by Edward J. Lawler. Greenwich, Conn.: JAI Press.

—. 1991. *Social Influence*. Mapping Social Psychology. Milton Keynes: Open University Press.

—. 2005. Explaining the Nature of Power: A Three-Process Theory. *European Journal of Social Psychology* 35:1–22.

Turner, John C., Michael A. Hogg, Penelope J. Oakes, Stephen D. Reicher, and Margaret S. Wetherell. 1987. *Rediscovering the Social Group: A Self-Categorization Theory*. Oxford: Blackwell.

Turner, John C., Penelope J. Oakes, Alexander S. Haslam, and Craig McGarty. 1994. Self and Collective: Cognition and Social Context. *Personality and Social Psychology Bulletin* 20:454–463.

Turner, Mark. 1996. *The Literary Mind*. New York: Oxford University Press.

Ulfgard, Håkan. 1998. *The Story of Sukkot: The Setting, Shaping, and Sequel of the Biblical Feast of Tabernacles*. Beitrage zur Geschichte der biblischen Exegese 34. Tübingen: Mohr Siebeck.

Ungerer, Friedrich, and Hans-Jörg Schmid. 1996. *An Introduction to Cognitive Linguistics*. London: Longman.

Uro, Risto. 2007. Gnostic Rituals from a Cognitive Perspective. Pages 115–137 in *Explaining Christian Origins and Early Judaism: Contributions from Cognitive and Social Science*. Edited by Petri Luomanen, Ilkka Pyysiäinen, and Risto Uro. Biblical Interpretation Series 89. Leiden: Brill.

Uro, Risto, and Istvan Czachesz, eds. forthcoming. *Cognitive Science Approaches in Biblical Studies: Proceedings of the Mind, Society and Tradition Section in 2007 and 2008 [Preliminary Title]*.

Walcot, Peter. 1988. Images of the Individual. Pages 1279–1290 in *Civilization of the Ancient Mediterranean: Greece and Rome*. Edited by Michael Grant, and Rachel Kitzinger. New York: Scribner.

Vardoulakis, Dimitrios. 2004. The Vicissitude of Completeness: Gadamer's Criticism of Collingwood. *International Journal of Philosophical Studies* 12:3–19.

Verhagen, Arie. 2005. *Constructions of Intersubjectivity: Discourse, Syntax, and Cognition*. New York: Oxford University Press.

Westerholm, Stephen. 2006. Paul's Anthropological 'Pessimism' in Its Jewish Context. Pages 71–98 in *Divine and Human Agency in Paul and His Cultural Environment*. Edited by John M. G. Barclay, and Simon J. Gathercole. Library of New Testament Studies 335. London: T & T Clark.

Veyne, Paul. 1987. The Roman Empire. Pages 5–234 in *A History of Private Life: From Pagan Rome to Byzantium*. Edited by Paul Veyne. Cambridge, Mass.: Harvard University Press.

White, John Lee. 1986. *Light from Ancient Letters*. Philadelphia: Fortress Press.

Whitehouse, Harvey. 2004. *Modes of Religiosity: A Cognitive Theory of Religious Transmission*. Cognitive Science of Religion Series. Walnut Creek, CA: AltaMira Press.

Whitehouse, Harvey, and Luther Martin, eds. 2004. *Theorizing Religions Past: Archaeology, History, and Cognition*. Cognitive Science of Religion Series. Walnut Creek, Calif.: AltaMira Press.

Whorf, Benjamin Lee. 1956. *Language, Thought and Reality: Selected Writings of Benjamin Lee Whorf*. Cambridge, Mass.: MIT Press.

Williams, Garrath. 2003. Blame and Responsibility. *Ethical Theory and Moral Practice* 6:427–445.

Wilson, Bryan R. 1970. *Religious Sects; a Sociological Study*. New York: McGraw-Hill.

Wilson, Stephen G. 1995. *Related Strangers: Jews and Christians, 70–170 C.E.* Minneapolis: Fortress Press.

Wolter, Michael, ed. 2005. *Ethik als angewandte Ekklesiologie: Der Brief an die Epheser*. Serie Monografica di "Benedictina". Sezione biblico-ecumenica, 17. Roma: Abbazia di San Paolo fuori le mura.

Yee, Tet-Lim N. 2004. *Jews, Gentiles, and Ethnic Reconciliation: Paul's Jewish Identity and Ephesians*. New York: Cambridge University Press.

Yuki, Masaki. 2003. Intergroup Comparison Versus Intragroup Relationships: A Cross-Cultural Examination of Social Identity Theory in North American and East Asian Cultural Contexts. *Social Psychology Quarterly* 66:166–183.

Zetterholm, Magnus. 2003. *The Formation of Christianity in Antioch: A Social-Scientific Approach to the Separation between Judaism and Christianity*. London: Routledge.

—. 2008. The Didache, Matthew, and Paul: Reconstructing Historical Developments in Antioch. Pages 73–90 in *Matthew, James and the Didache: Three Related Documents in Their Jewish and Christian Settings*. Edited by H. van de Sandt, and J. Zangenberg. SBL - Symposium 45. Leiden: Brill.

—. 2009. *Approaches to Paul: A Student's Guide to recent Scholarship*. Minneapolis: Fortress Press.

Zimbardo, Philip G. 1969. The Human Choice: Individuation, Reason and Order Versus Deindividuation, Impulse and Chaos. Pages 237–307 in *Nebraska Symposium on Motivation 17*. Edited by David Levine, and William J. Arnold. Lincoln, Neb.: University of Nebraska Press.

Zlatev, Jordan, Timothy P. Racine, Christopher Sinha, and Esa Itkonen, eds. 2008. *The Shared Mind*. Converging Evidence in Language and Communication Research 12. Amsterdam: John Benjamins.

Index of Authors

Index of Passages

Bible

Other than the Bible

Itero

www.ehs.se/itero

1. Åke Viberg, *Symbols of Law: A Contextual Analysis of Legal Symbolic Acts in the Old Testament.* 2021. First published 1992 by Almqvist & Wiksell International.
2. Thomas Kazen, *Jesus and Purity* Halakhah*: Was Jesus Indifferent to Impurity?* 2021. First published 2002 by Almqvist & Wiksell International. Corrected reprint edition published 2010 by Eisenbrauns.
3. Åke Viberg, *Prophets in Action: An Analysis of Prophetic Symbolic Acts in the Old Testament.* 2021. First published 2007 by Almqvist & Wiksell International.
4. Thomas Kazen, *Issues of Impurity in Early Judaism.* 2021. First published 2010 by Eisenbrauns.
5. Rikard Roitto, *Behaving as a Christ-Believer: A Cognitive Perspective on Identity and Behavior Norms in Ephesians.* 2021. First published 2011 by Eisenbrauns.